UNTIL PROVEN INNOCENT

INNOCENT

UNTIL PROVEN

STUART TAYLOR JR. and KC JOHNSON

*Political Correctness and the Shameful
Injustices of the Duke Lacrosse Rape Case*

THOMAS DUNNE BOOKS / ST. MARTIN'S PRESS ⌇ NEW YORK

THOMAS DUNNE BOOKS.
An imprint of St. Martin's Press.

www.thomasdunnebooks.com
www.stmartins.com

Library of Congress Cataloging-in-Publication Data

Taylor, Stuart (Stuart S.)
   Until proven innocent : political correctness and the shameful injustices of the Duke lacrosse rape case / Stuart Taylor Jr. and KC Johnson.
      p.   cm.
   ISBN-13: 978-0-312-36912-5
   ISBN-10: 0-312-36912-3
   1. Rape—North Carolina—Durham.   2. Malicious accusation—North Carolina—Durham.
3. Rape—Investigation—North Carolina—Durham.   4. Trials (Rape)—North Carolina—Durham.
5. Lacrosse players—North Carolina—Durham.   6. Prosecution—Corrupt practices—North
Carolina—Durham.   7. Seligmann, Reade.   8. Finnerty, Collin.   9. Evans, David Forker,
1983–10. Nifong, Michael Byron.   I. Johnson, KC.   II. Title.
   HV6568.D87T39 2007
   364.15'32092275656 3—dc22   2007020856

First Edition: September 2007

10 9 8 7 6 5 4 3 2 1

Stuart Taylor:
To Sally, Sarah, and Molly

KC Johnson:
To my parents, Kathleen, Mike, and Darrion

CONTENTS

ACKNOWLEDGMENTS

This book has been a labor of love in large part because of the many wonderful people who were victims of or otherwise affected by this false rape accusation, and with whom we have had the great pleasure of becoming friendly.

Most of our research and writing took place as the legal case progressed. Even so, we benefited from the extraordinary cooperation of all three defendants' legal teams, consistent with their ethical constraints as lawyers in a pending case. Counselors to clients they knew to be innocent, Joe Cheshire, Brad Bannon, Kirk Osborn, Jim Cooney, Wade Smith, and Doug Kingsbery shared with us every aspect of the defense files and thinking except for matters that had been placed under seal by the court or were confidential as a matter of law or professional ethics. Brad Bannon, in particular, went above and beyond the call of duty to answer dozens of our questions, however minor the detail. Steve McCool was also most helpful.

Dave Evans, Reade Seligmann, and Collin Finnerty—the three falsely accused players—their parents, and other family members patiently answered our numerous questions over a several-months period. They gave willingly of their time even as charges were still hanging over them.

Bob Ekstrand and Bill Thomas, who represented unindicted players, spent many long hours responding to our questions and were immensely helpful as well as courageous in speaking out against the abuses of a district attorney who had a great deal of power to hurt their practices. Stef Sparks also spent many hours tirelessly educating us on details of the case.

District Attorney Mike Nifong and the police officers discussed herein did not respond to repeated requests for comment.

We conducted dozens of interviews, either in person or via e-mail, with current and former members of the Duke men's and women's lacrosse teams, their families, and their coaches. Not one request for information was denied. We would especially like to acknowledge assistance from Mike and Sue Pressler, Larry Lamade, Jerry Crotty, Bruce Thompson, Thom Mayer, Bob Wellington, Sally Fogarty, Ben and Tricia Dowd, Everett and Rita Flannery, Steve Henkelman, and Bill and Tara Nick. Also the current and former players who agreed to interviews: Danny Flannery, Peter Lamade, Devon Sherwood, Bo Carrington, Tony McDevitt, Jay Jennison, Ryan McFadyen, Brad

Ross, and Michael Catalino. We also thank Taylor Price for insights into his friends Reade and Collin.

Duke President Richard Brodhead, Chairman Robert Steel, Provost Peter Lange, and Senior Vice President John Burness were responsive to our questions and generous with their time even though aware that we might well be critical of their actions. We appreciate their professionalism and civility.

For background on Durham politics, we are especially grateful to guidance from Jackie Brown. For background on Duke, we benefited from students including Kristin Butler, Stephen Miller, and Seyward Darby; 2006 graduates, including Adam Chandler; and a number of people who, troubled by the direction their university took in this affair, gave off-the-record assistance.

Robin Muller provided outstanding research and memoranda concerning media coverage, other unjust prosecutions, and rape law. Among several astute bloggers who helped inform us via private exchanges as well as the Internet, special thanks to the Liestoppers crew, to Bill Anderson, and to Mike Gaynor.

We are grateful to the dozens of people who read drafts of portions of the manuscript. Their suggestions dramatically improved the final product. Special thanks to the Presslers, Harvey Silverglate, Peter Berkowitz, Bill Bryson, Barry Scheck, Margaret King, Steve Remy, Kristin Butler, Danny Flannery, William Wolcott, Eric Ferrero, and (again) Bob Ekstrand and Stef Sparks.

Stuart thanks Charlie Green and his colleagues at *National Journal* for their patience with his long absences and his wife, Sally, for her patience with his long presence and her moral support. KC thanks his department chairman, David Troyansky, for agreeing to a last-minute course release, freeing time to complete the manuscript.

We are also grateful to Gail Ross, who was immensely helpful in finding a publisher for the book and ironing out various problems, and to Tom Dunne and John Parsley of St. Martin's Press for giving our book a home and helping us make it better.

We invite readers who are concerned about the legal injustices detailed in these pages to visit the Association for Truth and Fairness at http://www .truthandfairness.org/. The Association was formed to help defray the more than $5 million in legal fees associated with defending against the injustices visited by law enforcement officials upon the three defendants and their teammates.

UNTIL PROVEN INNOCENT

1. DREAMS OF GLORY

T HE DURHAM HEAT BURNED through Devon Sherwood's jersey as he waited for the lacrosse team he longed to join to come from the locker room. It was his eighteenth birthday, September 16, 2005. Shifting his feet on the green turf, he pondered the challenge ahead.

The lanky freshman had been a good high school goalie in Freeport, Long Island—good enough to be recruited by five small colleges and offered a probable starting position by prestigious Williams.

Duke had been a different story. A lacrosse powerhouse, it had come within a goal of winning the national championship in May 2005. This year's team was even more loaded with talent, and widely seen as the one to beat in 2006. Mike Pressler, the 2005 NCAA lacrosse coach of the year, could fill his twelve scholarship slots with high school all-Americans and near all-Americans. Devon had not made that cut.

He chose Duke anyway. His father, Chuck, had played lacrosse for Duke. And when Devon and his parents had toured the campus, Pressler had greeted them warmly, encouraging Devon to try out as a walk-on.

Few walk-ons make the roster in big-time college sports. Even fewer get playing time. And Duke was as big-time as lacrosse gets. So Devon's excitement was tinged with apprehension as the forty-five blue-helmeted figures came jogging onto the field. They formed two perfect lines, in full battle array, down to the fierce-looking face masks that in a few months would—along with charges of gang rape and racism—fix the team's image on the nation's television screens.

Showtime, Devon thought. Will I win their respect? Will they accept me?

One by one, the forty-five figures came up to the rookie, shook hands, introduced themselves, wished him luck. They didn't have to do that, he thought.

Two weeks and dozens of saves later, Coach Pressler called Devon into his office. Was he having a good time? Was he ready for the commitment and hard work expected of a Division I athlete? Devon was ready. He would be the third-string goalie. But he was sure he had to be the happiest person alive. Happy, and eager to improve. He had big shoes to fill. Chuck Sherwood, Duke's first African-American lacrosse player, had set goalkeeping records, including most saves in a game.

Now Devon would be the only black guy on a team with forty-six white guys. His contributions to team culture included a rap song incorporating every teammate's name or nickname, depending on which rhymed better. Everyone had at least one nickname. Devon's was "D-Wood."

The practices were grueling: at least fifteen hours a week in the fall and twenty-two hours in the spring of lacrosse drills, scrimmages, running, and weight lifting. Plus a full course load. Plus, for Devon, getting to know as many of Duke's other six hundred black undergraduates as he could.

Many of the other lacrosse players hung together off as well as on the field, acquiring a reputation for clannishness, in part because there were so many of them, and for going around in large, sometimes loud, often conspicuous groups, and for drunken revelry that stood out even at a legendary party school. In fact, aside from their visibility, their behavior was not atypical of many other Duke students, but it made the lacrosse players an unusually inviting target for those displeased with the Duke status quo.

One of the nation's ten top academic institutions, Duke could fill most seats in every entering class with high school valedictorians. It had also earned a national reputation as a hedonistic scene of wild antics and rampant sexual "hookups"—mostly one-night stands—marinated in oceans of alcohol.

Fraternities and sororities, informally ranked, dominated the social scene, which was mostly off campus because of Duke's strict drinking rules. With the young women as eager for sexual conquests as the guys, the female-male ratio and the balance of sexual power favored the alpha males, especially at Duke. Indeed, more than one sorority hired male strippers for its own initiation, a fact that became public in 2006 but was all but ignored by the media.

Inevitably the most extreme parties worked their way into the media as if they reflected normal affairs. A January 2005 bacchanal, for instance, brought national publicity. Police raiding an off-campus rental house jammed with two hundred students found coeds in bikinis, emulating the movie *Old School* by wrestling in a kiddie pool full of baby oil while beer-swilling boys watched and cheered. The scene was reminiscent of the raucous Saint Ray fraternity parties in Tom Wolfe's *I Am Charlotte Simmons*. Set at fictional Dupont University, which Wolfe modeled largely on Duke, the novel tells the story of a sheltered but extraordinarily bright student from a small North Carolina town who arrives in search of intellectual challenge and emotional growth. What she finds is a place where star athletes outrank star students and the route to social acceptance is a booze- and sex-obsessed culture of hard partying male athletes and scantily clad sorority girls. Charlotte dutifully, if unhappily, takes that route.

At Duke, as at Wolfe's Dupont, it was not all fun. Some women brought impressive academic and other credentials, only to become "unhappy, insecure girls all fighting to get rammed by someone of status," wrote Dukeobsrvr, an anonymous student blogger. All this provoked much gnashing of teeth and agonizing among Duke faculty and administrators, especially those concerned about equality and dignity for women.

"Men and women agree the double standard persists: men gain status through sexual activity while women lose status," complained a high-level, female-dominated group chaired by then-president Nannerl O. Keohane, a major 2003 report by the Steering Committee for the Women's Initiative at Duke University on the lives of women at Duke. "Fraternities control the mainstream social scene to such an extent that women feel like they play by the men's rules. Social life is further complicated by a number of embedded hierarchies, from the widely understood ranking of Greek organizations to the opposite trajectories women and men take over four years, with women losing status."

Most students took a less jaundiced view. What feminist professors and some others saw as hedonistic excess, many female students saw as being liberated and proud. "Duke was best summarized by a 'Work hard, play hard' mentality," recalled a 2006 grad. "While some burned the candle too close, others were able to handle successfully all of their responsibilities and took pride in doing so."

The party scene—or what was left of it after various purges by the Duke administration in recent years—was only one of Duke's many parts. Most students either stayed away from the wild parties to focus on academics and extracurricular activities or worked as hard as they played.

Most—but hardly all—of the forty-seven lacrosse players were in the latter category, and something like a bunch of big-man-on-campus fraternity brothers. "In the order of the social universe of Duke undergraduates," Peter Boyer wrote in *The New Yorker*, "the lacrosse players ranked at the top of the dominance hierarchy."

Whether this reflected unhealthy arrogance or a healthy self-confidence was in the eye of the beholder. "'Laxers,' as lacrosse players are universally known, tend to be the most desired and most confident guys on campus," wrote Janet Reitman in *Rolling Stone*. "They're fun. And they're hot." A more jaundiced view of some of the players came from Carly Knight, a third-year student. After the gang-rape allegations against the team broke, she told the *Chronicle*, the school's newspaper, that they exuded "an extreme amount of arrogance," urinated out their windows, kicked in the door of a friend several times, and were generally disruptive during frequent parties in a room near hers. To such caricatures, Chris Kennedy, an associate athletic director and the administrator closest to the team, had an obvious retort, if one often ignored in the spring and summer of 2006: "The lacrosse players didn't become among the most popular students on campus because they treated people boorishly."

The laxers, together with the baseball team, were the leaders of the pack at the most spectacular, and notorious, regular party scene of all—a Saturday morning, pre-football-game festival of keg parties, binge drinking, beer bonging, outrageous costume wearing, and other hijinks known as Tailgate, held in a parking lot near the stadium. The laxers "are credited with helping to transform tailgate from a small pre-game gathering to a campus-wide drinking event in the last several years," reported *The Chronicle*. One highlight was a foam machine and pit for collective, booze-soaked dancing. But the lacrosse station at Tailgate attracted the most attention because of the players' habit of colorful, often wild, costumes and the obvious fun the players had at the affair.

This was the main opportunity for the laxers to cut loose; they began rigorous training for the spring season in early February and were busy playing games and practicing during the spring break and post-exam Myrtle Beach bashes enjoyed by many other Duke students.

Much of what went on at these parties would strike most people—if not left-wing professors or right-wing Christian conservatives—as good clean fun.

A student later recalled the tradition with fondness:

Some tailgates had every [lacrosse team] member dress like a WWF wrestler from the eighties and each person mock-wrestled in front of close to a hundred or more tailgaters. The last tailgate party was amazing. About ten guys from the team stayed up all night and built a foam pit that probably measured twenty feet by ten feet and had blue tarp on the sides so that the foam could rise almost three to four feet. The deans, including Dean Sue [Wasiolek], were amazed. There are countless letters from people to coach Pressler saying how amazing our tailgates were. Our tailgates were positive. One alum wrote that since he had overcome cancer it was the best part of his new life.

But there was an uglier side to Tailgate. The liability-shy university had pushed the inevitable student drinkathons off campus, and as a foreseeable consequence many students were falling-down drunk by early afternoon. (No lacrosse players were cited for such behavior.) There was some fighting. And with Duke's football team expected to take a drubbing most of the time—it was the weakest of the major Duke teams, and in the 2004, 2005, and 2006 seasons defeated only one Division I opponent—many students treated Tailgate as the main event, showing up at the football games late or not at all.

Things got so out of hand that the new baseball coach made a show of banning his team—whose image had been tarnished by a recent steroid scandal—from Tailgate. At the request of the administration, Mike Pressler let his team attend but laid down a rule requiring all lacrosse players at Tailgate to leave as a group fifteen minutes before game time and watch at least the first half. They had to check in with the coach before entering the stadium, so he could see whether any had had too much to drink; on a few occasions, several players recall seeing Duke president Richard Brodhead as they went in to watch the football game. He was, they said, always cheery, telling them it looked like they were having a good time.

Players complied with Pressler's dictate and went in to the game, but they were virtually alone in doing so. Administration hopes that other students would follow were dashed. So the university forced those who stayed at Tailgate to leave at halftime, perhaps adding to the incidence of drunk driving.

Overall, despite the laxers' "reputation for some drunken, boorish behavior," Donna Lisker, director of Duke's Women's Center, told *Sports Illustrated*, "fraternities are a bigger problem." Still, administrators and faculty tended to associate the laxers with the worst excesses of Tailgate and of the party scene as whole.

The lacrosse players also symbolized Duke's large investment of resources in having nationally competitive Division I athletic teams. This emphasis was rare among the nation's the top academic institutions. "We bond over athletics," explained Seyward Darby, a nonathlete who was editor in chief of *The Chronicle* in 2005–2006. "It gives me a sense of pride in my university." The policy also helped Duke attract some quality students who could have gone to Ivy League schools.

But the emphasis on sports gave many Duke professors a sense of shame about their university. Especially those who were still infected with Ivy League envy even after Duke had soared to the fifth ranking for overall quality in the *U.S. News & World Report* annual college issue. These academics deeply resented what they perceived as Duke's bending of admissions standards and use of scholarship funds to build a championship-caliber lacrosse team. That the lacrosse players by and large compiled academic records indistinguishable from a typical group of fifty Duke nonathletes passed without notice from faculty members who resented their status.

Bending admissions and hiring standards and targeting scholarship money to attract more black and Hispanic students and professors was one thing. The Ivies and all other major universities did that, too. And most academics support racial and ethnic diversity (although not intellectual diversity) with the fervor of religious believers.

Bending admissions standards to build a lacrosse team was something else, especially since most team members were the kind of prosperous white boys whom many professors considered overrepresented already.

On campus, this position was championed with particular ferocity by cultural anthropology professor Orin Starn, who wanted Duke to drop "to Division III in the longer term or even just have club sports teams. Students could just as well learn the lessons of leadership, competition, and teamwork competing at the Division III or club level." Money now spent on athletics could then be transferred to "deserving African-American and other applicants from underrepresented groups to strengthen Duke diversity and excellence." Leaving aside the probable unconstitutionality of race-based scholarships under recent Supreme Court precedents, neither Starn nor any of his faculty supporters ever supplied evidence that funding for athletics had taken away from Duke offering academic merit scholarships.

Other professors, meanwhile, objected to the idea of athletics—especially male athletics—altogether. They saw sports as reinforcing ideas such as competitiveness and merit-based success that are out of favor in the contemporary academy. "The 'culture' of sports seems for some a reasonable displacement for the cultures of moral conduct, ethical citizenship and personal integrity," wrote Karla F. C. Holloway, a professor of English who would emerge as a vehement critic of the lacrosse players, in the journal *Scholar and Feminist Online*. Such attitudes, she hyperbolically claimed, reinforced "exactly those behaviors of entitlement which have been and can be so abusive to women and girls and those 'othered' by their sports' history of membership." Holloway cited no evidence for any of these crude, contempt-filled stereotypes of athletes.

Many professors and some students also harbored deep resentment of the affluent social class into which a majority of the lacrosse players were born. More than half of the players came from rich or near-rich families and had gone to northeastern prep schools where lacrosse is big. Many planned to make big bucks in fields like investment banking. Assisted by the influential lacrosse network, eight of the ten seniors on the 2005–2006 team planned to begin careers on Wall Street after graduating. Pressler put together a dossier of the job offers to distribute to parents of recruits, pointing out that his players had great success after graduation.

These tensions reflected two tranformations of Duke's culture over the previous two decades that put athletes—and many other students—on a collision course with thier increasingly radical professors. First, Duke joined schools such as Stanford, the University of Texas, and the University of Michigan as a perennial contender for the Sears Cup, awarded for the cumulative performance of all of a school's NCAA sports teams. Like Stanford, Duke wrote off football and focused instead on men's and women's basketball along with sports perceived as bastions of the upper class—such as golf, tennis, and lacrosse. To attract better athletes, the institution spent more on sports and athletics facilities. The number of student athletes on financial aid increased from 194 in 1984 to 308 in 2001. And the Athletics Department as a whole, led by men's basketball coach Mike Krzyzewski, became more autonomous after Coach K forced the administration to hire his friend, Joe Alleva, as athletics director.

At the same time, more important, Duke sought to join the Ivies, Stanford, and MIT among the nation's leading academic institutions. It chose to do so, however, on the cheap: bypassing the sciences (where the combination of salary and lab costs for a new hire ran around $400,000), the school focused on bringing in big-name humanities professors, for whom the only start-up cost was salary. Politically correct leftist professors were in vogue nationwide, and the leftward slant of Duke's humanities and social sciences faculty accelerated in 1995, when President Nannerl Overholser "Nan" Keohane named History professor William Chafe as her new dean of faculty. As he explained in a 2002 "State of Arts and Sciences Address," Chafe focused on using new faculty hires to eliminate the "tendency to think of Duke as a place of wealth, whiteness and privilege." Diversity, rather than traditional conceptions of academic excellence, would be the prime criterion in choosing new professors for Duke. In a 2002 column, Economics professor E. Roy Weintraub pointed out the obvious flaw in this approach, which abandoned "the development of an ever-more distinguished faculty." "Have we," Weintraub wondered, "chosen to settle for using our resources to achieve a more diverse faculty instead of a more intellectually distinguished one? The record of the past decade seems to indicate that the answer is 'yes.'" In this, as we, shall see, Duke was hardly alone.

In a 2007 blog posting, former Duke professor Stuart Rojstaczer accurately described Duke's two-track path to excellence as a looming train wreck. "The humanities," he wrote, "are dominated by far left politics and many of these star faculty members were very much on the political left. Duke had never had this level of leftist slant before. . . . Many could care less about college athletics and some were openly dismissive. They were different. They tended to be urban. They tended to be Eastern. They tended to fit into the culture of the South and Durham poorly. Duke was an oasis for them." Coupled with Chafe's emphasis on far-left diversity hires, by early 2006 Duke's faculty had grown well out of step with mainstream student opinion.

Meanwhile, the men's lacrosse team was seen as symbolic of a way of life despised by many left-leaning Duke professors and administrators and a much smaller group of students. This resentment was fed by the preexisting stereotype—up and down the East Coast—of lacrosse players as a privileged, conceited, drunken, boorish, even thuggish mix of rich-kid entitlement and big-jock swagger.

This stereotype was to pervade the media coverage once gang-rape charges placed the Duke team in the spotlight. Explained *Newsweek*: "Strutting lacrosse players are a distinctive and familiar breed on elite campuses along the Eastern Seaboard. Because the game until recently was played mostly at prep schools and in the upper-middle-class communities on New York's Long Island and outside Baltimore, the players tend to be at once macho and entitled, a sometimes unfortunate combination." The same article also suggested, without specifics, that they "sometimes behave like thugs."

Among those who read such stuff with mounting disgust was Stefanie Williams, who went to high school with three of the Duke players in Long Island and managed the University of Maryland men's lacrosse team. "I watched kids I grew up with get labeled racists, misogynists, white supremacists and hooligans," she later wrote in *The Diamondback*, Maryland's student newspaper. "I defended the guys on our team who had often walked me home from a bar, let me crash on their couch, hung out with me on away trips, picked me up when I needed rides, grabbed lunch with me, helped me in my classes and stuck up for me when other guys got too rowdy. . . . While . . . race-baiting journalists continuously commented on the 'white culture' behind lacrosse, no one seemed to mention the hours of community service that 'culture' encouraged teams to give back."

Whatever validity the lacrosse-thug stereotype might have as to some players, at some colleges, in some years, the 2005—2006 Duke team was branded with it by dozens of journalists and thousands of others who had never met a Duke lacrosse player. People who properly shunned racial and gender stereotypes had no hesitation asserting that the Duke team had it coming because lacrosse players were a bad bunch, and probably racists to boot.

That's not how they seemed to Devon Sherwood. "I received nothing but love and appreciation and thoughtfulness from my teammates," he reflected after the tumultuous 2005–2006 academic year had passed. "People were looking out for me. They never treated me differently from the all-Americans, Matt Zash and Matt Danowski. I felt more accepted by this team than ever before in my lacrosse career. It was like a big family."

The lacrosse players were also like family to Sue Pressler, Mike's wife. She helped recruit them. They played with the Presslers' two girls, fourteen-year-old Janet Lynn and eight-year-old Maggie. And she shared their hopes and dreams for a national championship and happy, productive lives. "This class of 2006 seniors, they were always special," Sue later reflected. "They were cohesive. There was something magical about this group. I had knee surgery when they were freshmen, and along with the flowers the team sent me, the freshmen sent their own flowers. I thought, 'My gosh, I love these kids.'"

A more mixed but on balance highly positive verdict came from a seven-member faculty committee that investigated the culture of the lacrosse team and Coach Pressler's leadership from 2001 to the spring of 2006. The gist: Even more than most Duke students and athletes, lacrosse players drank much too much. They were much too loud when drunk. Those living and partying off campus often disturbed the neighbors. They were often cited by Durham police for noise and open-container violations. And those shy of twenty-one often got caught drinking illegally.

But apart from the disputed rape charge, the lacrosse players' infractions, though numerous, ranged from minor down to trivial. They had been involved in no serious misconduct. They had no record of racism, sexism, violence, or bullying. They studied hard. They got good grades, among the best of any Duke athletic squad, and better than any other lacrosse team in the Atlantic Coast Conference. Every member of the Class of 2006 graduated with a grade point average above 3.0. They enrolled in the same kinds of classes as most other Duke students. Of the seniors, two majored in economics, two in engineering, one in public policy, and five in history. Five of the squad's ten seniors made the honor roll in each of their four years at Duke: captains Dave Evans, Matt Zash, and Bret Thompson, and Erik Henkelman and Glenn Nick. The team's graduation rate was 100 percent.

Because many lacrosse players planned careers in business, banking, and consulting, they often supplemented their academic majors with a seven-course "markets and management" cluster. Given their career aims and the need to avoid conflicts with their practice schedule, it was common for several players to enroll in the same class. Such situations often foster academic-integrity problems, as when fraternity brothers or sorority sisters "share" papers from previous years. But the 2006 Duke lacrosse team's academic-integrity record was impeccable.

The team also had a good record of community service, especially with a reading program that targeted black and Hispanic children in the Durham public schools. They showed respect and consideration for the people who did menial jobs for the team, minorities, and women. And even more than past Duke teams, the 2005–2006 team had formed a tight bond with the women's lacrosse team. The two teams practiced side by side.

When the legal case against the players collapsed, defenders of the rush to judgment would fall back on the new mantra that the Duke lacrosse players were "no choirboys" or "no angels." The implication seemed to be that traits shared by the vast majority of college students nationwide could justify the selective public trashing of the lacrosse players' character by the authorities, the media, and many Duke professors and administrators.

Some Duke administrators and others continued to float innuendos, despite the evidence, suggesting that members of the 2005–2006 lacrosse team had been involved in boorish or even thuggish conduct that the committee had somehow missed. But when pressed for examples, these detractors had little to offer. Two Duke grads did cite a case in which lacrosse players broke up a party at a local restaurant by getting into a brawl, with people smashing beer bottles on each other's heads. "I remember seeing a guy who I somehow knew to be a lacrosse player, on top of someone else, pounding them with his fist," one grad recalled. But that occurred in the spring of 1997, years before any member of the 2005–2006 team had arrived at Duke.

More recent data from Duke's Judicial Affairs Office are telling: In the six academic years ending in 2006, there were a total of 377 reported incidents of academic dishonesty (such as cheating and plagiarism) by Duke students; 46 reported incidents of physical abuse, fighting and endangerment; 20 incidents of alleged sexual misconduct; 171 alcohol-related medical calls; and 96 incidents of drug-related misconduct. None of these involved lacrosse players, excepting one accused of smoking pot in his room in 2001.

Not that all was idyllic. Not all the younger players always loved all the seniors, any more than kids always love older siblings. There were tensions inherent in the need for the seniors to step up to leadership roles, the arrival of a new group of freshmen, the competition for scarce playing time, the annual ritual of any team that Sue Pressler called "herding to get everyone on the same page to achieve the goal." And while both men's and women's teams were loaded with talent and were contenders for national championships, the high expectations brought pressure. "The spirit for both teams at times seemed forced, trying to find a new identity from the previous year's team," reflected an assistant coach for the women's team much later. "The girls' team found that identity as their season went on." The boys' team never got the chance.

As the season began in February 2006, they dreamed of winning the national championship that had barely eluded Duke the previous spring. "Duke is loaded this year," the 2006 Yearbook edition of *Face-Off* reported. "Just about everybody's back and the [Blue] Devils are ready to run and gun their way back for another crack at the title." Then senior Casey Carroll, one of the best defenseman in the country, tore his ACL during practice on March 6. He was out for the season. "That was devastating, just devastating," Sue Pressler recalled later. It was not the same team without Casey. They struggled to beat Loyola of Baltimore on March 12, in San Diego. After the game the team had a ceremony to give Casey the game ball. But a game ball was no compensation for an end to his college lacrosse career.

"It's not unlike a death when your sport ends," Sue Pressler explained. A tall, athletic woman who was captain of the swimming team at the University of Michigan, a swimming coach at Ohio Wesleyan University, and a tenured faculty member in Physical Education, teaching Exercise Physiology and Kinesiology, Sue understood the passion of young athletes for their sport. "These lacrosse players are some of the most elite student athletes in the country," she explained, at a time when they were being reviled as the shame of the country. "These kids are driven. They have a passion for their sport. They have a passion for the classroom—okay, a few not as much, but many do. They do things that you can't teach. It's beautiful, and part of it is that they would die for each other. I understand 'work hard, play hard.' Did they ever let the door slam in your face? I doubt it. They were everything you'd want your kid to be—polite, courteous young men who are diligent and stick to task."

Casey Carroll had one chance of coming back the next year and finishing out his Duke lacrosse career. If they made it to the finals of the national championship, as it happened, they would have played enough games for him to qualify under the arcane rules for such matters. All his teammates would have to do for him to qualify would be to run the table against all of the best lacrosse teams in the country.

Soon afterward, a cruel fate would turn such dreams into life-changing nightmares. Especially for three players who would have been ranked by acquaintances as among the least likely Duke students to be accused of a brutal gang rape: Dave Evans, Reade Seligmann, and Collin Finnerty.

The twenty-two-year-old Evans, a senior, was one of four cocaptains, and a vocal leader for the defense. Devon Sherwood called him "Big Dave." In fact, Evans was a bit smaller than the average laxer. But, Devon explained, the five-foot-ten, 190-pound Evans "plays big. He's a physical player, a leader with a positive attitude and a sense of responsibility."

Rob Bordley, a legendary coach at Landon School, outside Washington, who had been Dave's academic adviser and coached him in lacrosse and football, recalled him as unusually "mature, serious, thoughtful, well-liked, and really respected" among his peers. Dave "worked hard, he wanted to succeed," both on the field and academically, Bordley said. "He was a great teammate that cared about his peers. He was actively involved in the community service program and was quick to come to the aide of a friend who needed support during a difficult time." Bordley added that "I cautioned him against going to Duke because I didn't think he had the innate athleticism to play at that level. I thought he was a little too small. But he was a very smart, tough athlete, and at Duke he became sort of the quarterback of the defense."

These leadership qualities had been noted by adult mentors from Dave's childhood. Bill Moulden, a summer camp director and former Green Beret sergeant, saw in him a "tenacious spirit" and a "lead by example" disposition. "Dave was always a joy to have on-board," Moulden recalled. "You could always, as in *always*, rely on him to lead the way. First into cold water, first to a muddy beach, when ordered to jump he would be airborne as the last syllable still hung in the air. The more difficult the task the faster his response."

Lacrosse is a game in which pure determination and hard work can go a long way. Dave made himself a three-year starter on the Duke team, was its defensive player of the year as a sophomore and won its Nutcracker Award as a junior. The Nutcracker Award went to the team's hardest hitter of the previous year.

Evans threw himself into his academic work and partying as well as practicing and playing lacrosse. A multitasker, he often did homework while watching TV, listening to music, and instant-messaging on his computer. He was fiercely goal-directed. After his sophomore year, while friends were at the beach, Evans worked for Senator Elizabeth Dole to build his résumé. He interned with Merrill Lynch the next summer and with UBS in Durham for part of his junior year, while carrying a full courseload and a demanding practice schedule.

On the party scene, he loved the limelight and was a prankster with a sardonic sense of humor. He showed up at Tailgate dressed in a range of wild costumes.

Generally self-confident, Evans was also so affectionate in the presence of a stunning, statuesque girlfriend that another female friend called him a "puppy dog."

Collin Finnerty, a twenty-year-old sophomore, was "a sweet-tempered, shy, considerate kid in a big body, this baby face, this deep voice, a Jolly Green Giant." So said Yani Newton, a member of the women's team. She got a kick out of his repeated displays of appreciation after she had once folded his clothes, instead of just dumping them, when she needed to use the dryer in which he had left them.

Collin stood six feet five. At 175 pounds, he was thin, with a conspicuously freckled visage that would earn him the moniker "baby-faced" in the nation's press. Not a big talker, Collin made friends easily. He had a warm, welcoming smile, a ready laugh, a self-effacing manner. At Chaminade, a Roman Catholic school in Mineola, Long Island, he had combined athletic stardom with a perfect disciplinary record. He met his first girlfriend, Jess, in middle school and was still dating her when he was at Duke and she at Boston College. (Jess's two brothers both switched their lacrosse jersey numbers to 13 in Finnerty's honor.) With athletic ability in sports ranging from basketball to skiing, Collin also was an accomplished guitar player, and friends noted his unusually discerning ear for music, especially his ability to ferret out rarely heard songs that soon would become popular.

Collin's reserved demeanor and unusually mild disposition masked a personal warmth often unseen by the outside world but familiar to those who knew him well. "Collin literally has no temper," his girlfriend, Jess, observed. "The only way I can even tell he's mad is if he takes a really deep breath, and then that's it." Throughout the year-long ordeal that was to befall him and his family, he tended to keep his feelings inside, lest he upset his friends or family.

Dr. Bradley Hammer, Collin's academic mentor at Duke, praised "Collin's deeply sensitive creativity, critical and profoundly analytical thinking skills, and the cogency in which he discourses himself." Hammer recalled Collin's "special rapport with his fellow students," which flowed from a combination of "his hard work, diligence, genuineness, and overwhelming likeability." Hammer gave Collin an A in freshman research writing, but the student's character most stood out: "his sense of genuine good-heartedness and devotion to hard work and critical reflection" gave him "a distinct and rare maturity for a young man his age."

Collin's record had a small blot that would grow to gargantuan proportions in the fun-house mirror that is the national media in a feeding frenzy. He and two friends were arrested and charged with simple assault after a November 2005 shouting match outside a bar in Washington's Georgetown area had ended in a brief brawl. It was treated as no big deal then. But once the rape scandal erupted, Collin would be widely accused of beating up a gay man in a homophobic hate crime. In fact, while his two antagonists accused Collin of using antigay slurs, nobody involved in the scuffle was gay. Collin never thought they were gay. And he never hit either of them. On these points the prosecution and Collin's defense lawyers were agreed.

Still, because this trivial episode intersected with the rape charges, Collin would regularly be deemed the worst of the worst, a caricature of an out-of-control, misogynistic, homophobic frat boy. This was a description that no one who knew him would remotely recognize. More, perhaps, than anyone else, Collin would suffer from the harsh, distorting glare of the media.

Reports of the character of Reade Seligmann by numerous people who had encountered him in his home town and high school and at Duke were all glowing. Seligmann, who was twenty-one in the spring of 2006, had one of the most impressive athletic résumés at Duke: football and lacrosse captain at high-powered Delbarton School, in Morristown, New Jersey. High-school all-American in lacrosse both junior and senior years. Selected as a senior to play in the National High School Senior Showcase. All-conference, area, and league in football. Rushed for forty-one touchdowns in his junior and senior years. Recipient of the award given annually to the student who best embodied the school's ideals of strong character, integrity, and desire to excel (the "Red" Green '56 Fighting Spirit Award). Six foot one, 225 pounds. Recruited by every Ivy League school and lots of others.

When he was not too busy winning state championships, Reade volunteered in Appalachia and poor areas of New York City. He inspired praise like this: "If I had a son, I would hope he could be like Reade. I have been teaching at the high school level for 24 years, and I have never said or written that about another student." So said his religion teacher, Patricia Crapo, in a college recommendation.

Near the end of Reade's junior year, Abbot Giles Hayes, the monk who oversees the Roman Catholic school, wrote him a letter. It said: "I cannot help but notice the respect and admiration that your teammates have for you; no, more than teammates, all the kids here, and maybe especially the younger kids."

Reade would probably have gone to Harvard, which wanted him. But his father, Phil Seligmann, had suffered financial setbacks as a result of the September 11, 2001, attacks, both because of the nature of his international trade finance business clients and because his office was shut down for weeks after the Twin Towers fell. With four sons to put through college, the family could not pass up the 90 percent scholarship offered by Mike Pressler. So Reade went south.

At Duke, Reade was one of two members of the lacrosse team with a Jewish heritage, on his father's side. He hung out with teammates less than did most lacrosse players, was unusually popular with other students, had a devoted girlfriend in his class, and made the ACC academic honor roll.

But there had been setbacks. Reade missed most of his freshman season after breaking his hand the first week of practice. Then he did so much running to keep in shape as to cause a hairline fracture in his foot.

As the 2006 season began, Reade was healthy, eager to prove himself, and vying to move from third to second midfield. Pressler told him to lose weight. The coach also pushed him to make more aggressive use of his size and strength. "This kid can be a freight train," Pressler thought. "Run through him, Reade. Run through him," the coach would shout during practice.

Reade was such a worrier that he was nicknamed "Frazzle." He and Yani Newton talked about how they were feeling at practices, how well they were playing, and how much playing time they might get, and they bucked up each other's morale at a regular breakfast before Reade's African-American history class. "If I was having a bad day, Reade was the guy I'd want to give me a big hug, and he'd always have a funny story that would crack you up," she recalled later. Yani was the only African American on the women's team and Reade the only white student in that history class. The professor, Raymond Gavins, would later sign an April 6 faculty statement that strongly suggested the players' guilt.

Dave, Collin, Reade, and some of their teammates would not have gotten scholarships at Duke but for their lacrosse stardom, and not all would necessarily have been admitted. Lacrosse put them over the top. But they were all solid students at Duke. So were most of their teammates. Coach Pressler demanded hard work in the classroom as well as on the field.

Devon Sherwood found that out after getting subpar grades in his first midterm exams. Soon thereafter, the coach walked up to Devon's locker and told him to take off his headphones. "You know what I'm here to talk to you about, don't you?" Yes, Devon said. "We can't have this on our team. You're capable of better." Devon understood. He knew what he needed to do. Pressler turned and walked away. After practice, he announced that everybody could go except Devon. Now he's calling me out publicly, thought the freshman. But this was not for show. The coach explained that one of the captains, Dan Flannery, was going to line up student tutors to help Devon study. Dan drove Devon to the off-campus, rented house he shared with Dave Evans and Matt Zash. Within two days Devon had two tutors.

He also had a new work ethic. His grades got better, rising from a 2.7 GPA to a 3.0. Pressler was proud. That meant a lot, Devon later recalled, coming from "the best coach I'd ever had, a man of loyalty and honor."

Every weekend, Devon later recalled, "Coach Pressler said to us, 'Protect yourselves and look out for each other. You have so much going for you, and so much to lose.'"

2. AN UGLY SCENE:

DUKE MEETS DURHAM

PRESSLER'S WARNINGS SOMETIMES FELL on deaf ears. On Monday, March 13, 2006, the captains hosted the stripper party that was to bring them and their team so much pain and cost their coach his job.

The locus was the rented, run-down Evans-Flannery-Zash house where Danny had taken Devon Sherwood to help him find tutors. The address was 610 North Buchanan Boulevard, in the genteel Trinity Park neighborhood across Buchanan from Durham's walled East Campus.

It was spring break. The campus was largely deserted. But most lacrosse players had returned Sunday night to resume practice after beating Loyola College, 9–7, in a game played on a neutral field in San Diego. "Now," Coach Pressler told a reporter after the game, "we look ahead to the most difficult weeks in Duke lacrosse history." He meant the games against North Carolina, Cornell, and Georgetown. His words proved prophetic in a very different sense.

The team had a light running-and-weight-lifting practice Monday morning. Team tradition called for a bonding party that week. Their classmates were living it up on spring break, and all they had had was a cold, rainy trip to supposedly sunny San Diego. They were tired and spent and needed some fun. The previous year, unbeknownst to the coach, they had gone to Teasers Gentlemen's Club, a local strip joint, with a dozen members of the women's team in tow. But Teasers had recently been cracking down on fake ID cards. Concerned that many of the younger players would be turned away or get in trouble with fake IDs, some of the seniors had a bright idea: Instead of taking the team to the strippers, bring the strippers to the team.

Dan Flannery did an online search for female escort services. The first two sites he found had disconnected phone numbers; the third was Allure Escort Services and Bunny Hole Entertainment. He called Allure and slightly lowballed the number of guys who would be there, estimating twenty to thirty. He asked for white girls. The agency said they would call back in fifteen minutes and that the number of guys didn't matter. The woman called back to offer two girls in their late twenties, one Hispanic, one with brown hair and blond highlights. The woman said the pair had worked together several times before and measured about 36–25–35. For $400 each, they would arrive at 11:00 P.M. and dance for two hours. Flannery agreed.

A credit card was needed to confirm the reservation, the agency told Flannery. He hadn't expected this. Worried about identity theft, he gave the woman his credit card number, but then blurted out that his name was Dan "Flannigan." That decision—which Flannery never tried to hide from police—would later be cited to prove a conspiracy by *all* the players to conceal their *first* names at the party.

More than one top Duke administrator later compared the hiring of strippers, with perfect hindsight, to bringing a stick of dynamite into the house.

In fact, this sort of thing was not uncommon at Duke. The basketball team, which enjoyed godlike status on campus, had hired strippers for a party just two weeks before. Over the 2005–2006 academic year, fraternities, sororities, and athletic teams hired strippers for more than twenty parties. This tally, never challenged by Duke, was computed by a lacrosse player's father after the players had been trashed by their university and held up to national scorn in the media for hiring strippers. The father did some old-fashioned investigative reporting that none of the hundreds of professional journalists covering the story ever thought to do. He opened the yellow pages, found four "escort" agencies, called them up, and asked what services they offered and what experience they had with Duke parties. Plenty, it turned out.

Indeed, while the lacrosse players were at Duke taking a break from practices, conditioning, and games—no spring break for them—many of their classmates and other students around the country were partying around the clock at Myrtle Beach, Panama City, Cancun, and other magnets for college kids on spring break. A brief search through webshots.com, a photo hosting service, on April 21,2007, brought up 293,165 photos under "spring break party"; 62,242 under "spring break drunk"; 40,934 under "spring break beer"; 6,427 under "spring break naked"; and 53,359 under "strippers." Youtube has thousands of soft-porn videos of student sexual activities over spring break.

Across town that afternoon, in southern Durham, twenty-seven-year-old Crystal Mangum got a call from Tammy, at Angel's Escort Service. There was a job for her that night, dancing for a group of guys at a bachelor party at 610 North Buchanan.

Durham is sandwiched between two more upscale cities. Raleigh, the state capital, is fourteen miles to the southeast of Duke's north Durham cam-

pus. Six miles to the southwest lies Chapel Hill, a smaller town that is home
to the University of North Carolina's flagship campus. UNC is famously Duke's
archrival in basketball, lacrosse, and other sports. The region is called the Research Triangle, due to the concentration of high-tech companies attracted by
the universities' research facilities and the educated workforce that they provide, with the nation's highest number of Ph.D.'s per capita.

But Durham's $23,000 median per capita income is just over half the
$41,000 in annual tuition and fees paid by a single Duke student. The city's
210,000 people are 44 percent African American, and there are substantial
pockets of poverty. Some 15,000 Durhamites work mostly unskilled and low-
skilled jobs at Duke, the city's largest employer.

Psychologically marinated in the tortured racial history of the old South,
many black employees resent the perceived arrogance and condescension of
Duke students. Some Dukies are cavalier about making messes for employees
to clean up. Some employees call Duke "the plantation." And with 86 percent of the students coming from out of state (with New York, Florida, California, Maryland, New Jersey, and Texas, in that order, the most common
home states after North Carolina), most have even less in common with
North Carolina blacks than do North Carolina whites.

The disrespectful attitude of some students is not the only source of resentment among Durhamites. Many, black and white alike, harbor the ele-
mental, age-old resentment felt by people who don't have much money for
people who do. Such class animus usually just smolders. Sometimes it erupts.
The animus is not confined to the poor. It is lodged deep in the bones of
many a news reporter and professor, among others.

"Duke is the shining castle on the hill," Joseph B. Cheshire V, a prominent lawyer from Raleigh once explained. "And people don't like the shining
castle on the hill." Cheshire, who takes pride in his family's efforts over five
generations to salve wounds left by slavery and racism, has represented many
poor black defendants. Beginning in late March 2006, when he became Dave
Evans's defense lawyer, he would get a dispiriting lesson in the power of racial
bias against fortunate white people.

Duke's proximity to resentful Durhamites has made town-gown relations
more delicate than at most universities. A work stoppage by black employees
could shut the place down. A small race riot could scare away applicants for
years. And whenever Durham crime leaks into Duke territory, chills run
down the spines of university administrators.

Durham's mayor, Bill Bell, and the city manager, the police chief, and a
majority of the city council in 2006 were black. These officials owed to black
bloc voting—orchestrated by the powerful Durham Committee on the Affairs

of Black People—their political dominance of a city with slightly more white than black voters. Michael Biesecker, Durham bureau chief of the Raleigh *News & Observer,* described the committee as "a venerable group in Durham that played a key role in the local struggle for civil rights. Its endorsements carry strong weight with many of the city's black residents." The committee was especially critical in encouraging racial bloc voting in elections for the Durham School Board, where a 4–3 split between white and black members had remained constant after 1993. Together with leading black ministers, the committee has power to send Duke's prestige plummeting.

So Duke presidents—now Richard Brodhead—their staffs, and board members have worked very, very hard to keep black Durhamites as happy as possible. They do their utmost to be on friendly terms with local political leaders, who in 2006 ranged from Mayor Bell and North Carolina NAACP president William J. Barber II to District Attorney Michael Nifong, who is white. Duke has launched a variety of programs to share its wealth with Durhamites, including free care at Duke's hospital.

Mangum did not come from the lowest stratum of Durham society. Daughter of an African-American retired mechanic who still works on cars in his front yard, her parents lived together in the house where she and her (then) two children also lived. She was said to be taking courses at North Carolina Central University (NCCU), a historically black college in southern Durham, although virtually no one on campus appeared to have any contact with her before the fall of 2006.

Mangum was not leading the kind of life that most college students aspire to have. She had graduated from Hillside High School in 1996, gotten married, and joined the navy. But she was discharged after becoming pregnant with another man's child (she divorced her husband of seventeen months) and repeatedly showing up for work drunk. Delois Burnette, Mangum's former minister, told the *News & Observer* that soon after she returned to Durham, it was clear that she had a drinking problem. She had copped a misdemeanor plea in 2002 to avoid a felony trial for stealing a taxicab, leading police on a high-speed chase, driving at a pursuing cop who had exited his car, and hitting the squad car when he jumped aside, visibly laughing all the while. She had claimed in 1996, at age seventeen, that she had been gang-raped by three men at age fourteen and in 1998 that her husband had taken her out in the woods and threatened to kill her. Her father later said she made up the former incident.

Mangum had a long history of psychological problems. Doctors at UNC Hospital diagnosed her with hypertension, anxiety, and bipolar disorder—a condition that causes severe mood swings. She had abused narcotics and spent a week in a state mental hospital in the summer of 2005. She was also prescribed two antipsychotic drugs, Depakote and Seroquel, that year.

Mangum found what for her was steady work from January into March 2006 as an "exotic dancer"—stripper—under the name "Precious" at the Platinum Pleasures Club, in Hillsborough, north of Durham. She had a pattern of passing out onstage. "It was just constant, every night," former manager Yolanda Haynes later told reporters, while adding that she never saw Crystal take drugs or drink. Three nights before the March 13–14 lacrosse party, Haynes sent Crystal to the bathroom after she had started pulling a female customer's hair and making sexual advances toward the customer. The manager later found Crystal naked and passed out cold in the bathroom. She had to be dragged and carried out to the parking lot, still unconscious, by four people. She was so heavy that they accidentally dropped her onto the gravel, probably leaving scratches and bruises, Haynes said.

Mangum also did private performances on the side. The weekend of March 10–13, Mangum had at least four private hotel room engagements with various escort customers. (Some called this prostitution.) She made approximately 20 to 25 calls to at least eight escort services that weekend for jobs. (With understatement, defense attorney Jim Cooney said that "we were able to track down at least one of those customers. We were comfortable with what his testimony would have been.") She performed for a couple with a vibrator during one hotel visit. According to a statement to the police by Jarriel Johnson, one of her "drivers" (some called them pimps), he took her to a Holiday Inn Express on Friday at 2:20 P.M., picking her up half an hour later. Then to her parents' home in Durham, his parents' home in Raleigh, and the Platinum Club until 4:30 A.M. Saturday. Then to a job at the Millennium Hotel from 5:15 to 6:15 A.M. Then to her parents' house for some sleep.

Later Saturday, after Mangum had hosted a visit from Matthew Murchison, the man she sometimes described as her boyfriend, Johnson went to pick her up about 5:30 P.M., played with her two kids while she got ready, and eventually "we drive around downtown Raleigh to find this guy" she had met. No luck. They bought Chinese food, checked into a hotel, waited for the guy to call. When he did not, Mangum and Johnson had sex while watching TV. He went home about midnight. On Sunday he found Crystal at the same hotel "with an older gentleman that she says he wants to see her perform." Johnson waited in the car. Then they drove to his parents' house. By then Crystal and Johnson weren't getting along. While he was driving her back to Durham, she had him pull over, got out, and started walking down the road, telling him to leave her alone. Johnson gave chase in the car, urging her to get back in. Finally she did.

On Monday afternoon, Mangum asked Johnson to take her to a job that night at the "bachelor party." He agreed but later canceled because his phone had been on the blink since she had spilled her drink into it the day before. So she lined up Brian Taylor, her other regular "driver." Her father drove her to Brian's house, where she had two twenty-two-ounce Icehouse beers and took a shower before heading for 610 North Buchanan.

Lacrosse players had been drifting over to the party since about 2:00 P.M. "We were all playing Beirut"—also known as beer pong—"hanging outside, and watching TV," Danny Flannery was to tell police three days later. A neighbor noticed them drinking beer in the backyard while playing washers (similar to horseshoes).

Coach Pressler allowed legal drinking forty-eight or more hours before the next game. But some of the drinkers were underage. And the indoor-outdoor drinking party at 610 North Buchanan evoked a different kind of town-gown problem. The many loud, raucous parties in the off-campus houses rented by 20 percent of Duke's students annoyed and sometimes infuriated their older neighbors. Especially in Trinity Park, a neighborhood of grand old houses, multifamily apartments, trendy restaurants, and seedy little houses like the one rented by Evans, Flannery, and Zash. Many professors, retired professors, and other professionals live there.

Student renters and their guests were known for "screaming at the top of their lungs at two in the morning, urinating on lawns, throwing beer cans around, driving fast, that sort of stuff," Francis Conlin, a mechanical engineer, later complained to *The New York Times*. And leaving their own yards full of trash after staggering off to bed.

Raucous drinking parties are routine at campuses around the country, of course. What caused so much tension at Duke was a university policy since the mid-1990s banning the huge keg parties in and near the dorms that had once kept the party scene centered on the campus, where students are required to live for three years. The exiling of fraternities from the campus main quad in 2002 only increased the demand for off-campus party houses.

This unofficial policy of exporting the drinking problem beyond Duke's boundaries made sense from a legal standpoint. It would help the university escape liability if students were injured or killed while drunk, as occurred in a 1997 case at MIT. A freshman named Scott Krueger drank himself to death there in a fraternity initiation that occurred in university-owned housing. But liability avoidance cannot negate the reality that many college kids are so determined to find ways to get drunk that closing off one option often drives them to more dangerous or disruptive alternatives.

Indeed, the Duke policy did lead to disruption, especially in Trinity Park, where it inflamed residents against students. Dukies in quest of big drinking parties congregated in the sixteen Trinity Park houses rented by groups of seniors, especially fraternities. On weekends, hundreds would spill across Buchanan Boulevard and wander the streets looking for parties. Police recorded well over two hundred calls from neighbors complaining of noise or alcohol violations from 2001 through 2004.

At the outset of the 2005–2006 academic year, Duke officials tried to stuff the genie back in the bottle by agreeing to a Durham Police Department crackdown on Duke's own students. This policy shift involved overt discrimination, with Dukies selectively arrested for petty infractions that would earn other Durhamites mere citations.

Durham police and state Alcohol Law Enforcement officers tried to scare returning Duke students straight by hitting 194 of them with drinking and noise citations in late August 2005, including ninety-one at one party alone (in a search later ruled illegal, since it occurred without a warrant). Such steps could bring at best a temporary respite, however. When Evans and Flannery got noise citations for a loud party on January 10, for example, it was the fourth time police had been called by neighbors to their house since September. And theirs was not even in the top ten Dukie-rented Trinity Park houses in generating complaints to police. That said, these were petty allegations: Upon finding Flannery not guilty of the charge later that spring, Durham County District Court Judge David LaBarre said, "It seems to me this court and all other courts can make better use of its time than dealing with such cases as this."

Duke next decided to block students from renting in Trinity Park by buying houses from the landlord, putting them under owner-occupancy covenants, and then reselling them to nice, quiet adults. The purchase of fifteen houses, including 610 North Buchanan, went through on February 28, two weeks before the lacrosse team annoyed the neighbors with its stripper party.

The Duke administration's assiduous efforts to kill off the party scene, off campus as well as on, amounted to "nothing short of an administrative ransacking of this school's social life," fumed Matt Sullivan, a graduating senior and former managing editor of *The Chronicle*, in a May 1, 2006, article. "Deans, cops, neighbors, nerds, and the shadow of the Ivy League have gradually and systematically pulled the rug out from underneath the backbone of this school's identity: fun. . . . This is not about [Duke president] Dick Brodhead's master plan to ruin your life. This is about a change in priorities for a university stuck between a rock and a hard place without a clue as to what made my class and I want to come down South instead of go to goddam Harvard."

The administration, Sullivan explained, had put "a stranglehold on its students' release valve [by] cutting off anywhere to cut loose on the campus where we pay them to live . . . forcing two mainstay fraternities off campus [and] appeasing nutso neighbors by having Dean [Stephen] Bryan and the Duke Police chase kids down Watts Street [in Trinity Park] and secretly buy up students' homes when that didn't calm them down. . . . Who would've wanted to spend four years at a place like this? Duke rained on our parade."

This cold rain would soon give way to a raging hurricane. The two women dancers were due to arrive at 11:00 P.M. on March 13, 2006. Almost forty lacrosse players (and two other students) had gathered in the small living room. The players had cleaned up the messy room that afternoon to make it presentable for the dance. Evans collected $25 per player to cover the agreed-on $800 and a keg of beer. Most sat around drinking and listening to music. A few had partied hard for most of the day. Others, like Reade Seligmann, who had been playing golf all afternoon, spent little time at the party. Still others, like Bo Carrington, drank nothing at all and left before the strippers arrived. Matt Zash wanted no part of the strippers and watched TV in his room.

The first dancer, Kim Roberts, arrived between 11:05 and 11:15 in her own black Honda Accord. She wore jeans and a T-shirt and carried a large bag. Flannery assumed that she must be the Hispanic dancer. In fact she was part black, part Asian, light-skinned, and thirty-one years old. Flannery showed Roberts his ID (a real one) at her request and explained that this was not a bachelor party but a get-together among friends on the lacrosse team, all Duke students. Roberts smoked a cigarette and chatted with Flannery before going inside. In statements made afterward to police, they agreed that the conversation had been pleasant and nonconfrontational.

The front door was blocked by a couch that had been moved to make just enough room for dancing. Roberts entered the house with Flannery and Evans through the back door, collected her $400, met a few of the guys, chatted with Flannery while Evans made her a whiskey and diet Pepsi. She was friendly and outgoing. Everyone waited for the second dancer to arrive. And waited.

Flannery and Evans had Roberts call the escort agency to find out the story. Brian Taylor and Crystal Mangum had gotten lost. Finally he dropped her off about 11:40 P.M., a time verified by an 11:43 P.M. receipt from a nearby gas station where Taylor stopped after the dropoff. She was already clad in her skimpy dancing outfit: a white teddy, a see-through red sparkling top over a white bra, white underwear, white stiletto high heels. Although very late, she made no attempt at small talk and offered no apology to the players for tardiness.

The two women met for the first time in the backyard. Kim introduced herself as "Nikki" and Crystal as "Precious." They had a smoke. Crystal went inside and collected her $400. Then they went into the bathroom shared by Dave Evans and Matt Zash, where Kim changed into her outfit and they discussed their plan for the dance. Someone knocked and handed them two drinks. Crystal spilled hers into the sink. They both sipped Kim's rum and Coke.

One of the older players went into the living room and said that the women had finally both arrived but were not as expected. They did not bring bodyguards, as dancers usually do, and were not white or Hispanic, as the agency had described. The consensus was to proceed anyway. They had been waiting a long time, and it would be rude to send the dancers away. Devon Sherwood, recently arrived from the airport, jokingly welcomed the idea of nonwhite dancers. Someone else said, "D-Wood's gonna love it." Most of the guys tried to have fun and make the best of it. Flannery led the women into the living room to do their show.

The women started "dancing" at exactly midnight, according to one of more than twenty time-stamped photos taken by a team member. The guys were seated on couches and on the floor, smiling and lighthearted at first. But within ten or twenty seconds the smiles were gone, the cheering had stopped, and the mood had turned sour, the photos show.

Mangum, who was supposed to be the experienced lead dancer, could neither dance nor speak coherently. She fell to the floor as she tried to take her shoes off. The guys assumed she was dead drunk or on drugs. Roberts got down and they simulated oral sex. Then Mangum put her face into Roberts's lower anatomy in a way that many of the guys found disgusting. The women stood up. Many of the guys were close enough to reach out and touch them. None did. Roberts, too, projected annoyance and dismay about her dancing partner's condition.

She recalled the scene months later in an on-camera interview with the late Ed Bradley of CBS News's 60 Minutes.

BRADLEY: *"At some point, you said that she seemed intoxicated or—"*

ROBERTS: *"Yeah, something was going on, you know, where we were stumbling over each other, falling against each other, maybe almost tripping each other. So it started to get a little uncomfortable."*

The photos show some guys looking away. One looked at his feet. One was sending a text message on his phone. Another had his thumb pointed down. Another was passed out with his head flopping down on his chest. By 12:02 Ryan McFadyen was in the other room with his back turned, holding his cell phone. Then Matt Zash, already in a bad mood after an argument with his mother, went to his room with Ryan and Ed Douglas and watched David Letterman.

Reade Seligmann, seated on the floor, was shrinking back in one photo with a look of distaste. "I didn't like the tone of the party," Reade later told Ed Bradley. "And I just—it made me uncomfortable. I mean, it's as simple as that. I wasn't—it was a boring party, and I just didn't like the tone." Collin Finnerty didn't like it, either. "It wasn't fun to watch," he said months later. "People were talking over them. Maybe they expected everyone to be loving it, and maybe that's what happened. It was not appealing at all." "It was kind of boring, to be quite honest," Devon Sherwood recalled in another on-camera interview months later, this one with ABC's *Good Morning America*. "We were just sitting around. And there was nothing to it. It was very boring. I was itching to get out of there, because it was. I'd rather be going to sleep personally, to tell you the truth."

Roberts asked who would step up and take off his pants so the women could "play with it." No takers. "Do you have any toys?" a player asked, meaning sex toys. "No," replied Roberts, saying they would "use your dick but it would be too small."

The same guy leaned back on his stool and picked up a broom propped against the wall. "Why don't you use this?" he said in a joking tone. Or words to that effect. A few players recoiled. None thought that the comment was threatening or intended to offend the women. But Reade Seligmann, for one, thought the broom comment was a repulsive, offensive thing to say. He decided it was time for him to leave a party that had made him uncomfortable from the start.

Roberts thought so, too. She waited several seconds, and then exploded in rage. Whipping around on the offending player, she yelled curses, walked toward him, roughly pushed him aside with her forearm, spilling his beer, and stormed out of the living room, headed for the back door. Mangum followed, yelling and screaming, tripping, stumbling, and banging into walls as she followed Roberts through the house, while leaving her right shoe behind in the living room.

The performance was over. It had lasted four minutes, from midnight to 12:04 A.M., time-stamped photos show. And everyone in the house was angry, with the possible exception of one guy who had passed out. Roberts had not minded the banter about sex toys, she later told Ed Bradley, in one of many inconsistent statements that she ended up giving over the next several months. But when the partygoer with the broom said, "We'll just use this on you," as she recalled his words, "I started to think, what if he really did want to use a broomstick? What if?"

BRADLEY: *"Did you feel threatened, intimidated?"*

ROBERTS: *"Definitely. All of that. Not necessarily completely threatened that he might use that actual broomstick on me, but threatened that, if he would say that and I've only been on this dance floor for ten minutes, what's the next step? You know what I mean? What's next? What's the next thing they might say?"*

Roberts did not leave in any great hurry, however. Dan Flannery and Dave Evans caught up with the women in or near Dave's room. Roberts yelled that they could not talk to her that way, that they had disrespected her, that "I don't need to be doing this." Mangum was also yelling, loudly and incoherently.

"We tried to apologize and reason with the Hispanic stripper," Flannery later told police. "The black stripper was mumbling and stumbling. I was apologizing to the Hispanic stripper and she offered to give me a private dance that I refused." Roberts then offered to give her cell phone number.

The conversation between Flannery, Evans, Roberts, and Mangum spilled outside the house. Worried that they could be cited for a noise violation or for public indecency (since Roberts was topless), Flannery persuaded the strippers to go back into the house, saying that there would be apologies all around. But then Roberts saw the guy who made the broomstick comment, shouted at him again, and stormed into the bathroom, with Mangum following. Roberts angrily shut the door.

Some of the guys were almost as angry as Roberts. "Guys thought that we might have been hustled when they said that they were leaving," Evans later said in another Ed Bradley interview. "We paid $800 and they were there for five minutes, and naturally guys got upset." Evans told the women that if they were leaving they should give the money back—a demand echoed by many of the guys still in the living room. Others shrugged it off and talked about whether they should go to the Teasers strip bar after all.

While Flannery and Evans were talking to Roberts and the incoherent Mangum in Evans's room and outside the house, Reade Seligmann was making phone calls. He made eight calls on his cell, including six to his Duke girlfriend, between 12:05:37, which was ninety seconds after the dancing had stopped, and 12:14. The last call was to a taxi driver named Moezeldin Elmostafa, who picked up Reade and teammate Rob Wellington at 12:19.

The cabbie took Reade and Rob to an ATM, where a security video shows Reade taking out cash between 12:24 and 12:25, then to the Cookout Restaurant, where they ordered carryout food, and then to their dorm. Reade gave Elmostafa a big tip and swiped in at 12:46.

Back at the party, one guy told Evans he wanted to take back the money from Evans's bathroom, where Mangum had left her things. Another went into the bathroom and grabbed some money. Evans said this was stupid because her driver would come back with a gun and kill them. He took the money, gave it to Flannery, and told him to return it to the women. It's unclear whether that happened.

Mangum and Kim went back into Evans's bathroom and locked themselves in for five to ten minutes. According to Roberts's subsequent statement to police, she told Crystal she wanted to leave, but Crystal wanted to stay and make more money. "She was uncontrollable at this point and was yelling at the boys who were knocking at the door to leave us alone," Roberts said.

Some guys feared that the women might be doing drugs in the bathroom. Flannery slid money under the door to get them to leave. Defense lawyers later theorized that Mangum was painting her nails, because photos suggest that she left reddish stains on the railing of the back stoop a few minutes after leaving the bathroom.

The women left the bathroom about 12:15 or 12:20, taking all their stuff (except the unreturned money and Crystal's shoe), plus Evans's toiletries kit. Crystal was behind Kim.

The guys wanted Kim to resume dancing, she later told Ed Bradley. But while they did nothing threatening, she said, she was intimidated by their size and loudness. She ran to her car with breasts exposed, got in, and changed her clothes. Flannery followed, still apologizing. Kim lost track of where Crystal was for a few minutes—or so she told Bradley. But this assertion was inconsistent with her earlier police statement as well as the recollections of lacrosse players. They said that the women were close together every minute until both left the house.

By this point, many of the laxers (including Colin Finnerty) had also left the house. Kyle Dowd, a senior, had told the underclassmen to leave, lest they get in trouble with Pressler for attending a party with underage drinking. Still, some of the team members were hanging around outside, heated and agitated, yelling about being scammed. When Mangum arrived at the car, Evans later told police, she "was circling the car yelling. Her boobs were exposed and I thought that we were going to get a noise violation and that she was going to get a 'public nudity' charge." Roberts was sitting in the car. By then it was close to 12:25 A.M. A neighbor, Jason Bissey, was watching the scene from his porch in the apartment house across the alley. "I noted that the skimpily dressed woman had exited the car, saying something to the effect that she would go back into 610 to retrieve her shoe," Bissey later told police.

ROBERTS (*TO ED BRADLEY*): "*She obviously wasn't hurt or—because, you know, she was fine. . . . She wouldn't have went back in the house if she was hurt. She was fine.*"

BRADLEY: "*What'd she say?*"

ROBERTS: "*'There's more money to be made.'*"

Crystal headed around the house into the backyard. At 12:26 A.M. she made a cell call to Centerfold, another escort service for which she worked. Between 12:30:12 and 12:31:26, a succession of five time-stamped photos show her standing on the back stoop with one shoe on, her clothes still skimpy but unmussed. In a 12:30:47 A.M. photo she was peering into Dave Evans's toiletries kit (she had apparently stolen it from his bathroom), teeth showing in what looks like a smile. In others she was apparently trying to get in the back door, which Zash had locked, while holding the screen door open.

Then came a six-minute, photo-free period during which any rape would have to have occurred, unless Crystal had decided to go back into the house to retrieve her shoe *after* being gang-raped, kicked, beaten, and strangled. During that period, Zash told police, Crystal was cursing and pounding so hard on the back door that he feared she would break it. He did not let her in. The four to six guys left inside searched for her shoe but could not find it. A couple even considered calling the police, but held off, worried that doing so would ensure that Pressler would find out about the party. Evans, meanwhile, left by the front door, walked to another lacrosse house, a few yards away, rented by fellow senior William Wolcott, who had left the party just after the dance ended. Evans called his girlfriend.

Some guys heard a thump out back. They found Crystal sprawled on the back stoop, apparently passed out. She had fresh cuts on her right buttock and right outer heel, matching the pattern of the screen door's two jagged edges, in a 12:37:58 photo. It also showed new red stains on the black metal railing. Wet nail polish?

A player picked her up. She no longer had her black purse. One of the players put her arm over his shoulder and carried her to Kim's car, helping her into the passenger seat in a 12:41:32 photo. He asked Roberts to take her off their hands.

"By this point," Kim wrote in her statement for police, "it seemed that the fellas may have been ready for the evening to be over." But she noticed that Crystal did not have her purse and asked if she had "the most important thing, her money." Crystal said she did, but seemed incoherent, still insisting that there was more money to be made. Kim locked her in the car and went to the back of the house to look for Crystal's things. This solicitude for Crystal's money was prompted by Kim's instructions from the escort service: Bring back all $800 and then you'll get paid your share.

Finding nothing, Kim headed back to her car about 12:50, through a crowd of the team members who were still complaining about being scammed. She vented her anger by trash-talking them in a loud voice, especially one who made a rude comment.

"I called him a little dick white boy, who probably couldn't get it on his own and had to pay for it," Roberts recalled with a laugh in her 60 *Minutes* interview. "So he was mad, and it ended with him calling me the N word. And it echoed, so you heard 'nigger' once and then you heard, 'Yeah, you nigger, nigger, nigger.' You know what I mean? . . . [I] obviously provoked that remark. But then . . . he could have said 'black girl.' He didn't have to go that route."

Zash recalled hearing secondhand that the comment was: "We wanted white girls, not n——." Whatever the context, that one use of the N word, by one lacrosse player, in response to Kim's racial taunt, was to launch countless thousands of false media reports over the next year to the effect that the lacrosse players had hurled multiple racial slurs at the two women while they were inside the house doing their dance. In fact, all three defendants-to-be had left the party before the racial taunts and did not hear them.

By all accounts, Roberts stopped and screamed something like "Fuck Duke. I'm calling the cops. That's a hate crime." Then she drove off with the seemingly passed-out Mangum in the passenger seat. One of the guys walking back toward Duke's East Campus yelled, "Hey, bitch, thank your grandpa for my nice cotton shirt."

The guys still lingering outside took off, fearing a police raid or a visit from Crystal's driver or both. At 12:53 A.M., Kim called 911, saying that she and a girlfriend had been driving (or walking, she said at one point) past 610 North Buchanan and that guys had yelled racial slurs at them. Her assertions were, she later acknowledged, lies.

Durham police sergeant John C. Shelton arrived at the house two minutes later. Nobody was home. After other officers arrived, Shelton shone a light through the window. He saw only scattered beer cans and bottles, a keg, and plastic cups.

The party was over. But not the anger. The anger was just beginning to do its work.

3. SO MANY STORIES, SO FEW INJURIES

A S KIM ROBERTS DROVE AWAY from 610 North Buchanan, she asked her passenger if she had her money. No response. Where did she live? No response. She was basically out of it, Roberts later told police.

Roberts tried to get Mangum out of the car. "I . . . push on her leg. I kind of push on her arm," Roberts said months later, to Chris Cuomo of ABC's *Good Morning America*. "And clear as a bell, it's the only thing I heard clear as a bell out of her was, she said—she pretty much had her head down, but she said plain as day, 'Go ahead, put marks on me. That's what I want. Go ahead.'"

This remark "chilled me to the bone," Roberts told Cuomo. But she had kept it to herself for more than seven months, never mentioning it to the police or to the many journalists who had asked what light she could shed on whether Mangum's rape claim was a fabrication.

Roberts's statements to Cuomo might seem powerful evidence for the defense. But she would also be easy to discredit. These were the latest in a parade of inconsistent statements. In the beginning she told police the rape claim was a "crock." Then she told reporters it might be true. Then she veered back again.

Unable to dislodge her unwanted passenger, Roberts drove to a Kroger twenty-four-hour grocery store two miles from the lacrosse house—passing up a police station a mile away—and asked the security guard for help. At 1:22 A.M., the guard called 911. Sergeant Shelton responded. He called in that the woman was "just passed-out drunk."

Roberts told Shelton that she had made the earlier 911 call after picking up the other woman as she was being pelted by racial slurs from men while walking past 610 North Buchanan. This claim, like the 911 call itself, was a lie, Roberts later admitted.

Mangum seemed unconscious. But Shelton concluded that she was faking after she switched to mouth breathing when he put an ammonia capsule under her nose. Similar suspicions about Mangum faking various conditions would arise again and again during the ensuing weeks. Shelton tried to pull her out of the car, as Roberts stood by. Mangum grabbed the emergency brake and held on. He got her out with a "bent-wrist come-along." She collapsed on the ground. Shelton and Officer Willie Barfield got her into Barfield's patrol car. Clad in one white high-heeled shoe and a skimpy see-through outfit, she would not speak and had no ID.

Shelton decided that she met the criteria for involuntary commitment as a danger to herself or others. He told Barfield and Officer Joseph Stewart to take her to the Durham Access Center, a facility for processing patients addled by mental illness or drugs. He also said authorities should send someone to check on her children. Mangum knew what that meant, having been involuntarily committed before, for a week, in the Holly Hill Hospital in Raleigh the summer before. This time she might be locked up for a night. Or for a lot longer.

Mangum had said nothing about rape during the first ninety minutes after leaving the party. Not to Roberts. Not to the security guard. Not to the three cops who had attended to her. This silence changed after she arrived at Durham Access about 1:55 A.M., identifying herself as "Honey" and saying she did not want to go to jail. A nurse, who thought Mangum's thinking disorganized, asked if she had been raped. Prompting a patient with such a question violated the center's policies. Someone eager to avoid involuntary commitment could seize on the suggestion. That's just what Mangum seems to have done. She nodded yes to the nurse's question. The nurse later told police she had been unable to speak coherently and acted psychologically hurt. Mangum also said at Durham Access, Barfield later reported, that "Nikki" had taken all her belongings, including phone, ID, and $2,000 cash.

It was when she was complaining about her missing money that she started to cry. But her nod in response to the rape question was her ticket out of involuntary confinement. Barfield took her to the Duke University Medical Center emergency room for treatment and a sexual assault workup, arriving about 2:40 A.M.

"While being interviewed at Duke, her story changed several times," Durham police officer Gwendolen Sutton reported. Mangum told Sutton that she "ended up in the bathroom with five guys who forced her to have intercourse and perform sexual acts" and "later stated that she was penetrated by all five." That Brett had penetrated her vagina with his hands and penis. Also that "Nikki" had stolen her money and cell phone.

But when Sergeant Shelton questioned her, she said that after her performance "some of the guys from the party pulled her from the vehicle and groped her" but nobody "forced her to have sex." Shelton walked out to the parking lot and called in to the watch commander. The woman had recanted the rape allegation, he reported. Then he heard that she had told a doctor she had been raped. Shelton went back and asked Mangum again if she had or had not been raped. She said that she did not want to talk to him anymore, started crying, and said something about being dragged into a bathroom.

A Duke campus cop, Christopher Day, overheard the Durham cops and wrote in his report that "she was claiming that she was raped by approximately 20 white males at 610 N. Buchanan" and "changed her story several times." He added that "Durham police stated that charges would not exceed misdemeanor simple assault against the occupants of 610 N. Buchanan." Day did not mention the accuser's race.

A female Durham police officer, B. S. Jones, asked Mangum at 3:50 A.M. what had happened. She said that "Brett knew the deal" and "the guys weren't with it" and Nikki "had taken her purse and phone." Then she "began to sleep again and told me all she wanted to do was go home." Officer Jones did not report her saying anything about being raped.

Did Mangum want out? Did someone nudge her to go forward?

Three doctors and five nurses examined her between three and nine or ten in the morning. In a departure from standard procedures, several hours passed before a forensic nurse arrived for the examination. And then Duke Hospital provided only a trainee sexual assault nurse examiner (SANE), another irregularity.

This process included taking samples for a rape kit to be given to police for comparison with the DNA of any suspects: panties and other clothing, cheek scrapings, oral, vaginal, and rectal swabs, and a pubic hair combing, a process performed by a senior resident at the hospital, Dr. Julie Manly.

Now Mangum seemed alert and responsive, not drunk or impaired. Her hysterical behavior and crying suggested that something might have happened to her. But the doctors and nurses were unanimous in finding no physical evidence of the attack described by Crystal—that is, a brutal assault by three, five, or twenty varsity athletes, lasting a half hour. No bruises. No bleeding. No vaginal or anal tearing. No grimacing, sweating, changes in vital signs, or other symptoms ordinarily associated with the serious pain of which she complained.

Dr. Manly performed a thorough physical examination for any signs of sexual assault. The only physical evidence of trauma, she noted, was three small nonbleeding cuts on Crystal's right knee and heel. Manly later said that she left the ER on the morning of March 14, 2006, believing that Mangum had been raped. The patient's histrionic behavior suggested to Manly a traumatic experience, and the doctor also had seen fluid in Crystal that she believed was semen. But Manly started doubting this diagnosis after learning that the state crime lab had found no male DNA matching any lacrosse player in Mangum.

The last nurse to see Crystal Mangum had no such doubts. Tara Levicy, the "SANE nurse," was to play a little-known but critical role in bringing about the prosecution of the lacrosse players.

A strong feminist who had played a part in a *Vagina Monologues* production and who saw herself as an advocate for rape victims, Levicy was later to acknowledge that she had never doubted the truthfulness of a single rape accuser.

Levicy took notes during Dr. Manly's pelvic examination. Crystal's head, back, neck, chest, breasts, nose, throat, mouth, abdomen, and extremities were all normal, with no sign of rectal penetration or trauma. Levicy noted that Dr. Manly had found "diffuse edema of the vaginal walls." Edema means swelling. As Kathleen Eckelt, a longtime Maryland forensic nurse who trains SANE nurses in her home state, observed, "Edema, diffuse or otherwise, is *not* an injury. It is the body's *response* to an injury, an infection, or a disease or inflammatory process of some sort." According to Eckelt, diffuse vaginal wall edema could have several possible causes. Smoking. Sex within twenty-four hours of the vaginal exam. Frequent sex. Tricyclic antidepressants or other medications with properties similar to them—such as Flexeril. Crystal Mangum fit all four categories.

Mangum told the three doctors and first four nurses who spoke with her that she had been raped vaginally and had great pain "down there," rating it a 10 on a scale of 1 to 10. But she specifically denied any anal or oral penetration or other physical assault. She also denied having tenderness of the abdomen, chest, back, head, neck, or extremities. And she denied using any alcohol, tobacco, or drugs that night.

Then, during her interview with Levicy, Crystal contradicted much of what she had told the other three doctors and four nurses. Now she said she had been penetrated orally and anally as well as vaginally. Now she said she had been pushed, pinched, and kicked "in my butt" and had lost fake fingernails scratching at an assailant. Now she complained of pain not only in the vaginal area but also in the anus, face, shoulders, chest, abdomen, back, buttocks, and legs. Now she said she had had an alcoholic drink and was taking Flexeril, a muscle relaxant with side effects, including badly impaired judgment when combined with alcohol.

Crystal specifically denied to Levicy that she had been choked and repeated her denials that she had been hit by hand or fist—statements that she would later contradict.

Levicy's standardized Sexual Assault Exam Report included a checklist interview and a narrative interview. According to Levicy's four pages of notes of the narrative interview, Crystal said that after the dancing had started, the men were getting excited and "Nikki" was pushing her into a sexual "three-some." This development scared Crystal. She "stormed out of the house" and out to the car. Nikki helped a lacrosse player drag Crystal back out of the car and into the house as she protested no. "Adam," "Brett," and "Matt" took off her clothes. They held her by both legs, pinched, pushed, and kicked her. "Matt said I'm getting married tomorrow I can't do this. Adam said yes you can and then that was Matt put his private part in me and he did not use a condom and he said oh yeah I love black pussy. . . . They kept calling me nigger bitch. . . . They kept grabbing me and said I swear I'll kill you if you don't go through with this. . . . Adam came around back and put it in my butt. . . . Matt put it in my mouth and that's why my breath smells so bad."

Mangum's claim that "Matt said I'm getting married tomorrow" was a clear sign—albeit ignored by the police and prosecutors who later pressed charges—that her entire story was a fabrication. No Duke lacrosse player or other guest at the party was getting married the next day, or any time soon. But it's not hard to imagine where Mangum might have gotten the idea: Tammy, at Angel's Escort Service, had told her that she would be dancing for a group of guys at a bachelor party.

Matt raped her vaginally and orally, Crystal said. Adam raped her anally. Brett did not penetrate her. She had told Officer Sutton that Brett had. Then the three dressed her, and Nikki, who had been on the other side of the door, helped them clean her up with a towel and take her to the car. Nikki drove her away. Then she "took all my money and everything" and pushed her out of the car. Levicy later recalled Mangum telling her the attack occurred at about 1:00 A.M.

Over the subsequent ten months, Levicy would repeatedly tell police that she thought Mangum had been raped, adjusting her theories to bat aside new evidence that the charge was false. Levicy later said that she had never seen a sexual assault victim behave hysterically in the way that Mangum did at Duke Hospital that night but dismissed the comparison as insignificant, since "no two sexual assault victims behave the same way." Shrugging off the absence of physical evidence of sexual assault, she would also explain away the lack of lacrosse-player DNA in Crystal with a feminist slogan: "Rape is about power, not passion." Dr. Anne Burgess, a pioneer in treatment of rape victims, would later tell defense attorneys that Levicy's analysis was fatally flawed. But for Nifong, Levicy was an ideal witness.

Next evening, March 15, Mangum went to her regular hospital, at the University of North Carolina, and added some dramatic new twists. Duke Hospital had sent her away without any pain medications, a situation that she appeared eager to remedy. Now she said she had been knocked to the floor several times and had hit her head on the sink. Now she said the rapists had assaulted her with hands and fists, contradicting what she had said at Duke Hospital. Now she was limping and complaining of tender muscles, acute pain in her knees and neck, and trouble moving her head. And now she explained that she had been "drunk and did not feel pain" while telling doctors at Duke Hospital the day before that (among other things) she had had nothing to drink.

"Due to the patient's long psychological history," including bipolar disorder, anxiety, and hypertension, one UNC physician wrote, "she is at very high risk of narcotic abuse, and at clinic, we have recommended not to prescribe the patient any narcotics." But a second physician prescribed more Flexeril and fifteen doses of Percocet, a powerful narcotic painkiller.

Three days later, Crystal Mangum was back at the Platinum Club, saying, "I'm going to get paid by the white boys," according to H. P. Thomas, the strip club's security manager. She said nothing about being raped or assaulted. And on March 23, 24, 25, and into the early hours of March 26, Crystal was dancing her regular routine, according to Platinum Club records. Again she said nothing about rape. On March 28 and April 3, Crystal was back at the UNC hospital, asking for more narcotic painkillers and complaining of extreme pain in her neck, back, and knees from the alleged assault on March 14.

4. POLICE:

BUILDING A CASE WITHOUT EVIDENCE

EVERY POLICE DEPARTMENT HAS good cops, in-between cops, and bad cops. And this investigation—initially by police, and later by Durham district attorney Michael Nifong—could be a model for a criminal law exam question on ways to muddy the truth and finger innocent suspects, whether by incompetence or by design.

Within hours after Crystal Mangum had convinced the cops at the Duke Hospital on March 14 that her rape claim was a lie, a sergeant named Mark Gottlieb heard about the case. As soon as he learned that Duke students had been accused of gang rape by a black woman from Durham, the burly, forty-three-year-old detective went out of his way to take over the investigation.

Gottlieb had spent years as a domestic violence investigator and took pride in being a victim's advocate. He also hated Dukies and had an ugly history of abusing them, according to allegations by Duke students who dealt with him before the lacrosse case surfaced. They told *The Chronicle* that he filed false reports in their cases; displayed an attitude of ethnic bias by threatening to report to his supposed consulate an immigrant who was a naturalized U.S. citizen; engaged in excessive force; and failed to respect their constitutional rights.

Gottlieb got under way slowly. There was no detailed interview of Mangum until March 16, two days after her initial parade of inconsistent statements to cops, doctors, and nurses. No signed statement for another *three weeks*, a stunning deviation from sound police practice. No effort to interview Kim Roberts for almost a week, another stunning deviation. Or to interview Mangum's "driver," Jarriel Johnson, until April 6.

Police and prosecutors grossly misrepresented the Duke Hospital records by swearing in court papers that "medical records and interviews . . . revealed the victim had signs, symptoms, and injuries consistent with being raped and sexually assaulted vaginally and anally." There was also no investigation into the ample signs that Mangum was a prostitute whose activities with multiple sex partners and a vibrator could account for the "diffuse edema" that was the only conceivably relevant sign found at the hospital.

This sorry (at best) record came in what DA Nifong was to call a case of towering importance that "talks about what this community stands for" and that involved "one of the worst things that's happened since I became district attorney." Were Nifong and Gottlieb trying to find out whether Mangum was telling the truth? Their actions—and omissions—suggest not.

The lacrosse captains' first inkling that their stripper party would end up being more than a waste of money and a bad memory came during a March 15 team outing at a bowling alley. Coach Pressler got an urgent message from Sue Wasiolek, Duke's dean of student affairs. Dean Sue, as she liked to be called, told Pressler that the team had hired two strippers for a party. One had claimed she had been gang-raped. Police did not consider her credible, and Duke's top campus cop said it would "go away."

Pressler called his four captains aside and confronted them. They admitted hiring strippers but swore that nobody had touched them. Devon Sherwood saw the captains huddled with Pressler. Something's wrong, he thought. Had coach found out about the stripper party? That would be big trouble.

So it would. But the enormity of the charge eclipsed Pressler's anger about the strippers. He was not worried that it could be true. Pressler knew these young men very well. But he was worried about where this could go. Calling Dean Sue back, Pressler handed the phone first to Flannery and then to Zash. They said it was a lie. Dean Sue advised them (they later recalled) to cooperate with police and tell them the truth. She added that they should not hire attorneys, nor should they tell anyone about the allegations. Flannery clearly recalls Dean Sue saying: "Don't tell anyone. Not even your parents." (She has denied this.) The fewer people who knew about the allegations, she said, the better. And nothing would come of this.

That same night, a team member sent an e-mail to friends back home containing racist (or at least racially insensitive) comments about the two strippers. Other than the two racist responses to Kim Roberts's taunts as she was leaving the party, this player's remarks are the only documented instance of any racial comments by any of the forty-seven players, ever. And there is no evidence at all of racist remarks by Dave Evans, Reade Seligmann, or Collin Finnerty.

Gottlieb and Detective Benjamin Himan, his twenty-seven-year-old chief investigator, got around to interviewing Mangum at her house just before noon the next day, March 16, more than two full days after the alleged rape. She seemed shaken and could barely sit down, Himan later wrote. His handwritten notes, however, contained no hint of this alleged difficulty. Nor did her performance some thirty-six hours later at the Platinum Club.

Again she contradicted all of her previous accounts, on numerous points. For the first time she said that she had been strangled and hit as well as kicked. And now "Nikki" had begun morphing from the rapist-accomplice and thief portrayed in Levicy's notes into a sympathetic soul sister, as Crystal would later depict her.

The police had not yet seen Levicy's notes. Gottlieb and Himan may not have been fully aware of the many other inconsistencies underlying the skepticism of the police who had seen Mangum at Duke Hospital two days before. Crystal may well have seemed traumatized during the March 16 Gottlieb-Himan interview. And that morning, Himan later reported, he had been told by Tara Levicy that "there were signs consistent with a sexual assault during her test." So it's quite possible that Himan and Gottlieb—unlike the police at the hospital—believed that Crystal had been raped.

One point of consistency with her account to Levicy was Mangum's claim to Gottlieb and Himan that her assailants had called one another "Matt," "Brett," and "Adam" and that Adam had carried her to the car. This claim made prime suspects of four players on the team with those first names. The police later would add the two other residents of 610 North Buchanan, Dan Flannery and Dave Evans, bringing the list of total suspects at that point to six.

After describing what the three had done to her in vivid detail, Crystal was far from vivid when asked what they looked like. She was sure that they were white. But according to Himan's handwritten notes, she recalled little else except that "Adam" was "short, red cheeks fluffy hair chubby face, brn"; "Matt" was "heavy set short haircut 260–270"; "Bret" was "chubby." The lacrosse team had no players that came close to matching the descriptions she gave for "Matt" or "Brett."

Police immediately ruled out one of the team's three Matts as a suspect because he did not remotely resemble any of Crystal's three descriptions. That was Matt Danowski. He is tall and lean—much like Collin Finnerty. That's why neither player's photo was among the thirty-six that police showed Crystal on March 16 and 21, in the hope that she might be better at recognizing faces than at describing them.

Gottlieb had Officer Richard Clayton show her photos of twenty-four of the forty-six white lacrosse players just after seven the evening of March 16, and another twelve photos (twice apiece) on March 21. Asked then for a better description, she could recall nothing further. They all looked alike, she said. She added that she had drunk a twenty-four-ounce beer before the party and performed with a vibrator for a couple in a hotel room not long before that.

These pictures, all from the Duke lacrosse Web site, were arranged in six arrays of six photos, with one prime suspect in each array. Officer Michele Soucie looked on. "This is harder than I thought," Mangum told Clayton. But still she picked five faces. Four she identified with 100 percent certainty. The fifth was Reade Seligmann, whom she identified with only a "70 percent" confidence level; she did not recall where she had seen him at the party. She did not recognize Dave Evans at all when twice shown his picture on March 21.

Of course, Crystal's inability to identify any attackers did not necessarily mean that she had not been raped. This was especially true given that she clearly had been drunk or otherwise impaired the night of the lacrosse party. But unless her memory could improve with the passage of time—an unlikely scenario—no individual lacrosse player could properly be charged with assaulting her unless he was turned in by others at the party or implicated by physical evidence such as DNA.

According to forms signed by both Clayton and Mangum at the time, she was asked, as to each photo, "Is this the person you saw that sexually assaulted you?" And Crystal's father, Travis Mangum, told Associated Press reporter Emery Dalesio that she had identified her attackers in the March 16 lineup. But later Clayton contradicted this, asserting that she had identified only people that she believed attended the party.

This reason for this reversal—which came in an undated, unsigned, typewritten memo prepared by Clayton after the indictments of Evans, Finnerty, and Seligmann—is not hard to imagine. Crystal had told the doctors, nurses, Gottlieb, and Himan that there had been three rapists, not four or five. And the four faces she picked with certainty on March 16 and 21 did not include any of the three eventual defendants.

These March 16 and 21 photo sessions, on top of the hopelessly vague descriptions, showed that even if Mangum was raped, she had no idea who had done it. Her picks also could be seen as suggesting that she was willing to hurl a rape charge at players picked randomly.

Brad Ross, one of the four whom she picked with certainty, could conclusively prove that he was not even in Durham the night of the party. And her identifications of others were all flawed by various mistakes.

The police and prosecution did their best to cover up this powerful evidence of innocence, in violation of the spirit—if not the letter—of a landmark 1963 Supreme Court decision.

In *Brady v. Maryland*, the justices held that due process of law requires police and prosecutors to hand over to the defense all exculpatory evidence—all police notes, witness statements, scientific tests, and other evidence that might raise doubt as to a defendant's guilt. Unlike Warren Court decisions that excluded evidence of guilt to deter police from cutting constitutional corners, the *Brady* rule was designed solely to protect the innocent. But many police and prosecutors comply grudgingly or not at all. Sometimes they hide or destroy exculpatory evidence. Sometimes they withhold it on the pretense that it is not really exculpatory.

Such evasions and violations have been uncovered in thousands of cases (claims the Death Penalty Information Center), including most of the more than 120 cases in which men convicted of murder have been exonerated and released from death row.

Prosecutors withholding evidence has been a major issue in North Carolina in recent years. The first, and best-known, case involved the prosecution of Alan Gell, in which prosecutors withheld notes of interviews with *eighteen* people who saw the victim, Allen Ray Jenkins, alive after April 3, the day that prosecutors claimed that Gell killed Jenkins. The relevance of this date? After April 3, Gell was either out of state or incarcerated on unrelated charges and therefore could not have committed the crime. In the appeals process, Gell's representation changed (eventually including two attorneys involved in the lacrosse case, Joe Cheshire and Jim Cooney). The conviction was overturned, and a new trial led to Gell's acquittal—after this demonstrably innocent man had spent over nine years in prison.

Shortly after the Gell case revelations, an even more blatant instance of prosecutorial misconduct was brought before the state bar's Disciplinary Hearing Committee. In 1996, Jonathan Hoffman was sentenced to death, based largely on the testimony of his cousin, Johnell Porter. But the prosecutors in the case, Union County DA Kenneth Honeycutt and Scott Brewer, never revealed the extent of a sweetheart deal they had cut with Porter in exchange for his testimony. They even altered documents they provided to a judge describing the extent of their activities on Porter's behalf. After conviction, Hoffman's attorneys uncovered the withheld evidence; Hoffman, like Gell, received a new trial. The State Bar later investigated and charged the two prosecutors with ethical violations, but the charges were dismissed as filed too late.

These outrages spurred the state legislature in 2004 to adopt a law designed both to end the evasions of *Brady* and to give defendants fair notice of *all* evidence in the prosecution's hands, including all documents, photos, videos, and other evidence in their case files. The open discovery law required prosecutors to turn over everything in their files to defense attorneys, in every case.

Efforts by police and prosecutors to hide evidence of innocence have persisted, however. They include simply omitting such evidence from investigative documents.

In an undated forty-nine-page memo summarizing his activities during the first two months of the investigation, Himan devoted two pages to Crystal Mangum's March 16 account of what had been done to her. But he mentioned neither her hopelessly vague descriptions of the alleged assailants nor the March 16 and 21 photo sessions. These omissions were no accident, defense lawyers surmised. By the time Himan prepared this memo, Seligmann and Finnerty had been indicted and Evans was about to be. Himan was well aware that Mangum's vague descriptions were wildly inconsistent with Finnerty and Seligmann and hardly consistent with Evans. Himan also knew that Crystal had passed over Evans's photo without picking him.

Himan's memo was unsigned and typewritten as well as undated, a record-keeping method that proved to be a trademark of the Gottlieb team. This approach made it impossible for readers to tell whether the memo's author recorded actual observations and witness statements or concocted them much later to suit the prosecution's theory.

It is easier to keep the truth out of some documents than to erase it entirely, however. Cops are compulsive note takers. Memories fade. In order to have something to refresh their recollections months or years later when testifying at trial, they typically takes notes during witness interviews. That's what Himan did—at least in the investigation's early days.

Notes taken during initial interviews of witnesses have the virtue of being prepared before police, defense lawyers, or other interested parties have had a chance to pressure or coach the witnesses to change their stories. Many witnesses—especially those whose own problems put them in the power of police or prosecutors—are glad to change their stories to please police. But in their initial interviews, even bad cops cannot easily discern what may turn out to be evidence of innocence, or know how to avoid jotting it down.

A tape recording of a witness interview would, of course, be far more reliable than any officer's notes. That's one reason why cops and FBI agents almost never tape witness interviews. (The other reason is that witnesses may be less candid if they know they are being taped.) An exact record of what witnesses said would often end up helping to exonerate a suspect targeted by police or prosecutor. So notes jotted during witness interviews, imperfect as they are, tend to be the most reliable record of what witnesses saw and heard. Contemporaneous notes are far more reliable than subsequent documents, such as Himan's typed memo, and carefully scripted trial testimony.

Only by the open discovery law's requirement that Nifong turn over Himan's handwritten notes and other documents created on March 16 and 21 did defense lawyers find out about Mangum's extraordinarily sketchy descriptions of her alleged assailants and self-discrediting photo-ID sessions. And that was not until May 17.

The March 16 Gottlieb-Himan interview would have been a logical time to obtain a signed, handwritten statement from Crystal about who had done what to her. But police and DA Nifong waited for *three more weeks* to do that. Why? Because a statement on March 16 would have dramatized Crystal's inability to describe or identify her assailants while adding still more contradictions to the many inconsistent stories she had already told. Gottlieb and his team needed time to work on her.

Meanwhile, Mangum had money on her mind. It was two days after her meeting with Gottlieb and Himan that she told the security manager of the strip club she would get paid by the white boys. Crystal's mother subsequently met with Willie Gary, a big-time Florida plaintiffs lawyer with a private jet he called the *Wings of Justice*, and would tell *Essence* that she was "very much interested" in "getting Gary involved."

Gottlieb and Himan used Crystal's March 16 remarks to obtain a warrant to search 610 North Buchanan. At about 9:00 that night, after practice, Dave Evans was napping in his room when "I woke up to thundering knocks on my door like it was going to be broken down." Matt Zash and Dave yelled back and forth about who should see what it was. Then Dave heard: "Police! Freeze! Don't move! Put your hands up!" He ran into the living room. "There were all these cops with their flashlights in our eyes," he later recalled.

"It was like you were in a movie or something. The next thing you know, they were patting us down, going through our pockets, yelling, 'Why didn't you answer the door? Why didn't you answer the door?' I said I was sleeping. They said, 'Who was in the backyard? Who was trying to run out the back door? Why are the window shades down?'"

The cops said they had a search warrant and read from it. These were lies, Evans and Zash interjected, asking for a chance to tell what had really happened. Gottlieb picked up the $160 on the living room table. Police demanded to know where Mangum's wallet and cell phone were. On top of the refrigerator, the guys said; we found it in the backyard. "Yeah, sure you did," sneered Gottlieb. "We kept telling them we would help them in any way, gave our passcodes and stuff," Evans recalled. "I said I would take a polygraph."

When Danny Flannery arrived home from dinner with teammate William Wolcott to find his house being searched—with his name on the warrant as the guy who had ordered up strippers—he, too, asked for a chance to tell the true story. To Flannery's utter bafflement, Clayton accused him of having assaulted a police officer weeks before. It was Danny's twenty-second birthday. Several officers surrounded him. He thought he was about to be beaten up, as Clayton summoned the officer to identify Flannery as his assailant. He noticed one officer help himself to slices of his birthday cake. Then the officer who had been assaulted arrived, checked Flannery out with a flashlight, and said that Flannery hadn't been the guy. Later, when Wolcott came by the house to return Flannery's car keys, Gottlieb accosted him, saying, "If you cover up anything, you'll go to jail for just as long as the rapists." Wolcott replied that he had no idea what Gottlieb was talking about, since nothing had happened at the party.

The three captains helped police find much of what they were looking for in the house. Flannery showed Gottlieb the Allure Web site. He repeatedly told Himan that if the police had any questions about what happened, all they had to do was to track down Kim Roberts. Zash went through the garbage to dig out Mangum's five fake fingernails. The three guys had left her makeup bag, ID, and $160 of the $400 in cash specified in the warrant on the counter. The police also took towels and rugs from the two bathrooms and the students' cell phones and computers. The fact that Evans, Flannery, and Zash had not gotten rid of all this "evidence" during the nearly three days since the alleged rape would, one might think, have struck the police as evidence of innocence, had the police been competent and honest.

After a while the cops calmed down, started joking around, got the guys to turn on the TV and started watching the NCAA basketball tournament. Gottlieb became friendly, asking if Dave wanted some food. The police assured the three that they were not suspects and were free to leave. Instead they volunteered to go downtown to be interviewed at the police station.

The three were taken into separate rooms, with Himan interviewing Evans, Gottlieb interviewing Flannery, and Michelle Soucie interviewing Zash. At the end of the interviews each was told to write out what he recalled by hand. While Dave was starting to write, Gottlieb walked in and said: "I want to give you some advice. Tell us the truth or you're going to jail for the rest of your life." Flannery heard another officer talking about how contradictory the accuser's stories were.

Evans, Flannery, and Zash did not invoke their constitutional rights. They answered every question. They wrote and signed detailed statements. They voluntarily gave DNA, blood, and hair samples, knowing that if any of their DNA were found in or on Mangum it would mean decades in prison. (Gottlieb said that negative tests would rule them out as potential suspects.) Critically, in light of events to come, they gave police passwords to their e-mail and instant messenger accounts, so the authorities could immediately access all e-mails they had sent and received. Finally, they asked to be hooked up to a polygraph machine for lie-detector tests. Police usually jump at the chance to polygraph suspects. The Gottlieb team refused, saying that DNA would make or break the case and that lie detectors couldn't be admitted in court.

The police seemed to be having a good time putting the three captains through the wringer. At one point, Gottlieb came out and showed the captains two rape kits, saying that one of them had already been cleared. Just joking, he said. Then Clayton, on the phone with another officer, told Evans that police had found cocaine in his room. Evans said the claim was crazy. "Just kidding," Clayton replied.

It feels like they are just going through the motions, thought Evans. The truth will set us free. Flannery was also convinced that the police did not believe the accuser. At the end, Gottlieb shook their hands and said: "Everything's going to be OK. Don't worry about it." Police told them not to mention any of this to their teammates or anyone else. This reinforced Dean Sue's keep-it-quiet message, which she reaffirmed repeatedly.

Throughout all this, Evans, Flannery, and Zash behaved the way people do when they have nothing to hide. Not that this would do them any good. Before long, the police and Nifong would convince the world that the lacrosse players had all been uncooperative, putting up a "wall of silence."

The Evans, Flannery, and Zash accounts were confused as to the chaotic sequence of events and inconsistent on details. But on the main issues they meshed well with one another, with subsequent statements by Kim Roberts, and with more than twenty subsequently disclosed, time-stamped photos taken by a teammate at the party. "The case should have ended right there," blogger William L. Anderson later wrote. "Police should have told the district attorney that there was no evidence for rape other than the numerous conflicting stories told by a woman whose previous criminal behavior and dishonesty were well-known to the Durham police. In most other cases, that is *exactly* what police would have done."

It was past 4:00 A.M. on March 17 when Himan dropped them back at their house, exhausted, stripped of computers and cell phones, frazzled. Before they left the station, Gottlieb and Clayton both said not to tell anyone else about being questioned—the more people who knew, the cops said, the worse it would be for the captains. As long as the players were telling the truth, both cops said, this would all go away.

After a few hours' sleep, they met with Pressler and associate athletic director Chris Kennedy, a friend of Pressler's whose son had cocaptained the 2005 lacrosse team. Kennedy said that the captains needed to tell their parents—which they did immediately—and that they would need attorneys. Kennedy, too, had been told by other Duke administrators that the allegation wasn't regarded as credible. Even so, he informed the captains, he regarded the incident as a failure of leadership—on Flannery and Evans's part for organizing the event in the first place, on Zash's part for simply stating his objections but then allowing the plan to go forward. How, Kennedy asked them, could they have made themselves vulnerable by bringing a woman such as Mangum into their house?

The captains made no argument. They mentioned to Kennedy that, as Evans had told police, they had thought about calling the police as Mangum's behavior grew more erratic, but feared that doing so would bring the party to Pressler's attention.

When he called his father from Pressler's office, Dave later recalled, "I told him I was in trouble, something bad had happened, I didn't need him to yell at me, I just needed him to listen to me. And that's what he did. From that point [he didn't dwell on] how stupid we had been, which I freely admitted."

On Dean Wasiolek's recommendation, Kennedy suggested a Durham lawyer named Wes Covington, who had quietly handled other scrapes for the athletic department in the past. Wasiolek had once worked for Covington and considered him wonderful. He struck Pressler as a folksy Southern type who exuded confidence that he knew how to work the system in Durham.

Covington was not so well thought of by Duke's top in-house lawyers. And he had been suspended from the State Bar for six months in 2000 for ethics violations. But nobody told the players that.

Evans, Flannery, and Zash went to Covington's office the next day and told him their stories. Covington barely took notes, instead writing down a word or two on his legal pad and then circling it repeatedly for effect. He advised them to keep quiet, including not talking to anyone from the university, and said that Gottlieb was a "prick." Covington spoke about his good relationship with Dean Sue, said that he had handled cases like this one frequently, and assured them that the problem would "go away." (Wasiolek used the same phrase with Pressler.)

Evans wondered how Covington could be so confident while at the time stressing how bad it was that Sergeant Gottlieb was involved in the investigation. But the lawyer came across as a good ole boy, with a distinct drawl, who knew how to work the police. He joked that he couldn't meet for long because he had to get to Greensboro for an ACC basketball tournament game. Covington left it unclear whether he was representing the captains and who, if anyone, was his client.

Evans's parents reached Covington late that morning, by phone, while driving to Durham from their home in Annapolis. Covington's friends in the Durham Police Department believed the three boys had fully cooperated, the lawyer said, and everything would go OK. Covington added that they should not retain him, or anyone, as Dave's lawyer. Not yet, at least. The police would presume the guilt of any students who came in with lawyers. Better for Covington to tell the cops he was not representing any lacrosse player. And better for the Evanses not to mention the issue to anyone else.

That afternoon, March 18, at Koskinen Field, Duke fell behind a weak North Carolina team, 6–0, but rallied for an 11–8 win. "None of those who knew about it [the rape charge] could sleep," Evans later recalled. "Others had no idea what was going on. We came out really flat and unfocused and frazzled and we got the win but it was ugly. It's just hard when you're going through that to focus on the game." After the game, the four captains, along with their parents, headed back to 610 North Buchanan. There Rae Evans, Rita Flannery, and Bruce Thompson ripped into their sons for the decision to have the party. The four captains sat quietly, knowing their parents were right. But they figured the worst was now over.

Bruce Thompson, Bret's father, a Washington executive with Merrill Lynch, called Covington on the morning of March 20. Once again Covington stressed that hiring individual lawyers would backfire. The way to go, he advised, was that "I'm going to be unofficial legal adviser to everyone." It was unclear who would pay Covington. But he told Thompson, "I do this all the time for them," meaning for Duke. If everybody followed his advice, Covington told Thompson, there would be nothing to worry about. The woman's story was internally inconsistent, not credible. Covington had an old friend and former client in the police department, a man named Hester. "We're going to get this swept under the rug," he asserted.

Covington met with his friend at 2:00 P.M. Later he called Thompson to report that "my guy" needed to talk with the detective in charge to put this to bed. Covington would call back as soon as he knew more.

While Covington was trying to kill the case quietly, Detective Himan finally got Kim Roberts, the most important witness, on the phone at 10:10 A.M. on March 20, six days after the alleged rape. Roberts got right to the point.

"She stated that she heard that Ms Mangum was sexually assaulted, which she stated is a 'crock' and she stated that she was with her the whole time until she left," Himan later wrote in his forty-nine-page memo. "And the only time she was alone was when she would not leave and that time period was less than five minutes." Himan had no reason to disbelieve her.

Next Himan called Coach Pressler. They set up an appointment for all forty-six white team members to be interviewed by Durham police at the Duke police headquarters two days hence, on March 22, at 3:00 P.M. Any players who were not at the party would be excused, and the interviews of the others would be brief, just one to two minutes apiece, Himan said. He gave Pressler the impression that the police did not believe the woman and were dotting the i's and crossing the t's, wrapping things up. No lawyers would be present.

This plan was a good one, Wes Covington later told Pressler. Sergeant Gottlieb had said the accuser was not credible.

Himan neglected to mention to Pressler or Covington that the police planned to pressure all forty-six players to give DNA samples and mug shots as well as interviews. Nor did he reveal that the police would feel free to subject some or all of the forty-six to detailed grilling, in separate rooms. That's what they had done with Evans, Flannery, and Zash despite virtually identical assurances that they would only have to "answer a few questions." Indeed, that's what police almost always do when they are trying to get their targets to make voluntary statements: Lull them into a false sense of security.

It's possible that the police tipped from disbelieving to believing Crystal Mangum because of Gottlieb's first meeting with Tara Levicy, on March 21. The SANE nurse already had told Himan that Mangum had shown injuries consistent with a sexual assault in the March 14 exam. Now, she gave Gottlieb the records she had created the morning after the alleged rape. Levicy also— contrary to accepted medical practice—dramatically expanded upon those records to bolster her assertions that a rape had occurred. Did Mangum exhibit the effects of "blunt force trauma"? Gottlieb asked. Yes, replied Levicy. (The SANE nurse later stated that in her mind, since Mangum claimed to be in pain, that alone proved blunt force trauma.) Moreover, claimed Levicy, Mangum had screamed hysterically after being left alone in the examination room with a male rape crisis counselor. Levicy would later state that she couldn't remember this man's name, but that she believed he was "white" and "soft-spoken."

Levicy didn't tell Gottlieb that she personally had never viewed the only objective "injury" discovered in the March 14 exam, Dr. Manly's diagnosis of "diffuse edema in the vaginal walls." So Gottlieb never spoke to Manly about her exam—either on March 21 or any time thereafter. Nor did any other representative from Durham law enforcement. Defense attorney Doug Kingsbery later speculated that "after speaking with Levicy, the authorities felt like they had the 'perfect' witness, and did not need to interview Manly. It could have only gone downhill from there."

Wes Covington met with David and Rae Evans, Bruce and Kathy Thompson, and Rich Zash, Matt's dad, for the first time on March 21, before the team's game against eighth-ranked Cornell. They got together over lunch at the Washington Duke Inn, a fancy place often crowded with Duke big shots. Covington said it was a good idea for a few key players to give interviews to police, as had Dave, Matt and Danny. The captains, he continued, had provided a list of six other players who could back up their version of events.

No one would need a lawyer because Covington would be there. This was all Himan would need to complete the record and close the case without charges.

Covington also warned, however, that if Sergeant Gottlieb were involved, it would mean trouble. He hated "Duke and all Duke students." But, of course, Covington already knew that Gottlieb *was* involved, on the basis of his conversation with the captains. His inability to keep straight basic facts about the investigation called into question exactly who Covington was trying to help.

Tossing out words like "rape" and "prostitute" in a loud voice, Covington seemed oblivious to the people at nearby tables. Bruce Thompson cringed. He had an urge to tell the lawyer to pipe down and discuss this more privately. Thompson was also annoyed that Covington had not returned two phone calls that morning—and that his excuse was that he was on the phone all day with Wasiolek and Kennedy. This man is a buffoon, Thompson thought to himself. He is not working for our sons. He is working for the Duke administration. Here is Duke's lawyer telling us not to get lawyers, and sending all the players to be grilled by police while most of their parents are still in the dark.

It's time to get a real lawyer, Thompson thought. Maybe Duke will be mad at us and maybe the cops will presume guilt. But it would be better to take our chances on that than to put our son in the hands of this character. Or would it be? Thompson had a sleepless night, weighing the risks of the each approach. Within a few days the Thompsons had retained Bill Thomas, who was touted by lawyer friends as Durham's best and classiest criminal defense lawyer.

After interviewing Bret, Thomas had no doubt that he was telling the truth. Criminal defense lawyers are lied to by their clients every day. But this time, "I knew it in my heart when I finished my initial interview," the lawyer said later. "I absolutely adore Bret. He's an Atlantic Coast Conference scholar, a tremendous athlete. He's honest. I don't think I've ever been more impressed with a young man in my entire career. I'd be so proud to have any of my three sons grow up to be just like him."

The Cornell game was a bust. In a downpour, the top-ranked Dukies lost, 11–7. The dozen or so parents who had come to watch them play had never seen the team play so poorly. Something is wrong, John Danowski remarked. These kids aren't having any fun out there. Danowski, the lacrosse coach at Hofstra, had come to watch his son Matt. Larry Lamade, whose son Peter was a preseason pick for all-American as a junior, wondered why the usually dependable Evans and Flannery were missing easy ground balls, flubbing easy throws. The Thompsons looked ashen, other parents noticed.

We were awful, Pressler thought. This phony rape charge is draining the guys. Pressler did not discuss the team's sorry performance in his postgame talk. He told the boys that they would have to go to the Duke police station the next afternoon to give statements; he had been told that each player would be asked to spend only a minute or two with police, with no detailed interrogation. This was mandatory. Pressler wanted to get all this behind them and get on with the season. And the Duke administration had told everyone to cooperate with police.

Could Covington's mass interview plan have succeeded in quietly ending the investigation? "If you have faith in the system and faith in the people administering justice," Dave Evans later mused, "Wes Covington's approach would have worked. But something was wrong with the people running the system."

That night at 10:50, the phone rang in the senior Lamade's hotel room. It was Peter, calling from a criminal attorney's office. He was scared to say what it was about. Duke had told the team to keep it quiet. Don't worry Dad, said Peter, nothing happened. But I need you right now.

A few hours later, at 1.30 A.M., the phone rang in Ben and Tricia Dowd's modest Long Island home. Their son, Kyle, calling from the same attorney's office, reported that there had been an allegation of rape. When he called back at 3:00 A.M. to provide more details, Tricia Dowd told him not to speak to police without having a lawyer present and to round up the others on Covington's list and give them the same advice. Whenever he needed her, she added, she would come down to North Carolina.

"Mom," replied Kyle, "I need you."

5. COPS IGNITE FIRESTORM,
DUKE RUNS FOR COVER

PETER LAMADE AND KYLE DOWD HAD BEEN CALLING from the office of Robert C. Ekstrand, of Ekstrand & Ekstrand, who had heard about the Duke-brokered mass-interview plan that evening about six.

Bob and Samantha, his wife and law partner, had represented many Dukies charged with petty drinking and noise infractions, including several other lacrosse players. Bob also taught criminal law and procedure at Duke Law School, of which he was a 1998 graduate. The Ekstrands were plugged into the team through Samantha, who had been an assistant coach for the women's team for seven years until birth of her triplets, and their twenty-two-year-old paralegal, Stefanie Sparks, Samantha's sister. A 2005 Duke grad, Stef had played on the women's lacrosse team, was helping to coach it in 2006, and was friendly with most of the men's team.

On March 20, when Dan Flannery was at the office to discuss his ultimately dismissed noise citation, he brought up the rape investigation. Bob and Stef listened as Danny quickly rattled off the key points of what was happening. This seemed to Bob and Stef to be the real point of Danny's visit. He mentioned that the captains were working with Wes Covington, who Bob thought had done little, if any, criminal defense work. Not sure whether Danny was asking for his assessment of the situation, Bob did not express his mounting concern. Bob asked Danny if Covington represented him, and Danny couldn't say for sure; he thought Duke had hired him. That revelation hit Bob sideways. Bob could not believe that Duke had hired Wes Covington; Bob represented Duke and knew the University Counsel's office would not hire a lawyer in these circumstances or on the terms Danny was describing. Danny seemed to be asking Bob if he thought the approach they were taking was right. Bob did not, he later recalled: "Red flags were everywhere. There was Gottlieb, there was this horrific rape scene already memorialized in a public document (the search warrant), news reports recounting an alleged

gang rape at the home of three captains of the lacrosse team. Gottlieb, Gottlieb, Gottlieb. Now there's a lawyer I've never heard of, Covington, claiming
Duke hired him and he's gonna sweep this under the rug. There were so
many goddamn red flags flying up, the thing looked like Kremlin Square."
Bob did not tell Danny that, not then. Instead, Bob confirmed the one thing
he needed to know: Danny was taking this as seriously as he should. But
Danny had already given his statement and DNA to the police, and there was
no decision before him. There was no cause for Bob to describe the fear he
felt. Not just yet.

Before he left Bob's office, Danny reiterated that he was confident that
the allegations would soon be disproved and dropped. Danny and Stef turned
to discussing the team's quest for a national championship. They had just lost
to Maryland, and Stef gave Danny advice on how he as a leader could help
infuse the team with the right competitive spirit.

After Danny left, Stef asked Bob what he thought about Covington. Bob
said, "I don't know much, but I'm damn sure Duke didn't hire him." Bob had
also pulled up Covington's law firm's Web site. He showed Stef. "Criminal
law" was not on the list of practice areas on Covington's page. Bob told Stef,
"We need to make sure they don't make any more decisions without talking to
us. If that mass interrogation is ever scheduled, we need to know it right
away." Stef was sure she would know right away.

Stef noticed a worrisome article on the investigation in that day's *Chronicle*. It depicted an investigation of an alleged "gang rape" at 610 North
Buchanan. She showed it to Bob as soon as she could. They immediately recognized the address: Danny's house, widely known to be a lacrosse house. But
what leaped off of the page for both of them was the name of the lead investigator, "M. D. Gottlieb." With Gottlieb investigating these allegations and talking to the newspaper, the whole thing was about to explode.

She urged Bob Ekstrand, who was initially reluctant to butt into the case
uninvited, to protect those of the players who were already his clients in connection with petty drinking and noise citations. She also worked the phone to
get those clients and their teammates to come to the office.

Ekstrand needed no convincing that the mass-interview plan was potentially disastrous. There would be no defense counsel, no ground rules, and
no tape recording to prevent police from distorting what the players said.
Talking to police without the benefit of counsel was the most dangerous
thing in the world, the lawyer thought. And most of the players had not even
consulted their parents. The danger was compounded by the explosive nature of the allegations and the certainty of national media attention if they
became public.

Every single member of the team is in grave peril, Ekstrand worried. Anyone who told police that he was at the party but denied the rape allegation could be indicted as an accomplice. At worst, the DA could indict dozens of them and then use their status as defendants to attack their credibility as witnesses. The prosecutor could take this course even if the accuser could not identify any alleged rapists.

I have to stop this mass interview, Ekstrand thought. The lives of forty-six students are on the line. He picked up the phone and called his mentor, a nationally famed criminal defense lawyer—"the finest lawyer I know," Ekstrand liked to say. The mentor stayed in the background in the Duke case. The younger man quickly described the allegations and the mass interview plan. The answer was forceful: This is no time for subtlety. If you are going to save these students, you'll do it tonight. Get to it. Ekstrand hung up the phone. He looked at the note he had made of his mentor's words: "Nuclear Dimensions." He went to the conference room, where Stef had gathered a handful of team members. Ekstrand thanked them for coming. "We're getting in," he told Stef. "No one sleeps tonight." She should do whatever it took to get everyone on the team into the office that night. If they weren't in town, get them on the phone. If they are in bed, wake them up. As soon as you get them in here, we need to call their parents.

Ekstrand looked at the clock: 10:30 P.M. At three the next afternoon, forty-six team members were going to walk into a police station, most of them not even knowing why. Some did not know that the subject matter was rape, let alone that the police could claim that three among them had done it and the rest were accomplices. While police had assured Pressler that there would "just a few questions" to wrap up a routine investigation, Ekstrand didn't believe it. The cops would have the Identifications Unit on standby to take DNA samples. They would isolate each team member and employ the typical Durham police routine: Confuse them, lie to them, exhaust them, frighten them, and extract from them anything that fit the cops' theory of what had happened that night.

Gottlieb's involvement was especially alarming. Ekstrand considered him a rogue cop likely to do his best to frame the lacrosse players. Just a month before, Ekstrand had compiled a dossier showing the sergeant's harsh treatment of and disdain for Duke students, and what the lawyer saw as Gottlieb's pattern of bending the truth or even lying in court. Ekstrand had done this research at the request of a client whose daughter, a Duke student, had been arrested by Gottlieb. He had hauled the student and a female friend to jail while sneering that he would lock them up with a "crack whore" to show them what life was really like. They ended up in a cell with a blood-covered, drug-addled woman who said she had stabbed someone.

Gottlieb's basis for jailing the two women attracted the derision of other cops. It was a disputed charge that they had failed to prevent a nineteen-year-old from taking a can of beer from a cooler during a party at their home. That sort of thing happens thousands of times a year on college campuses all over the nation. It almost never lands anyone in jail—much less with a "crack whore."

Ekstrand's client wanted to know more about the cop who had done this to his daughter. From publicly filed arrest records, Ekstrand learned that Sergeant Gottlieb, a high school graduate who had spent nearly two decades on the force before earning his first promotion, had jailed several times as many Duke students as the Trinity Park area's three other supervisors combined. He had locked up sixteen over six months for such offenses as noise violations, drinking beer outside off-campus houses, or serving alcohol to minors.

Other Durham cops almost always dealt with such petty infractions by handing the students citations akin to speeding tickets; the fines could enrich Durham's coffers. And Gottlieb used a double standard to hammer Dukies. In the twelve months before the lacrosse players' party, he had let *nonstudents* walk away with no-jail citations after being charged with far more serious crimes, such as carrying a concealed .45-caliber handgun.

Gottlieb's crackdown on Dukies had made him a popular figure among Trinity Park residents angry about the loud, late, sometimes boorish partying by Dukies who rented houses there. Some students had laughed off the citations. It was to appease neighbors that Duke's administration had helped devise the police program targeting Duke's own students for selective arrest and prosecution on petty charges for which other Durhamites would not be arrested. Duke president Richard Brodhead was later to acknowledge this arrangement, which Duke called its Good Neighbor Policy.

But this crackdown had elements of a reign of terror. The year began with a series of planned, warrantless raids of student parties off campus. The police, joined by Alcohol Law Enforcement agents, raided several homes in pursuit of underage drinking. Once inside, police allowed no one to leave until they either proved they were over twenty-one, proved they had nothing to drink, or confessed. Those scenes played out again and again, though on a smaller scale, every weekend in the area around East Campus. Perhaps the most stunning incident occurred at the pool at an apartment complex that was home to mostly Duke students. One Saturday afternoon, after a football game, students gathered at the pool. Someone called in a noise complaint. A battery of officers showed up and began threatening to arrest anyone who didn't leave. One young man was told to leave, and he said he needed to grab his shirt, lying close by. When he turned, the officer and several others jumped on his back and he was thrown head first into the concrete. The student got up from this assault with blood flowing freely from a gash on his forehead. He was later acquitted on a charge of delaying an officer in conducting his duties.

Even in this atmosphere, Sergeant Gottlieb stood out. Several Duke students—all "young women and unimposing young men," Ekstrand wrote in his dossier—said that the sergeant had roughly handcuffed them, thrown one against a car, threatened others with deportation, illegally searched them, and lied to judges to get convictions without real evidence or to cover up his trampling of their constitutional rights.

In an October 2005 case, neighbors complained of Dukies (not lacrosse throwing beer cans, and smashing a bottle on the sidewalk. That was about 4:00 P.M. Things quieted down when the students went off to a Rolling Stones concert at Wallace Wade Stadium. It was some eleven hours later, at three in the morning, that Gottlieb led a ten-cop raid on the house. The police not only arrested and handcuffed all seven occupants, but they dragged one out of his bed and down the stairs with his head hitting the steps. All but one of the students were later found innocent of any offense. The one was convicted only of aiding and abetting another student who had a drink in an open container on a city street.

Gottlieb's behavior in this incident involved more than an apparent use of excessive force. One of the students Gottlieb arrested was Urosh Tomovich, a naturalized U.S. citizen of Serbian heritage. Outside the house, the cop told Tomovich, "You're going to be in the biggest trouble of your life." He made good on his threat when they arrived at the police station, telling Tomovich, "Do you need to speak to your consulate? We can deport you." The Duke student couldn't believe what he was hearing. "Why would I need to speak to my consulate?" he told Gottlieb. "I'm a U.S. citizen. I have a different last name, but I'm a U.S. citizen."

"In my judgment," Bob Ekstrand later recalled, "some of the tactics were outrageous, they appeared to be escalating, and I did not believe this would end well. I thought that, absent some intervention, a student was going to get seriously injured or worse. The students were seeing this happen over and over again to their friends. It angered them, and many were right to be angry. Up to that point, the kids were not responding out of their anger. Sooner or later, a cop was going to run into a kid who had seen enough and wouldn't stand for it. If the kid stands his ground, or says something to the officer, who knows where that leads? Why run the risk? Why not transfer Gottlieb to some other beat that wasn't filled with Duke students? No one wanted to sue; but we thought we were delivering to the City a very good reason to move Officer Gottlieb to a beat that kept him away from Duke students." Ekstrand's client passed the message and the Ekstrand dossier along to a high-level Duke administrator, saying that "you've got a rogue cop on your hands." The client urged that something be done before a student got seriously hurt or worse. It's unclear what happened next. But eleven days later, Gottlieb was transferred to another beat.

This transfer came three weeks before the alleged rape at 610 North Buchanan. Now Gottlieb had grabbed the lead role in the investigation. Ekstrand feared that he would go after the lacrosse players to take his revenge on Duke for his reassignment. The lawyer was not about to let his clients wander into Gottlieb's den without counsel or a tape recording. Not before they had consulted their parents, at least. Nor did Ekstrand have confidence in Wes Covington.

Ekstrand began calling parents of lacrosse-team clients, telling them about the rape charge and the mass-interview plan and advising against allowing their sons to participate. The horrified response of one father—a lawyer—was: My son is not talking to police about this until he talks to me. Meanwhile, at Stef's urging, Peter Lamade, Kyle Dowd, and most of the other players arrived at the Ekstrands' office that Tuesday night and in the early hours of the next morning. Bob and Stef worked with them until 8:00 A.M. Samantha was home with the six-month-old triplets.

Larry Lamade arrived shortly before midnight. Ekstrand briefed him until 1:30 A.M. A Washington lawyer, Lamade understood that it was serious business for suspects in any criminal investigation, no matter how innocent, to waive their constitutional rights and talk to police without lawyers. Especially when the suspects were college kids who have been admonished not to tell their parents, and the cop leading the investigation allegedly had a record of misconduct and animus against Duke students.

In an ideal world, a good cop would compare the students' stories with one another and all other evidence as it came in to figure out whether they were telling the truth. But even a good cop could be trouble if he or she had developed a theory of the alleged crime before all the evidence was in. Cops share the natural human tendency to bend new evidence to fit their preconceived beliefs rather than adjusting their beliefs to fit the new evidence.

Lamade was confident that there had been no rape. Peter had never lied to him about anything big. Tricia Dowd, who had taken a 6:00 A.M. flight from Islip, Long Island, and had also arrived at Ekstrand's office, quickly reached the same conclusion. Her son Kyle, who had stayed until the end of the party, assured her that nothing happened. It was not fear of the evidence but distrust of the Durham police that spurred Lamade to tell Coach Pressler a few hours after he had left Ekstrand's office, early on March 22, that the interviews must be postponed so the players could consult parents and lawyers first.

Pressler felt caught in the middle of a dispute among friends. He sent Lamade to Wes Covington. Lamade met with the lawyer twice that day, accompanied the second time by Tricia Dowd. Both were skeptical about the lawyer's approach, but held out hope that maybe Covington was really trying to help their sons.

Covington acknowledged to Lamade that Sergeant Gottlieb was running the investigation. Gottlieb had told Covington that the matter would probably be dropped soon with no charges, but only if the lacrosse players gave statements to police. Covington admitted to the two parents that Gottlieb appeared to be biased against Duke kids. But the lawyer wanted to go ahead with the mass interview anyway.

What does submitting to police interrogations do for my son or the other team members? Lamade asked. Nothing, Covington admitted. But it might help the captains, who were the most exposed. Whom do you represent? Lamade pressed. I'm not really representing anyone, Covington responded. "I'm here to kind of fix this. And I'm advising Duke." Lamade concluded that Covington was playing fast and loose with the lives of Peter and his teammates on the remote chance that the lawyer could bury the matter quietly and thus please his real client: the Duke administration, or part of it.

All well and good, if it worked. But if it did not, the Covington approach might well help the cops railroad innocent students into prison. At Lamade's insistence, Covington had his assistant, Andy Peterson, tell police that the interviews would be postponed for eight days. Peterson made it clear in an e-mail to Gottlieb that this was only a postponement, not a refusal to cooperate: "The young men will be available for questioning Wednesday, March 29th at 3 P.M. at the Duke Police Department." He explained that the players needed time to consult parents and perhaps lawyers.

Lamade returned to Covington's office at about 4:00, this time with Tricia Dowd. Again Covington urged that some or all of the players submit to uncounseled interviews. On their way out, Dowd told Lamade, "This guy's some kind of flake." Covington, she added, was violating "Law 101" by telling innocent people to submit to police interrogation without counsel. The Duke administration was prepared to take this risk with its students. Larry Lamade and Tricia Dowd were not about to take this risk with their sons.

Lawyers? As Covington had predicted, the cops treated this as a sign of guilt—or, Ekstrand thought, as an excuse to publicize the rape allegation and put pressure on the players and the university. The police essentially declared war. Within hours, Himan went to Assistant District Attorney Tracy Cline, who was the DA's rape specialist, a rape victim herself, and the highest-ranking African American in the office. The police and prosecutors started work on an application for a nontestimonial identification order (NTO) to force all forty-six white lacrosse players to give DNA swabs and upper-torso photos that would show any scratches from Crystal Mangum's fingernails. Meanwhile, two plainclothes cops came prowling around a Duke baseball game that afternoon, asking people where to find the lacrosse team. They left after being told that there was no practice that day.

Himan also conducted a more detailed interview with Kim Roberts at a police station that same day, March 22. Her seven-page handwritten statement contradicted Mangum on all important points. Not one player had touched either woman, as far as Roberts had seen or heard. The women had lingered in and around the house without fear for forty-five minutes after the dancing had stopped. Crystal had said nothing about being raped either then or during their half hour in the car together after leaving the party.

Roberts did say that a player's comment that he would "use the broomstick on us" had made her "uncomfortable." She also reported one of the players shouting "nigger" as she drove away, without mentioning how she had provoked him by screaming her own racial taunt about "limp-dick white boys." Roberts cited no other racial slurs, let alone the barking chorus alleged by Crystal Mangum.

While Roberts was at the police station, Gottlieb and Clayton served her with an outstanding arrest warrant for flagrantly violating the terms of her probation on a 2001 conviction, for embezzling $25,000 from a photofinishing company where she had worked on payroll records. She got out on $25,000 bond. But unless she could wangle a sweetheart deal, she faced trial and a likely prison term on the parole violation charge.

The NTO application was ready by the next day, March 23. As a matter of constitutional law, Nifong had to show probable cause to believe not only that Crystal had been raped, but also that each of the forty-six lacrosse players whose DNA was sought had participated in some way. The latter proposition was a huge stretch. Some players could prove they had been nowhere near the party that night. Durham defense attorney Alex Charns—a specialist in civil liberties who had authored a book on the FBI's relationship with the Supreme Court—told a reporter: "I can't imagine a scenario where this would be reasonable to do this so early in the investigation. It seems unusual, it seems overbroad, and it seems frightening that they're invading the privacy of so many people."

The application, signed by top Nifong assistant David Saacks, portrayed Crystal's most recent and horrifying allegations as established fact. It added an allegation that Crystal had never mentioned in her long March 14 interview with Tara Levicy: "she was clawing at one of the suspects' arms in an attempt to breath [*sic*] while being strangled." The application also twisted into a threat the tasteless but joking comment about using a broom as a sex toy that Evans, Flannery, and Zash had described in their interviews a week earlier.

"One male stated to the women 'I'm gonna shove this up you' while holding a broom stick up in the air so they could see it,'" the DA's application asserted. Where had this claim originated? Crystal had said nothing like it to the SANE trainee. Nor had anyone else mentioned the broom comment to police until after Evans, Zash, and Flannery had done so. Roberts had said in her signed, March 22 statement that she had become "uncomfortable" when someone had allegedly "said he would use the broomstick on us." But she had not described this remark as threatening. And both women had been comfortable enough to spend the next forty-five minutes in and around the house.

The conversion by police and Nifong's office of a tasteless joke into a sinister prelude to gang rape was just one of a succession of false and misleading statements in the March 23 application. The document claimed that "medical records and interviews . . . revealed the victim had signs, symptoms, and injuries consistent with being raped and sexually assaulted vaginally and anally." This description did not correspond to the records and was highly misleading as to Levicy's interview, but the SANE trainee had told Gottlieb and Himan things at odds with her own written report.

The application by Nifong's office omitted all of the large body of evidence that the rape charge was probably false. It mentioned neither Mangum's many prior inconsistent stories; nor her inability to describe specifically or identify a single assailant; nor her incapacitated condition; nor Roberts's statements to Himan that the rape charge was "a crock" and the women had been apart less than five minutes; nor the cooperation of Evans, Flannery, and Zash; nor their denials of the rape charge and offers to take lie-detector tests. Nifong's office also neglected to inform the court that Mangum had failed to identify anyone as an assailant after being shown photos of the six initial prime suspects and thirty other players.

The NTO application abandoned the earlier police theory that players named Adam, Matt, and Brett were the prime suspects. Now all forty-six white players were suspects. Perhaps to compensate for the absence of probable cause to take DNA samples from all forty-six white players, the application stated that they had concealed their identities by using first-name aliases and uniform numbers. Police had no evidence to substantiate this claim. And it was contradicted by Kim Roberts's statements that Flannery had showed her his ID when she asked to see it and that she had spoken with "Dan" and "Dave" when she had first arrived. Roberts's recollection confirmed the police statements by

Flannery and Evans that they had introduced themselves to and spoken with Roberts.

These deceptions in the NTO application fooled not only Judge Ronald Stephens—a former district attorney who had been Nifong's boss—but also the media and many others into thinking that the accuser must have been raped. The application contained only one bow to procedural fairness. It declared: "The DNA evidence requested will immediately rule out any innocent persons, and show conclusive evidence as to who the suspect(s) are in the alleged violent attack upon this victim."

This was nothing short of an assurance by District Attorney Mike Nifong's office that he would end the case and admit the players' innocence if the DNA results proved to be negative.

Mike Pressler heard from Wes Covington that a court order was in the works and then called Ekstrand. "What the hell is a nontestimonial order?" he asked. Ekstrand hurried over to the team's windowless meeting room as Pressler's players gathered. The order, with the judge's signature, came in by fax at 3:11 P.M. Ekstrand huddled in the hallway with Pressler and his assistants to read it. In the process it became clear once and for all that the cops' assurances to Wes Covington and Mike Pressler that they were just wrapping up a routine investigation had been a ruse. It was also clear that Nifong had bought into the same rape allegations that had seemed so incredible to the cops who interviewed Mangum at Duke Hospital.

"Cooperation" was dead. Nifong and the police had killed it. Their March 23 application and subsequent statements showed that their agenda was not to find the truth but to make the accuser's charges stick.

Ekstrand thought that the order might well be unconstitutional. But he had no desire to challenge it. DNA is the innocent suspect's friend, he thought. Police can lie about what witnesses say in interviews. But DNA does not lie. In addition, North Carolina law required prosecutors to immediately turn over test results to defendants who comply with such an NTO order. So the players would get copies of the proof of their innocence, which they then could publicize to the world. As for Pressler, he hoped that the DNA results would come back soon enough for his team to resume its quest for the national championship. Dave Evans heard Wes Covington complain that Ekstrand was trying to take over as lawyer. Dave pulled Covington aside and asked, "Are you my lawyer?" Covington did not respond directly, saying something about how he had an arrangement with Dave's dad and had things worked out with the authorities.

Back in the meeting room, Ekstrand told the players that each of them needed to go to the police crime lab to be swabbed and photographed. Pressler moved his eyes down the six rows of seats as they took this in. Not one flinched. Not one asked about challenging the order. Not one brought up his constitutional rights. Kyle Dowd called his mother, who had returned to New York, from outside the meeting room to fill her in. He said that everyone wanted to submit their DNA, since "we have nothing to hide." Tony McDevitt told himself, "Fine, take it, I don't care. I know I did nothing wrong. Go ahead, take my DNA." And, he recalled, "There were forty-six other guys saying the same thing as me."

Eager to get everything behind them, forty-six lacrosse players piled into cars and headed for the police lab. All except Devon Sherwood. He had attended the party. But Mangum had said her assailants were white. The coach took Devon aside and said, "You don't have to go." Devon was not happy. He wanted to stick with his team. And when Devon noticed later that the New York *Daily News* had said that the "lone" black player had been exempted, the word rankled. Not the "only" black player. Not the "sole" black player. The "lone" black player. The media made it sound as though he were kept off in a segregated corner of the locker room.

News of the mass trip to the police lab quickly spread. Contrary to another of Gottlieb's promises, the police had tipped off the newspapers. Two reporters called Pressler within five minutes after the team members had left for the crime lab, where a reporter and photographer were waiting for them. This extinguished the fantasy of some Duke administrators that Wes Covington could make this go away quietly. But there was still no sense of urgency. Not enough, at least, to prevent Richard Brodhead and board chairman Robert K. Steel from flying by private jet to Atlanta that afternoon to watch Mike "Coach K" Krzyzewski's top-ranked basketball team play Louisiana State University in the NCAA tournament.

Stef Sparks intercepted some of the players as they arrived, telling them to cover their heads. She and Ekstrand did not want the guys' faces on the front page under a "rape" headline. They also feared that Mangum might finger any lacrosse player whose picture she saw in the paper.

Some players thought it weird to be hiding like this. It seemed to them like the sort of thing that mafiosos and murderers do. Not innocent college kids. A Duke official later said: "That was the worst thing they could do. It sent the wrong signal." And that's how the police-orchestrated perp walk would play in the media.

Inside the crime lab, Gottlieb told Ekstrand that Covington was going to "bring his guys in" to get on with the mass interviews that had been postponed. How about your guys? he asked. "My guys are wondering who invited the press," Ekstrand responded. "Why don't we get through this" first? Most of the players had not yet spoken with their parents. If any interviews did go forward,

Ekstrand thought, they would have to be videotaped, and with counsel present. But he did not tell Gottlieb that.

The DNA swabbing and photographing was no big deal. Team members cracked jokes. They made sure the police understood that any scratches or bruises in the photos came from their contact sport, not from any rape victim. Gottlieb made nice: Lacrosse player John Walsh recalled that "they were treating it to make it seem like it was nothing." Gottlieb told everyone that the cops appreciated them coming down. Just cooperate and we'll get through this mess. This will all blow over. But, Walsh realized later, "I think they sort of knew that it was a bigger deal than we did."

The first sign of how big a deal the case would become appeared on the front page of the next day's *News & Observer*, the Raleigh newspaper that was the Triangle's leading news source. It depicted the hiding of the players' faces as a sinister move "to conceal their identities."

Ekstrand thought that hiding their faces was worth the cost. He also knew that once innocent suspects start talking, they can be trashed as liars for getting minor details wrong. And this was a case in which the only way to get an acquittal would be to prove to a certainty that there had been no sexual assault. As a practical matter, "reasonable doubt" would be no defense. Any public misstep could be disastrous. The only safe strategy was silence, Ekstrand advised. That meant no-commenting to friends as well as to the media.

Bob and Samantha Ekstrand and Stef Sparks also needed time to interview the more than thirty players who were or would soon be their clients before anyone issued any detailed statements. While they were confident that there had been no sex of any kind—much less a brutal gang rape—they needed the interviews to make a convincing case to other, newly retained defense lawyers, among others. From the first night they were in the case, Ekstrand and Sparks began working on what they thought might be a way to prove the actual innocence of all forty-six suspects. They used an old device in a new way. They were building a time line of digital evidence, one that was transformed into a "digital alibi" for each team by mapping onto the foundation time line each individual's personal metadata (his cell phone calls, the cellular panels that received his phone's signal, his Duke card swipes, his credit card transactions). Each of these digitally recorded events put each team member at a particular place and a particular time. Each player would have a digital alibi to accompany the testimony of those he was with at the time.

Some players seemed to be in more jeopardy than others, especially the three who lived at 610 North Buchanan, the others named Matt, Bret, and Adam, and the one who had held up the broom. They would need separate counsel, Ekstrand thought. With more and more lawyers becoming involved, nobody could speak for the whole group. It would take time to coordinate any joint statements. And with the authorities threatening to indict any team members who had been at the party as accomplices unless they supported the bogus rape claim, any statement, no matter how true—such as, "I was there the whole time and nobody touched her"—could have been suicidal.

This strategy of silence had an enormous cost in public relations. For four long days, no one associated with the team publicly denied the rape charge. During this period, they were demonized as gang rapists by police, by Nifong, by professors, and by the media, while Duke president Richard Brodhead tarred them as at best bad actors and at worst heinous criminals.

With the lacrosse players being savaged in the media on an hourly basis every day from March 24 on, the Evanses and some other parents wanted to put out a statement proclaiming their innocence, or at least consult a public relations expert confidentially on how to respond to the situation. But Bob Ekstrand, Larry Lamade, and others objected to breaking the team's silence, and with so many team members and parents and lawyers involved, consensus on any course of action was unattainable.

Meanwhile, when Sue Pressler told fourteen-year-old Janet about the rape allegation, the child thought for a minute and then said: "Mom, I don't believe it. Even if someone tried to do anything inappropriate to the girl, Zash and Flannery would have been saying, 'You've got to come through us.' If they were there and they say nothing happened, then nothing happened." During the ensuing months, eight-year-old Maggie asked over and over again: "Oh, Mom, why did the boys have to go to that party?" "They didn't go to the party, they had the party," Sue responded the first time. Later, Maggie said: "Oh Momma, if Daddy had found out about the party, the boys would still be running."

While silent in public, the four lacrosse captains did convince three top Brodhead subordinates privately that they were innocent on March 24, in a 2:00 P.M. meeting. Duke executive vice president Tallman Trask III and athletics director Joe Alleva told the captains that "we can't move forward" unless they heard everything about the party. Some of the captains said that their lawyer (Bob Ekstrand) had told them to keep quiet because whomever they spoke with could be called as a witness. Trask became angry. He asserted that there was a faculty-student privilege and that he would fight in court if the authorities demanded that he disclose what the captains told him, Dave Evans later recalled. (No such privilege is recognized by the law in North Carolina or anywhere else.)

But the captains were still reluctant to go against their lawyers' advice. Finally Pressler said, "Guys, just tell him what happened," and they did. At the meeting's conclusion, the administrators all said they believed their students. "I've always believed you," added associate athletics director Chris Kennedy, whose unequivocal belief in the players' innocence soon left him frozen out of the decision-making process.

The captains effusively thanked Alleva and Trask for listening to them and left the meeting in good spirits. On his way out, Flannery shook Trask's hand. The executive vice president confided that he had been in a similar situation in his youth. I got through it, he said, and so will you. "Beat Georgetown," he added. Alleva then told Trask and Pressler that the team would have to be punished for hiring strippers and underage drinking. Pressler agreed, saying he would discipline the players who attended the party, with multigame suspensions for organizers, once the dust had cleared. Trask suggested making them rake yards and clean up around the Trinity Park neighborhood.

But other forces in motion that day would obliterate this business-as-usual approach. Brodhead was besieged by activist professors and protesters on his return from watching LSU upset Duke's basketball team in Atlanta Thursday night, 62–54, with Duke star J. J. Redick going three for eighteen in his last college game. In a March 24 faculty meeting, professors demanded that Brodhead order all of the lacrosse players to talk to police—never mind their constitutional rights—and disband the team. Paul Haagen, chairman of Duke's Academic Council, told the N&O, "There was a sense of, 'This is sad, and it's terrible.'" The assembled professors seemed to have little doubt that a rape had occurred.

Also on March 24, Nifong's extraordinary role as head of the police investigation was formalized when Captain Jeff Lamb ordered all Durham police "to go through Mr. Nifong for any directions as to how to conduct matters in this case." This arrangement contradicted the department's official chain of authority: Officers in District 2 (which covers the area around Duke) reported to Commander Ed Sarvis, who was subject to orders from Chief Steven Chalmers. Yet Sarvis was bypassed, while Chalmers entirely absented himself from the investigation, claiming a need to tend to his sick mother, who lived right there in Durham.

The same day that Nifong assumed personal control of the investigation, Durham police corporal David Addison unleashed a battery of falsehoods to the media. The statements made the case national news and dominated the front pages of both local newspapers the next day and the national news. Addison told *The News & Observer*, the Durham *Herald-Sun*, CBS News, and ABC News that there was no doubt that "a brutal rape . . . occurred within that house," as he put it to ABC. His falsehoods to *The Herald-Sun* included:

- He said that there was "really, really strong physical evidence" of rape.
  In fact, there was none at all.

- He asserted that all forty-six white lacrosse players had refused to cooperate with police. In fact, not one had refused. Evans, Flannery, and Zash had fully cooperated, requesting lie-detector tests that police refused to administer. And it had been the district attorney and cops, not the team, who had broken off cooperation after the postponement of the other interviews.

- Finally, Addison stated that all of the players had "denied participation or knowing anything." In fact, the only three interviewed by police had given detailed accounts of what had and had not happened.

Moreover, in his capacity as liaison for Durham CrimeStoppers, a private organization that gave cash for anonymous tips leading to arrests, Addison released a statement unequivocally asserting that a crime had occurred and adding some editorial comment: "The Duke Lacrosse Team was hosting a party at the residence. The victim was sodomized, raped, assaulted and robbed. This horrific crime sent shock waves throughout our community."

Dozens of subsequent public statements by Nifong over the next ten days exuded similar certitude that the lacrosse players were rapists, and similarly mangled the evidence. The only question seemed to be which three had done it and how many others could be charged with aiding and abetting. These confident proclamations of guilt by the authorities had a gigantic effect on public opinion.

Just the day before, Duke's senior vice president for public affairs, John Burness, had held a meeting in which Bob Dean, the chief of the Duke campus police, had stressed that police did not consider Mangum or her rape claim to be credible. But "when I saw Addison quoted," Burness later recalled, "I had one of these 'Holy S——' moments. It was a stunning statement. When the police and the DA make that strong a claim, with no ambiguity, you think that they must have something."

From that day forward, the Duke administration, as well as the lacrosse players, lived inside a pressure cooker. "Every day there was some new thing," Burness later recalled. "If I got three hours of sleep it was a good night, and it went on for months. The media were all vilifying our kids, and not just lacrosse players." The administration was also under public attack, almost entirely for failing to rush to judgment against the lacrosse players as fast as Duke's faculty and the media themselves were doing.

The day of the Georgetown game, Saturday, March 25, dawned gloomy and foreboding, in more ways than one. Tens of thousands of newspapers, painting the team as a bunch of racist brutes and rapists, landed on doorsteps around the Raleigh-Durham region. From the start, the only two papers with substantial circulation in Durham played the "Duke lacrosse rape" story as a morality tale of white, rich, privileged, racist, swaggering, drunken jocks brutalizing a poor African-American mother struggling to work her way through college.

When the police and Nifong demonized the lacrosse players and canonized the "victim," the media were happy to provide unskeptical coverage, as *The Herald-Sun* did in its March 25 front-pager quoting Corporal Addison. And when an opportunity presented itself for journalists to do their own demonizing and canonizing, they seized it with relish. Among local papers, *The Herald-Sun*, with far more Durham circulation than any other newspaper (about 45,000 in spring 2006, but falling fast), was incomparably biased in the more than three hundred articles and twenty unsigned editorials it churned out in 2006, savaging the lacrosse players and downplaying or omitting altogether the ever-growing evidence of innocence.

But *The News & Observer*, with daily circulation of almost 180,000, including 10,000 in Durham County, was just as bad in its early coverage. Among the most journalistically irresponsible articles of the entire case was *The N&O*'s five-column, front-page article on March 25, which set a standard soon to be followed by *The New York Times* and other national news organs. The headline: "Dancer Gives Details of Ordeal." The word "alleged" was conspicuously absent. The subhead cited "A Night of Racial Slurs, Growing Fear, and, Finally, Sexual Violence." No "alleged" there either.

The rest of the article was also studded with phrases pervasively slanted to imply guilty lacrosse players and a virtuous accuser: the authorities' "vowing to crack the team's wall of solidarity"; the "victim"—the article always described Mangum as the victim—"struggling not to cry"; her father's concern that "someone hurt his baby"; her two children and "full class load at N.C. Central University."

Then there were neighbors' complaints of a long-running *Animal House* scene with "drunken antics and loud music"—quotes that were slyly unspecific on whether the worst antics were at the lacrosse house or (as police reports showed) the ten or so other Duke party houses nearby.

The article concluded by portraying the chairman of Duke's Academic Council, law professor Paul Haagen, as hinting he thought the players guilty. The story said that Haagen cited studies showing "that violence against women is more prevalent among male athletes than among male students in general," and singling out "helmet sports," such as football, hockey and lacrosse, for particular notice. The concluding quote: "These are sports of violence. This is clearly a concern." Yet, as Haagen recalled later, reporter Samiha Khanna took the quotes wildly out of context: he had grave doubts about Mangum's story, and Khanna spent most of her interview with him fishing for negative quotes about the players at a faculty meeting that day.

Billed as an interview with the accuser, the article was studded with falsehoods, all damning to the lacrosse players. The piece stressed the "victim's" claim that the players were "barking racial slurs" during the dance so aggressively as to drive both her and Kim Roberts to tears. This claim was contradicted by Roberts and everyone else who attended the party.

It claimed that the accuser had reported the rape to police only after her father had visited her at Duke Hospital. This assertion was contradicted by every relevant police report and (later) the father himself.

Samiha Khanna and her editor, Linda Williams (the highest-ranking African-American woman on the paper's news staff), also chose to omit Mangum's statement during the "interview" that Roberts, too, had been raped. Nor did the reporter dig up such evidence as the accuser's claim that Roberts had been an accomplice in the rape.

Such discordant notes would have complicated the morality tale that Khanna and Williams so clearly wanted to tell, a tale of virtuous black women brutalized by vicious white men. Williams later justified the omission of Mangum's comments about Roberts on legal grounds: "If we had printed that utterance [about Roberts]—an admitted speculation without the slightest foundation to suggest the possibility of truth—it would have been a conscious act of libel." The gist: Printing Mangum's utterances about the lacrosse players was great; printing her utterances about a fellow black dancer would be libel.

The News & Observer also allowed the "victim" to hurl her charges from behind a veil of anonymity, as virtually all news organs do in all rape cases, even when publicly available evidence shows that the rape claim is a hoax. The newspaper—once again omitting the word "alleged"—explained that its policy was "not to identify the victims of sex crimes." Such anonymity is *never* extended to men accused of rape, even when it is clear that they are victims of malicious lies by false accusers, nor is it extended to the alleged victims of virtually any non-sex crime. Such policies invert the once-cherished constitutional presumption of innocence, but they have become so routine as to seem unremarkable.

Duke administrators understood that the spectacle of the alleged rapists taking the field at 1:00 P.M. would keep the media pot boiling and bring hordes of protesters. Indeed, a Duke professor named Faulkner Fox, who lived in Trinity Park, had sent out an e-mail that morning calling for a silent protest at that day's game, with signs such as DON'T BE A FAN OF RAPISTS. She also recommended a candlelight vigil outside 610 North Buchanan that evening.

Brodhead decided that something dramatic needed to be done. So Alleva appeared without warning in Pressler's office at 11:30. Duke was going to forfeit the Georgetown game and the one after it. Pressler asked why. To punish the players for hiring strippers and underage drinking, Alleva said. Never mind that Duke had no rule against stripper parties. Never mind that there had been more than twenty such parties at Duke that year, including the basketball team's, and that underage drinking was and is rampant among athletes as well as other students at Duke and around the country.

Pressler was especially angry that the Georgetown players and coach, his friend Dave Urick, had come all this way for nothing. The Georgetown team was already warming up in the stadium. Pressler made Alleva tell Urick. The Duke players were in the locker room, dressed for the game. Alleva also told them about the two forfeits, adding that there would be no further penalties unless criminal charges were brought. And then he left, with a breezy "See ya" that the players would often repeat as a leitmotif for the contempt in which they held Alleva. Pressler sent the team to do some running and weight lifting while he had to break the word to the fifty or so Duke parents who had come to watch their sons play. Some, it turned out, had already heard the news from parents of visiting Georgetown players, who had already warmed up on the field.

Many of the senior parents, meanwhile, were at the Washington Duke Inn discussing plans for a graduation party for their sons. During a lull, Rich Zash, Matt's father, turned to Tricia Dowd and said, "I think the worst is over." She replied, "Rich, the worst is yet to come." About a minute later, someone came in and said the Georgetown game was canceled.

As the women's lacrosse team returned to their locker room in the Murray Building from practice, Coach Kerstin Kimel saw Georgetown players and parents milling around at the field with no sign of the Duke team or coaches and knew something was wrong. While she was in her office meeting with a recruit, members of the press started banging on the locked Murray Building door, trying to get in, demanding to see Pressler. She went to the door, told them that the building was locked on the weekends, and said that neither Pressler nor anyone else associated with the program was available. A little while later, *The N&O*'s Samiha Khanna, whose egregiously one-sided article had run on the front page that morning, somehow got into the building and walked into Kimel's private meeting, saying she wanted to speak to Pressler. Kimel told Khanna and her photographer that they weren't allowed in the building and asked them to leave or she would call campus police.

The Duke parents felt that the forfeit would make their sons look guilty in the eyes of the world. And many were almost completely in the dark about what had been going on. Meeting without lunch in the team's windowless, airless meeting room, they vented their fury and sense of betrayal from noon until past 5:00 P.M. at Alleva, Wasiolek, Trask, and Larry Moneta, the vice president for student affairs.

Despite repeated requests from parents that day and later, Brodhead refused to meet with them. This, parents noted, was the same Duke president who had found time to fly to Atlanta two days before to watch Coach K's basketball team. Now he was distancing himself and the university from its own lacrosse players at their hour of peril. Brodhead's decision poisoned the relationship between the president and the parents from the start.

Moneta and especially Trask came across to the parents as blunt, even arrogant. Moneta dodged questions about the administration's actions. Trask rolled his eyes and threw his head back as parents were speaking. When Trask himself was speaking, he often looked at the floor or out the door. Alleva repeated his promise to the players that there would be no more punishments absent criminal charges. While stressing that the party was "inconsistent with Duke's values," he admitted that no university rule had been broken and he could cite no other forfeiture of a game to discipline a team in Duke's history. The parents had already been infuriated by John Burness's comments on local television stations the night before to the effect that if the rape charges were true it would be deplorable—without much emphasis on the possibility that the charges were lies. "I said, 'You have to shut up Burness,'" Bruce Thompson recalled later. "'This guy is a disaster. He's out there just ripping into us.'"

Dean Wasiolek bore the brunt of the parents' anger. How could she urge all members of the team to talk to police without consulting parents or attorneys? Parents demanded. Wasiolek said she would have done the same had her own son been involved. This from a woman with a North Carolina Central law degree. Lashing back, Wasiolek chided the parents for criticizing Duke administrators but not their sons' stripper party. False, parents retorted: They had upbraided their sons for the party. And their sons had apologized. But the administration's response was grossly disproportionate to the misconduct.

"How in the world," Larry Lamade asked Wasiolek, "did you think you could sweep this under the rug knowing that Durham is one of the most racially divided cities in the country and the accuser is black?" According to Lamade, the dean—apparently oblivious to the front-page articles in that morning's News & Observer and Herald-Sun—responded: "She is?"

Stef Sparks, waiting in the hallway with Bob Ekstrand, could hear the anger spilling out of the room every time the door opened. She saw Tricia Dowd come out crying hysterically. At one point she heard Trask on the phone, saying, "I just told them something else."

Meanwhile, the team had convened in the weight room upstairs from the parents' meeting with Duke officials. Some players were upset that the captains had not told them what was going on. The captains explained that they had been admonished by police, by Pressler, and by Duke administrators to keep quiet.

At the much longer meeting downstairs, parents reviled Wes Covington, the Duke administration's would-be fixer. Wasiolek admitted that she didn't know much about his (sparse) criminal defense credentials. Trask trashed Bob Ekstrand, whose own credentials included teaching criminal law at Duke's own law school. "You ought to fire that guy," he told the parents. Expressing anger at the scuttling of the Covington sweep-it-under-the-rug plan, Trask also implied, to the astonishment of some parents, that all would be well had they refrained from consulting lawyers.

Moneta said that Duke would do what it could to accommodate team members who needed to vacate their off-campus housing to avoid harassment or worse. He also promised that the administration would not tolerate any faculty harassment of the players. Duke would live up to the first commitment. Not the second.

Alleva, Trask, and Wasiolek (but not Moneta) repeated their assurances that they believed the players to be innocent, with Wasiolek reiterating that Duke police had assured administrators that the rape allegation was not credible and would eventually go away. But when parents pleaded for the university to say so publicly—the only way to avoid an implication of guilt—the answer was no. No more statements would come from Duke today, announced Trask, who had been in and out of the room to take phone calls, presumably from Brodhead's office. Parents pressed: Could Duke at least promise not to make statements that would harm their sons? The administrators offered no guarantees. Trask eventually agreed that any additional comments from Duke would be given to the parents in advance so they would not be caught by surprise.

Finally the Duke officials left. The parents stayed to hear Bob Ekstrand say that his investigation had shown the rape charge to be a lie and explain how the DNA would prove this result. Meanwhile, Richard Brodhead was rushing to compound the beleaguered players' problems and break Trask's promise to their parents.

At 6:00 P.M., on the heels of three top Duke officials telling the parents that they believed the players innocent and that no further statements would be forthcoming, Brodhead led much of the world to believe them guilty. "Physical coercion and sexual assault are unacceptable in any setting and have no place at Duke," the president began, in his first public statement on the rape claim. "The criminal allegations against three members of our men's lacrosse team, if verified, will warrant very serious penalties."

Then Brodhead got to mentioning that "there are very different versions of the central events. No charges have been filed, and in our system of law, people are presumed innocent until proven guilty." In a sense, it made for a reasonably balanced statement. But as refracted by foreseeable media distortion, Brodhead's statement was not balanced at all. *The News & Observer, The Herald-Sun,* and the Associated Press all quoted Brodhead's opening line— "Physical coercion and sexual assault are unacceptable in any setting and have no place at Duke"—words that at the very least implied that the president believed a rape had occurred. None quoted his qualifier about the presumption of innocence. *The Herald-Sun* summarized the point, while *The News & Observer* and AP ignored the qualifier altogether.

Brodhead also urged the team "to cooperate to the fullest with the police," without mentioning that Evans, Flannery, and Zash already had done so. This implicit reproach became a mantra of Brodhead and his subordinates: The lacrosse players, they repeatedly suggested, were at fault for invoking their constitutional rights not to submit to untaped interviews with cops whom they had been warned were bent on framing them for a nonexistent crime.

Finally, Brodhead stressed that the March 13 party was "inappropriate to a Duke team member," applauding Alleva's forfeitures of two games. He did not mention the many other stripper parties at Duke, or the absence of any rule against them, or the extraordinary nature of any Division I team canceling a game in such an abrupt fashion, less than two hours before it was to start.

"That was the day we all realized that Duke was not on our side and was not going to do anything to protect its students," a parent later wrote. "That was the day Brodhead turned his back on our sons." Tricia Dowd later recalled leaving the meeting room with "a horrible feeling knowing we weren't going to get their help. I felt despondent at the realization that Duke wasn't going to stand beside our sons." Other parents clung to the hope that Brodhead would do the right thing once the DNA had cleared the team.

The captains felt an even greater sense of betrayal by Duke administrators. "They would go into a room and say we believe you, but that's not what they put out to the world," one captain later recalled. "That's why you feel stabbed in the back."

About the same time that Brodhead released his statement, his senior vice president for public affairs, John Burness, sent an e-mail to Duke's board of trustees. He reported on the team captains' meeting with Trask and their absolute denial that anything happened, noting that "Dr. Trask is inclined to believe the players." Burness added: "The students have hired an attorney who, for perhaps understandable reasons, has urged them not to say anything. While that may be a sound legal strategy, it leaves them vulnerable to the woman's version of events filling a vacuum and the students appearing to be uncooperative. . . . The situation is further complicated by the behavior of the lacrosse team over many years which for those predisposed to be angry with them, presumes their guilt. . . . We simply do not know what actually happened, which is why the [police] investigation is so important." Burness offered no specific examples of bad behavior. Indeed, the worst examples of pre-stripper-party lacrosse-player behavior that were ever documented were routine college-kid stuff: loud parties, having an open beer while sitting as a passenger in the back seat of a car, and (in two cases over a several-year period) public urination.

To Burness, this e-mail was an even-handed update of the situation. To lacrosse players and parents who learned of it later, Burness's language about "appearing to be uncooperative" and the "behavior of the lacrosse team over many years" seemed another dagger in the back from the Duke administration.

Over the next few days, as the story exploded into a media firestorm immolating the lacrosse team, the players and their parents believed that public comments such as those of Brodhead—and, they suspected, private comments by Duke officials to reporters—were feeding the fire, and inspiring such coverage as the April 1 *New York Times* headline: "Team's Troubles Shock Few at Duke."

Lacrosse parents also circulated reports of a succession of negative comments about their sons' characters over the ensuing months by Burness, and by Duke board chairman Bob Steel, in private conversations with people at Duke and elsewhere. Burness also ran down the lacrosse players in off-the-record comments to news reporters. (Some of the reporters repeated these comments to others, who in turn repeated them to the authors; there were striking similarities in the Burness language reported by these different sources.) Bruce Thompson, father of cocaptain Bret Thompson, quoted one such journalist saying that Burness had motioned him to turn off his tape recorder and then launched into an attack on the team, saying: "These are bad guys, be careful about them," while offering no specifics beyond the usual complaints about lacrosse players being big drinkers and loud partyers with what some other students saw as an arrogant swagger.

Asked by one of the authors to respond to these lacrosse parents' complaints, Burness acknowledged telling reporters and others that the lacrosse players were "no choirboys" and the like. But he stressed that in the frenzy of late March, "I and President Brodhead were somewhat alone in trying to slow down the train of folks rushing to judgment." As an example, he cited a March 29 interview with MSNBC's lacrosse-team-bashing Joe Scarborough in which Burness stressed that the players had "been in contact with the police" (which was not what the police were telling the media); "have consistently said . . . that there was no sexual activity"; that "no one has been charged"; and that the team's past scrapes with the law for "drinking and acting obnoxiously" should not be equated with "something as horrific as sexual assault." But these tepid comments were lost in the noise.

"The only information that was out there was making these kids seem demonic, and everything pointed to guilt," a Brodhead aide later explained. He stressed that "the kids hadn't said publicly that it didn't happen."

Privately the kids all had, of course, said that it didn't happen, and that the DNA would prove it. They had said this emphatically to Pressler and Wasiolek on March 15, to police on March 16, to Brodhead subordinates Trask, Alleva, and Kennedy on March 24, to Covington and Ekstrand, to their parents, and to others. By then they were all being grilled by parents and lawyers who were admonishing them not to sacrifice themselves to cover up for a teammate. "The best gauge of what did not happen here," Collin Finnerty's father Kevin later recalled, "was that you can't keep forty-six kids under that kind of pressure and not have someone crack if they have something to hide. They were grilled by their parents, by their lawyers, by their girlfriends. None ever varied from the theme that nothing happened. If something had happened, somebody would have broken down and confided it."

The captains had also issued denials not only to police but also to Brodhead's executive vice president, vice president for student affairs, dean of student affairs, athletics director, assistant athletics director, and lacrosse coach. They all said the same to Brodhead himself when he finally met with them. But that was three long days after Brodhead had begun with the words "physical coercion and sexual assault" in his first public comments about the team. Brodhead would later stress that he was just about the only major figure in the news who gave even lip service to the presumption of innocence, a bedrock principle of criminal justice and American culture, while the police, the district attorney, the media, and the professors rushed to presume guilt. True. For a while.

That same evening, March 25, protesters held a candlelight vigil outside 610 North Buchanan. Carrying candles and signs reading REAL MEN DON'T PROTECT RAPISTS, dozens of protesters chanted "Shame!" and sang hymns. Duke professor Faulkner Fox told reporters: "The students need to realize they live in a community, and people are going to talk back if they do something, or potentially do something, that is disrespectful to women." How one is to judge people for what they "potentially do" Fox did not reveal.

Having found no one home at their targeted house, the protesters moved on to a nearby residence rented by two other lacrosse players, William Wolcott and K. J. Sauer. Looking outside, the two players noticed people screaming, banging on the windows, demanding that they come out and "confess." Fearing for their safety, Wolcott called Larry Moneta and asked for Duke police protection. Moneta said no. Call the Durham cops, the dean suggested. What good would that do? Wolcott asked: The Durham cops were already there, standing outside the house, supervising the mob. The two waited until things quieted down, left by the back door, and walked to Wolcott's car. Forced out of their home, Wolcott and Sauer moved to another, more secure, off-campus apartment.

A few hours after these protesters had chanted and sung "This Little Light of Mine" on Crystal Mangum's behalf, their "victim" was pole dancing in almost acrobatic fashion at the Platinum Club. A videotape that ended up in the hands of defense lawyers showed her clad in a thong and skimpy top, grabbing a floor-to-ceiling pole and lowering herself into a squatting position, buttocks almost on the floor, stretching her right leg toward the ceiling and waving it to either side of the pole. The stripper demonstrated none of the ills of which she had complained earlier that day on her second post-party visit to UNC Hospital, where doctors could detect no physical problems and denied her request for more Percocet.

Another protest, held by people who came to be called "potbangers," assembled outside 610 North Buchanan again the next morning, Sunday, March 26, before nine o'clock. "We are having a 'Cacerolazo,' or a pots & pans protest, because it is a tool women all over the world use to call out sexual assaulters," proclaimed an announcement posted on a local Listserv. "Y'all, a sister—an NCCU student and a mom of two—has been brutally assaulted, and we need to get together and make a big noise!" Another protester asserted that they needed to apply pressure because "the individuals who have information about this incident refuse to share the information." He added: "I'm not sure I understand the 'innocent until proven guilty' statements that have been put forward."

"There is a sense that Duke students need to be protected from Durham, but rapes are happening off East Campus at the hands of Duke students," Manju Rajendran told the assembled media. (None mentioned that she was an outsider with no connection to Durham.) Potbangers carried signs reading, YOU CAN'T RAPE AND RUN, IT'S SUNDAY MORNING, TIME TO CONFESS, and even CASTRATE. They demanded that Duke fire Pressler, expel everyone who attended the party, and disband the lacrosse program. They chanted: "Who's protecting rapists? They're protecting rapists! So, who are the rapists? They must be the rapists!"

Nobody was inside. Evans, Flannery, and Zash had fled to avoid continuing harassment and in fear of being physically attacked, even shot, by self-appointed avengers.

At the time, these and other protests seemed spontaneous. In fact, they were carefully planned by people with other agendas. As soon as the first reports linking the lacrosse team to the alleged rape surfaced, on March 24, two groups had mobilized to exploit the case for their own purposes. The first was a loosely aligned network of local "progressive" activists, who saw an opportunity to strike back at a society they viewed as oppressive toward minorities, women, and the poor. These included figures on the leftist fringe of Triangle politics, such as the People's Alliance, which calls itself "a progressive community organization focused on "gay/lesbian/bisexual/transgender rights," the environment, "economic justice," and opposing U.S. foreign policy. Also active were staffers of the *Indy*, the Triangle's alternative weekly paper.

The second group included a handful of habitual protesters, some of whom happened to be in Durham for other matters. Manju Rajendran, the lead speaker at the potbanger protest, had come to Duke as a panelist for "Mic Check: The Hip Hop Generation Has Something to Say," where she joined Professor Mark Anthony Neal, who would later help lead faculty attacks on the lacrosse players. Rajendran described herself as "a twenty-five-year-old artist, activist, and biologist" who had worked with Hip Hop Against Racist War before arriving in the Durham area. Rann Bar-On, a Duke graduate student in math who was active in radical anti-Israel groups such as the Palestine Solidarity Movement, organized an anti-lacrosse-player group named Durham Responds. It sought to use Mangum's rape charge to force Duke to change its curriculum and spend money on various radical causes.

While such protesters focused on issues national and global, the Trinity Park Association concentrated on local affairs. In 2000, when two home-invasion rapes occurred in the neighborhood, it had established a Listserv to discuss crime and related matters. By 2006 the Listserv carried frequent complaints about the raucous partying and drunkenness of Duke students in rented houses. The Trinity Parkers' grievances were against all Dukies who partied in their neighborhood. But when the rape allegation came along, many saw the lacrosse players as perfect scapegoats. "Shame on them," read one message on the Trinity Park Listserv. "Shame on the parents who raised them. Who are this [sic] so-called 'men' who shout racist slurs and have no respect for women, authority, indeed, for anyone? Who do they think they are?"

Faulkner Fox used the Listserv to issue her call for protests. Later, she declined to discuss her motivations.

That Sunday morning, March 26, also brought a sanctimonious sermon condemning the lacrosse players by Father Joe Vetter at Catholic mass in the Duke Cathedral. Two team members and parents were there. Afterward, Rob Wellington's father, Bob, confronted the priest, saying that 70 percent of the players were Catholic and that they needed the priest's support. The response: "Tell them to confess their sins first."

Devon Sherwood was not exempt from harassment. E-mails rained in accusing him of letting down his race. One exhorted him to turn against his teammates and be a "young black soldier." Another said that he should "rot in hell" if his teammates went down. "I was like, whoa, this guy wants me to rot in hell," Devon recalled months later in an interview with Chris Cuomo of ABC's *Good Morning America*. "Like, he doesn't even know. He doesn't even know who I am. . . . What my favorite food is or anything like that. He doesn't know me at all."

The lacrosse parents were shocked that Brodhead would not meet with them or their sons that weekend. "He had just made news all over the country," one parent later recalled, "and he couldn't come down and talk to us or the team?"

All that weekend Samantha Ekstrand heard from mothers worried that their sons would be assaulted by vigilantes. Samantha was worried, too. The biggest protest yet was planned for Monday morning. With the university's blessing, it was to be held on Duke's main quad, which the lacrosse players had to traverse to get to and from class. Might they be attacked by an angry mob?

Already, Bo Carrington, who was recognizable as one of the tallest lacrosse players on the team, had been surrounded by a group of African-American students while walking across the quad in the middle of Duke's West Campus. "You know what happened that night!" shouted one member of the crowd. "Why aren't you saying anything?" As the crowd dispersed, a fellow student in one of Carrington's classes came running up and asked: "Bo, why don't you tell me what you know?"

But nobody wanted to hear what Carrington knew: He had left the party (without drinking any alcohol) before the strippers had arrived because he considered such entertainment distasteful. And he was confident that the rape charge was a lie.

The Ekstrands wanted official excused absences from class for any players who feared for their physical safety. Bob called Larry Moneta Sunday night. He got nowhere. Then Samantha tried her luck. Moneta first claimed that he had no authority to do anything. Samantha pressed, again and again. Finally the dean allowed that any players in trouble with professors for unexcused absences could ask him for help later. This was no guarantee, Samantha protested.

"Samantha, what do you want from me?" Moneta finally demanded.

"I would like for you to believe these kids and support them," she said.

"Well, frankly, Samantha, I don't believe them."

Also on that Sunday, Durham mayor Bill Bell spoke by phone with Brodhead. While the Duke president would later deny feeling pressured, Bell complained publicly the next day about the team's supposed "code of silence" and urged Duke to cancel the whole season to "send a strong message to the community."

Most Duke students—although not the ones that the media loved to feature—were more open-minded than the protesters and Larry Moneta. "We wanted desperately to be able to reasonably doubt the allegations," Adam Chandler, a senior, recalled later, after winning a Rhodes scholarship. "It was inconceivable to us that any Duke student would act in such a violent manner, especially as part of a group in a premeditated attack. But at first, we had nothing to give any legs to the view that we wanted to support. And it was literally the only topic anyone could talk about in those days."

The morning of March 27, it seemed like everyone was talking about a column by the *N&O*'s Ruth Sheehan. Entitled "Team's Silence Is Sickening," it began: "Members of the Duke men's lacrosse team: You know. We know you know. Whatever happened in the bathroom at the stripper party gone terribly terribly bad, you know who was involved. Every one of you does. And one of you needs to come forward and tell the police."

Ruth Sheehan would later come to a dramatically different view about events of that evening and the authorities' handling of the inquiry. But during the early days and weeks when the story was hot, the possibility that nothing deep and dark had happened in that bathroom—nothing at all—was off the table as far as the DA, the cops, the media, and the Duke faculty were concerned.

6. THE MOST DANGEROUS POWER:

ENTER NIFONG

The prosecutor has more control over life, liberty, and reputation than any other person in America. . . . While the prosecutor at his best is one of the most beneficent forces in our society, when he acts from malice or other base motives, he is one of the worst. . . . [T]he citizen's safety lies in the prosecutor who tempers zeal with human kindness, who seeks truth and not victims, who serves the law and not factional purposes, and who approaches his task with humility.

So said one of America's legal giants, U.S. Attorney General Robert Jackson, in a famous 1940 speech to an assemblage of United States attorneys. Jackson later sat on the Supreme Court and served as chief American prosecutor of Nazi leaders at the Nuremberg war crimes trials.

It has long been a bedrock principle of justice that the duty of every prosecutor is not to "win a case, but that justice shall be done," as the Supreme Court said unanimously in 1935, in *Berger v. United States.* "As such, he is in a peculiar and very definite sense the servant of the law, the twofold aim of which is that guilt shall not escape or innocence suffer. . . . It is as much his duty to refrain from improper methods calculated to produce a wrongful conviction as it is to use every legitimate means to bring about a just one."

North Carolina's Rules of Professional Conduct for lawyers recognize these duties. Section 3.8 requires that district attorneys and their assistants "refrain from prosecuting a charge that the prosecutor knows is not supported by probable cause." The official comment to this section states that "a prosecutor has the responsibility of a minister of justice and not simply that of an advocate; the prosecutor's duty is to seek justice, not merely to convict."

Most trial judges act as passive umpires enforcing rigid legal rules. So the prosecutor is the only player in the criminal justice system whose judgment, intelligence, and sense of proportion can intercede to stop the meat grinder from chewing up people who are either completely innocent or (more often) don't deserve the harsh punishments prescribed for them.

Prosecutors—and especially district attorneys in small cities such as Durham—also have enormous power over the very defense lawyers who are supposed to take them on. The bread-and-butter work of most local defense lawyers is making deals with the district attorney's office: reducing a serious charge to a lesser included offense; giving a defendant an affordable bond to get out of jail while his case is pending; and more.

"If a prosecutor decides that Joe Smith isn't going to get any more deals," explains a North Carolina defense lawyer, "then unless Joe Smith has a lot of power, his practice is going to start drying up." Most defense lawyers thus will pay a big price if they take on or publicly criticize a prosecutor who is treating the lawyer's client unfairly, or failing to comply with his obligations to hand over evidence, or engaging in any other form of prosecutorial abuse. And a lot of defense lawyers will go a long way to ingratiate themselves with their local district attorney.

So it was not surprising that reporters who inquired into Mike Nifong's reputation after the lacrosse case had put him under a spotlight found Durham defense lawyers to speak well of him—even including the lawyers representing some of the lacrosse players.

And in North Carolina, district attorneys even have the power to pick which of several judges will try their biggest cases and hear the biggest motions. This is a byproduct of the state's unusual system of rotating judges in and out of most cases after a few months, combined with the DA's power to control the scheduling of cases for trial. The DA can simply delay the trial if he thinks that he will get a more sympathetic hearing from the next judge due to rotate in. And since judges gain prominence and reelectability by presiding over big cases, the system gives them a special incentive to ingratiate themselves with the local DA—and not to cross DAs who abuse their powers.

Michael Byron Nifong (*NIE*-fong) was a career prosecutor who thought of himself as exceptionally ethical. He had his share of admirers. Few, however, ever accused him of the kind of humility identified by Robert Jackson as a critical safeguard against abuse. "I have," Nifong asserted on his campaign Web site, "earned the reputation among my colleagues in the court system as a prosecutor of the highest level of professional skill."

Born in 1950, a native of Wilmington, North Carolina, Nifong went with his father, a treasury agent, to blow up moonshiners' stills when he was a kid. His parents were both Duke grads. But he graduated from Duke's archrival, the University of North Carolina at Chapel Hill, in 1971 and was known for hating Duke and Dukies.

Coming of age during the Vietnam era, he registered as a conscientious objector with the Selective Service. After graduating from college, Nifong worked for a year as a math teacher and three years as a social worker before going to the University of North Carolina Law School. He received his J.D. in 1978.

Patsy McDonald, a law school classmate of Nifong's who now practices law in Maryland, recalled him as a nondescript, mediocre student. "Nifong spent a lot of time in the student lounge watching game shows like *Dialing for Dollars, Bowling for Dollars*, and playing cards, mostly bridge. He was neither one of the better players nor one of the better students. He wasn't on law review and did not get Order of the Coif," the award given to top law students at UNC. McDonald also remembered Nifong developing a "deep-seated antipathy to lacrosse players" while at law school. UNC's law library overlooks the lacrosse field, with a large window from which students in the library can watch practices and games.

Nifong wanted to be a prosecutor and try cases. Yet his mediocre academic record prevented him from getting a job offer. After being turned down for positions in Raleigh, Greensboro, and Durham, he volunteered to work for free for the Durham district attorney. Before long, he received a paid position as an assistant DA in Durham. Within two years, Nifong was trying felony cases in Superior Court.

In the late 1980s, Nifong, then married with a young daughter, entered into a relationship with Cy Gurney, the (married) district administrator of the Durham Guardian Ad Litem Office, which pairs volunteers with attorneys to represent abused and neglected children in court. Gurney got pregnant, and both divorced their spouses. Nifong and Gurney were married several years later, in 1998, when their son was eight years old.

This minor scandal had no effect on Nifong's career. By the mid-1990s he was assigned to the biggest cases and was promoted to chief assistant DA. By the late 1990s he had tried more than three hundred felony cases and taken thousands of guilty pleas. Nifong loved trials. He had self-confidence and a certain flair. In a 1995 murder trial, Nifong flopped onto the floor in a prone position—saying, "I hate to do this in a suit"—to illustrate his theory that the defendant had been prone when he fired. He was known for taunting defense lawyers and wisecracking in court. In one case, when defense attorneys asked for a continuance, he ridiculed them as "poultry," and told *The Herald-Sun* that they were "a bunch of chickens."

"When you got in there, it was about winning," he told a *News & Observer* reporter in 2005. Nifong showed this attitude in a 1994 rape case with some similarities to the Duke case. A woman claimed that Timothy Malloy, a convenience store clerk, had pulled a gun from his waistband and raped her orally, then vaginally (with ejaculation), then anally. Malloy's defense was that they had had consensual, vaginal sex. Most of the evidence supported his story.

Medical reports showed no physical evidence of injury or anal or oral sex. Malloy had been wearing sweat pants held up by flimsy elastic that could not have supported a gun. No gun was ever found despite a thorough search of the store and Malloy's car. A newspaper deliveryman testified that just after the incident, he saw Malloy and the woman talking and thought they were friends. She was very drunk, had told inconsistent stories to police, and had made numerous false statements in the past on job and credit applications.

Still, Nifong took the case to trial. The defense lawyer shredded the woman's credibility for hours. When it was Nifong's turn for rebuttal, he skipped over the evidence of innocence as though it were inconsequential. He asked the woman only whether she had taken an oath on the Bible to tell the truth and if she had told the truth. She said yes. Nifong sat down. The jury's verdict was not guilty. The question that lingered was why Nifong had forced a probably innocent man to go through the ordeal of a rape trial in the first place.

Was it that Nifong thought that all self-described rape victims are entitled to put their story before a judge and jury, as he would suggest during the lacrosse case? No. He had dismissed as unworthy of prosecution two other rape claims that resembled the Duke case. The first, in 1989, involved a twenty-one-year-old woman who accused four lawn-care workers, all black or Hispanic, of forcing their way into her car and sexually assaulting her. Nifong had the men immediately arrested and charged. But when he learned of "numerous demonstrably false statements" by the accuser, he dismissed all charges.

A decade later, Nifong investigated the rapes that had roiled Trinity Park. Police arrested a homeless black man, Leroy Summers, based solely on an identification by one of the rape victims. But the State Bureau of Investigation lab reported (after more than three months) finding another man's DNA. Nifong dismissed the charges. "Results of DNA testing exclude the defendant as the perpetrator of this crime," he wrote—a view that would contrast starkly with his blithe dismissal of exculpatory DNA evidence in the lacrosse case.

By 1999, Nifong had slowed down, following prostate cancer surgery and radiation and hormone therapy. Shortly after the Summers case was dismissed, then-district attorney Jim Hardin put Nifong in charge of negotiating pleas in traffic court, which had been ravaged by scandal. Hardin saw Nifong as an ethical person who would clean it up.

In that job Nifong became known as the traffic ticket king; *The New Yorker* would describe his new position as a publicly funded "semi-retirement." Lawyers lined up like supplicants outside his office while Nifong enjoyed his collection of more than five thousand CDs. When the hard rock started blasting through the door, it signaled that Nifong was open for business to negotiate pleas for speeding tickets, revoked licenses, and the like.

He also earned a reputation for bluster, a volcanic temper and unpredictable moods. "Is Mike on his meds today?" lawyers would ask. One Durham attorney said to *The News & Observer*, "Working with Mike, you never knew from one day to the other who you'd be dealing with. He would curse you, scream at you, call you names over nothing." After an argument with a Chicago resident over the prosecutor's refusal to settle a traffic ticket, Nifong proclaimed: "My name is Mike Nifong and I'm the chief asshole of the Durham County district attorney's office."

In April 2005, North Carolina governor Michael Easley, a Democrat, named Jim Hardin, Durham's elected DA, to the bench. The major candidates to succeed Hardin—all assistant district attorneys, like Nifong—had significant weaknesses. David Saacks didn't live in Durham and had no desire to do so. Tracey Cline, though an African American, had a poor relationship with leaders of the Durham Committee on the Affairs of Black People. Many people had doubts about Freda Black's legal ethics. On the recommendations of both Hardin and Judge Ron Stephens, Hardin's predecessor as district attorney, the governor chose Nifong to fill out the remaining twenty months of Hardin's term. In return, Nifong promised Easley that he would not run for a full term, thereby minimizing the risk that the interim appointment might politicize the office before the next election.

The twenty-six-year veteran of the office seemed a logical choice to some at the time. One was Bill Thomas, perhaps Durham's top criminal defense lawyer. "I've known Mike Nifong for twenty-seven years," Thomas said later, after the lacrosse case had made him a strong critic. "I have never before had a problem with Mike Nifong professionally. We tried some very serious cases opposite each other, including murder and armed robbery cases, and I never had a problem with his ethics. He was a careful lawyer who paid careful attention to his cases."

To others, he seemed a man flawed by wild mood swings, an ugly temper, a petty-tyrant attitude, and a tendency to presume guilt, a characteristic of many a career prosecutor who has never represented a defendant, let alone an innocent one.

Just after his appointment, Nifong confessed that he had been "kind of cocky" when he was trying cases, but had learned something through age and his battle with cancer. "What you may lose sight of when all you're worried about is winning," Nifong told *The N&O*, is that "this is really supposed to be about justice."

Nifong soon would be worried about winning again. In one of his first acts as district attorney, he fired Freda Black, a longtime rival in the office. She was better known because she had helped win the conviction of Michael Peterson, a novelist and former mayoral candidate, in a celebrated 2003 murder trial. Soon after her dismissal, Black made preparations to run in 2006. She secured a position in the law offices of Jerry Clayton, a well-connected local attorney who was eager to have an ally in the DA's office. With her name recognition, she seemed like a strong candidate for what would be an open-seat primary. And few doubted that she would fire Nifong as soon as she took office.

With his career on the line, Nifong abandoned his promise to Easley and decided to run for a full four-year term. He told associates he needed the extra time in office to receive the maximum pension. Under North Carolina's pension plan for government employees, Nifong had a strong financial incentive to make the race. If he served out a full term as elected DA, Nifong's pension would increase by $15,000 annually. He told Jackie Brown, who managed his primary campaign, "I really don't want this job; I was the last one on the list. I just need three years and seven months for retirement. You won't have to worry about running another campaign for me."

To enjoy a full four-year term, Nifong had to win a May 2, 2006, primary election. Roughly 80 percent of Durham County's voters were Democrats or independents who could vote in the Democratic primary, an electorate divided almost evenly between whites and blacks. No Republicans were expected to run, so the winner of the May primary would presumably be a shoo-in for the fall election.

Though his last election contest had been in student government, Nifong had some political assets before the lacrosse case broke. He had the behind-the-scenes backing of Hardin, Stephens, and other big-name figures within the county Democratic Party. He scored a coup in landing Jackie Brown, a close ally of Mayor Bill Bell, as his campaign manager. And in early 2006, he launched a major fund-raising drive. Between January 1 and February 19, he took in just over $20,000, outpacing Black, who had outraised him in 2005. Lacking significant financial support from the business or educational communities, or from grassroots organizations, Nifong got his campaign funds almost exclusively from local lawyers who did business with his office. Such a fund-raising strategy is risky: no private-practice lawyer wants to be remembered as a major donor to the candidate the current DA defeated to win her office. To continue to attract contributions, then, Nifong had to be perceived as a likely winner.

Nifong frequently described himself as a prosecutor, not a politician, and his performance on the campaign trail proved the point. He was especially awkward in dealing with black voters. Despite nearly three decades in public service, Nifong had few personal or professional connections with African Americans. In a voter guide published in *The Herald-Sun*, he listed attending church and working with his son's Little League as his two major community activities; neither involved much interaction with blacks.

Nifong's first major outreach efforts suggested intent to pander based on a simplistic view of African-American preferences. In January 2006, the interim district attorney appeared at a local church, where he addressed a group called Parents of Murdered Children. According to a *Durham News* columnist on the scene, Nifong promised toughness on crime but then generated outrage by lecturing the mothers, "You have to remember that when there's a murder, two mothers lose their sons. There's another mother whose son will spend the rest of his life in prison." In unison, the crowd shouted, "No!" One mother ridiculed Nifong's claims that the mothers of criminals and victims suffered equally: "She can visit her son in prison. If I want to talk to my son, I got to talk to dirt!"

Nifong's approach reflected a one-dimensional, almost caricatured view of black people. Because prominent black leaders are well to the left on issues of criminal justice, Nifong seemed to assume that this all-black audience of mothers would feel the same.

Disliking Freda Black and turned off by Nifong, the city's African-American leadership considered the third candidate in the race, defense attorney Keith Bishop. Bishop had never run for office before, nor had he ever prosecuted a case. Moreover, in 2001, the State Bar had sanctioned him for unethical conduct, claiming that he improperly delayed a civil case in order to block the defendant's attempt to depose a witness. His candidacy therefore seemed a long shot at best. But he was black, a plus in Durham.

As Black continued to raise money from Durham's business community, aided by Jerry Clayton, her well-connected mentor, Nifong's campaign stagnated. He proved reluctant to campaign personally. His wife tended to focus on peripheral issues, such as letters on the campaign Web site, hiring bands for campaign rallies, or ensuring that shooting stars would appear on the campaign's lawn signs. And his fund-raising dried up. The donors, it seemed, had concluded he couldn't win. They understood that sticking with a loser in this election could cost them a lot more than a few campaign contributions. Between February 20 and April 1, Black outraised Nifong by a margin of greater than four to one.

As his fellow lawyers abandoned him, Nifong could have thrown in the towel. Instead, needing to keep pace, he loaned his campaign nearly $30,000, money that this longtime government servant could ill afford to risk losing with his son bound for college in three years.

Racial politics also threatened to squeeze Nifong. Bishop, as the sole black candidate, seemed to be the front-runner for the endorsement of the Durham Committee on the Affairs of Black People, which traditionally had carried enormous weight with Durham's black voters. Freda Black, meanwhile, enjoyed much higher name recognition than the appointed incumbent, and had the advantage of being the only woman candidate in a constituency where 57 percent of the registered voters were female. If Black received a majority of the white vote and Bishop garnered a majority of the African-American vote—probable outcomes before March 13—Nifong had almost no chance of winning. In a private poll taken by the Black campaign that was completed on March 27, Black enjoyed a whopping 17-point lead on the incumbent. And if Freda Black prevailed, she would surely fire Nifong from the only law office that had ever employed him, as he had fired her. Who would employ him then?

Professional oblivion loomed. Then came Crystal Mangum and her spectacular rape charge. And everything changed.

Nifong met with Gottlieb and Himan on March 27 to be briefed on the case, including SANE trainee Tara Levicy's misleading suggestions that she had seen physical evidence "consistent with rape." Nifong probably "was sold a bill of goods by Gottlieb" and might have initially believed that Mangum had been raped by Duke lacrosse players, in the view of Bill Thomas.

Gottlieb and Himan also showed the DA a newly discovered, seemingly bloodcurdling e-mail that one of the players, nineteen-year-old Ryan McFadyen, had sent to the whole team just over an hour after the stripper party ended. The e-mail said that McFadyen planned to have some strippers in his dorm room but that, instead of dancing, "i plan on killing the bitches as soon as they walk in and proceeding to cut their skin off while cumming in my duke issue spandex."

The other lacrosse players recognized this for the extremely sick joke that it was; some immediately recalled the horror book-movie that McFadyen had mimicked. But to Nifong, who had always disliked Duke, the e-mail may have signaled that these lacrosse players were a depraved bunch, and quite capable of gang rape.

It was also convenient for Nifong to believe this version of events. The black community was understandably outraged at the lurid, initially uncontested story of a local woman being brutally gang-raped by white Duke lacrosse players "barking racial slurs," as *The News & Observer* described them on March 25. So suddenly the black vote was in play. Nifong's best hope was to make the rape case the campaign's main event. At the least, he could garner publicity and match Freda Black's name recognition. At best, he could use the case to inflame the black community and win over minority voters who would otherwise support Bishop.

And that's what Nifong did.

On March 27—two days after Duke president Richard Brodhead's March 25 statement that seemed to lacrosse parents to imply that their sons were guilty—Nifong began a media barrage unheard of for a prosecutor in Durham, or anywhere else. Declaring that he would personally handle the case because it "talks about what this community stands for," he spent over forty hours that week giving at least seventy media interviews and press conferences.

In fiery language, Nifong declared that medical evidence made it clear that the "victim" had been raped by Duke lacrosse players. False. Fanning the flames of racial and class hatred, he suggested the rampant use of racial slurs. False. The entire team was a "bunch of hooligans" who had formed a "wall of silence" to protect their three rapist teammates. False.

He said the players' "daddies" would buy them expensive lawyers. He asked "why one needs an attorney if one was not charged and had not done anything wrong." He threatened the entire team with prosecution for "encouraging or condoning" rape if they did not "cooperate." He said that the DNA tests would show that there had been a rape, then said the opposite after gleaning that the DNA tests would likely be negative. He compared the accuser's claims to cross burnings and a quadruple homicide.

At a March 27 meeting with Bob Ekstrand, who urged the district attorney to await the dispositive DNA results before charging anyone, a blustering Nifong threatened all the players with prosecution. As Ekstrand recalls, Nifong said: "If you've come here to ask me questions instead of telling me what you know about who did it, then we don't have anything to talk about. You're wasting my time. You tell all of your clients I will remember their lack of cooperation at sentencing. I hope you know if they didn't do it, they are all aiders and abettors, and that carries the same punishment as rape."

Ekstrand had no more luck when, later that same day, he offered to sit down with Richard Brodhead or anyone whom Brodhead might designate to walk through the large body of innocence that Ekstrand had already accumulated. This included a time line based on time-stamped photos and cell-phone records starkly contradicting the accuser's version of events. "I wanted to give them the confidence they needed to withstand pressure that would be brought to bear before the DNA tests came back negative, as we knew they would," Ekstrand later explained. He also offered to arrange a briefing by his mentor, one of the nation's most famed lawyers. But after Ekstrand's offer had been relayed to Brodhead, the lawyer was put off, as he was when he made similar offers on subsequent occasions. "I said, 'I'll come to his house or meet in somebody's basement at 3 A.M. if he'll listen to me," Ekstrand recalled later. But it seemed that Brodhead and Nifong alike were taking pains to avoid seeing or hearing the evidence of innocence.

Brodhead would later explain in an interview with one of the authors that "we kept a degree of distance and not by accident. . . . Duke had to be very careful not to seem to intrude in the case or to try to manipulate it." He said that if Duke had done its own investigation by interviewing witnesses, it could have been accused of witness tampering. But it would not, of course, have been witness tampering to listen to a lawyer (Ekstrand) explain why the evidence in his hands proved the innocence of the Duke students who were his clients.

What was the basis for Nifong's certitude of guilt? It was not any interview of the "victim." Chief investigator Nifong never interviewed her about the facts, as he would admit months later, to the astonishment of rape prosecutors across the country. It was not Mangum's hopelessly vague descriptions of the alleged rapists. Nor was it her inability to identify as rapists any of the thirty-six photos she viewed on March 16 and 21. Nor information from anyone else at the party: Roberts (as well as all of the players) had seen no evidence of rape, and their stories directly contradicted Crystal's in almost every respect. Nor anything said by the police officers who had dealt with Crystal the night of the alleged rape and who disbelieved her wildly changing story.

Instead, Nifong repeatedly based his accusations on the March 14 exam at the Duke hospital. He told Dan Abrams, host of MSNBC's *Abrams Report,* "I am convinced that there was a rape. Yes sir." Why? asked Abrams. "There is evidence of trauma in the victim's vaginal area that was noted when she was examined by a nurse at the hospital," Nifong answered. "And her general demeanor was suggested—suggestive of the fact that she had been through a traumatic situation."

This assertion was misleading in multiple ways. The hospital records, some of which Nifong had not yet seen, contained no evidence of rape. They said nothing about "trauma in the victim's vaginal area." Tara Levicy had noted nothing about vaginal trauma in her report of the exam. In short, apart from Mangum's rapidly changing, self-contradicting, and far from credible stories, and whatever Levicy had told Gottlieb and Himan, Nifong had no evidentiary basis at all, ever, for his assertions that the woman he came to call "my victim" had been raped.

This problem did not stop him from embarking on the most flagrant serial smearing of innocent suspects ever to unfold in a national spotlight. A
sampling from the first two days of the Nifong media offensive:

- MARCH 27: "In this case, where you have the act of rape—essentially a
  gang rape—is bad enough in and of itself, but when it's made with
  racial epithets against the victim, I mean, it's just absolutely uncon-
  scionable. . . . The contempt that was shown for the victim, based on
  her race was totally abhorrent. . . . My guess is that some of this stone
  wall of silence that we have seen may tend to crumble once charges
  start to come out."

- "The information that I have does lead me to conclude that a rape occurred. . . . I'm making a statement to the Durham community. . . .
  This is not the kind of activity we condone, and it must be dealt with
  quickly and harshly."

- "We don't know who the assailants are, but we know they came from
  this group."

- MARCH 28: "The thing that most of us found so abhorrent, and the reason I decided to take it over myself, was the combination gang-like rape
  activity accompanied by the racial slurs and general racial hostility.
  There are three people who went into the bathroom with the young
  lady, and whether the other people there knew what was going on at
  the time, they do now and have not come forward."

- "I would like to think that somebody has the human decency to call up
  and say, 'What am I doing covering up for a bunch of hooligans?'"

In each of these statements, Nifong misled the public by omitting facts
inconsistent with the demonic portrait he was painting: The three residents of
the house had helped police search it; had voluntarily given detailed statements, DNA, their e-mail passwords, and hair samples without lawyers; and
had unsuccessfully asked police for lie-detector tests. All team members had
provided DNA samples without hesitation. And not one player had refused to
talk to police if appropriate safeguards were provided.

The local papers took Nifong's inflammatory statements as gospel and
threw gasoline on the flames. The N&O reported on March 28 that in the past
three years, fifteen of the forty-seven Duke lacrosse players had been charged

with misdemeanors, mostly involving drinking and noise. Out of context, this seemed striking. But the article made no effort to put this number in perspective, as it could have done by reporting that Dukies who did *not* play lacrosse had racked up *more than one thousand* alcohol-related disciplinary violations in the past three years. That information was on Duke's Web site. Also lost in the noise were the facts that the charges against the laxers were all petty—six for underage drinking, two for an open beer in a car's passenger area, four for noise, two for public urination, and the like—and that as of then no player had been convicted. (One was convicted months later on noise and open container charges.) Four were found not guilty. Most, as *The N&O* reported but others ignored, entered plea deals that left them with clean records.

Not to be outdone, *The Herald-Sun* published an editorial on March 28 that was remarkable both for its factual errors and for its certitude that a rape had occurred: "When police officers arrived at the house with a search warrant on March 16, none of the players would cooperate with the investigation. Later, under threat of further penalty, 46 members of the team were DNA-tested by police . . . the allegations of rape bring the students' arrogant frat-boy culture to a whole new, sickening level. . . . We agree that the alleged crime isn't the only outrage. It's also outrageous that not a single person who was in the house felt compelled to step forward and tell the truth about what happened."

Also on March 28, Nifong and the police promoted their claims that the lacrosse players were racists by releasing a tape of the 911 call that Kim Roberts had made just after leaving the lacrosse party—the same call that Roberts had admitted to police, at least twice, was a lie. "I was driving down near Duke's campus, and it's me and my black girlfriend. It's right outside of 610 [North] Buchanan [Boulevard]," the caller said. "And I saw them all come out of, like, a big frat house, and me and my black girlfriend are walking by, and they called us 'niggers.'"

There was something very strange about this call, thought Adam Chandler, a Duke senior on his way to a Rhodes scholarship, and many other Dukies who called up the tape on the Internet. It sounded staged. The caller had segued from "driving" by the house to "walking" by. She had repeated three times, with emphasis, the number of a house that bore no number visible from the street. And she had sobbed in a way that sounded very fake.

But in the media, these fishy signs were overwhelmed by expressions of horror from Nifong, from dozens of Duke professors, and from President Brodhead. All treated this 911 call as undisputed evidence of racism among Duke lacrosse players.

Nifong told the media that he did not know the identity of the 911 caller. On March 28, Police Department spokesperson Kammie Michael went even further, e-mailing a *Herald-Sun* reporter that "the caller was not the woman who accompanied the [alleged] victim to 610 North Buchanan." This official deception created the false impression that numerous lacrosse players had rampantly hurled racial slurs at four black women, both outside and inside the house, scaring a passerby into calling 911. In fact, Kim Roberts had admitted to Sergeant Shelton that she had been the caller on March 14. And she had confirmed that she was the caller in her written statement on March 22. Police also knew that Roberts had lied to the 911 operator about what she had been doing at the house, and perhaps about other matters as well.

These statements, coming from the district attorney and a police spokesperson under his command, had an even bigger impact on public opinion than the March 24 statements by Corporal Addison that had made such an impression on John Burness. "If a prosecutor gets up and says, 'I know that certain things happened,' the white middle-class norm is to believe that it must have happened," Peter Lange, Duke's provost, later explained. "Could we really believe that Nifong would be out making stuff up to help his election? Look at the damage he'd be doing to our community, to Duke, to these kids. Could he really be that morally corrupt? It was hard to believe that."

"In the early days of this story," Duke president Richard Brodhead reflected after the flames had receded, "DAs were people who carried a certain amount of credibility. So you have reputable papers reporting what the DA said about the likelihood the crime had occurred, and speaking with considerable confidence. And if a lot of people then formed the conclusion that they knew what had happened, how could one be surprised? One other thing I'd ask you to remember is, it was a long time before the students made the case for their innocence in any effective way. They made no public statement about it for several days."

And in the minds of black faculty members and black Durhamites familiar with the long history of oppression of blacks by law enforcement and favoritism toward whites, especially in the South. Nifong's confident assertions rang even more powerfully true. No white prosecutor would act this way with white boys unless he had really solid evidence, many blacks, thought: White prosecutors never do that.

Little did they—or Nifong's other enablers—know that Nifong had privately conceded that he did *not* have solid evidence. At his March 27 meeting with Gottlieb and Himan, just before the DA began his barrage of public statements, the three discussed the many evidentiary holes in the case. According to subsequent testimony by Himan, Nifong asserted bluntly: "You know we're fucked."

7. THE DEFENSE FIGHTS BACK

DAVE EVANS'S PARENTS, RAE FORKER and David C. Evans, had never experienced anything remotely like seeing their son under attack by a mob. This was a student athlete who had never engaged in serious misconduct, who had succeeded at everything he had attempted by sheer hard work and force of will. But since his bathroom was the scene of the alleged rape, Dave was especially at risk to be targeted by Nifong. The Evanses—she a prominent Washington lobbyist, he a senior partner at one of the nation's largest law firms—decided that they needed the very best criminal defense lawyer they could find.

They found their way through a friend of a friend to Joseph Blount Cheshire V, who headed his own nine-lawyer firm in Raleigh, the state capital. Sporting his signature goatee and bow tie, sitting in a rocking chair in his homey office, walls covered with honors for generations of his ancestors who had practiced law in the state, Cheshire impressed Rae and David Evans greatly at their first meeting. "He was just talking to us in just-a-friend-of-the-family kind of way," Rae Evans later recalled. "He said, 'I've got boys.' He presented himself as someone who was interested in our son, not somebody you had to prove something to."

At age fifty-eight, Cheshire had tried cases in eighty-five of North Carolina's one hundred counties and fourteen other states, representing clients who were black or poor whites in about a third of his cases. In the process, Cheshire had long since transcended his distinguished pedigree as the fifth in a line of prominent lawyers named Joseph Cheshire, with roots in North Carolina going back to 1651. This Joe Cheshire was known both for his courtroom skills and for his extraordinary willingness to take on prosecutors, and even judges, who mistreated his clients.

"Joe is simply the best leader and lawyer with whom I have ever worked," says James P. Cooney III, of Charlotte, another top defense lawyer whose five-hundred-lawyer firm, Womble Carlyle, is North Carolina's largest. "He always checks his ego at the door, does not care who gets credit, and always tries to make sure that everyone on the team is valued and respected. Joe is also a true warrior. With him at counsel table, there is no question that he will do what is right and strategically correct and if that requires confronting an opponent or a judge, then so be it."

During the second Alan Gell murder trial in 2004, Cooney recalls, "the judge was trying to exclude as much of our illustrative evidence of body decomposition as possible—claiming that all I was doing was putting on a show in front of the jury in order to convince them (silly me, I thought that was my job). At the break, Joe confronted him in open court, told him that he was wrong, and said that Alan Gell had gotten railroaded at his first trial and he was not going to let that happen again. I had never seen anything like that and just knew that Joe was going to jail. The judge turned red and just stormed off the bench—he still did not let the evidence in, but Joe communicated the force of will that every trial lawyer needs in order to win a case. Joe later told me that he was convinced he was going to jail, too, and was surprised he was not held in contempt, but that he thought that was what needed to be done. He cares deeply about fairness and justice. While that sounds corny, it is the essence of Joe."

One reason that Cheshire could afford to go after unfair prosecutors and judges was that with a statewide practice, he did not depend on the good will of any one district attorney or judge. He got on well with most of them. But "I built my career on going to counties and trying cases that other lawyers were afraid to try," Cheshire was to explain after battling Nifong for months, "because if they did the district attorney's office would punish them for the rest of their lives."

While Dave Evans's parents were getting to know Cheshire, Coach Pressler pushed for a meeting with Brodhead to give the four captains a chance to convince the president of their innocence, as they had convinced Trask, Alleva, Wasiolek, Kennedy, and Pressler himself. Pressler got the meeting, stressing that it was time the president gave his students a personal hearing. The coach, the only Duke official who was standing up in defense of his players, was told moments before the March 28 meeting that he could not attend.

Just before the captains went into Brodhead's office, Dave Evans was introduced to his lawyer for the first time, by phone. Joe Cheshire's advice was clear and firm, as Dave later recalled it: "His basic message was get out there and fight, don't just sit timidly back and let people say these awful things about you. You are a captain. Go fight for your team."

The captains told Brodhead their stories in an emotional encounter that was also attended by Duke associate counsel Kate Hendricks, faculty representative Kathleen Smith, and Bob Ekstrand, then representing all four captains and many of their teammates.

Brodhead, sweeping his hand around the room as if drawing a protected circle, declared that "everything you say here will stay within these walls," or words to that effect. That promise was good for no more than three weeks, when Duke officials offered to disclose to Nifong voluntarily, with no court order, all conversations between Brodhead, other administrators, and members of the team. This would come as no surprise to Bob Ekstrand. But it made no difference to him. The lawyer had advised the captains to speak freely with Brodhead because they had nothing to fear from the truth.

"The main things I told the students," Brodhead later recalled, "were, 'Tell the truth, whatever it is. It's not going to get better by telling some portion of it now and some portion of it later. Tell the truth.' I also said that they were telling me things that the world had not heard them say and I urged them to state their case more fully. . . . These kids expressed significant contrition to me. They were mortified, they were mortified by the shame they had caused to themselves, their teammates, their families, their university. They mentioned all these things at the same time that they fervently denied the rape charge. And I said to them, 'Whatever it is that is true, you should acknowledge and you should find a way to do it as quickly and fully as you can, and then draw the line between that and what you didn't do.' "

The captains decided beforehand that Dave Evans, the most eloquent among them, would handle most of the talking. Evans spoke with emotion during the meeting about how much Duke meant to him and how badly he felt that the party had caused so many people so much pain. Smith was crying. Brodhead's eyes filled with tears. He said that the captains should think of how difficult it had been for him. They needed to be held accountable for their actions, which had put him in a terrible situation.

Ekstrand felt his blood starting to boil. Here, he thought, is a comfortable university president wallowing in self-pity in front of four students who are in grave danger of being falsely indicted on charges of gang rape, punishable by decades in prison. The lawyer bit his tongue and said nothing. Dan Flannery, also holding his tongue, thought to himself that the players already *had* been held accountable for their actions: They had forfeited two games, an unprecedented punishment for their offenses.

Evans reiterated that nothing had happened at the party. Flannery sternly added, "*Absolutely* nothing happened." On the edge of his seat, he looked Brodhead in the eye and said that nobody had touched the woman. "It meant everything in the world to him that the truth of it be understood," Ekstrand later recalled. Flannery left with a clear and firm recollection of a wet-eyed Brodhead saying, "I hope for all of our sakes that you're telling the truth. I believe you are telling the truth." Ekstrand had a similar recollection. Flannery called his parents immediately after the meeting to pass on to them what Brodhead had said; other captains did the same.

In an interview months later, however, Brodhead had a different recollection of what he had said: "We were a bunch of human beings together in a situation where there were some people in a real emergency . . . it was painful to contemplate the degree of this emergency. . . . I wasn't sitting there convulsed with tears. I didn't have to get my hanky out. But I'd have to say it was a very moving account. [But] I said nothing to them to express my certainty of their innocence . . . because I did not have that certainty. That's part of what made it such a painful thing. You know, this was a situation where people were meeting and speaking on a deep, grave level. That's where we were. And I heard what they were telling me and I knew that I did not know the truth."

Whether or not Brodhead uttered the words "I believe you," it is undisputed that he said nothing suggesting disbelief of the captains' vows that there had been no rape. While asserting that they should learn from the event, he voiced no dissatisfaction about the extent of their cooperation with police. He also urged them to make a public statement asserting their innocence.

The captains, convinced that Brodhead believed them, eagerly adopted his suggestion that they publicly proclaim their innocence. After having been hammered in the media for five days, they had had enough of the no-comment strategy. They drafted what became the first public denial of the rape claim by anyone associated with the lacrosse team, with the help of Rae Evans and Bob Ekstrand. The statement was issued by Duke that day, March 28.

It declared that the lacrosse players were all innocent of rape and—far more important—the DNA results would prove it. The captains also expressed "sincere regret over the lapse in judgment in having the party on March 13 which has caused so much anguish for the Duke community and shame to our families and ourselves." Such a public apology, Duke in-house counsel David Adcock had said, might make it easier for Brodhead to resist faculty pressure to cancel the season. But Brodhead did not resist for long.

"Sports have their time and place," Brodhead declared in a press conference hours after meeting with the captains, "but when an issue of this gravity is in question, it is not time to be playing games." The very same "issues of gravity," of course, had been in question four days before when the captains met with Duke administrators and had received word that the Georgetown game would proceed as planned. And these very same issues had been in question three days before, when administrators had assured parents that the suspension would last for two games, not the entire season.

Public relations, not any new evidence against the team, dictated the administration's reversal of course. As Bob Steel later said to Peter Boyer of *The New Yorker*, "We had to stop those pictures [of the players practicing]. It doesn't mean that it's fair, but we had to stop it. It doesn't necessarily mean I think it was right—it just had to be done." A more legitimate argument for stopping the season might have been to protect the players and avert riots. But neither Brodhead nor Steel ever invoked that justification.

Brodhead also said during the March 28 press conference that the captains had assured him that there had been no sex of any kind at the party. But he ratcheted up his rhetorical attacks by asserting hyperbolically that the party had been "wholly inappropriate to the values of our athletics program and the university." Once again, no mention of how common stripper parties (to say nothing of underage drinking) were at Duke. No mention of the absence of any Duke rule against them.

The Herald-Sun editorial page, which had all but declared the players guilty, celebrated Brodhead's March 28 remarks, commending him for "doing the right thing" and adding that the players "have themselves to blame for the current trouble."

Dave Evans went from the March 28 Brodhead meeting to Joe Cheshire's office in Raleigh, twenty miles away. He was very personal, very compassionate, like a father with a son in trouble. But the lawyer made it clear that he needed to be very sure that Dave was telling him the truth. Cheshire and his thirty-six-year-old partner Brad Bannon, a slim, studious lawyer known for his mastery of every detail of every case on which he worked, then met with Dave alone in Cheshire's office from 3:00 to 6:00 or 7:00 P.M., going through every detail of what had happened that night two weeks before.

Well before the end of the interview, Cheshire was sure: "He instantly answered every question that I had. He consistently answered every question that I had. He described the situation he was trying to control, with this woman with her boobs out yelling outside his house. Everything about him and about his demeanor showed that he was telling the truth. He didn't destroy evidence. He gave a statement to police. He volunteered to take a polygraph test. Everything he *did* was consistent with a person who's telling the truth."

Cheshire's background was enough like Dave's to give him confidence in his ability to discern whether he was the good kind or the bad kind of affluent youth. At age twelve, young Joe had been sent north to Groton, the preppiest of New England prep schools, where he spent six years. He struggled at first to catch up with kids who had come from far better schools. He still does a bang-up imitation of a New England–snob accent: "I go to Baah Haabaa in the summaa." He had played football, basketball, tennis, and squash in high school and tennis in college. And his two sons had both been lacrosse players, with one playing in college.

"I raised Dave Evans twice in my family," Cheshire later explained. "All of my sons' friends were like them and all of them were like Dave Evans. I knew what his life was like. I knew he was being completely and totally honest. I knew it from his body language. I knew it from his words. And I knew Dave Evans was incapable of doing what he was accused of doing. In defending Dave Evans, in many ways I was defending one of my own boys. I had an emotional connection to him, and to the attack on who he supposedly was, painting him as some kind of monster because he came from a nice family and had the advantage of going to good schools. And I had seen my own son getting up at five A.M. every morning to make it as a college lacrosse player. I knew that many of the people demeaning these boys had never worked that hard in their lives."

Brad Bannon was a harder sell. "When I first read in the newspaper that these rich white kids from Duke had raped a poor black woman from Durham, I found it easy to believe," Bannon later recalled. "My background wired me to believe that privilege and wealth would exploit poverty." Bannon's single mom had worked as a teenager with her own mother for John F. Kennedy's presidential campaign in West Virginia; she had worked as a teacher to support Brad and his brother. In college and law school, Brad had honed a sense of distrust for the exercise of privilege and power and an affinity for society's underdogs. He had become a defense lawyer because he saw criminal defendants as the ultimate underdogs. Bannon is not a Democrat, he says, "because the Democratic Party isn't liberal enough."

Bannon, like Cheshire, had been practicing criminal defense law long enough to know that most clients are guilty and many lie to their lawyers. And after all, it was unheard of for a district attorney to proclaim with such certitude that a rape had occurred unless he had the evidence to prove it.

But in this case, Bannon later recalled, "You just knew from the first moment, it was so obvious that he was innocent and was telling me the complete truth about everything and not hiding anything. He instantly and consistently answered every question I had." Cheshire added, "I don't remember anyone in my career who I believed like I believed Dave Evans who turned out to be a liar."

But Richard Brodhead was not acting as though he believed them. The next morning, March 29, he issued another statement hammering the lacrosse players, after listening to Kim Roberts's fishy-sounding—and false—911 call. "Racism and its hateful language have no place in this community," he declared. "I am sorry the woman and her friend were subjected to such abuse." Many Duke students had been voicing suspicion that the 911 call sounded staged. Now Duke's president unhesitatingly gave his approval to the caller's claims—which were lies, as she had admitted to police on March 14 and 22— without pausing to inquire whether they were true.

That same day, Alleva postponed the team's April 1 game at Ohio State because of threatened protests. On the same rationale he soon called off the April 8 home game against Johns Hopkins, which was to be a nationally televised rematch of the teams that had played for the 2005 national championship. If we were a big revenue maker like football or basketball, Mike Pressler thought to himself, no way would they have canceled.

Meanwhile, Nifong was continuing his media offensive. On March 29, the district attorney proclaimed: "The circumstances of the rape indicated a deep racial motivation for some of the things that were done. It makes a crime that is by its nature one of the most offensive and invasive even more so." He added, "My reading of the report of the emergency room nurse would indicate that some type of sexual assault did in fact take place." (The full report, it turned out, was not even *printed* until the next day.) For good measure, he attacked the players' character, stating, "It just seems like a shame that they are not willing to violate this seeming sacred sense of loyalty to team for loyalty to community."

Nifong's comments through March 28 never departed from the March 23 prosecution assurance that the DNA tests would clear the innocent as well as identify the guilty. But that afternoon the State Bureau of Investigation found that there had been no semen, blood, or saliva anywhere on or in Crystal Mangum. This result was powerful evidence of the falsity of her claim of a thirty-minute, three-man, three-orifice rape, with ejaculation and without condoms.

As soon as Nifong knew of the SBI DNA test results, a lightbulb should have gone off in his head. He must have realized that the claims that he was riding—to win the election, to save his pension, and to become famous—were almost surely fraudulent. Crystal Mangum had been thoroughly swabbed in all of the usual places by Dr. Manly for any traces of male DNA—including skin cells as well as semen—within hours of the alleged rape and without changing her clothes or bathing. It was not merely unlikely that three assailants could leave no trace of their DNA after an assault anything like the one described by Mangum, not to mention her initial tales of being raped by five or twenty men, forensic experts agree. It was virtually impossible. "The odds are tiny to zero that you're not going to find any sample from anybody," Arthur Caplan, chairman of the Department of Medical Ethics at the University of Pennsylvania, told *The News & Observer* months later. "It gets hard to imagine that some kind of forced or unwanted activity took place."

Nifong must also have understood the significance of the confident, carefully lawyered statement issued on March 28 by the four cocaptains that "the DNA results will demonstrate that these allegations are absolutely false."

Case closed. Except that, of course, the case was not closed. For another thirteen days, Nifong kept these results secret from defense lawyers and the public. And it was probably no coincidence that, on March 29, Nifong— completely reversing what his office had told the court six days before— declared that negative DNA tests would prove nothing. "How does DNA exonerate you?" Nifong mused rhetorically in an interview with *The N&O*. "It's either a match or there's not a match. If the only thing that we ever have in this case is DNA, then we wouldn't have a case."

"I would not be surprised if condoms were used," Nifong told *The New York Times, The Charlotte Observer,* and many others. But this claim was belied by Mangum's still-secret statements to doctors and nurses, to which Nifong had access, where she specifically denied that her attackers had used condoms. And even if condoms had been used, the assailants could not possibly have raped her in the way that she described without leaving skin (epithelial) DNA, sweat DNA, or hair DNA.

"We were just stunned at what he was saying," Brad Bannon recalled later. 'We had never seen anything like this before."

On March 29, Cheshire had his paralegal call Nifong's assistant to set up a meeting so that Cheshire could show the DA the already substantial evidence of innocence and try to persuade him to stop convicting the lacrosse players in the media. After a long pause, Nifong's assistant read what she described as his response: If Joe Cheshire wants to have his client charged, he can bring him down here and we can talk.

The next morning, March 30, Nifong was on TV attacking the lacrosse players again. He told viewers of CBS's *Early Show* that "no doubt" existed that a sexual assault took place. "The victim was examined at Duke University Medical Center by a nurse who was specially trained in sexual assault cases. And the investigation at that time was certainly consistent with a sexual assault having taken place."

Cheshire and Bannon decided that they had to take the offensive. On the morning of March 30, they sent a confidential complaint about Nifong's media attacks to the State Bar. "He has basically announced the criminal guilt of dozens of people for committing a racial gang rape, effectively saying they are either guilty as principals or aiders-and-abettors," the Cheshire-Bannon letter said. "He has untruthfully suggested no one has cooperated with law enforcement. . . . Thus, one can scarcely imagine anything *more* likely to materially prejudice an adjudicatory proceeding in the matter."

Then, at midday, Cheshire called a press conference in his office, the first by anyone connected with the defense. This was a highly unusual tactic in North Carolina, and one with which other lawyers were not comfortable. But Cheshire sensed that the only way to beat Nifong's savage attacks in the media was to go back at him in the media: "I came to the decision that we had to win the media war, and that if we didn't win the media war, we would be in trial." And while Cheshire never thought a conviction was a serious possibility, he did fear a hung jury; a city that had been driven into a race-based, class-based fury by Nifong's race-baiting attacks on the lacrosse players was not a good bet for fairness or justice. "The playbook was thrown out the window in this case," Bannon later recalled.

At the news conference, "I looked at the press and said, 'What the hell are you all doing?'" Cheshire later recalled. "'You've labeled them as rapists, as racists, as privileged. Let's start looking at facts. You people need to stop. You need to think about what you're doing. You people are wrong. You are going to be proven wrong. You are going to be embarrassed.'"

Cheshire added: "We believe that the DNA will show that this is not true. We believe that a full and complete and fair investigation will show that it is not true."

Bill Thomas, another well-respected Durham lawyer, representing Bret Thompson, said on the same day: "Each and every one of those young men who were present at this party categorically deny that any assault of any description took place. The entire Duke lacrosse team looks forward to the results of the DNA test in order to clear their names." James "Butch" Williams and Kerry Sutton, who represented Dan Flannery and Matt Zash, also said their clients were innocent. In addition to the four captains, a few other team members had retained individual counsel, while Ekstrand & Ekstrand continued to represent most others.

These lawyers were making a big, big bet that the DNA results would be negative. The bet would have backfired if the DNA of any lacrosse player was found on or in Crystal Mangum. They were obviously quite confident that the assault described by her was a figment of her imagination.

With these public comments, the defense attorneys also disavowed the usual fallback defense to a rape charge: Even if my client's sperm was found in the accuser, the sex was consensual. "When you see lawyers this experienced this convinced, you can bet there is a damned good reason for it," Bill

Thomas reflected later. "Without having seen the DNA evidence, we put our heads on the chopping block. I've never called a press conference in another case."

Why so confident? By that point, these lawyers had grilled the lacrosse players extensively about what had happened that night. They, and the parents, had sternly warned the students not to sacrifice themselves by covering up for any rapist teammates. Nifong had threatened team members who did not cooperate with long prison terms as accomplices. Yet not one player had wavered, not for a second, from their unanimous vows that there had been no rape and no sex. "I've never been in a case," Bill Thomas later recalled, "where all the lawyers were so sure an accusation was false. We knew it in our bones."

Nifong had to know that these defense lawyers' extraordinary statements reflected great confidence that his rape case was bogus. And he himself had not spoken with Crystal Mangum, Kim Roberts, or any other witness. Nor did the hospital records that he was citing contain any physical evidence of sexual assault. At this point, most prosecutors would have seen that Crystal's rape claim was almost surely a lie and moved toward dropping the case without charges, while reserving the option of going forward if there turned out to be a DNA match.

Not Nifong. He simply walked away from past statements that negative DNA tests would clear the innocent, closed his eyes to the mounting evidence of innocence, and blustered on. This despite the fact that his lust for the cameras was alarming his campaign manager, Jackie Brown, who feared it could backfire politically. His response to Brown's concern: "I'm getting a million dollars of free advertisements."

Hours after their March 30 news conference, Cheshire and Bannon faxed Nifong an extraordinary letter, throwing down the gantlet to the DA over his refusal even to listen to evidence of innocence. "In 33 years," Cheshire wrote Nifong the next day, "I have never seen such a request denied by a prosecutor, nor in such a manner. Your responsive comments, reported [to Cheshire's paralegal by Nifong's assistant] verbatim, seemed to suggest that I should call the Durham Police Department and have my client charged with a crime before you would have a conversation with me on a topic you have demonstrated no reluctance to discuss with myriad national and local news reporters over the last several days. . . .

"[You] have announced the criminal guilt of potentially dozens of people for committing a racially-motivated gang rape [and] inaccurately suggested that no one has cooperated with law enforcement." Adding that these remarks had "greatly prejudiced any court proceeding that may arise," Cheshire strongly suggested that Nifong had violated "the Rules of Professional Conduct related to pre-trial publicity" and urged him to cease his inflammatory attacks.

Nifong ignored the letter. And it soon became clear that for him this had become a personal battle against Joe Cheshire, the one lawyer who had taken him on at that point. "Nifong had never had anybody confront him in that way; he wasn't used to people fighting back," Brad Bannon said later. And the DA didn't like it. He had always resented Cheshire's pedigree: "Nifong would call Joe 'Joseph Blount Cheshire the Fifth,' as if that's some kind of criticism," noted Bannon. From then on, the DA treated Cheshire as a hated enemy.

The next day came three of Nifong's most incendiary statements, each of which would be cited months later when the State Bar filed an ethics complaint against him. Dismissing the defense attorneys' proclamations of innocence, the district attorney told USA Today, "There's been a feeling in the past that Duke students are treated differently by the court system. . . . There was a feeling that Duke students' daddies could buy them expensive lawyers and that they knew the right people. It's discouraging when people feel that way, and we try not to make that the case."

To ESPN, he asked why the lacrosse players were "so unwilling to tell us what, in their words, did take place that night? . . . And one would wonder why one needs an attorney if one was not charged and had not done anything wrong."

And, in his most spectacular appearance, he went on Dan Abrams's MSNBC telecast and theatrically reenacted how one of the players had supposedly choked Mangum during the rape. "Somebody had an arm around her like this," demonstrated Nifong, "which she then had to struggle with in order to be able to breathe, and it was in the course of that struggle that the fingernails—the artificial fingernails broke off. Now as you can see from my arm, if I were wearing a shirt, a long-sleeved shirt or a jacket of some sort, even if there were enough force used to press down, to break my skin through the clothing, there might not be any way that anything from my arm could get on to those fingernails." Photos would show that none of the players wore either jackets or long-sleeve shirts, and in most of her stories, Crystal never even claimed to have been choked, much less described the act with any specificity.

Section 3.8 of the North Carolina Code of Professional Responsibility for lawyers requires prosecutors to "refrain from making extrajudicial comments that have a substantial likelihood of heightening public condemnation of the accused." It is hard to imagine a more egregious succession of violations of that rule than Nifong's media blitz, in the view of many experts.

But demonizing the lacrosse players paid off for Nifong politically. Suddenly he was omnipresent on TV and lionized in *The New York Times* and other big media. As he later told the AP, "I must say that the single good thing about all the publicity that I've gotten is that so many people know my face now that it's really easy for me to meet people. Before, literally very few people had any idea who I was, so I had to go up and introduce myself to everybody. And now I don't have to do that."

Locally, he won powerful African-American support. Durham mayor Bill Bell gave Nifong a campaign contribution on March 31, sending a powerful behind-the-scenes message to the black community that the city's leading black politician would not be supporting Bishop. Mark Simeon, a politically active African-American lawyer who had run and lost to Nifong's then-boss in 2002, promised on March 28 to support Nifong, one day after Nifong's first public statements on the lacrosse case. Simeon later invited Nifong to speak at his church, telling the congregants that this was a "good prosecutor" who was also, Simeon said he had recently learned, a "good man."

With a struggling law practice—mainly traffic violations and small criminal matters—Simeon had grand visions of his own role in the potentially profitable rape matter. He landed Roberts as a client on March 30. "I will be there for her if and when she decides to pursue legal remedies," Simeon told *Newsweek*. He also hoped to put together a team to bring a multimillion-dollar lawsuit for the accuser, and asked an associate to contact Willie E. Gary, the big-bucks Florida plaintiffs' lawyer.

If all went well—ending in a conviction—that could bring Simeon a big referral fee. And perhaps Simeon's client Kim Roberts could be helpful in the conviction department.

Simeon also urged the powerful Durham Committee on the Affairs of Black People to support Nifong. Keith Bishop, a former officer of that group, ended up with its endorsement, but only barely. In the group's initial tally, neither Bishop nor Nifong received a majority, a stunning change from the political situation before the lacrosse case broke. In the second ballot, two delegates who supported Freda Black switched over to Bishop, seeing him as the weaker challenger to their preferred candidate.

With Bell, Simeon, and other prominent black leaders backing Nifong, the committee's endorsement proved a nullity, as Bishop could never consolidate black support. Nifong also won the support of most other local groups with political clout, including the far-left Durham People's Alliance, the Friends of Durham, the *Indy*, and the Fraternal Order of Police.

Reflecting on events several months later, Duke law professor James Coleman told 60 Minutes, "I think that [Nifong] pandered to the [black] community by saying, 'I'm gonna go out there and defend your interests in seeing that these hooligans who committed the crime are prosecuted. I'm not gonna let their fathers, with all of their money, buy you know big-time lawyers and get them off. I'm doing this for you.' You know, what are you to conclude about a prosecutor who says to you, 'I'll do whatever it takes to get this set of defendants?' What does it say about what he's willing to do to get poor black defendants?"

At the time, though, Nifong was riding high. His new ally, Mark Simeon, brought him not only political clout but fashion advice. *Newsweek* reported that Simeon told Nifong to "lose the plaid shirts and to start wearing black suits, light shirts and power ties," since "women like power."

Nifong had plenty of power. He also had a big problem: With the primary a month away, the case that he was hyping to save his job was falling apart.

8. ACADEMIC McCARTHYISM

*I chose Duke to be my home for four years. And to see your professors . . .
go out and slander you and say these horrible, untrue things about you
and to have your . . . administration just . . . cut us loose for, for, based on
nothing. Duke took that stance that "we wouldn't stand for this behavior."
They didn't want to take a chance on standing up for the truth. I can't
imagine representing a school that didn't want to represent me.*
— READE SELIGMANN, *on* CBS News 60 Minutes, *October 15, 2006*

ONE GROUP TOPPED EVEN Nifong's inflammatory attacks on Duke
lacrosse players. That was the Duke faculty.

More than ninety of the activist professors who dominate campus discourse were quick to denounce the lacrosse players, based solely on Nifong's media offensive.

So did the leftist minority of students, such as Venis Wilder, who asked rhetorically in a *New York Times* interview: "Is this going to be a team of rich white men who get away with assaulting a black woman?" Small but vocal crowds of leftist students continued their daily protests, capturing more media attention than the thousands of others who were skeptical of the rape charge. Brodhead met with them on March 29. They included a group called Concerned Citizens at Duke University, who passed out a statement that "the university is cultivating and sustaining a culture of privilege and silence that allows inappropriate behavior to plague the campus."

"If you were at a university where the president meted out punishment based on what he reads in the newspaper," Brodhead told them, "it would be a pretty dangerous place." But Brodhead was already meting out punishment based on public clamor. And Duke and Durham were already becoming pretty dangerous places for lacrosse players, and some other Dukies as well.

Coincidentally, the week of March 27 had been declared Sexual Assault Prevention Week at Duke. Hundreds of students and Durhamites marched across campus that night in an annual Take Back the Night rally—a common event on college campuses nationwide. Among them was sophomore lacrosse player Ryan McFadyen, who a week later would suddenly be suspended and forced to flee town for fear of being harmed. He casually chatted with an acquaintance after the rally, only to see his classmate taking down notes; she was now a reporter for *The Chronicle*. McFadyen stated, "I completely support this event and this entire week. It's just sad that the allegations we are accused of happened to fall when they did."

The march, which had been planned for months, triggered one of the darkest events yet, as student activists joined with the potbangers to heighten public pressure on the alleged lacrosse-team rapists. Late on the afternoon of the March 29, the campus was flooded with wanted posters. They showed the photos (from the Athletics Department's Web site) of forty-three of the team's forty-six white players, coupled with a demand that someone come forward to identify the rapists. Senior Dinushika Mohottige was the only person to publicly admit that she distributed the posters. She said she did so because "I'm so outraged by how heinous the crime was. But more than that, it's the lack of compassion the lacrosse team has shown for the victim."

"The day those [wanted posters] appeared was probably the most awkward day of the term," freshman Michael Catalino recalled later. "It seemed like every single car had a wanted poster on its windshield, and the entire wall at the main campus bus stop was covered with the posters." Tony McDevitt saw his and his teammates' photos posted on a tree as he was returning from a late afternoon run on East Campus. "I don't think I'll ever forget it," he later said. "I was thinking, 'What kind of society is this?' I ripped it down." Recalled Bo Carrington: "It was scary. I went out and took down as many of them as I could. It reminded me of Western days with a wanted poster." McFadyen tried to laugh it off, taking one of the posters and hanging it up in his room. He told some of his teammates that variety was the spice of life, and they should just look at this episode as something that kept things different. He continued to believe that the truth would soon be out and the case would die.

A few students supported the lacrosse players. Members of the wrestling team had started wearing Duke lacrosse gear around campus to show their solidarity. Wrestlers spent the evening of the March 29 going around campus and tearing the posters down. But for the most part, McDevitt recalled, in late March and early April "it felt like we were betrayed by the students. Everyone on campus believed we were guilty, except for people who really knew us." Carrington agreed: "People who knew the team had the real story, but it seemed like everyone else was the enemy. Our fellow students had no trust in us unless they had a personal relationship with one of us."

But "the faculty was a hell of a lot worse than the students," Mike Pressler later recalled. "It was appalling. These are our educators." These professors pressured Brodhead in angry meetings to take up the cry. And they soon got their way. Looking back on the affair in January 2007, *News & Observer* columnist Rick Martinez noted that in normal conditions, faculty obsessions with race, class, and gender "are more comical than consequential" and have little effect on the outside world (which ignores them), except in distorting hiring patterns at universities nationwide. But at Duke in 2006, by creating the public impression that the students' own professors believed them guilty, "this self-generated culture of pseudo-oppression helped send the three players, their teammates and Pressler down the river for an alleged crime that is supported by scant evidence."

Like the media, many professors—and not only the radical fringe—were initially swayed by Nifong's public comments and the initial silence from the lacrosse players. All but ignored were the captains' March 16 cooperation with police, their confident March 28 prediction that the DNA would soon clear them, the similar predictions by defense lawyers, and the unlikelihood that they would go out on such a limb without strong reasons for confidence that no rape or sex of any kind had occurred.

But while many of the journalists misled by Nifong eventually adjusted their views as evidence of innocence and of Nifong's conduct came to light, the activist professors did not. Resolutely refusing to reconsider their initial presumptions as new facts emerged, they served as enthusiastic cheerleaders for Nifong, with whom they had little in common besides their opportunism. For many months *not one* of the more than five hundred members of the Duke arts and sciences faculty—the professors who teach Duke undergraduates— publicly criticized the district attorney or defended the lacrosse players' rights to fair treatment. Not even after enough evidence had become publicly available to establish clearly both the falsity of the rape charge and the outrageousness of Nifong's actions—widely seen as the worst case of prosecutorial misconduct ever to unfold in plain view.

The majority of Duke's arts and sciences faculty kept quiet as the activists created the impression that Duke professors en masse condemned the lacrosse players. Several months later, John Burness explained their silence: "I think people just go about their business doing what they do and were not paying attention." But, as some admitted privately to friends, they were also afraid to cross the activists—black and female activists especially—lest they be smeared with charges of racism, sexism, classism, homophobia, or right-wingism.

That's what would happen to a chemistry professor who—months after the team's innocence had become clear—became the first member of the arts and sciences faculty to break ranks with the academic herd. It took less than twenty-four hours for the head of Duke's women's studies program to accuse him of racism in a letter to *The Chronicle*.

Leading the rush-to-judgement crowd at Duke was Houston A. Baker Jr., a professor of English and of African and African-American Studies. He showed his mettle in a March 29 public letter to Duke administrators that boiled with malice against "this white male athletic team"—a team whose whiteness Baker's fifteen-paragraph letter stressed no fewer than ten times. He demanded the "immediate dismissals" of all lacrosse players and coaches, without acknowledging their protestations of innocence or the evidence. He assailed "a 'culture of silence' that seeks to protect white, male athletic violence." He denounced the lacrosse players as "white, violent, drunken men . . . veritably given license to rape, maraud, deploy hate speech." He bemoaned their alleged feeling that "they can claim innocence and sport their disgraced jerseys on campus, safe under the cover of silent whiteness." Treating as gospel Kim Roberts's transparently bogus 911 report of being pelted with multiple racial epithets as she drove (or walked) past the lacrosse house, he asserted that the lacrosse players' "violence and raucous witness injured [a black woman] for life." He stereotyped them as embodiments of "abhorrent sexual assault, verbal racial violence, and drunken white, male privilege loosed amongst us."

For such insights, Baker was in demand among TV hosts such as MSNBC's Rita Cosby and CNN's Nancy Grace. He was also quoted in newspapers local and national, including *The New York Times* and *USA Today*.

Baker provided a window both into his soul and into the indifference of many academics to fact after a critic e-mailed him, "You will owe a big apology when the truth comes out, but I doubt you will be man enough to issue it."

Retorted the professor: "Who is really concerned about whether a woman was actually raped or not? Are you a perfect idiot?" Baker tossed out a litany of false charges of misbehavior by lacrosse players, such as that they had "beat up people who were gay," before closing:

"ALL of 'official' American history is a lie, Pal!! Where did YOu [*sic*] go to school??? . . . Good lorad [*sic*], all you people think you an [*sic*] go 'ah hah,' and the polar caps will not melt, or the levees will hold. You live in a white supremacist fantasy land. . . . Whew! Have you read recently? Anything? . . . And, get over yourself, buddy. Get smart before you write to a professor, OK. Read SOMETHING."

In a subsequent (June 10) e-mail, Baker wrote, with no basis in fact, that "46 white guys on the Lacrosse Team at Duke . . . may well have raped more than one woman." And in still another e-mail, sent to the mother of a lacrosse player, Baker called her son and his teammates "farm animals."

Despite such displays of viciousness, Baker was a big deal in the academic world. A past president of the Modern Languages Association (the major academic organization of English professors), Baker was such a big name in academia that Vanderbilt would hire him away from Duke at the end of the academic year. The chair of Vanderbilt's English Department, Jay Clayton, hailed his new hire as "one of the most wide-ranging intellectuals in America today in any field of the humanities. He is prolific and writes to an audience far broader than academic specialties."

Baker's last academic monograph was published more than fifteen years ago; since the early 1990s, he has devoted himself to slim books geared toward nonacademic audiences. Take, for instance, his 1993 *Black Studies, Rap, and the Academy*.

In a devastating review, drama and music critic Terry Teachout characterized the book as "a veritable *omnium gatherum* of latter-day academic clichés." He noted that Baker had managed to misspell the names of S. I. Hayakawa, Carol Iannone, Catharine MacKinnon, and Salman Rushdie. Teachout also described Baker's views on rap as, "controlling for polysyllables, mostly indistinguishable from those of the average thirteen-year-old, and . . . in any case asserted rather than demonstrated." The book's thesis, wrote Teachout, was: "(1) Black studies is an indispensable part of American higher education. (2) Rap is a creative and authentic expression of the urban black experience and should thus be taken seriously by academics, particularly those working in the field of black studies. (3) Anyone who disagrees with (1) or (2) is a racist."

Many Duke students, such as senior Adam Chander, were enraged by Baker's hate-filled antics. But Baker had plenty of Duke faculty companions in his crusade.

Not far behind was Peter H. Wood, a history professor who touted his background as a lacrosse player at Harvard and Oxford and as coach of women's lacrosse when it was a club sport at Duke. Wood coauthored a U.S. history textbook that bills itself as emphasizing "the lives and labors of women, immigrants, working people, and persons of color in all regions of the country," based on "an expanding notion of American identity—one that encompasses the stories of diverse groups of people." He teaches courses in African-American and Native-American history. His scholarship and teaching reflect an unmistakable slant on the American past.

In late March and early April, Wood's status as the first Duke professor to have criticized the lacrosse players—back in 2004—made him something of a folk hero among the faculty. At the time, Wood had penned a letter to the dean claiming that lacrosse players had failed to take his Native American History class seriously, by "giving priority to unnecessary athletic commitments created by the coaching staff, such as a practice called during class time at 10 A.M. on a

Friday." Such events, Wood suggested, were "signs of a developing problem." In 2006, he touted this prophecy as if missing a class were a precursor to gang rape.

Duke students often miss one or two classes per semester for extracurricular commitments, but no record exists of Wood ever complaining about students missing his classes for, say, debate or theatrical requirements. And Wood misrepresented the 2004 episode. The players' absences had been approved by the appropriate dean because they had to travel that afternoon to the University of Virginia, where they could not practice, for a big game the next day.

As soon as the lacrosse case generated media attention, Wood reveled in his newfound celebrity status. He reviled the lacrosse players indiscriminately in a succession of interviews in *The New York Times*, *Vanity Fair*, *The New Yorker*, and various North Carolina newspapers. On March 31, he told the *Times*—in remarks that fit in with the new story line—that "lacrosse players on campus stood out for their aggression, which he said was in some ways endemic to the violent nature of the game they played." And, apparently content to practice the kind of racial and group stereotyping against which he preached in his classes, Wood added: "The football players here are often rural white boys with baseball caps or hard-working black students who are proud to be at Duke. . . . Too often, there seems to be a surliness about some lacrosse players' individual demeanor. They seem hostile, and there is this group mentality."

Baker was widely perceived on campus as an extremist. And Wood came across as a caricature of a burnt-out professor. But on March 31, a far more respected and serious scholar threw his weight behind the anti-lacrosse jihad in a guest column in *The Chronicle*. That was history professor and former dean of the faculty William Chafe, a figure of great prestige for his scholarly work on the civil rights movement. He associated the lacrosse players with "white slave masters [who] were the initial perpetrators of sexual assault on black women" and "white men [who] portrayed black women as especially erotic, more driven to sexual pleasure and expressiveness than white women." He fantastically suggested that the whites who lynched Emmett Till—a fourteen-year-old black boy viciously beaten, shot, and drowned after he allegedly whistled at a white woman in Mississippi in August 1955—provided an appropriate historical context through which to view the actions of the lacrosse players. And shedding unintentional light on the intellectual seriousness of his column, Chafe misidentified the year of Till's lynching, one of the major events in the history of the American civil rights movement, claiming that the boy's death occurred in 1954.

Reasoning from the premise that the team had "hired a black woman from an escort service to perform an erotic dance," Chafe explicated the "intersection of racial antagonism and sexual exploitation" and "this latest example of the poisonous linkage of race and sex as instruments of power and control." Never mind that Flannery had asked for white strippers, and the agency had said it would send a white and a Hispanic dancer.

Chafe also stressed that "whether or not a rape took place, there is no question that racial epithets were hurled at black people." Never mind that the only epithet came from a student whom Kim Roberts had "obviously provoked" by calling him "a little dick white boy," as she would laughingly tell Ed Bradley of 60 *Minutes*.

Chapter 6 of the *Duke Faculty Handbook* opens: "Members of the faculty expect Duke students to meet high standards of performance and behavior. It is only appropriate, therefore, that the faculty adheres to comparably high standards in dealing with students. . . . Students are fellow members of the university community, deserving of respect and consideration in their dealings with the faculty." Unlike Baker, Chafe, Wood, and like-minded figures, many Duke professors adhered to the handbook's guidelines despite the stress imposed by the lacrosse case.

Sam Veraldi, an instructor in the markets and management program, had four lacrosse players in his spring 2006 senior capstone class. Danny Flannery and William Wolcott had become close to Veraldi's family. Indeed, they had been returning from a dinner at Veraldi's house the night of March 16, when the police did their search of 610 North Buchanan. Flannery had strung up a stick for Veraldi's son, who was new to lacrosse and competing for a spot on the varsity squad at his high school, and the players had outfitted the boy with their Duke gear. Veraldi and his family were steadfast in providing moral support and friendship. Each week he held the four players after class to get an update on how they were holding up, offered his home as a refuge if they needed a place to stay, and encouraged them to keep their heads up.

Rhonda Sharpe, a visiting professor of economics, taught six lacrosse players including cocaptains Dave Evans and Matt Zash in her Sports Economics class. An African-American woman, she e-mailed each lacrosse player saying that if things were tough, they could come in and talk to her—an offer that several of the players accepted. The class usually began with her asking, "What's new in sports today?" but Sharpe said right away that she was not going to discuss this issue in class out of fairness to the class members who were on the team. Several other lacrosse players, such as Tony McDevitt and Kyle Dowd, said they wished the Duke faculty had more people like Rhonda Sharpe in spring 2006.

History professor Thomas Robisheaux also taught several lacrosse players, including Bo Carrington and Danny Flannery. After the allegations became public, Carrington went to see Robisheaux in his office to get everything on the table. ("We all," Carrington recalled, "had to feel out our teachers" for their response to the affair.) Robisheaux provided a sympathetic and nonjudgmental ear, and talked about past race relations in Durham to try to explain the reaction. He went out of his way to treat Flannery in the same way that he approached all other students in the class, avoiding a judgment on the case one way or the other. After the term had ended, Flannery e-mailed Robisheaux that "it speaks volumes of your character that you did not pre-judge my team, and use your classroom as a platform to voice your personal views about our situation. My teammates and I truly appreciate professors like yourself and I just wanted to express our gratitude. Both my parents are college professors and I know how happy it makes them to know you are one of my teachers. Many of my teammates," Flannery concluded, "have shared their negative experiences with their parents and the stories have traveled among the parent group."

As Flannery suggested, other professors used their power to direct classroom discussion to practice their own petty brand of vigilante justice. One was Reeve Huston, who had five members of the men's lacrosse team, one member of the women's team, and some fifteen other students in his U.S. labor history class. In late March, Huston opened a class by saying that he needed to break his silence on the lacrosse episode and talk about what he had concluded from his research on the topic: There was a long-prevalent problem of alpha males assaulting black females in America and there had been a sexual assault at 610 North Buchanan.

As the professor spoke, Ryan McFadyen text-messaged Rob Schroeder, asking if they should walk out. Huston plowed ahead, declaring it obvious that an "ejaculation had occurred." Jay Jennison added the quote, with a bubble around it, to a cartoon that he was drawing of Huston's antics. This would later provide a moment of excitement for Detective Himan, who—on discovering the cartoon—thought he had made an investigative breakthrough.

Senior Casey Carroll had had enough. He got up and left the room. McFadyen, Schroeder, Jennison, and Breck Archer followed their teammate. As they left, Huston said, "Don't worry, this won't affect your grade." The female lacrosse player remained. She later reported that Huston had devoted the entire session to his "analysis" of the case. Several other students approached McFadyen later to express agreement that Huston's remarks were out of line. When asked via e-mail about his behavior, Huston refused comment.

Down the hall from Huston's class, several other players were taking Professor Sally Deutsch's course in U.S. history during the Gilded Age. The Monday after Nifong began his publicity barrage, Deutsch departed from the syllabus and announced that she would discuss how white men, especially in the South, have disrespected and sexually assaulted black females. "We all knew what she was doing," lacrosse player Tony McDevitt later recalled. "A couple people asked questions to try to get her off track, but she persisted. It lasted a half hour. She clearly wasn't sympathetic." Deutsch subsequently asserted that because her course dealt with themes of race and gender, it was appropriate for her to use class time to offer her take on the background to the incident. When asked by one of the authors whether she had also had adjusted her planned topics to examine the case through the equally relevant historical legacy of race-based prosecutorial misconduct in the South, Deutsch did not reply.

Yet another history professor, John Thompson, got into the act through an e-mail sent to the two lacrosse players in his Canadian history class, including Collin Finnerty. After assuring the two that he didn't believe they had committed the crime, Thompson wrote: "Whether the alleged rape and assault took place or not, the men in question must step forward and take responsibility for their actions—whatever those actions were. If they are innocent, a court will decide. By not stepping forward, they unfairly shame not only the whole lacrosse team, but also shame all of the rest of us at Duke. [If] these 'men' are too cowardly to step forward, it is your duty as real men to identify them. Please understand that manliness doesn't mean remaining silent to protect cowards."

But Thompson's own e-mail had already admitted that maybe there had been no crime at all. Indeed, the lacrosse players had unanimously said that and the DNA evidence would back them up. How were the "cowards" to "take responsibility," and how could his students "identify them," if there had been no crime? In response to a request for comment from one of the authors, Thompson said he didn't remember sending the e-mail, and that in any case federal law might preclude him from discussing its contents, because he sent the missive to students.

Students who sympathized with the lacrosse team were not immune from similar treatment. Elizabeth Chin spent the spring 2006 term as a visiting professor in Duke's cultural anthropology department, where she taught a course called Girl Culture/Power. The students, Chin later wrote in *The Chronicle of Higher Education*, included some "well-off white women who were in the most elite sororities at Duke," plus three males, "several heterosexual women of color and a handful of what I affectionately thought of as my radical feminists." She did not explain how she determined her students' sexual orientations.

When an anti-lacrosse rally coincided with a class meeting, Chin instructed the students to go outside and listen. "After a while," she wrote, "I noticed that, one by one, the sorority girls were going back inside." (Many of these "girls" knew members of the men's lacrosse team.) Chin continued: "When I went after them, their pain and frustration were obvious. 'It's just not fair being targeted as a group,' wailed one woman."

"Wailed." Had a white male professor at Duke (or many another universities) spoken in such a tone about those whom Chin "affectionately thought of as my radical feminists," he could have faced charges of sexual harassment.

Making clear her conviction that the lacrosse players were rapists and her displeasure with anyone who disagreed, Chin noted that her class's "olive branch" to the "sorority girls" was an assertion by a "radical woman" that she, too, knew a man who "had raped someone."

Meanwhile, on the evening of March 29, African-American Studies professors Wahneema Lubiano and Karla Holloway converted a student gathering on black masculinity to a discussion of the lacrosse case, in which the overwhelmingly African-American audience spoke of the rape as an established fact. Lubiano later said that she diligently took notes of the speakers' words, although she never produced them. Nor did she ever state how she determined that the speakers at the gathering—which included, according to several witnesses, students and professors from UNC and NCCU as well as many Duke graduate students—were Duke undergraduates.

Professors like Lubiano, Holloway, Chin, Deutsch, Huston, and others trained in the race-class-gender approach generally consider American society deeply flawed, with the majority and the powerful oppressing women, minorities, and the poor. For these faculty members, the lacrosse case was too tempting not to exploit. And they did not hesitate to vent their class hatred against their own students.

In this respect, the statement was fully consistent with the group's educational philosophy. As one critic of the team, Maurice Wallace, explained in a 2003 interview with *The Herald-Sun*, "I have a responsibility to all of my students—every single one of them—to disabuse them of all of the national, racial, middle-class, gender and sexual myths they've been taught to comfort or flatter themselves and, of course, the people who, perhaps unknowingly, miseducated them." Wallace appeared to have little interest in the traditional approach of teaching students something of the liberal arts. For him and his allies, teaching was about politics and little else.

Take the career of Grant Farred, a professor of literature who recalled his mentor, the anti-Israel scholar Edward Said, as "a model for being engaged in political activities outside the university." Farred's 2005 book, *Phantom Calls*, examined the cultural significance of an event in a 2005 NBA playoff series. It exemplifies what can pass for scholarship in contemporary academia.

Houston Rockets coach Jeff Van Gundy had complained about "phantom calls" against his team's star center, Yao Ming, a native of China. That in itself was not such a big deal to sportswriters and fans. But Van Gundy had also claimed that an NBA referee had told him that league officials had ordered the referees to call more fouls against Yao. This charge touched off a media explosion. It called into question the integrity of the game. And when Van Gundy couldn't substantiate it, he was fined $100,000, then the largest fine in the history of the NBA.

Farred, in his ninety-five-page, pamphlet-length book, argued that the critical aspect of the story was not Van Gundy's claim of an anti-Rockets conspiracy, the focus of virtually all contemporaneous press coverage. Instead he said the crux was—well, take a guess.

If you guessed that the crux was Van Gundy's use of the phrase "phantom calls" to describe unfair officiating against Yao, you are getting warm. If you further anticipated Farred's claim that this remark "unleashed a racial politics that was foreclosed during the rhetorical skirmishes that erupted around the 'fouled' Asian body," you are so warm as to exhibit stellar qualifications for a tenured position at almost any modern university.

Van Gundy, it turns out, had powers that no one imagined. "By positioning Yao as the symbolic victim of the American racial phantasmatic and his refusal to name the race or racism, by 'mediating' Yao, in Kundera's sense, Van Gundy makes possible a discussion about the condition of racial politics as it pertains to African-American players in the NBA."

Soaring further above mere reality, Farred went on to suggest that Van Gundy's complaint might come to be viewed as a critical point in the development of globalization: "The 'phantom calls' reveal how the migrant Asian subject of globalization is, in the moment of crisis or the experience of direct address, precariously close to the kind of non-belonging with which the raced subject perpetually lives." While the NBA might have been able to discipline Van Gundy for his comments, Farred concluded that the United States will not be able to use the "neo-liberal, imperial imaginary" to hold back China. In this respect, "Yao represents the spectral presence of Chinese capital within America. He is, precisely because of his complicated ideological heritage, the most profound threat to American empire."

This nonsensical stuff was not just academic writing at its most absurd. It also revealed a mind preconditioned to see racism everywhere, even where it clearly doesn't exist. A mind that takes in an everyday occurrence in the NBA—a coach complaining about fouls called on his best player—and spews out: "NBA is once again fraught with the ghostly presence of race, now refracted through the Asian body." A mind quite similar to those of thousands of other professors around the country, all feeding on the hard-earned savings of parents who think they are buying their kids a good education.

In a 2007 essay, Duke graduate student Richard Bertrand Spencer co-mented on the large number of "professional black activists" who formed a major faction in the anti-lacrosse protests. Many in this cohort, he noted, "have achieved tenure with little or nothing in the way of publications or research," and therefore "can only justify their presence at Duke—and their six-figure salaries—through their campus politics. The lacrosse case gave them some-thing to do."

Perhaps no figure better embodied Spencer's thesis than Wahneema Lu-biano, whose career provides a glimpse of the kind of professor Duke's human-ities and (some) social sciences departments have actively recruited in recent years, beginning with the presidency of Nannerl O. Keohane in 1993 and con-tinuing into the Brodhead years. As an African-American female active in gay and lesbian causes, Lubiano, who labels herself a "post-structuralist teacher-critic leftist," was almost an ideal candidate for a university eager for "diver-sity" hires. On paper, her credentials were good: Her Ph.D. in literature came from a quality institution (Stanford). But in nearly two decades as a professor, she compiled a thin scholarly record while blurring the lines between her job and political activism. This approach generated an enthusiastic following in some academic quarters. But it also set in motion a pattern of unusual con-duct that culminated during the lacrosse case.

Professors, especially at an elite institution such as Duke, normally are tenured on the basis of their research qualifications. Yet Lubiano, who re-ceived her doctorate in 1987, has failed to publish a scholarly monograph. (She edited one book, a collection of conference papers from high-profile African-American authors.) Those who relied solely on Lubiano's word for her publication record, however, would have supposed a far more robust per-formance. The Black Cultural Studies Web page states that a Lubiano manu-script entitled *Like Being Mugged by a Metaphor: "Deep Cover" and Other "Black" Fictions* was forthcoming from Duke University Press—in 1997. On Lubiano's official Duke Web page, which was "last modified" on November 17, 2006, *Like Being Mugged by a Metaphor* is listed as forthcoming—in March 2003. (This time, she did not disclose the name of the press preparing to publish the book.) Yet the current Duke University Press Web page, nearly a decade after Lubiano listed the book as poised to appear, contains no listing of *Like Being Mugged by a Metaphor*. The book still has not appeared at this writing.

Like Being Mugged by a Metaphor isn't the only manuscript for which Lu-biano has flexibly interpreted "forthcoming," a description usually reserved for manuscripts that a press has accepted for publication. The Black Cultural Studies Web page from 1997 lists a volume called *Messing with the Machine: Politics, Form, and African-American Fiction* as "forthcoming" (no date supplied) from New York's Verso Press, which bills itself as the "largest English-language radical publisher in the world." And Lubiano's official Duke Web page claims that *Messing with the Machine* was "forthcoming" as of March 2003. Yet Verso's catalog contains no trace of *Messing with the Machine*.

When asked about the discrepancy between her claimed and actual publication record, Lubiano sent a two-sentence reply, "Do not email me again. I am putting your name and email address in my filter."

Lubiano's current record of scholarly publications is confined to essays, most of which have appeared as chapters in books edited by others. (In contrast to journal articles, book chapters usually are solicited and do not go through a peer-review process.) Her essay titles include such only-in-academia topics as "Shuckin' Off the African-American Native Other: What's Po-Mo Got to Do with It?"

Lubiano's scholarship has condemned the Western intellectual tradition ("Western rationality's hegemony," she complained in one essay, "marginalizes other ways of thinking about the world"), celebrated the Ebonics movement, and proclaimed herself as "at the mercy of racist, sexist, heterosexist, and global capitalist constructions of the meaning of skin color on a daily basis." "Many whites," she asserted with her usual antiwhite racism, "might not ever be persuaded by appeals to reason, to what we 'know' and agree to be 'truth'—that all men/women were created equal, for example."

The Manhattan Institute's Heather MacDonald, who attended a conference at which Lubiano spoke, recalled the atmosphere:

> The final impression left by the conference had less to do with the substance of the debate about the "academic culture wars," numbingly familiar as it is, than with its style. After hours of being bombarded with impenetrable syntax and utterly predictable slogans, one stumbled out of the conference hall profoundly depressed by the state of academic speech.

Lubiano is candid about her approach to her job as a professor: For "university intellectuals," she contended, "sabotage has to be the order of the day." She views her job as engaging in "a deliberate attempt on the part of the historically marginalized to reconstitute not simply particular curricula, but the academy itself." As a result, she considers herself entitled to use her job to advance her political agenda. "Whether I'm thinking, teaching, or engaging in politics (including strategizing)," she wrote, "I think that it is part of my privilege, my work, and my pleasure to insist that those three activities are not clearly demarcated."

In many ways, Lubiano resembled Nifong—a rogue in her profession, someone who had advanced while doing comparatively little, though a figure who escaped the notice of the outside world. Like Nifong, she couldn't resist exploiting the lacrosse case. Unlike Nifong, she was treated with deference by the Duke administration and the hundreds of Duke professors who were her peers even after the evidence had obliterated her position.

Duke's arts and sciences faculty had already showed itself to be skewed toward extremist views, with the more moderate majority silently indulging the antics of their more radical colleagues, long before the lacrosse case. One example was the effort of cultural anthropology professor Diane Nelson to disrupt a March 7, 2006, speech by David Horowitz at Duke. Horowitz, a 1960s radical turned conservative, is known for sometimes inflammatory denunciations of the ideological one-sidedness of the contemporary academy. Nelson organized a group of students to heckle and laugh loudly at Horowitz during his remarks. She sent an e-mail urging women attending the affair to take off their T-shirts. A student who shared her distaste for Horowitz nonetheless described Nelson's conduct as "immature" and as "making a mockery of the concept of free speech." Nelson's next notable contribution to academic discourse would be to join the faculty attack on the lacrosse players.

Duke's faculty hiring policies made it especially vulnerable to this group-think atmosphere. The first numerical documentation of the dramatic transformation of Duke's faculty (outside the sciences) came in early 2004, when a survey by the Duke Conservative Union disclosed that Duke's humanities departments contained 142 registered Democrats and 8 registered Republicans. Faculty members' commentary about this finding shed revealing light on their mind-set in hiring new colleagues.

John Thompson, then chairman of the History Department, dismissed as insignificant the DCU's finding that his department contained thirty-two registered Democrats and zero registered Republicans. Instead, he suggested that his department was not *sufficiently* leftist, since "the interesting thing about the United States is that the political spectrum is very narrow." Philosophy Department chairman Robert Brandon declared the survey results unsurprising: "If, as John Stuart Mill said, stupid people are generally conservative, then there are lots of conservatives we will never hire." The ideologically one-sided nature of the academy, Brandon explained, was a natural development. Just as "players in the NBA tend to be taller than average . . . members of academia tend to be a bit smarter than average. There is a good reason for this."

Do the parents who pay for all this understand that so many professors of Romance studies, literature, English, art, and history see their main job as critiquing contemporary society from a one-sided perspective?

Academic ideals used to include dispassionate analysis of evidence and respect for due process. No more. In the lacrosse case, Duke's faculty not only failed to stand up for procedural regularity, but a substantial faction of it gleefully joined the rush to judgment. Those professors also clung to that judgment even after a mountain of evidence had proved it wrong. The activists and others determined to fit the university even more tightly into the straitjacket of political correctness saw the lacrosse scandal as the opportunity of a lifetime. The affair provided a chance to exploit the assumed (and never questioned) victimization of a black woman to skewer privileged white males as much because of who they were as because of what they (allegedly) had done.

As Ed Bradley noted after examining the case for *60 Minutes,* the "biggest surprise for us was the presumption of guilt." In a more blunt assessment, Thomas Sowell, a former UCLA economics professor who is currently a senior fellow at the Hoover Institution at Stanford University, wrote months after the lacrosse firestorm: "The haste and vehemence with which scores of Duke professors publicly took sides against the students in this case is but one sign of the depth of moral dry rot in even our prestigious institutions."

So it was that the elite university's faculty publicly celebrated the targeting of its own students by a local prosecutor as he publicly committed what many experts came to see as the most egregious prosecutorial misconduct of our era. And if Duke president Richard Brodhead disagreed with his faculty's statements and actions, he never said so.

Asked why, in an interview by one of the authors as the case was winding down, Brodhead said:

> *I believe that the president of the university's role is to protect the space of discourse, not to advance his particular views. Whenever the president speaks, it's read as an exercise of authority. . . . And therefore I have an obligation to dig deeper than my personal opinions. A university president's obligation to protect the sphere of free speech in all its rough and tumble is not well served by attacking or defending individual utterances of individual faculty.*

Would Brodhead have had the same reluctance to exercise his own right to free speech had it been a group of presumptively innocent *African-American* Duke students being smeared as gang rapists by the district attorney, with dozens of Duke professors joining the mob?

9. POLITICALLY CORRECT SENSATIONALISM

IN LATE MARCH, the journalistic echo chamber quickly spread the image of drunken, disorderly, publicly urinating lacrosse thugs around the world. Nifong whipped the national media into a feeding frenzy with his public assertions on March 27 and thereafter that the lacrosse players were clearly guilty of raping the "victim," of pounding her with racial slurs, and of forming a "wall of silence" to cover it up.

It was extremely unusual—all but unprecedented—for a district attorney not then reputed to be a nut or a crook to hurl such accusations with such certitude at anyone, let alone at an athletic team bidding to bring the national championship to a top-tier academic institution. And it was understandable that in the early days reporters and others would wonder: Why would a woman make up such a charge? And why would a prosecutor embrace it so confidently unless he had the evidence to prove it? So the initial coverage in the national media was bound to highlight Nifong's charges, the claims that lacrosse players had hurled racial slurs at black women, and the anti-lacrosse team protests, including the March 29 Take Back the Night march.

Far less understandable was the sparse coverage of the four captains' public statement on March 28 that the rape charge "is totally and transparently false"; that the "team has cooperated with the police" and "provided authorities with DNA samples"; and that "the DNA results will demonstrate that these allegations are absolutely false." This prediction put careful journalists on notice not only of the claim of innocence but also of defense lawyers' confidence—after grilling the lacrosse players and investigating other evidence—that the DNA would set them free.

USA Today ignored the statement entirely in a March 30 article that, instead, stressed that "the flier being distributed outside Duke's student union Wednesday night looked like a wanted poster: 40 faces of young men, smiling smugly for the camera." Reporter Sal Ruibal reached out for a gratuitously pejorative adverb to describe a bunch of kids smiling for their official photos.

"These men are wanted on the Duke campus," Ruibal continued. "Their fellow students want them to come forward about what happened in a shabby off-campus house March 13. Police say the athletes have refused to cooperate with their investigation."

Ruibal also interviewed enough students to find one who said without evidence or explanation that "there's a culture of rape at Duke" and that the alleged attack at the lacrosse party was "just another example of the abuse of privilege that exists on many levels at Duke."

Chimed in columnist Christine Brennan: The lacrosse players were "giving us all a whole new definition of the word teamwork. . . . Perhaps if no one is found guilty of any criminal activity in this unseemly affair, the collective silence of the Blue Devils someday will be seen as admirable. For now, though, the sports world's vaunted concept of team is reaching a frightening extreme." Months later, appearing on CNN's *Reliable Sources*, Brennan described the time as "an awful performance, an embarrassing time, I think, for journalism. . . . I think some people lost their minds in this story." She did not mention her own contribution to this performance.

On March 30, John Feinstein, Duke alumnus, bestselling author, and nationally prominent sportswriter, urged the administration to cancel the lacrosse season immediately and revoke the scholarships of every lacrosse player who would not speak with authorities. He imagined himself in the role of the Duke president, lecturing the players: "We know you had this party. We know it got out of hand. None of you is man enough to come forward and say what happened. You were witnesses to a crime. We're shutting down the program and *you're all gone.*"

Since Nifong would speak to the players *only* on condition that they confess, or reveal which of their teammates committed the "crime," the sportswriter, then, wanted the university to give its students an ultimatum: implicate their teammates in a crime they knew did not occur or lose the financial wherewithal to attend college.

In this atmosphere, *The New York Times* initially stood out for its reasonably balanced coverage. The first *Times* reporter to conduct detailed interviewing about the evidence in the rape case was sportswriter Joe Drape, who authored or coauthored articles that appeared on March 29, March 30, and March 31. In each article, he quoted Nifong (including one of the district attorney's most outrageous statements: "I'm disappointed that no one has been enough of a man to come forward") but also presented a defense viewpoint. The March 29 article quoted the captains' statement that "the DNA results will demonstrate that these allegations are absolutely false." The March 30 article downplayed the players' previous "minor infractions" and—ironically, in light of events to come—contained positive quotes by Delbarton headmaster Luke Travers and Phil Seligmann.

Drape's March 31 article especially stood out from the pack. He highlighted comments by defense lawyers challenging the accuser's credibility, vowing that the DNA would prove the lacrosse players innocent, and pointing to the fishy features of Kim Roberts's 911 call. Drape quoted Bill Thomas providing an unanswerable reply to Nifong's taunts: "Everyone asks why these young men have not come forward. It's because no one was in the bathroom with the complainant. No one was alone with her. This didn't happen. They have no information to come forward with." Defense lawyers and others interviewed by Drape saw him as a sharp, aggressive reporter who called one of them back at least ten times with follow-up questions and who was pushing hard for the truth. And the more he pushed, the more Drape came to believe that Mangum was not credible and her rape charge was probably false.

Bruce Thompson and his attorney, Bill Thomas, realized that the team needed to do more to get out its side of the story. Encouraged by Drape's performance, Thomas provided all the evidence of innocence then in his possession to the *Times* reporter. Thomas was expecting a great article, but in early April Drape called him and said there would be no article because he was "having problems with the editors." "From my perspective," Thomas recalled later, "the interest of *The Times* in defense information came to a slow crawl with the departure of Drape."

And soon after Drape privately told people at Duke and, presumably, at the *Times* that this looked like a hoax, his byline disappeared from the Duke lacrosse story. The word among people at Duke and defense supporters, including one who later ran into Drape at a race track, was that the editors wanted a more pro-prosecution line. They also wanted to stress the race-sex-class angle without dwelling on evidence of innocence. They got what they wanted from Drape's replacement, Duff Wilson, whose reporting would become a journalistic laughingstock by summer, and other reporters including Rick Lyman, who led a long article on March 31 with a neighbor's complaint about Duke students—including lacrosse players—who rented houses nearby: "Screaming at the top of their lungs at two in the morning, urinating on lawns, throwing beer cans around, driving fast, that sort of stuff." Lyman closed with a female Duke student's guilt-presuming quote: "Is this going to be a team of rich white men who get away with assaulting a black woman? People are really watching to see how Duke is going to respond."

People who got their news from the national media would hardly have suspected the fact that a larger number of Duke women—soon to be a lop-sided majority—thought the lacrosse players were probably innocent. But the lacrosse players' sympathizers did not put on noisy demonstrations.

Times editors also got what they wanted from sports columnist Selena Roberts. Her March 31 commentary, "Bonded in Barbarity," seethed hatred for "a group of privileged players of fine pedigree entangled in a night that threatens to belie their social standing as human beings." Virtually presuming guilt, Roberts parroted already-disproved prosecution claims that all team members had observed a "code of silence," and described a search warrant as a "court document." (A tiny correction ran six days later.) She likened team members to "drug dealers and gang members engaged in an anti-snitch campaign."

Roberts also took a swipe at Duke itself, in a passage that was read with care and consternation by top Duke administrators, who cared far more deeply about their image among readers of the *Times* than about almost anything else: "At the intersection of entitlement and enablement, there is Duke University, virtuous on the outside, debauched on the inside. . . . Does President Brodhead dare to confront the culture behind the lacrosse team's code of silence or would he fear being ridiculed as a snitch?"

The message was clear: Lynch the privileged white boys. And due process be damned.

Detective Himan could barely contain his glee. On March 31, he e-mailed several of his criminal justice instructors at the University of Pittsburgh at Bradford: "The media has scooped this case up and has made it a very popular story. . . . Its [*sic*] not every day you make the NY Times."

Despite the passionate commitment to "diversity" in her Duke columns, Roberts didn't practice what she preached in her personal life. She lived in Westport, Connecticut, a bastion of rich whiteness. Of its 25,598 residents, 24,560, or 95.5 percent, are white. Westport has a grand total of 292 African-American residents. Barely 1 percent of Roberts' townsfolk, in other words, are black. The median family income in Westport is $153,131, more than $100,000 greater than the median family income for the United States as a whole. And a grand total of 104 families live below the poverty level. Barely 1 percent of Roberts' townsfolk, in other words, are poor. The town Web site has forms for people who need to store their boats—either on water or on land—and for residents-only tennis and golf facilities. Roberts, as an affluent columnist, has the right to live wherever she can afford. Yet, judged by the severity with which she condemned others for exhibiting insufficient sensitivity to minorities or the poor, it smacks of hypocrisy to see that she chose to live in a lily-white, upper-class suburb.

But the campaign of the *Times* Sports Department in the Duke case was very much in character: politically correct politics without the scrupulous attention to facts that is applied by the best *Times* reporters, no matter how liberal their politics may be. In 2002 the Sports Department had distinguished itself by "turning the paper into a laughingstock by hounding the Augusta National Golf Club" to admit rich women along with rich men, in the words of Jack Shafer, the distinguished press critic for *Slate*, an online magazine. It was fine to criticize the club for its sexist admissions policy. But few serious journalists thought it was worth a prolonged crusade including dozens of stories using the thinnest of pretexts to keep a tired subject alive.

It speaks volumes that top editors at the *Times* left the Duke case in the Sports Department for so long. The sports reporters (excepting Joe Drape) as well as sports columnists at the *Times* showed in the Duke case that they were incapable of giving serious coverage to a story that—the *Times* never seemed to figure out—was about prosecutorial oppression of innocent men, not white male oppression of black women.

Now at the head of the guilt-presuming pack, *The New York Times* vied in a race to the journalistic bottom with trash-TV talk shows hosted by the likes of Nancy Grace, CNN's egregiously biased, wacko-feminist former prosecutor, and Joe Scarborough, MSNBC's preachy, right-wing blowhard. By late March, CNN, MSNBC, NBC, and Fox TV trucks were filling the parking lots, grabbing random students for interviews, turning the campus into a freak-show set. The team's forty-six white members had been branded as depraved racists from coast to coast.

New York magazine media critic Kurt Andersen conveyed the dynamic months later, beginning with a quote from "a *Times* alumnus": " 'You couldn't *invent* a story so precisely tuned to the outrage frequency of the modern, metropolitan, *bienpensant* journalist.' That is: successful white men at the Harvard of the South versus a poor single mother enrolled at a local black college, jerky superstar jocks versus $400 out-call strippers, a boozy Animal House party, shouts of 'nigger,' and a three-orifice gangbang rape in a bathroom." The academics and media were not about to let mere evidence get in the way of a delicious "morality play that simultaneously demonized lacrosse, wealth, the white race, the South, and the male sex," as Charlotte Allen later wrote in *The Weekly Standard.*

While reporters sharpened their spears, cameramen hovering at lacrosse practices chose to shoot the team from a distance, through a chain-link face, rather than from inside the practice arena. The effect was to make them look a bit like caged animals.

"The authorities were leading the lynch mob and the press was behind them clapping and screaming," defense lawyer Joe Cheshire later recalled. "We knew that we were screwed."

He added: "These people descend, they somehow uncover every phone number you have, every address you have, and they're on you every day, all day. They are like fish in a feeding frenzy. They're very bright and they're very manipulative and alluring to your ego. . . . It was stunning to me how they leapt to a conclusion, and their absolute unwillingness to listen to anything that wasn't what they had already decided they wanted to be true. What I've found out about those folks is that they're kind of in a way like Nifong. They're like bullies. They try to goad you into being strident and getting down in the gutter with them. But if you challenge them, sometimes they all of a sudden stop and say, maybe we don't want to look foolish. Maybe we should take a step back and reexamine what we have reported to see if it really is correct.

"We knew that unless we turned this lynch mob mentality around, our clients might have to endure the worst of all fates for an innocent person, a trial."

These and other news accounts "stoked the image of the lacrosse team as a swaggering pack of white, privileged beer-drinkers with a string of misdemeanor charges, and the accuser as a hard-working state college student stripping to stay in school and support her two children," as *U.S. News & World Report* later reflected.

Like the district attorney, the cops, and the academics, few of the journalists initially covering the story were either careful or focused on searching for the truth. Nor, initially, did they seem interested in Nifong's political motive for seemingly trashing prosecutorial ethics with his preprimary publicity barrage.

"What was coming to our door from the media every morning was so far from what we knew to be the truth of what happened, it was the most bizarre thing you could experience," Sue Pressler recalled. "It was stunning. At four P.M. Mike would turn on the TV and say, "What are they going to say we did today?"

It was also open season on the lacrosse players among TV talk-show hosts, with the exceptions of MSNBC's meticulously fair Dan Abrams and ABC's Chris Cuomo.

Nancy Grace of CNN took special joy in excoriating the lacrosse players, cheering on guests who did the same, and hectoring those who dared to suggest the possibility of innocence. In a March 31 program, Grace falsely suggested that the lacrosse players had refused to provide DNA samples voluntarily. Then she asserted: "There's really no good reason why, if you're innocent, you won't go forward and go, 'Hey, you want my DNA? Take it. I insist.'"

On she rambled, from presumption of guilt to false statement of fact: "The first line of defense is, I didn't do it. The second line of defense is, I did it, but it was consensual. The third line of defense is, She's a hooker. Now, let's just say we get DNA back. They'll immediately claim consensual. But what about those nails torn off?"

Grace enlisted prosecutor Holly Hughes, whom she described as a former head of a sex crimes unit, in a tag-team trashing:

HUGHES: *"And based on the bruising and the beating and the broken nails, Nancy, this is rape. If, in fact, there's DNA, they can say consent all they want, but the other evidence speaks volumes, and it's going to negate that."*

GRACE: *"But of course, you know, Holly, . . . you've got these probably rich kids, lacrosse players, claiming consent or I didn't do it. . . . If there had been evidence, I'm sure it was flushed down the commode or gotten rid of, innocently or not. . . . The Blue Devils! It may not be just a nickname at Duke University."*

Grace then noted—apparently oblivious to her self-contradiction—that "the fake nails were still there in the bathroom" and Mangum's cell phone was still out in the open when police searched the lacrosse house almost three days after the alleged rape.

Grace also brought on Jennifer Minnelli, a neighbor of the lacrosse house, who accused the Duke students, without evidence, of "date rape" and "driving while intoxicated," among other crimes. Then came a Duke graduate student and participant in the potbangers' organization, Serena Sebring, who said there was "clear evidence of some sort of an assault having happened" and faulted Duke administrators for being "exclusively concerned with the legalities" rather than with her own safety.

Grace next moved to clinical psychologist Dr. Patricia Saunders, who at Grace's invitation ridiculed a lacrosse team defender who cautioned against rushing to judgment and asked how viewers would feel if these were their own sons:

GRACE: *"What if this girl was your girl? You know, I'd burn the place down, for Pete's sake!"*

SAUNDERS: "*I think that statement really reveals some of the underlying prejudice, and elitism, and classism, as well as probable racism, that, what if these were your boys, as if the boys were the ones who mattered and not the young woman. This is outrageous, Nancy.*"

One of the few oases of common sense in this wretched media landscape was Duke's own student newspaper, *The Chronicle*. Setting a tone for coverage that would consistently outclass almost all in the national media, *The Chronicle* published an April 3 editorial noting that student protesters and professors who demonized the lacrosse players were "guaranteed front page coverage in the nation's biggest newspapers [and their] fringe views are slated for prime time." But it stressed that far more students reserved judgment while awaiting the evidence. "You'd hardly believe that," the editorial said, "if you've read any major newspaper or turned on your television in the past few days."

And "when the nation's most respected and widely consumed media are showing Duke students openly professing our status as a 'white supremacist' university, suspicion of the protesters is entirely warranted. . . . The frequency of protests is tied directly to the presence of media.

"To the media and their customers around the world: There are some among us, undergraduate and graduate students alike, who think Duke breeds cultures of hate, racism, sexism and other forms of backward thinking. Several thousand others of us are inclined to civilly disagree."

The bias driving media coverage of the Duke case had many roots. "When this case first made national news," Sharon Swanson of *The News & Observer* reflected later, "I was viewing the scenario through the prism of white liberal guilt. I felt somehow responsible that young black women were still being exploited by affluent young white men in the South. I stereotyped the entire Duke lacrosse team."

Also at work was the attitude underlying a hoary slogan long embraced by reporters as the essence of their trade: "Comfort the afflicted and afflict the comfortable." How many of those who glory in this idea ever stop to ask themselves whether *all* of "the comfortable" *deserve* to be afflicted? Should every child born into an affluent family be afflicted for that alone? A stunning array of journalists and academics—many quite comfortable in their own right—exuded exactly that attitude in their gleeful sneering at the "privileged" Duke lacrosse players.

Amid this mass demonization of the lacrosse players, the media offered a steady stream of quotes and commentary suggesting that the players were receiving especially *favorable* treatment because of their race. Wrote syndicated columnist Leonard Pitts: "Imagine if the woman were white and reported being raped by three black members of the basketball team. You'd have to call out the National Guard." In the (London) *Independent,* a student at NCCU was quoted as saying, "If the tables had been turned and two white women had been raped by the [NCCU] football team, the whole team would be in jail. They would not be walking around." Another NCCU student, Spirit Mitchell, told CBS, "If it was a Duke student and it was Central's football team, the situation would have been handled totally differently."

Such assumptions were dramatically refuted by the low-key reactions of the authorities, academics, and the media themselves to several other recent cases involving allegations of sexual assault by white women against black and Hispanic football players. The contrasting reactions to the Duke case and to these other cases suggest that any racial double standard in dealing with alleged sexual assaults by college athletes is the opposite of the one supposed by the conventional wisdom.

- In 2005, at Wake Forest University, also in North Carolina, a white undergraduate accused four black football players of sexual assault. The district attorney in the heavily white county, Jim O'Neill, a former Duke lacrosse player, avoided public comment. The police did not use the case to exploit racial fears. Nobody was thrown in jail. Local papers covered the allegations in a dry, fact-based fashion. The rape claims attracted almost no national attention. The players' professors and administration did not publicly condemn them. They were not suspended from school. Their coach allowed them to keep practicing with the team (while temporarily suspending them from games). Eventually the DA declined to file charges against the students, whose defense was that the sex was consensual, and all four played on the 2006 ACC champion Wake Forest squad.

- In January 2006, four students at historically black Virginia Union University (with annual tuition between $13,000 and $19,000) were accused of raping a white, out-of-state student at the University of Richmond (annual tuition, $42,610). Two of the four played on the football team; one had been quarterback. The five had attended a party, and the woman had left voluntarily with the Virginia Union students, who said the sex was consensual. The case received little media attention. The University of Richmond paper avoided mention of the accuser's race. And when attorneys representing two of the players were asked whether their black clients were demonized by comparison with white college athletes accused of sexual assault, they scoffed. "That hyperbole isn't borne out by the facts," said one. Another noted that the Duke and Virginia Union cases "are being treated differently, that's for sure." As *Richmond Times-Dispatch* columnist Mark Holmberg concluded: "The Duke/VUU cases may show that columnist Pitts has it backward—that we're more alert for white-on-black, rich-on-poor crime."

- In April 2006, just after the Duke case hit the news, Los Angeles police arrested University of Southern California's Hispanic backup quarterback, Mark Sanchez, on suspicion of sexual assault. Sanchez was caught on tape entering a bar with a fake ID; two witnesses who saw him enter his apartment building later that night said he was drunk. The USC team had a history of brushes with the law, and Sanchez himself had been investigated for underage drinking and breaking a window at a fraternity party. But though the story received considerable short-term play in the Los Angeles media, it never went national. The district attorney avoided inflammatory race-based rhetoric and other assaults on Sanchez's personal character. And after an investigation, the charges against Sanchez were deemed noncredible and dropped. He returned as the backup quarterback on the 2007 Rose Bowl champion team.

- Another California case involved an allegation of sexual assault against former University of California running back Marshawn Lynch, just after Lynch had announced his decision to turn pro. Lynch is African American. No articles on the case mentioned the race of his accuser. Alameda County senior deputy district attorney Kim Hunter told reporters that Lynch denied all charges; that the accuser had offered contradictory versions of events; that the accuser had no visible injuries or photographs of injuries; and that a third witness contradicted the accuser in every way. "No one is saying that the victim isn't entitled to the feelings she's having, but I have an ethical obligation," Hunter concluded. "If I don't believe I can prove it to twelve jurors, then I can't ethically charge the case." The Lynch allegations received almost no national attention.

In none of these cases did the media construct a metanarrative styling the accused as personifying broader social ills involving sex, class, or interracial rape. That is precisely what the media did to the "privileged" Duke lacrosse players.

In fact, more than one-third of the forty-seven lacrosse players came from families of modest means. Four were sons of retired New York City firefighters. Other parents included a bricklayer; a medical office worker; a beauty parlor proprietor; a science teacher; two nurses; a respiratory therapist; a school administrator; a 7-Eleven franchisee; two public school teachers, one of them a widow; the Hofstra lacrosse coach; a Johns Hopkins professor; and two professors at the City University of New York.

The Duke team's "privilege" quotient may well have been less than that of the reporting and editing staff of *The New York Times*. In the heady days of March and April, however, such inconvenient facts were ignored.

10. RICHARD BRODHEAD'S TEST OF COURAGE

DUKE HIRED RICHARD BRODHEAD away from Yale University in 2004 to replace departing president Nannerl Keohane in large part because the highly regarded English professor and later dean of Yale College was much admired for brilliance, eloquent speeches rich with literary allusions, sensitivity, and wry wit. Despite these impeccable qualifications, Brodhead, to a much greater extent than most Duke figures involved in the lacrosse affair, appeared to allow personal distaste to affect his judgment.

Brodhead reacted with deep, visceral disgust to the nature of the stripper party that had plunged him, as well as the lacrosse players, into this crisis. "From our point of view," he later told *60 Minutes*, "this was an evening of highly unacceptable behavior whether or not the rape took place."

As a wry observer noted: "It was like he'd never been to a college campus. Drinking! Strippers! Wild parties!"

Brodhead had been courted ardently by Robert K. Steel, who grew up near Duke's East Campus, attended Durham public schools, and graduated from Duke in 1973. Steel was the first Durham native to chair the university's board of trustees since 1924. He got this position the old-fashioned way: by making tens of millions of dollars on Wall Street, as vice chairman of Goldman, Sachs & Co., before retiring in 2004.

But Brodhead had been on probation with the faculty's powerful activist wing for debasing himself, in their view, on his very first day as Duke's president. That was June 28, 2004. Duke's wildly successful and widely celebrated basketball coach, Mike Krzyzewski, had been offered a reported $40 million to become coach of the Los Angeles Lakers. Coach K, as he was widely called, seriously considered taking the job. Losing the rock-star basketball coach would be a most inauspicious way for Brodhead to begin his presidency.

So desperate was he to persuade the coach to remain that he joined crowds of students shouting "Coach K, please stay." Brodhead even jumped into a human chain forming the letter K outside Cameron Indoor Stadium. Coach K stayed. But many professors were disgusted by their new president's groveling. It had been an embarrassing demonstration that at Duke the status of the self-regarding academics was far below that of a man who taught over-sized kids how to toss balls through hoops.

Brodhead performed much better in the eyes of campus activists in the fall of 2004, when Duke hosted the annual conference of the Palestine Solidarity Movement, the U.S. student arm of the International Solidarity Movement. The ISM had a stated goal of destroying the state of Israel "by any means necessary." It described suicide bombings as "noble." It also demanded that all colleges divest from companies doing business in Israel. A conference organizer, the soon-to-be potbanger Rann Bar-On, refused to sign a statement condemning terrorism. "We don't see it as very useful," he told *The Herald-Sun*, "for us as a solidarity movement to condemn violence."

More than 92,000 Duke students, alumni, and other concerned citizens signed a petition urging Brodhead to deny the PSM permission to hold its conference at Duke. Rejecting this request out of hand, the president told Duke's trustees: "At its core, this decision tested the university's commitment to academic freedom. All ideas are not equal, but it is a foundational principle of American life that all ideas should have an equal opportunity to be ex-pressed, and the right of free speech is not limited to speech we approve of."

Extremist groups of both left and right could, of course, exercise their un-doubted rights to free speech without being given privileged access to the Duke campus. And it is hard to imagine Brodhead giving similar access to a neo-Nazi or white supremacist group.

In both the Coach K and the PSM affairs, Brodhead, a somewhat shy man, showed that in time of crisis he did not project the image of a confident commander. Bob Steel, the tough, forceful captain of finance, was a very dif-ferent sort.

Steel was determined that the $532,000-a-year president he had chosen would succeed. He was the power behind Brodhead throughout the lacrosse crisis. With tight reins on the thirty-seven-member board, Steel conferred with Brodhead on every major decision. They took special pains to avoid of-fending Duke's leftist professors and Durham's black leaders and populace.

Bob Steel was the adult paradigm of what the leftists despised about their stereotype of the lacrosse players and their parents: rich, privileged, white, and reaping (or on their way to reaping) huge sums by presiding over finan-cial manipulations of the despised capitalist system.

But Steel knew as well as Brodhead that both activist professors and black

Durhamites had the power to do terrible damage to the university's hard-won reputation as a top-tier school. The professors could run down Duke in the media and among peers at other elite schools. Black Durham, a large proportion of Duke's 30,000-member work force, could shut the place down by protesting or even just staying home. And signs of Duke-Durham tensions surely could threaten Duke's status in the competition for top students.

"Being a university president," Brodhead would reflect almost a year after being plunged into the lacrosse crisis, "is one of the very, very interesting things to be doing on this earth." In the year 2006, he experienced the full irony of the ancient Chinese curse: "May you live in interesting times."

"We had to worry that things might blow," a Duke official later recalled. "What if there were riots in Durham? Durham didn't blow, but that was a concern."

Against this background, Brodhead articulated a policy of broad deference to the criminal justice process. When urged to criticize Nifong for prosecutorial misconduct—after months of revelations of what were widely seen as clearcut violations of the rules of legal ethics—Brodhead declared that the university "can't speak with certainty of matters that only the criminal justice system can resolve."

This stance contradicted a long tradition of academic leaders speaking out against procedural abuses in the criminal justice process—most prominently the Sacco and Vanzetti case and the trumped-up charges against African-American activists in the civil rights struggle.

And on at least two occasions Brodhead himself had intervened in legal matters to promote due process at the behest of students. In 2003, as a dean at Yale, Brodhead signed a letter to the New York Board of Parole urging the release of inmate Kathy Boudin, a former member of the Weather Underground who was serving a sentence of twenty years to life for felony murder and robbery. Her son, Chesa, was then a student at Yale, and his campaign to earn parole for his mother had become a cause célèbre on the radical left.

Then, in 2005, a Duke graduate student in cultural anthropology, Yektan Turkyilmaz, was placed on trial in Armenia on charges that seemed politically inspired: Turkyilmaz, a Turk, had been researching the Armenian genocide. His adviser, Orin Starn, was one of the leaders of the Duke campus left, which rallied to his cause. In a letter to the president of Armenia, Brodhead asked him not merely to intervene in the case but to release Turkyilmaz outright.

Brodhead took a dramatically different approach to the lacrosse case. For more than eight months, he acquiesced without a peep of protest in a pattern of prosecutorial abuse of Duke student athletes that would come to be seen as perhaps without parallel in modern American history. Criticizing Nifong for violating the ethical rule against "heightening public condemnation of the accused," Brodhead and Steel knew, would infuriate many faculty members and black Durhamites.

Beyond that, Brodhead joined Nifong and the activist professors in publicly and repeatedly assailing the lacrosse players, albeit in more muted ways. This policy had the effect—and, critics said, the intent—of entering an alliance of convenience with the oppressor of forty-six of Duke's own students in order to appease activist professors and black Durhamites.

In early April, a lacrosse team parent called John Burness and offered a briefing in which defense lawyers would tell Burness and others at Duke everything they knew, including an already substantial body of exculpatory photos, timelines, witness statements, and more. This evidence, the parent told Burness, would show all team members to be innocent and Duke should see it before doing anything rash. The parent, who took notes, recalled Burness rejecting the offer out of hand, saying that "I know everything I need to know" and launching into a "diatribe" against the team by asserting that what had happened was all their fault and that their bad behavior over the years had made people believe the charges. When the parent said the "bad behavior" involved things like open beer can violations, Burness said (according to the parent) that this was not true and there were "two or three real bad actors on that team." Burness provided no specifics. Not then. Not ever.

Burness, asked by one of the authors to respond, did not dispute that he had rejected any briefing by the defense—because "the University was relying on the legal system to get to the truth and it was not the university's role to be the judge and jury." He did not recall saying that "I know everything I need to know" and denied any mention of "two or three real bad actors." Burness added: "He clearly was frustrated that Duke was not more supportive of the kids and their innocence. I do recall telling him at the end of the conversation words to the effect that it was worth remembering that the players and the university would not be in this mess had the party not been held and that part of the difficulty was that the team's behavior over the years around alcohol had contributed to the storm we were in and also to people's willingness to believe the events of 14 March could have occurred. But that doesn't qualify as a diatribe."

Brodhead himself, much like Burness and Nifong, appeared to take pains to avoid exposure to the evidence in the case. He would later turn down an offer from an indicted student's parents to give Brodhead or his designee unrestricted access to *all* of the evidence in the DA's own files. (The defense received evidence in installments, beginning on May 17 with 1,278 pages, because the open discovery law required Nifong to hand it over.) The parents assured Brodhead that the DA's files would show him that the criminal charges were false. Brodhead refused to look at them or assign a subordinate to look. Ironically, even as he went out of his way to *avoid* examining the discovery information, Brodhead publicly complained about his difficulties in having to base decisions on incomplete information.

Whether intentional or not, the Brodhead-Steel approach perfectly served Nifong's interests. In late March, Nifong asserted with certitude that Duke lacrosse players had gang-raped the "victim," had used "abhorrent" racial slurs, and were now hiding behind a "stonewall of silence." Brodhead and Steel knew or had good reason to know that much of what Nifong was saying was untrue. But they acted as though they were quite content with Nifong's convicting the lacrosse players in the media and inflaming racial passions against them. Duke administrators continued calling on team members to "cooperate." "Duke effectively gave Nifong a green light to act," lacrosse parent Bruce Thompson later recalled.

Nifong, in turn, praised the Duke administration. While saying that the lacrosse team "has not been fully cooperative," he added that "the university, I believe, has done pretty much everything they can under the circumstances. They, obviously, don't have a lot of control over whether or not the lacrosse team members actually speak to the police."

Brodhead was later to claim that he did not focus on what many considered to be Nifong's flagrant violations of the ethical rules against publicly demonizing targets before trial because hardly anybody else was raising that issue then. Perhaps he did not notice that precisely this issue had been the central complaint of the defense lawyers from their first press conference, on March 30 and afterward. The *News & Observer*'s front-page article began:"Defense lawyers representing members of the Duke University men's lacrosse team say prosecutors are trying to convict their clients in public in a rape investigation before any charges have been filed." It quoted Joe Cheshire as saying, "The fact that the D.A. is out in public saying these boys are guilty is just extraordinary."

Later, on April 19, Brodhead could have heard an indictment of Nifong's conduct on MSNBC's *Abrams Report* from David Freedman, a North Carolina lawyer with expertise in legal ethics: "You had a district attorney coming out and making potentially unethical statements, saying he believed a crime occurred, which he should not do. He should not be commenting on the evidence. He took an adversarial position from the start. . . . It's not the D.A.'s job to get a conviction. It's the D.A.'s job to make sure justice is done, to make the truth is found out and rather than rushing and doing indictments two weeks before the primary is held."

Brodhead could also have heard about Nifong's ethical violations from Bob Ekstrand. Ekstrand's notes for a meeting he hoped to have with Brodhead had the pretrial publicity rules at the top of the list of things to discuss, as objective proof that what Nifong was doing was forbidden. But Brodhead refused to meet with Ekstrand.

While Brodhead shunned any and all dealings with advocates for the players, strong pressure came at the president from a different direction. On March 29, Brodhead met with local and state NAACP leaders, including state conference president Rev. William J. Barber II. The next morning he convened with Durham's black leaders. These included Mayor Bell, NCCU chancellor James Ammons and Provost Beverly Washington Jones, County Commissioner Phil Cousin, Mignon Schooler and F. Vincent Allison of the politically powerful Durham Committee on the Affairs of Black People, Rev. James Smith, president of the Interdenominational Ministerial Alliance of Durham, Rev. Frederick Davis, and Rev. William Turner. Duke's John Burness and community affairs chief MaryAnn Black also attended.

On campus that afternoon, an emergency meeting of the Academic Council was called. Less than 10 percent of Duke's full-time faculty members attended, but the lacrosse team's most vehement critics appeared in full force. While administrators cautioned against precipitous action, none proved willing to confront the faculty extremists. The meeting illustrated the thesis of *New York Times* reporter Richard Bernstein's 1995 book, *Dictatorship of Virtue*, that "in the era of political correctness and craven university administrations, the charge of racism, unsubstantiated but accompanied by a few demonstrations and angry rhetorical perorations, suffices to paralyze a campus, to destroy a reputation, and to compel an administration into submission."

From administration members came three cautionary messages that they were soon to abandon. First, at Brodhead's request, Trask answered complaints about the lacrosse team's disciplinary problems. Since the players tended to do things in a group, he explained, when one is found with an open container, several others may be cited for the same offense. Trask said that he had inquired into the team's disciplinary issues the summer before and that "as much as I would have liked to have found something," the problems had been handled appropriately. Trask was to suggest the opposite seven days later, in an interview with *The New York Times*.

Second, Brodhead warned against making an example of the lacrosse players if it meant treating them more harshly than Duke had treated other students in the past for similar conduct, including hiring strippers and racial slurs. But Brodhead himself had already done just that when he approved forfeiting the Georgetown game.

Third, Brodhead suggested that for Duke to seek to fix its cultural problems by scapegoating the lacrosse team would suggest to the world that Duke's problems were extraordinarily serious. Exactly one week later, on April 6, eighty-eight Duke faculty members did exactly what the president had cautioned them to avoid. Brodhead would say nothing by way of criticism or even disagreement.

Most of the professors at the Academic Council meeting leveled vitriolic attacks against the team. One speaker claimed that Duke, as an institution, tolerated drinking and rape, and the lacrosse incident reflected a university problem from the top down. Another suggested punishing the team by suspending lacrosse for three years and then making it a club sport. A third asserted that the team embodied the "assertion of class privilege" by all Duke students. A fourth called on the university to do something to help the "victim."

Three professors dominated the meeting. Houston Baker stated as a fact that African-American women had been "harmed" by the lacrosse players and claimed that students in his mostly white, female class were terrified of the lack of an administration response. In a subsequent e-mail, Baker claimed that when he used the word "harmed," he was merely referring to the party itself, not any physical harm experienced by Crystal Mangum or Kim Roberts. He did not say how the knowledge that some male students had hired strippers for a party would have terrified female Duke undergraduates.

Wahneema Lubiano alleged favoritism by Duke toward the team and demanded a statement from Duke denouncing the players. She never supplied any evidence to bolster her claims. And Peter Wood gave an embellished version of his letter from two years before, claiming that he had described the team as out of control, and demanded a hard line against the athletic director, coach, and team. Wood's remarks received robust applause.

"I have never heard presumably intelligent, careful, balanced people being so completely over the top," Steve Baldwin, a chemistry professor, later recalled. "It was the most disgusting display I've ever seen in my life."

Initiating a pattern that would continue throughout the case, the student leadership on campus approached the issue far more responsibly. The night before the emergency Academic Council meeting, the Student Government spent two hours considering its response to the crisis. Two senators demanded a resolution encouraging the administration to enforce the Duke Community Standard, especially in regard to student athletes—with the insinuation that the lacrosse players had violated the standard. An even more radical proposal came from a senator named Chauncey Nartey, who demanded that the lacrosse team be prevented from practicing until Nifong completed his investigation.

Nartey did not inform his fellow senators that two days before, on March 27, he had attempted to achieve his goal unilaterally. He sent the Presslers an e-mail whose menacing subject line read: "WHAT IF JANET LYNN WERE NEXT???" Nartey would later explain that he intended no threat. He took the time to ferret out the name of Pressler's older daughter, he said, because he wanted to get the coach's attention. That way, Nartey hoped, the coach would read Nartey's earlier e-mail: "SOME THINGS ARE MORE IMPORTANT THAN WINNING A FEW GAMES. END THE SEASON UNTIL THE ALLEGED RAPISTS ARE FOUND! YOU'LL BE A MUCH BETTER COACH FOR IT."

Whatever Nartey's intention, in the vigilante atmosphere of the time, the Presslers feared for their children. On March 31, Sue Pressler filed a report with the Duke Police.

More temperate members of the Student Government resisted Nartey's efforts, and his resolution was tabled. Sophomore Matt McNeill spoke for the level-headed majority, urging his colleagues to respect due process: "You need to investigate the entire situation before you make charges against anyone." Eventually, the Student Government settled on a public letter affirming that it would continue to monitor the situation and expressing its support for Sexual Assault Awareness Week.

Support for due process seemed in short supply off campus. A blog launched to support the accuser ran a logo of two AK-47 assault rifles crossing and called for retaliation against the team. The site then went on to list the addresses of ten players, calling for readers to take justice into their own hands. One lacrosse family, living in Durham, had to move out of their house for fear of attacks.

Meanwhile, the resentment of Duke students among the half of the city's population that was black—and many whites, especially Duke professors— was coming close to a boil. Tales of violence and threats by black Durhamites against Dukies spread. At 3:00 A.M. on March 31, two Duke students in a car were blocked in by another car at the drive-through window at Cookout Restaurant, where Reade Seligmann had stopped after leaving the stripper party seventeen days before.

Young black men approached the Dukies' car, screaming that "this is Central [NCCU] territory" and that Duke kids weren't welcome because "they're going to rape our women." When the driver leaned out the window to hear, someone bashed him in the back of the head, knocking him unconscious. As he and his female companion drove off, they were briefly pursued by the same car that had blocked them.

Late that afternoon, at least three cars drove by a house on North Buchanan Boulevard with passengers pointing fingers in the shape of a gun or making other menacing gestures at students on the porch. At 9:00 P.M., in an e-mail to all Duke students, Moneta noted some of these events and warned of rumored "threats of 'drive-by shooting' of the lacrosse house in the Trinity Park area." By then, Dave Evans was going home every weekend to Maryland because he was scared that something might happen to him.

The news of the attack on Duke students at the Cookout outraged at least one critic of the lacrosse players, political science professor Kim Curtis. She was not outraged by the attack, however, but by the reporting of it. This news, Curtis complained, might contribute to "raising the temperature about black on white violence (and about lies in general)." Curtis suggested conducting "research on this [Duke] student" and making it public. Her damn-the-facts-be-politically-correct attitude was typical of Duke's activist faculty.

Provost Peter Lange pushed back forcefully on April 3 in a sharp, eloquent rebuke to Houston Baker's public attack on the lacrosse players, which had been addressed to Lange. Saying that he was "disappointed, saddened and appalled to receive this letter from you," Lange added, "A form of prejudice—one felt so often by minorities whether they be African American, Jewish or other—is the act of prejudgment: to presume that one knows something 'must' have been done by or done to someone because of his or her race, religion or other characteristic." Noting the uncertainty about what had happened at the lacrosse party, Lange declared, "We will not rush to judgment nor will we take precipitous actions . . . playing to the crowd." For a brief moment it seemed as though the Duke administration was beginning to take a stand against irresponsible faculty.

But two days later, on April 5, Brodhead did just what Lange had pledged not to do, in a dramatic way. Confronted with a crisis of epic proportions, with Duke's hard-won reputation at risk, he faced his ultimate test of courage. And in an extraordinary moral meltdown, he threw in his lot with the mob.

The day began inauspiciously for the lacrosse players, with *The New York Times* reporting Collin Finnerty's arrest on assault charges outside a bar in Washington four months before. A man named Jeffrey Bloxsom, the *Times* said, had claimed that Finnerty and two friends had beaten him without provocation while "calling him gay and other derogatory names."

This highly misleading allegation was to morph into dozens of news reports that Finnerty had beaten up a gay man in a homophobic hate crime. This despite the facts that Bloxsom was not gay and never claimed that Finnerty had thought he was. Few news media reported that police had dismissed the scuffle as "an argument between two young guys who were sizing each other up." Or that there was no prosecution claim that Finnerty had even hit anyone. Or that he and his friends had been put into a "diversion" program requiring only twenty-five hours of community service to keep their records clean.

What blew the lid off of the lacrosse story on April 5 was a single e-mail made public that day about noon. It was the same one that Ryan McFadyen had sent after the party to his teammates, and that Gottlieb and Himan had showed to Nifong nine days before. And it ignited what Sue Pressler, the coach's wife, called "a day of hysteria."

Police had quoted the e-mail's language about killing and skinning strippers in a March 27 sealed warrant to search McFadyen's dorm room for evidence of "conspiracy to commit murder," among other things. Judge Ron Stephens, the former district attorney who almost always gave Nifong what he wanted, unsealed the warrant on April 5, formally at the request of the Nifong-friendly *Herald-Sun*. Nifong did not release the reply e-mails from other players confirming that McFadyen's "kill and skin" e-mail was a joke, not a threat.

The timing of the e-mail's release was highly suspicious. The moment was a strategic one. The day before, Mangum's failure to recognize Mc-Fadyen had cleared him as a suspect in the rape case. The DNA results giving the lie to Mangum's rape allegations were in Nifong's hands. State law required him to give the results to defense lawyers. Nifong needed something to distract attention from this near-conclusive proof that there had been no rape. The media sensation over the McFadyen e-mail and Richard Brodhead's apocalyptic reaction to it gave the DA just the distraction he needed. "They released Ryan's e-mail because they already knew the DNA was negative," Mike Pressler would later surmise.

The six-foot, five-inch McFadyen was a bright, affable guy with an off-beat, sometimes sick sense of humor. His e-mail was sick indeed. It was also quite obviously a joke, a point all but ignored by the media as they spun into paroxysms of delighted rage. "Warrant: Player Wrote of Plan to Kill Other Strippers" was the subhead in *The Herald-Sun*'s story the next day.

Many Dukies immediately recognized the e-mail as a pale imitation of the book and movie *American Pyscho*—a point the media *entirely* ignored. *American Psycho* is a first-person narrative in the voice of Patrick Bateman, a crazed Wall Street banker who tortures and kills several women. It was assigned material in at least three Duke courses, including a freshman cluster called "Forging Social Ideals" and the English Department's "Companionate Love" and "Literary Grotesques: Of Gods and Monsters, *Richard III* to *American Psycho*." The *American Psycho* DVD was available in the freshman library.

The passage mimicked by McFadyen is on page 304 of the 1991 paperback edition. It should be read only by people prepared to stomach prose far more horrifying than anything that any Duke lacrosse player ever dreamed up:

I start by skinning Torri a little, making incisions with a steak knife and rip-ping bits of flesh from her legs and stomach while she screams in vain, beg-ging for mercy in a high thin voice. . . . While Tiffany watches, finally I saw the entire head off—torrents of blood splash against the walls, even the ceiling—and holding the head up, like a prize, I take my cock, purple with stiffness, and lowering Torri's head to my lap I push it into her bloodied mouth and start fucking it, until I come, exploding into it.

The McFadyen e-mail's play on this passage was: "tomorrow night, after tonights show, ive decided too have some strippers over to edens 2c. all are wel-come. . however there will be no nudity. i plan on killing the bitches as soon as the walk in and proceeding to cut their skin off while cumming in my duke is-sue spandex." Teammates instantly recognized the allusion. "I'll bring the Phil Collins," replied one, referring to a favorite singer of the crazed killer.

While Brodhead has always said that the McFadyen e-mail was a com-plete surprise to him when released on April 5, a copy had been given to the Duke campus cops eight days before. That was more than enough time to fig-ure out that it was a play on revolting course material assigned by Duke pro-fessors. And more than enough time to admonish McFadyen about his choice of literary models.

Duke administrators did neither. Instead, while news organizations and Durham leaders raged as though McFadyen had actually planned to kill and skin strippers, Brodhead immediately denounced the e-mail without qualifi-cation as "sickening and repulsive." He also approved the immediate suspen-sion of McFadyen, with no due process or opportunity to explain. That night, McFadyen and his father left Durham and drove straight through to their home in New Jersey. Avoiding the news trucks parked across the street from his house, he walked into the living room at 6:00 A.M. to see his mother and three sisters watching a TV broadcast of his face.

Brodhead did not stop with banishing McFadyen. Accelerating plans that had already been made, he canceled the team's season once and for all. He also appointed a gaggle of committees, to examine: (1) "persistent problems involving the men's lacrosse team, including racist language and a pattern of alcohol abuse and disorderly behavior"—a statement misleadingly suggesting that these Duke students were racists even while a race-pandering prosecutor was making an identical case to Durham voters and potential jurors; (2) his own administration's response to the crisis, especially complaints that it should have taken harsher action, sooner, against the team; (3) Duke's disciplinary process; and (4) "campus culture," including "personal responsibility," "consideration for others," and drinking. A fifth committee consisted of supposedly "wise figures" to advise Brodhead and the Board of Trustees.

Kowtowing to faculty extremists, the administration named Peter Wood as chair of the athletics subgroup of the Campus Culture Initiative. Two other fierce critics of the lacrosse team, Karla Holloway and Anne Allison, would head up the race and gender subgroups, respectively.

"Stacking the CCI with critics of 'white male privilege,'" *The Chronicle* editorialized months later, "suggests that the initiative was created to pacify countercultural professors, rather than to shape a new and improved campus culture."

In a "letter to the Duke community" that day, which could have been scripted by Houston Baker, Brodhead implicitly but unmistakably associated the lacrosse players with rape and "dehumanization," with "memories of the systematic racial oppression we had hoped to have left behind us," with "inequalities of wealth, privilege, and opportunity . . . and the attitudes of superiority those inequalities breed."

"This episode has touched off angers, fears, resentments, and suspicions that range far beyond this immediate case," Brodhead stated. It has "brought to glaring visibility underlying issues that have been of concern on this campus and in this town for some time . . . concerns of women about sexual coercion and assault . . . concerns about the culture of certain student groups that regularly abuse alcohol and the attitudes these groups promote . . . concerns about the survival of the legacy of racism, the most hateful feature American history has produced."

The tone of this "letter" was guilty, guilty, guilty. In 2,397 words, Brodhead never once mentioned the presumption of innocence. (The closest he came was a passing mention that "reaching certainty without evidence or process is a double wrong.") He barely acknowledged the *possibility* of innocence.

Brodhead's reference in this letter to unspecified pre–March 13 "reports of persistent problems involving the men's lacrosse team, including racist language and a pattern of alcohol abuse and disorderly behavior" was squarely refuted less than a month later by the faculty committee that Brodhead himself appointed on April 5 to investigate the team. It found not one iota of evidence that any lacrosse player had ever used racist language before the stripper party. (The committee was not asked to investigate two players' admittedly racist responses to a racist taunt from Kim Roberts as the women were getting into Roberts's car and driving away.) The committee also found that the lacrosse players' drinking and related petty misconduct was no "different in character than the conduct of the typical Duke student who abuses alcohol," as many and perhaps most were known to do.

What Brodhead's vilification of the lacrosse players had to do with Ryan McFadyen's sick joke the president did not explain.

"You wonder why they did this?" Bruce Thompson, father of Bret, said many months later. "It's all the faculty. They're terrified of the faculty. I believe that they were all thinking of what happened to Larry Summers." The reference was to the Harvard president who had recently been driven from office largely because some of his moves—albeit popular with many students—had offended hard-left (and many soft-left) professors. These professors demanded Summers's head—and got it.

Thompson also pointed out that many of Brodhead's April 5 actions seemed a capitulation (if not quite a complete one) to the demands listed by Houston Baker, the most openly hate-driven Duke professor of all, in the same March 29 "public letter" in which Baker had so viciously attacked "this white male athletic team" as the embodiment of "abhorrent sexual assault, verbal racial violence, and drunken white, male privilege loosed amongst us."

At a time when Duke students were in grave jeopardy from a prosecutor increasingly veering out of control, their own school, up to and including its president, was portraying them with grotesque exaggeration as a bunch of uncooperative, rowdy, drunken white racists who might well be rapists, too. Nifong, hoping to divert attention from the powerful proof of innocence in the soon-to-be-public DNA tests, could hardly have hoped for a more obliging helper than Richard Brodhead.

The Duke president's final April 5 move was to force, and brusquely announce, the "resignation" of Mike Pressler, even as he created a committee to investigate the team and the coach. "Sentence first—verdict afterwards," as the Queen decreed in *Alice in Wonderland*. Brodhead did not mention the fact that nobody had even accused the coach of doing anything wrong. Indeed, Brodhead's own committee would later find that Pressler had done *nothing* wrong.

Alleva had summoned Pressler that morning at ten to tell him that the rest of the season would be canceled. Chris Kennedy was also present. At a heated meeting, the coach protested that this decision would break the promise to his team and their parents that there would be no more punishments. Pressler jotted down later what was said:

PRESSLER: *"Joe, you believe the kids are right, you believe in the truth. What message does it send to students if we as educators say the truth only matters when it's convenient?"*

ALLEVA: *"It's not about the truth anymore. It's about the faculty, the special interest groups, the protesters, our reputation, the integrity of the university."*

PRESSLER: *"It's always been about the truth. If this was football or basketball you'd hire a thousand security guards."*

Pressler stressed that the DNA results clearing his players could come back any day. (Though Nifong had the results, he delayed turning them over to defense attorneys until April 10.) Pressler left Alleva thinking he had won a stay of execution for at least two days, by which time the DNA results might arrive. Alleva also promised the coach that his job was in no jeopardy—a promise to be broken that afternoon.

At about noon, Pressler's wife Sue called and said to come home immediately. Ryan's e-mail was all over the tube. Seeing it for the first time, the coach feared for his player's safety. He called around and located McFadyen at Bob Ekstrand's law office. On his way over, Pressler got a call from Alleva, who demanded to see him immediately. Pressler said it would have to wait until he had checked on Ryan's well-being. After doing that, he got to Alleva's office about 1:15.

With Chris Kennedy looking on, Alleva told Pressler that the season was canceled and he must resign immediately or face suspension and possible removal on worse financial terms. Contrary to previous assurances from Alleva that Pressler's job was in no danger, Brodhead would be announcing his resignation at a 4:30 P.M. press conference. Pressler felt he had had no choice. So much for the three-year contract that he had been given as a vote of confidence the previous June. He got his lawyer, hastily worked out a separation agreement, and met with his team at 4:30.

"Guys, our darkest hour has come," Pressler began. The season was over. The dream was dead. The coach was resigning, effective immediately.

Pressler's words broke the dam that had been holding back the lacrosse players' emotions during their ordeal. Hysteria filled the packed meeting room. Tears. Screams. Kids holding their heads in their arms, writhing as though in physical agony. Pressler's tears flowed, too. He spoke for forty minutes, thinking that this was ten times tougher even than giving the eulogy after his younger brother's fatal heart attack two years before.

"Fellas," the coach said, "you're not responsible for this. In the right time and venue I will tell our story so the world can hear the truth." Pressler had a hug and some affectionate words for every player. He had been coaching lacrosse for twenty-four years—at the Virginia Military Institute, West Point, Ohio Wesleyan, then sixteen years at Duke. This was one of his favorite groups of young men.

"If I had a son," the coach mused later, "and he was half the young man that any of these men are, I would be extremely proud. They are moral, highly motivated, and academically diligent. I feel very strongly about all of them."

Outside, the media waited. Coincidentally, they were at the athletics facilities because the Duke women's basketball team was scheduled to return from its trip to the Final Four. Sensing that something was up as lacrosse players came crying into the parking lot, the assembled journalists rushed over to get the scoop. Patricia Dowd shouted at the media to respect the team's privacy and told the players to return inside to shield themselves from the journalists. Several news reports the next day mentioned the action of a person they described as an "unidentified woman." Dowd was there with Melinda Wilson in an effort to provide the players with the security that Duke was not providing.

When Pressler got home, at least three TV trucks were lined up in front of his house. One blocked his driveway, tended by a guy who said he had a First Amendment right to park there. There seemed to be a reporter behind every tree, screaming for the coach to make a statement. More than forty neighbors and friends had come to the Pressler home as though for a wake; at least another sixty would as the evening wore on. They fended off reporters so that the coach could get to his front door. The somber gathering went past midnight. The phone rang constantly. A friend sat by the phone and filled a legal pad taking down sympathy messages, from other coaches, former players, old friends, admirers, recruits, and more.

Even as the sympathy calls came in, the media-academic complex was ratcheting up its libels. At 8:00 P.M. on CNN's *Nancy Grace* show, star guest Houston Baker said that lacrosse players had rampantly "urinated on people's houses, . . . used racial slurs, . . . been given special privileges so that they could make up courses in the summer and that they had showed up at these courses drunk and indifferent."

Every one of those statements was false or, at best, a grotesque exaggeration. Grace lapped them up with glee, enthusing that "someone has to speak out."

Then at 9:00 Baker shuttled to MSNBC's *Rita Cosby Live and Direct*. A student guest, Russ Ferguson, called the McFadyen e-mail "shocking and horrifying" but suggested that it might have been intended as a sick joke and should not be deemed proof of rape or intent to murder without some evidentiary inquiry.

Oozing condescension, Baker pounced: "I don't understand how some-body who is supposed to be an intelligent and elite university student or any group could suggest that that was—you know, that we need evidence sur-rounding this e-mail. It's sick."

Cosby piled on: "No, you're right. There is nothing funny about it."

And with that, Baker and Cosby floated the ludicrous innuendo that a sick joke by one lacrosse player had proved them all a bunch of rapists. Oth-ers in the media did the same. Former prosecutor Wendy Murphy, a prolific TV commentator on the Duke case, went on MSNBC's *Scarborough Coun-try* later that night to channel what the lacrosse players must have been think-ing after the (nonexistent) rape:

" 'I was entitled to do this. I'm a member of a wealthy white boy's school in a community that allows me to do what I want when I want.' They've got-ten away with a lot for a very long time. Why not go home and celebrate? You don't think you're going to get in trouble. If she does go to police, who's going to believe her? She's a black stripper. That's what they're thinking. That's what the e-mail reflects." Scarborough expressed no skepticism.

Murphy subsequently speculated on the reasons for Pressler's forced res-ignation: The coach "didn't tell [Duke administrators] the whole truth about what happened, he helped the guys cover up or encouraged it." The specula-tion was wholly without foundation.

When the last friend had left, Pressler tossed and turned all night on the couch. He got no sleep. His mind raced, thinking about what he had to do the next day, wondering what McFayden's e-mail was supposed to have to do with whether a woman was raped. It had not yet really hit the coach that his career and reputation had been ravaged—not for anything he had done wrong, but to suit the agendas of others. Indeed, Brodhead himself was later to admit to *Sports Illustrated* that Pressler had been found blameless by the faculty inves-tigative committee that Brodhead had named the day he forced the coach to resign.

As the administration terminated the season, faculty extremists applied a body blow. The April 6 *Chronicle* featured a full-page ad signed by eighty-eight Duke faculty members and put together by Wahneema Lubiano and Karla Holloway.

Five academic departments and thirteen academic programs were cited as having officially endorsed the statement, although none of the departments offi-cially voted on the matter, a violation of standard academic procedure. What became known as the Group of 88 included some of the faculty's leading names: Chafe. Alice Kaplan, a literature professor whose father was a prosecu-tor at the Nuremberg war crimes trials. Frank Lentricchia, a literature professor and prominent essayist. Alex Rosenberg, holder of an endowed chair in philosophy. Ariel Dorfman, an internationally renowned novelist, playwright, and human rights activist who fled with his family from Chile in 1973.

Asking, "What does a social disaster look like," the signatories stated without qualification that something "happened to this young woman [Mangum]," even though they based their judgment on nothing more than Nifong's uncorroborated allegations. The professors affirmed that they were "listening" to a select group of students troubled by sexism and racism at Duke. Yet of the eleven quotes purporting to come from students with whom these professors had been talking, eight contained no attribution of any sort, not even to anonymous Duke students. Nonetheless, according to the Group of 88, "the disaster didn't begin on March 13th and won't end with what the police say or the court decides."

The Group of 88 also committed themselves to "turning up the volume." As if the potbangers needed a faculty endorsement, the statement concluded, "To the students speaking individually and to the protestors making collective noise, thank you for not waiting and for making yourselves heard." By this point, of course, the protesters had plastered the campus with wanted posters showing the lacrosse players' photos; chanted outside 610 North Buchanan, "Time to confess"; and waved a banner proclaiming, CASTRATE. Neither in the statement nor subsequently did the signatories say why it was so important that the protesters not wait.

Group members were, however, fully aware that the DNA tests could be made public any day and that defense attorneys had bet their reputations that the DNA would exonerate the players. This could end the activist professors' chance to exploit the crisis for their own personal or pedagogical ends. Lubiano gave colleagues a deadline of forty-eight hours to decide whether to sign the statement; some had only had six hours.

In Lubiano's mind, the players could never be cleared, no matter what the evidence. Shortly after the Group of 88 ad appeared, she expressed pleasure "that the Duke administration is getting the point": The banging of pots and pans had hammered home that a specific claim to innocence mattered little. The members of the team, she noted, could be considered "almost perfect offenders," since they are "the exemplars of the upper end of the class hierarchy, the politically dominant race and ethnicity, the dominant gender, the dominant sexuality, and the dominant social group on campus." (Many months later, Lubiano would suggest that she didn't mean that *she* considered the players to be "perfect offenders," but the tenor of her springtime statements and actions belied this interpretation of her remarks.) Lubiano concluded by promising that the crusade to transform Duke would continue "regardless of the 'truth' established in whatever period of time about the incident at the house on N. Buchanan Blvd." and "whatever happens with the court case."

When the eighty-eight later came under criticism from bloggers and others for signing this statement, many complained that they had been taken out of context or misinterpreted. But student writers in *The Chronicle*, who were almost the only voices of reason amid the faculty's ravings, had seen the statement of the eighty-eight from the start for what it was.

"This absurd ad, which levied the untrue and indefensible charge that Duke is filled with racists, was officially endorsed by 20 of our academic departments and institutes and about 90 individual professors," wrote Stephen Miller in an April 12 column. "It is the hope of many activists, protesters and condemners to make a case not only for the excoriation of the lacrosse team, but also for sweeping social reform to address what they see as profound racial inequity." A *Chronicle* editorial the next day added: "This is but one example of the instances of radical, inflammatory discourse that obscures what should be our true aim: reasonable discussion."

Months later, Miller returned to the subject, lamenting that the lacrosse case had exposed a "shameful reality" that "while there are many good, decent and commendable professors on our campus, there are also a number of professors that are unethical, unbalanced and out of control. . . . Indeed, it truly is stunning to consider some of the disturbed people Duke hires to teach its students."

Duke engineering professor Michael Gustafson delivered a devastating retrospective assessment of the Group of 88's handiwork:

> *We have removed any safeguards we've learned against stereotyping, against judging people by the color of their skin or the (perceived) content of their wallet, against acting on hearsay and innuendo and misdirection and falsehoods. We have formed a dark blue wall of institutional silence; we have closed Pandora's box now that all the evils have made it into the universe; we have transformed students from individual men to archetypes—to "perfect offenders" and "hooligans"—and refused to keep their personhood as a central component of all this. . . . We have given to them all the responsibilities of being representational caricatures and stripped away any sense of their being individuals, making it ever so easy to sidestep the individual liberties and responsibilities in pursuit of some representational good. . . . Justice—for any and for all—demands distance from us.*

Who comprised the Group of 88? The signatories included only two professors in math, just one in the hard sciences, and zero in law. (Perhaps law professors hesitated to sign a statement deeming irrelevant "what the police say or the court decides.") More than 84 percent described their research interests as related to race, class, or gender (or all three). The Group of 88 was disproportionately concentrated in the humanities and some social science departments. Fully 80 percent of the African-American studies faculty members signed the statement, followed by women's studies (72.2 percent) and cultural anthropology (60 percent). Significant numbers of professors in romance studies, literature, English, art, and history signed as well.

At the other extreme, ten arts and sciences departments had zero signatories, including several in the hard sciences and economics. One explanation for this imbalance is that professors in such departments aren't as concerned about looking under every rock for traces (however microscopic) of white racism. Another is that, in the words of blogger William L. Anderson, a professor at Frostburg State University:

> The social status of the lacrosse players irked those [eighty-eight] faculty members. Here were young men who were socially popular, were overwhelmingly white and prep-school educated, were respectful to their professors, made high grades, majored in things like finance, and took well-paying jobs after graduation. In other words, they were the epitome of the bourgeoisie that the arts and sciences faculty have hated.

Some of the Group of 88 members' Web sites read like a *Saturday Night Live* parody of wacky professors. One signatory stated that his current project "argues that unless we attempt to read racialized trauma according to a more Freudian, Lacanian understanding for subjectivity we will continue to misunderstand why racial stigma persists and, more generally, why the laws humans create to protect against forms of discrimination leave in place a notion of the racialized subject as emptied of interiority and the psychical."

Another reasoned that "it was not merely military mobilization . . . that paved the path to war [in Iraq] but a highly gendered war talk." An example? Laura Bush's late 2001 comments about the plight of Afghan women, which allegedly "furthered the [U.S.] imperial project in her highly gendered appeal to a world conscience."

A third Group of 88 member began her career exploring "postmodernist theory about the individual and the body," and producing such academic works as an article about how "many urban-based gay male, lesbian, and mixed-gender sexually radical communities (such as leather and/or S/M groups) portray their interests in sexuality in terms of arousal and pleasure," leading to "the possibility that these sex groups are in the process of providing for us a new kind of ethic based not on individuality, but rather based on community." At the time of the lacrosse controversy, she was working on "a new project critiquing animal rights from speciesist perspective."

For the chance to sit at the feet of such figures—literature and Romance studies assistant professor Antonio Viego, modern Arabic professor miriam cooke (she doesn't capitalize her name), and women's studies associate professor M. Kathy Rudy, respectively—Duke students pay more than $43,000 a year in tuition and fees.

While the Group of 88 took charge of campus political dialogue, the Duke administration piled on. Also on April 6, Tallman Trask told *The New York Times* that the team's "previous boorish behavior" and misdemeanor charges had been a kind of red flag: "'I pulled all their disciplinary records a year ago,' he said, adding that he had found 13 citations for holding malt cans in public and two for public urinating." Trask's suggestion that the players were bad actors contrasted with his statements at the March 24 meeting with the captains that he had been in a similar situation in his youth and at the previous week's faculty meeting that the team's disciplinary record was no big deal.

Brodhead and Alleva told the other Duke head coaches at a meeting on April 6 that Pressler had resigned the day before because "he felt that he could no longer lead the team effectively." Dan Brooks, women's golf coach, retorted that Pressler would disagree with that assessment. So he did, when Brodhead's words got back to him. "I absolutely know my own faults," he told other coaches. "Lack of leadership is not one of them." He had resigned because he thought that might be the only way to prevent Brodhead from killing entirely a lacrosse program that the coach had devoted so much of his life to building.

Kerstin Kimel, who had asked Brodhead during his meeting with the coaches about protecting the guys' safety on campus and about the reports of in-class harassment by faculty members such as Huston, Deutsch, Chin, and others, eventually got a meeting with the president. He told her that the reports of abuse by faculty were exaggerated. When the Duke *Chronicle* asked about the same issue over the summer, John Burness conceded that "rumors" of abuse had occurred but implied that the administration had not investigated them. Looking back on springtime events, Kimel observed, "It doesn't seem right or fair to me that there was no accountability for faculty behavior. As coaches, we're in the kid business. This case exposed that their students aren't the priority of some faculty. The faculty are not invested in kids the way we would think."

Kimel's critique was equally applicable to the Brodhead administration.

Pressler's dismissal left his forty-seven players adrift. Duke provided them with little help. While Dean Sue reminded Pressler of the availability of Duke counselors for the players, their friends, or their girlfriends, the offer never reached the players. And as events got worse in the first two weeks of April, no follow-up from the administration occurred. Such a move, Bo Carrington noted, would at least have been a "weak gesture of support." But Brodhead's message was: no gesture, no support. Kerstin Kimel and Chris Kennedy did what they could on an ad hoc basis. The Duke's men's and women's lacrosse teams had become closer when both moved into the Murray Building a few years before and crossed paths daily. Kimel's office was the first one in the hall, and she provided a sympathetic ear for the guys. Josh Covaleski, a member of the men's team, worked in the women's lacrosse office as a work-study student (a program open only to students on financial aid). Several pairs of siblings— Crotty, Krom, Fogarty—were on both the men's and women's lacrosse teams. Kimel had gotten to know Reade Seligmann when he was recommending a family friend (Jessica McBride) as a recruit.

Meanwhile, by April 11 the administration had forbidden all members of the men's team to work out on their own practice field even though the field was open to members of the general public. "It was good to keep practicing," recalled Carrington, then a sophomore. "It helped keep us focused." The decision reinforced the players' sense that their university had turned its back on them and joined their persecutors. The team had already turned inward for support. After the Ohio State game was canceled, the seniors called a powwow in the weight room to allow players to express their feelings. "We couldn't talk to anyone else about it," noted junior Tony McDevitt. "Our parents weren't here; we couldn't talk to our professors."

The administration's dramatically different responses to Ryan McFadyen's sick-joke e-mail and the Chauncey Nartey e-mail that the Presslers had considered a threat, and about which all the players had heard, suggested at best a callous attitude toward the players and at worst a pernicious double standard.

On April 20, three weeks after Sue Pressler had turned Chauncey Nartey's e-mails over to the Duke police, the Brodhead administration incredibly named Nartey to be one of five students on the twenty-five-person Campus Culture Initiative. Larry Moneta was vice chairman of the initiative, which Brodhead told the Duke community was designed to "evaluate and suggest improvements in the ways Duke educates students in the values of personal responsibility, consideration for others, and mutual respect in the face of difference and disagreement."

Having forwarded the e-mails to Larry Moneta's office, Mike Pressler took copies along to help make his case for reinstating Ryan McFadyen when he went to see Moneta on April 25. "Do we need legal counsel here?" asked Moneta starchly. No, said Pressler, I just want to have a conversation.

The coach noted that McFadyen had been summarily suspended for a joking play on a sick work assigned by Duke professors. Nartey, Pressler said, had implicitly threatened harm to the Presslers' young children. Surely he deserved discipline at least as severe.

"That's not a threat or a suspendable offense," retorted Moneta. "That's an inference." Suppressing the urge to lunge across the table and throttle the man, Pressler yelled, "What? It's got my [child's] name in all caps!"

So: For his very sick joke, Ryan McFadyen was barred from the campus until he could go through the process of winning reinstatement months later. For putting the Presslers in fear of harm to their children, Chauncey Nartey was told to write an apology, which he did. Then, in an undergraduate population exceeding six thousand, he was one of five students entrusted with improving Duke's campus culture.

Why the double standard? Part of it was Moneta's instinct to appease—his detractors might say join—campus extremists. Part of it, apparently, was race: McFadyen is white. Nartey is black. Would Moneta have dealt so leniently with a white student who had sent an implicitly threatening e-mail to a black coach in a racially charged matter?

Dissenting from the politically correct line, on the other hand, proved hazardous at Duke. That's why only one of the more than five hundred members of Duke's arts and sciences faculty—chemistry professor and longtime Pressler friend Steven Baldwin—publicly objected to Mike Pressler being "hung out to dry."

"At the risk of arousing the wrath of the righteous," Baldwin wrote in an April 17 commentary in *The Chronicle*, "Coach Pressler is humble, reserved, thoughtful and honest to a fault. He has great integrity. . . . He was always more interested in his team members as people than as lacrosse players. . . . [H]e wanted to win the right way, with players who were students first and athletes second—players who would be a credit to Duke."

Looking back months later, defense lawyer Bill Thomas evaluated the administration's performance harshly. "Duke University," he lamented, "abandoned these three players and the entire lacrosse team. From the March 14 report of the Duke police, Duke had reason to know this was a false allegation. Duke has a responsibility to independently look at the evidence. When they dissolved the team and fired the coach, that sends a message that they believed the team guilty of misconduct. And that aggravated the adverse publicity and the atmosphere created by the people calling for castration and indictment and even death.

"The atmosphere was created by a false allegation. Leadership is lonely, and you can't lead by watching the print media, the television media. Buckling to adverse publicity is not leadership. Brodhead lacked the courage to stand up and support these boys and their team in their moment of greatest need, and in my view hung them out to dry. The Duke administration is partly responsible for all this."

As to Brodhead's rationale that he needed to defer to the criminal justice process rather than pronounce judgment on guilt or innocence, Thomas said: "It's not up to the criminal justice system to ruin the reputations of the entire team and fire the coach and end the season."

Brodhead had been on campuses all his life. And the conceit that pervaded the reactions of politically correct campuses, as well as politically correct media organizations, in the Duke lacrosse case was aptly described by Michael Barone of *U.S. News & World Report* as it wound down:

"The 'Group of 88' Duke professors, journalists for *The New York Times* and the Durham *Herald-Sun*, and heads of black and feminist organizations all seemed to have a powerful emotional need to believe. A need to believe that those they classify as victims must be virtuous and those they classify as oppressors must be villains. A need to believe that this is the way the world usually works.

"Except it doesn't. Cases that fit this template don't come along very often. In this country, black-on-white crime is far more common than white-on-black crime (black-on-black crime is far more common still)."

If a university president like Brodhead were to acknowledge this reality at a place like Duke, he probably would not be president for long. Not in the alternative universe that much of academia lives in today.

11. POLITICS TRUMPS LAW

Notwithstanding all the moral support that Nifong was getting from Brodhead, Duke's faculty, Durham's black leaders, and the media, he faced a bleak prospect at the end of March.

He needed to bring criminal charges before the May 2 primary to have much chance of keeping his job. And that would not be easy to do. The extremely powerful evidence of innocence could not be concealed from the public and the court forever. To review:

- The police who interviewed Mangum after she had left the March 13–14 lacrosse party found her rape charge incredible, and for good reason. She said nothing about rape to three cops and two others during the first ninety minutes after the party. Only when faced with the prospect of involuntary confinement in a mental health facility did she mention rape. This predictably got her released to the Duke Hospital emergency room for a rape workup, whereupon she recanted the rape charge.

- Then she re-recanted, offering a ludicrous parade of wildly implausible and mutually contradictory stories of being gang-raped by twenty, five, four, three, or two lacrosse players, with Roberts assisting the rapists in some versions and being terrorized by them in others.

- After settling on three rapists, Crystal Mangum gave police hopelessly vague descriptions and could not identify as a rapist any of the thirty-six lacrosse players whose photos she viewed on March 16 and 21. These included two eventual defendants: Dave Evans, whom she did not recognize at all, and Reade Seligmann, whom she was "70 percent" sure she had seen at the party, but not as a rapist.

• All of the other forty-odd people at the party had contradicted every important part of Crystal's various accounts. Kim called the rape claim a "crock" and said they had been apart less than five minutes.

• Contrary to claims by Nifong, medical records showed no physical evidence of rape or assault, let alone injuries consistent with Crystal's claim of being beaten, kicked, strangled, and raped anally, orally, and vaginally by three men in a small bathroom for thirty minutes.

• Above all, DNA tests by the state, which Nifong's office had said would "immediately rule out any innocent persons," did just that. The world did not yet know this. But Nifong did, no later than March 29.

• Crystal told the UNC doctors that she was drunk and on the muscle relaxant Flexeril, which can have side effects including badly impaired judgment when taken with alcohol.

• She had a history of narcotic abuse and bipolar disorder, a mental illness marked by wild mood swings from mania to depression, and had spent a week in a mental hospital in 2005.

• Her business was stripping and one-on-one paid "dates" with men in motel rooms, arranged by "escort" services.

• She had copped a misdemeanor plea in 2002 to avoid trial on multiple felony charges after she had picked a cabbie's keys out of his pocket during a lap dance, driven off in his cab, led police on the high-speed chase, laughed maniacally while driving right at a cop who had exited his car, and smashed her car into his when he jumped out of the way.

• This was not the first three-man rape she had claimed to have suffered, though Nifong, because he did no checking into her credibility, appears not to have known the details. A decade before, in the rural town of Creedmoor, fifteen miles north of Durham, she had told police she had been gang-raped—by three men, in a bathroom. She never pursued the charges.

- The lacrosse players had withstood enormous pressure from parents, lawyers, and the university, as well as from Nifong and the police, to spare themselves by fingering any guilty teammates—if any there were.

After the March 16 and 21 photo sessions it was clear that Mangum had no idea what her rapists (if any) looked like. By the end of March it should have been clear to any prosecutor that there probably had been no rape at all.

But Nifong had inflamed passions with dozens of guilt-presuming, race-baiting public attacks on the lacrosse players. Black leaders and voters made it clear that his only chance of winning the primary was to put his money where his mouth was by indicting lacrosse players for a rape that he must have known they did not commit.

Nifong's solution was to close his door to defense lawyers offering evidence of innocence and to rig a multiple-choice test with no wrong answers. On March 31, he took the extraordinary step of instructing police to conduct a *third* photo ID lineup, and the even more unusual step of showing Crystal (and telling her that she was being shown) photos of only the forty-six white lacrosse players. This decision flagrantly violated Durham, state, and federal principles for reliable identification procedures.

These principles stem from a universal recognition among experts that erroneous eyewitness identifications are the most prolific source of convictions of innocent people. Witnesses are supposed to identify suspects whom they clearly recognize as assailants. But many guess. Some lie. Some pick suspects whose pictures they have seen in the newspaper or on TV. Many pick whomever police point to through suggestive statements or body language, whether conscious or unconscious.

So familiar are these problems that the Supreme Court has long held unduly suggestive lineups and photo-identification procedures to be unconstitutional. Experts in policing have devised detailed guidelines to minimize the risk of erroneous identifications. All involve the use of at least five "fillers" (nonsuspects) for each suspect, to test whether the witness is fabricating the alleged crime or simply cannot recall what the perpetrator looked like. Various other safeguards protect against suggestiveness.

In 2004, North Carolina's prestigious Actual Innocence Commission recommended that:

- The individual conducting the photo or live lineup should not know the identity of the actual suspect [to avoid] misidentifications resulting from unintentional influences from those conducting the identification procedure.

- Witnesses should be instructed that the suspect may or may not be in the lineup.

- A minimum of eight photos [with seven fillers per suspect] should be used in photo identification procedures.

- Witnesses should not receive any feedback during or after the identification process.

- Fillers should resemble the witness's description of the perpetrator in significant features (face, profile, height, weight, build, posture, gait, voice, specific articles of clothing, etc.).

- When there is an inadequate description of the perpetrator, or when there is a suspect whose appearance differs from the description of the perpetrator, fillers should resemble the suspect in significant features.

The Durham Police Department adopted some of these recommendations in February 2006, in its General Order 4077 on Eyewitness Identification: The department required an officer uninvolved in the investigation to supervise the process; the officer, in turn, would instruct the witness that the lineup might or might not contain suspects. While the department did not adopt the AIC's recommendation for seven filler photos per suspect, General Order 4077 did require the department to use five filler photos per suspect in all lineups.

The police-run photo-ID sessions on March 16 and 21 complied to some extent with this Durham order. Clayton was a somewhat independent investigator; he told Mangum that "the person who committed the crime may or may not be included" and that "you should not feel like you have to make an identification"; and five fillers were shown with each of the prime suspects. But in an obvious violation, the "fillers" were other white Duke lacrosse players—i.e., witnesses to the alleged crime, and soon to be suspects.

Nifong tossed aside the March 16 and 21 photo sessions not because of these flaws, but because Crystal could not identify any assailants. Indeed, the outcome suggested that she would probably never be able to *reliably* identify any assailants. As Iowa State professor Gary Wells, a national expert on photo lineup identifications who had consulted with the Actual Innocence Commission, explained to *The News & Observer*, "Memory doesn't get better with time. That's one of the things we know."

Nifong dictated a process designed to allow and encourage Crystal to name three lacrosse players for him to indict. Almost any three would do, with little risk that she would pick one of the few who had not been at the party.

The district attorney instructed Gottlieb and Himan to show Crystal photos of all forty-six white team members and only them. By then they were all suspects, Nifong had said, even though she had identified as a rapist not one of the thirty-six whose photos she had previously viewed. There would be no fillers, let alone the 230 (five per suspect) required by the police department's rule.

In confining the lineup to members of the lacrosse team, Nifong ensured that Mangum would never see the photos of at least two people that police knew attended the party. On March 28, Himan—following up on information the captains had voluntarily provided him—had confirmed that two other Duke students, members of a fraternity, attended the party. But candidate Nifong had been telling the world that lacrosse players were the rapists. So lead investigator Nifong simply excluded the non–lacrosse players from the pool of suspects. (Subsequent DNA tests, made after Nifong obtained indictments, proved that the other two Duke students had no more connection to the alleged crime than did any lacrosse player.)

Violating another rule, Nifong allowed Gottlieb, the top police investigator on the case, to run the show. He also had Gottlieb tell Crystal that all the photos were of people the police believed attended the party, contrary to the requirements of General Order 4077. The planned lineup also deviated from common practice elsewhere in North Carolina—virtually every city or town of more than 15,000 people requires at least five filler photos in all lineups and has a standard policy of telling witnesses that the photo array might or might not include the suspect.

On April 4, starting at 11:29 A.M., Gottlieb carried out Nifong's instructions. The setting was a police station, with lots of cops in attendance and Clayton taking notes. Crystal was videotaped and audiotaped seated in front of a large computer screen showing head shots of the forty-six white lacrosse players for sixty seconds each. Gottlieb told her that it was "important" for her to the say whether she recalled "seeing any of the persons to be shown and to describe what they were doing." The whole setup almost screamed: You'd better pick some people.

Mangum's responses on April 4—as on March 16 and 21—demonstrated her unreliability in myriad ways, quite apart from the issue of which players she ultimately chose. More important, Nifong had access to information that proved her unreliability—and ignored it.

For instance:

- She said that she was 100 percent certain she saw Brad Ross "standing outside talking to the other dancer." With that identification, Ross became the only player that Mangum twice identified with 100 percent certainty as attending the party. But Ross had unimpeachable electronic records showing that he was in Raleigh visiting his girlfriend the night of the party. Said Iowa State's Wells: This flawed identification placed Mangum "in the questionable category of eyewitnesses who [are] capable of being positive and wrong. That's a red flag."

- She said that she didn't recognize the player who took the digital camera photos of her that would prove so critical in establishing the timeline.

- She incorrectly identified the team member who made the broomstick comment—choosing instead someone of a different hair color, body type, and height. In their statements, two of the captains had revealed the identity of the team member who made the rude remark.

- Other than the incorrect identification of Ross, Crystal failed even to recognize the three other team members she had described herself as 100 percent certain of seeing at the party in the March 16 lineup.

As for the supposed attackers, each identification also raised strong questions about Crystal's veracity. She actually identified four players as her possible assailants. Gottlieb, for reasons that are not clear, raced past her first identification to move on to the three players ultimately selected.

Crystal picked Collin Finnerty—even though Finnerty bore absolutely no resemblance to any of the three descriptions she had made on March 16. After being only 70 percent sure on March 16 that she even saw Reade Seligmann somewhere at the party, by April 4 she was 100 percent certain that Seligmann "looks like one of the guys who assaulted me." That would be enough for Nifong to indict.

When Dave Evans's photo came up on the screen for sixty seconds, Crystal—who had not recognized him at all on March 21—stared, squinted, leaned forward, then cocked her head to the side. After fifty seconds, she said, "He looks like one of the guys that assaulted me, sort of."

"OK. How, um, how sure of it are you on this image?" asked Gottlieb. "He looks like him without the mustache," Crystal said. "OK, so the person had a mustache," Gottlieb said. "Yes," she replied. "Percentagewise, what is the likelihood this is one of the gentlemen who assaulted you?" "About 90 percent," Crystal said. Evans never had a mustache—before the party, during the party, or after the party.

In one sense, Crystal's choice of defendants was unerring: The woman who had vowed to "get paid by the white boys" just happened to pick white boys from the wealthiest towns on the team, at least judging by the median incomes of the towns where they lived, as found on the Census Bureau's Web site.

Crystal's insistence that Evans had a mustache suggests another possibility. It would have been easy just to pick him. She had seen and spoken with Dave that night, with no mustache. So why insist that he had one? Was part of Crystal trying to get out of this by making picks that she thought could never hold up? Might this also have been a reason for picking other players with whom she had never even spoken?

Given the difficulty of retroactively putting a mustache on Evans, Nifong decided that his first two defendants would be Collin Finnerty and Reade Seligmann.

At the same time, with the SBI reporting no DNA matches to the lacrosse player, Nifong had Officer Soucie call Brian Meehan, the head of a private lab called DNA Security, Inc. It could perform more sensitive "Y-STR" testing, which isolated male DNA. Meehan seemed eager to be involved and offered to negotiate on price.

Also on April 4, Soucie recorded: "Mike Nifong stated that: Also need documentation on escort service and how they do business. Need to nail down what victim did on the day before arriving at 610 N. Buchanan so we can show that she did not receive trauma prior to the incident—with witnesses."

Implicit in the need to "nail down what victim did on the day before" was the fact that Nifong and the police had *not* nailed this down yet. Indeed, they had apparently not looked into Mangum's pre-lacrosse-party activities at all. Might the vaginal swelling ("diffuse edema") reported by the Duke hospital on March 14 have come from her energetic sexual activities *before* the lacrosse party? Nobody had checked. Instead, Nifong made multiple public assertions that the hospital report was conclusive proof of a rape.

Meanwhile, also on April 4, Nifong spurned an entreaty from defense lawyer Bill Thomas, who represented Bret Thompson and had known Nifong for twenty-seven years, to slow down his rush toward indictments and investigate the case thoroughly. If you plunge ahead, warned Thomas, you will be making a big mistake, and will look political as well. "He told me that he had interviewed the victim and that he believed her and she was convincing and he was going to proceed as he thought necessary," Thomas later recalled.

In subsequent statements to the court, Nifong would claim that neither he nor anyone from his office had ever interviewed the "victim" until more than eight months later.

The next day, April 5, every officer involved in the investigation convened to discuss what they needed to do before any indictments could be obtained. Once again, only Soucie provided detailed notes of the meeting, although all officers were required to do so. In her notes, Soucie said that the officers agreed they needed to speak to Devon Sherwood. They needed to interview, or try to interview, some of the players. They needed to touch base again with Kim Roberts. They needed to examine the captains' computers. They needed to talk with Matthew Murchison, described as Mangum's "boyfriend." They needed to obtain from her a precise timeline of her activities in the forty-eight hours prior to the party at 610 North Buchanan.

No record exists that Nifong did any of these things before proceeding with indictments.

Police did interview Jarriel Johnson, one of Crystal's "drivers," on April 6. That was when he described taking her to jobs in three hotels with three different men on the Friday, Saturday, and Sunday before the Monday-night lacrosse party and having sex with her himself that Saturday night. (He later amended this to a week earlier, which avoided contradicting Crystal's claim that she had not had sex for a week before the lacrosse party.) Johnson also described her behaving erratically and repeatedly demanding that he stop the car on the side of the road so she could walk away and urinate.

This was not the kind of evidence that Nifong wanted. So he simply didn't use it.

It was also on April 6 that the police, under Nifong's direction, finally got around to having Crystal herself write out and sign a description of the alleged March 14 rape. Coming twenty-three days after her initial interviews by police and medical personnel at the hospital, this delay in taking an official statement was unheard of. It reflected the extraordinary difficulty of getting her story straight.

The five-page statement contradicted all of Crystal's previous versions as well as Roberts's March 22 statement to police. In this version, Matt raped her vaginally and anally (not orally, as in her March 14 version) and "hit me in my face." (She had previously denied being hit in the face or anywhere else.) Adam raped her orally (not anally, as in her March 14 version), ejaculating into her mouth. Bret raped her vaginally and orally (which was two more rapes than Bret committed in her March 14 version).

And for the first time, Crystal said that the lacrosse players had started yelling racial slurs and threats during the dance itself. That "Nikki"—instead of stealing her money and helping lacrosse players rape her, as Crystal had charged on March 14—had joined her in running out to the car "screaming and crying." That Dan and Adam had apologized and lured them back with a promise of another $1,200. That Adam (not Matt) said he was getting married the next day.

Crystal also said—in a story explicitly contradicted by Roberts—that "three guys grabbed Nikki, and Brett, Adam, and Matt grabbed me and they separated us at the master bedroom door, while we tried to hold on to each other."

Had Nifong believed his "victim," he would surely have pressed to find out the identities of the three accomplices who had "grabbed Nikki." But in his March 27–April 3 media interviews, he had described *three* assailants, not six. So he ignored Crystal's claim. Indeed, the DA also quietly abandoned his earlier talk of prosecuting as aiders and abettors any and all lacrosse players who had assisted—or failed to prevent—the alleged assault.

After Crystal's April 6 statement, Nifong essentially stopped investigating, except for ordering more DNA tests from an expensive private lab, and focused on campaigning. The DA left undone much investigating that would have been done by any prosecutor whose goal was to find the truth. A truth-seeking prosecutor would have reinterviewed Roberts about the many contradictions between her and Mangum. Nifong did not, leaving it to CBS's *60 Minutes* and ABC's *Good Morning America*, which months later aired Roberts's revelations of dramatic new evidence that Mangum had fabricated the rape charge.

A truth-seeking prosecutor would have personally interviewed Crystal in detail. Nifong never interviewed her at all, and he did not have a representative of his office speak to her about the events of the night until December 21—when she would contradict virtually everything she stated on April 4 and 6. He would have asked Crystal, who had very clearly made many false and contradictory statements, to take a lie-detector test, as was publicly urged by one of Nifong's most prominent supporters, Duke law professor and former judge Robinson Everett. He would also have sought copies of the more than twenty photos taken by a lacrosse player at the party, which defense lawyers described as evidence of innocence. Not Nifong. He sent Gottlieb to the Raleigh NBC station *after* obtaining indictments to seek copies of the photos, which *The Abrams Report* had aired on national television.

A truth-seeking prosecutor who believed his own claims that lacrosse players might destroy evidence and that Finnerty and Seligmann were dangerous, violent rapists would have sought warrants to search their dorm rooms and to arrest them immediately after Mangum fingered them on April 4. Not Nifong. He waited *more than two weeks* to search their rooms and arrest them.

More stunning still, while pronouncing the lacrosse players guilty in the national media, Nifong repeatedly spurned offers by defense lawyers to show him evidence that they were innocent. Defense lawyer Joe Cheshire offered in an April 7 letter to Nifong to bring Dave Evans in to answer any questions Nifong might have. Nifong did not respond.

Other defense lawyers also tried to show Nifong evidence of innocence, with similar results.

It is unheard of for a prosecutor to pass up a chance to see defense lawyers' evidence, for three reasons. First, good prosecutors don't want to pursue charges against innocent suspects. Second, even bad prosecutors don't want to bring charges destined to blow up in their faces. Third, in the event that the case goes to trial, any prosecutor will be in a far better position to counter defense evidence about which he knows in advance.

Why did Nifong avoid pursuing so many obvious lines of inquiry? Why did he spurn defense lawyers' efforts to show him evidence of innocence? The most plausible explanation for Nifong's actions is what lawyers call willful blindness: Knowing that Mangum might say anything, Nifong did not want to hear her say that she could or would not go through with it. And knowing that the lacrosse players whom he was determined to indict had much exculpatory evidence, Nifong did not want to see clear proof of their innocence. In this respect the DA resembled Richard Brodhead, who had his own reasons for avoiding direct exposure to evidence of innocence.

By this stage, Nifong surely knew that once the rape case had run its course there would be efforts by lacrosse players, their parents, or their lawyers to seek his disbarment, as well as to sue him, for gross prosecutorial misconduct. Among the probable charges was violating a state bar ethical rule stating, "A prosecutor should not intentionally avoid pursuit of evidence merely because he or she believes it will damage the prosecutor's case or aid the accused."

Nifong could be accused of violating this rule, or even of criminally violating the lacrosse players' constitutional rights to due process of law, by refusing to look at evidence of innocence. Indeed, corporate executives are now serving long prison terms for willfully blinding themselves to avoid guilty knowledge of incriminating facts. One is former WorldCom CEO Bernard Ebbers, who was convicted of securities fraud based on the judge's instruction that he should be convicted if he "deliberately closed his eyes to what otherwise would have been obvious . . . in order to escape the consequences of criminal law."

But for Nifong to go after the lacrosse players *after being shown* clear proof of innocence would be an even more flagrant violation, one more likely to bring disbarment or suspension. Better, from this warped perspective, not to look.

Meanwhile, defense lawyers told reporters on April 9 and 10 that photos taken at the party established a time line inconsistent with the accuser's rape charge, including a photo of her with a with a smile on her face after the time of the alleged attack. Other photos, taken during the four-minute performance, showed her seemingly drunk or severely impaired, with bruises and scrapes on her legs.

The biggest defense bombshell came when the State Bureau of Investigation's report on the DNA evidence was finally delivered thirteen days after Nifong had learned of the results. Defense lawyers got a copy while meeting in the late afternoon of Monday, April 10, in Bill Thomas's downtown Durham office. After a quick study, they gathered on the courthouse steps nearby in front of the television cameras.

"No DNA material from any young man tested was present on the body of this complaining witness," Wade M. Smith announced. "The DNA was not present within her body, not present on the surface of her body, and not on any of her belongings or articles of clothing." Thomas added that none of Mangum's DNA was found anywhere in the bathroom where she had supposedly been kicked, beaten, strangled, had her head banged on the sink, and gang-raped anally, vaginally, and orally for thirty minutes. "We hope with this, Mr. Nifong will announce he is not going to pursue this case further," added Smith. "Mr. Nifong asked for these tests—a very extraordinary procedure—saying they would help clear the innocent."

"This report is a very dramatic report," Joe Cheshire said. "This report shows they're innocent." He explained that "our experts tell us that gang rape by three men would leave material to be examined," even if they were wearing condoms, as Nifong had (falsely) suggested. Collin Finnerty, seeing the news, did high fives with friends.

NCCU law professor Irving Joyner expressed more muted—and, it would turn out, fleeting—concern with Nifong's changing approach to DNA. "He seemed to be waffling there," Joyner told *The News & Observer*. "That's going to make him look weak and present the notion that he is trying to benefit politically."

The DNA confirmed what the defense lawyers already knew from many hours spent grilling their clients and many more hours investigating the other evidence. Several told friends privately that they would be proud to have their clients as sons.

Unbeknownst to the defense lawyers, Nifong, Gottlieb, and Himan had spent that same afternoon meeting with Brian Meehan at DNA Security, Inc., the private lab Nifong had hired to do more testing. Calling from the car on his way to the lab, Nifong told his campaign manager, Jackie Brown, that he was expecting important information. What Meehan told Nifong was even more devastating to the prosecution's case than what the defense lawyers would announce that evening. Meehan's analysts had discovered the DNA of as many as four males on the rectal swabs and panties from the rape kit, and none of it matched any lacrosse player. How could three violent, ejaculating (in at least one case), condomless rapists possibly have contrived to leave no trace of themselves amid all that other male DNA left over from earlier encounters?

These findings were virtually conclusive proof of innocence. So Nifong and Meehan agreed not to report them, as Meehan later admitted in court. They kept this secret—along with a similar finding of multiple-male-non-lacrosse DNA on the pubic hair comb—for more than six months, until doggedly brilliant sleuthing by defense lawyer Brad Bannon, Joe Cheshire's younger partner, cracked their scheme to hide this stunning evidence of innocence.

Nifong's instructions to DNA Security were, Durham defense lawyer Bill Thomas later explained, "the equivalent of telling a detective, 'Go get fingerprints from a crime scene and if you don't find any that match our suspects but you do find other fingerprints, I don't want you to report that.'" Nifong phoned Brown on his way back from Burlington: The tests results, he lamented, were not what he had hoped to receive. His mood—upbeat earlier in the day—was noticeably depressed during this phone call.

Instead of facing the truth, Nifong responded to the defense press conference later that night by saying: "The absence of DNA doesn't prove anything." He did not discuss what the absence of lacrosse-player DNA might mean when combined with the presence of DNA from multiple *other* males. Whether he even thought about this, or was so determined to see only any evidence pointing to guilt—of which there was none other than Crystal's inconsistent statements—is unclear. Indeed, to reconcile these DNA findings with her story would have required believing that *after* three men gang-raped her, she had sexual contact with between two and four *other* men before proceeding to Duke Hospital for the rape kit examination.

For most Duke students, on the other hand, "DNA day was a huge turning point," senior Adam Chandler recalled months later. "Nifong had said that the DNA would be the whole case, so when the DNA tests came back negative, I naïvely believed that the case could not go on." From that point forward, most Dukies were convinced that the rape charge was a fraud and Nifong a scoundrel.

Not so the media or the faculty. "The DNA kind of ruptured their story line," Chandler recalled. But their reaction was reminiscent of a Winston Churchill aphorism: "Men occasionally stumble over the truth, but most of them pick themselves up and hurry off as if nothing had happened." Still in a paroxysm of delight over Ryan McFadyen's "kill and skin" e-mail, most in the media were not about to let proof of innocence spoil their fun.

As Dave Evans and some teammates watched the defense press conference on television, he later recalled, "We were all elated at first. Finally we feel this vindication, that everybody's going to stop bad-mouthing us and making up these lies. We expected that everything would change with the DNA. We were watching all the talk shows so we could see what they were saying." Some saw the DNA as evidence of innocence, but "we change the channel and we see Nancy Grace and these people start making up these wild schemes and making up ways that it could have happened, explaining away the science with pure subjective irrational thought, instead of saying, 'My gosh, they were telling the truth.' And I realized that no matter what, people were against us. They just shamelessly start slandering us and making up reasons why there would be no DNA and find a way to make us guilty. They do it under the veil of the law. When Wendy Murphy goes out and compares me to Hitler, she's clearly out of her mind. But because they say she's a former prosecutor, she gets credibility."

As for the district attorney, Evans added, "at every juncture you'd expect Nifong to say, 'Well this is evidence we're going to take into consideration.' Instead, the response was always that doesn't change our mind a bit. The more we saw the blind approach Nifong was taking, that was what kept me awake at night."

The New York Times put the defense bombshell on the sports page. Reporters Duff Wilson and Juliet Macur rounded up people to dispute the defense claims, even obtaining a quote from Peter J. Neufeld of the Innocence Project, which has used DNA testing to free nearly two hundred wrongly convicted people. Neufeld's quote sounded skeptical of the defense's DNA case. But he explained later that this was because Duff Wilson had not told him "anything about any of the details in the case." The *Times* reporters also went out of their way to revisit McFadyen's "saying he planned to invite strippers to his dormitory room and kill and skin them," and to parrot the prosecution's assertion—later proven false—that "medical records and interviews that the police obtained by subpoena showed the woman had injuries consistent with being raped and sexually assaulted."

Times sports columnist Selena Roberts also picked herself up as if nothing had happened, declaring in a column the next day that "Duke's lacrosse members established a *Lord of the Flies* ethos in Durham." She praised the efforts of Durham's "hard-boiled district attorney," condemned the team's "atmosphere of degradation" and "symptoms of misogyny," and demanded that Duke initiate "a fresh discussion on race, gender and respect."

CNN's Paula Zahn, like most other major media figures, was not the least bit interested in what the DNA results might suggest. She complained of "what seems to be a concerted effort by friends of the defense to trash this alleged victim"—as if pointing out DNA results and other evidence casting doubt upon the accuser's story was somehow reprehensible. She was also outraged to hear Crystal Mangum called a stripper, even though this was undeniably true.

While most in the media gave the DNA bombshell modest play, some openly mocked it.

Former prosecutor Wendy Murphy, a favorite of CNN's Nancy Grace, because Murphy could always be counted on to spin evidence of innocence as proof of guilt, set the standard less than two hours after the April 10 defense press conference. The absence of a DNA match, Murphy claimed with a straight face, made the accuser more credible. How so? Well, "maybe what she said" to police was that the rapists did not ejaculate! (In fact, Crystal had said the opposite.) "What they did," Murphy explained, "was clam up and say, 'Let's stick together so we can get away with this.' Look, I think the real key here is that these guys, like so many rapists—and I'm going to say it because, at this point, she's entitled to the respect that she is a crime victim. These guys watch 'CSI,' and they know that it's a really bad idea to ejaculate on or in the victim."

The next day Murphy said on MSNBC's *The Situation* that Flannery, Zash, and Evans "have been, according to neighbors, reportedly been involved in not only carousing activity but other sexual offenses." This was false. Two days after that she asserted on Fox's *The O'Reilly Factor* that "all of them took the Fifth. All of them refused to cooperate." False again. None of them ever "took the Fifth" or refused to cooperate with police. Previously she had asserted that the accuser had a "torn genital area." False yet again.

Such stuff created a great demand for Murphy, who explained her premise on MSNBC: "I never, ever met a false rape claim, by the way. My own statistics speak to the truth." In her Duke lacrosse case commentary on Fox, MSNBC,

CBS, and CNN, Murphy compiled a record of demonstrably untrue statements, wholly unfounded speculation, and disregard for due process. Murphy is a former assistant district attorney in the child abuse unit in Middlesex County, Massachusetts, and adjunct professor at Boston's New England School of Law, focusing on sexual violence. She has regularly contended that the legal system discriminates against women. To many viewers she seemed an extreme feminist ideologue.

Wild speculation? "I bet one or more of the players was, you know, molested or something as a child," Murphy declared on *CNN Live*. Nazi comparisons? "Hitler never beat his wife either," she declared in dismissing a comment of MSNBC's Tucker Carlson that the lacrosse players had good disciplinary records. "So what?"

Ludicrous self-contradiction? Murphy told Carlson that the DNA tests had come back negative "because a broom handle was used, which by the way, doesn't produce DNA when you put it inside someone." False; even the accuser and Nifong had made no claim that a broom was used. Six days later, on May 2, Murphy mystified another guest on MSNBC's *Rita Cosby: Live and Direct* by declaring that "the broomstick DNA has not yet been revealed." Broomstick DNA? Police had never taken the broom from 610 North Buchanan because Mangum had never mentioned it during the more than sixty hours between the alleged rape and the March 16 search.

Presumption of innocence? "I'm really tired of people suggesting that you're somehow un-American if you don't respect the presumption of innocence, because you know what that sounds like to a victim? Presumption you're a liar."

So the DNA testing that had been seen as the crux of the case was now just a bump in the road.

The *Times*, like-minded journalists such as Paula Zahn and Wendy Murphy, and many other major news organs also chose not to report a revelation about the accuser's criminal record that appeared in some other publications on April 7. That was Mangum's June 2002 arrest after stealing a cab and leading police on a reckless high-speed chase. The detailed police report makes interesting reading:

"As she was feeling him up and putting her hands in his pockets she removed the keys to his taxi cab, without him knowing. He told her he would drive her home but needed to go to the restroom first. While in the restroom he was advised that she was driving off in his taxi cab." The cabbie called 911. An officer chased the woman at speeds up to 70 miles per hour in a 55-mile-per-hour zone, as she ran a stop sign and drove on the wrong side of the road with headlights off, finally stopping after trying to drive through a fence.

The report continues: The officer said he got out and told the woman to turn off the engine. She laughed, backed up the car, then drove forward again and nearly hit the deputy. The taxi slammed into the deputy's car and kept going, turning into oncoming traffic. Another officer chased her until the taxi got a flat tire. Officers boxed it in, pulled the woman out, and arrested her. Mangum registered a blood-alcohol concentration of 0.19, more than double North Carolina's 0.08 legal threshold for impairment. While being questioned, she "passed out and was unresponsive."

Mangum, whose driver's license had been revoked before the incident, was charged with a series of felonies, including assault with a deadly weapon on a government official. Under an extraordinarily lenient plea bargain, she pleaded guilty to four misdemeanors, served three weekends in jail, and was placed on two years' probation.

Duke's activist professors were no more interested in such insights into the accuser's character and credibility than was *The New York Times*. On April 12, the African-American Studies program convened yet another panel on the affair, this one bringing together Group of 88 organizer Wahneema Lubiano; Group of 88 member Thavolia Glymph, an assistant professor of history and African-American studies; and potbanger Serena Sebring, a Duke graduate student. A panelist complained that "since the DNA results were returned Monday, we [have been] moving backwards." Why? Because "students now feel issues such as race and gender no longer need to be examined." Advancing the Group of 88's pedagogical causes required setting aside the evidence that the players were innocent.

For Lubiano, there was no moving backward. In a blog posting three days after the DNA revelations, she dismissed the news as part of a "demand for perfect evidence on the part of the defenders of the team." (It was actually not the team's defenders but Nifong, of course, who had first stated that "DNA evidence requested will immediately rule out any innocent persons.") Even as the radical faculty saw the administration consistently accept their demands, she portrayed herself and her fellow extremists as so lacking influence that "we have to yell in order to be heard. . . . Regardless of the 'truth'"—meaning the small matter of whether anyone was raped—Lubiano asserted that "what people are asking is that something changes." She did not specify what change she wanted.

Others had more particular agendas. In an op-ed in the April 12 *News & Observer*, Orin Starn, a professor of cultural anthropology, sought to use hatred of the lacrosse team to promote his longtime goal of getting Duke out of all Division I athletic competition. Then, he said, students could focus on "pursuit of knowledge and learning"—such as, presumably, the kind of teachings offered by Wahneema Lubiano and Houston Baker.

Starn made some reasonable points: "Competing at the Division I level drains so much time and energy that athletes cannot do their best in the class-room, much less have anything like a well-rounded, broadening college expe-rience. Isn't it a sign that something's out of kilter when a great university like Duke is known before anything else for its basketball team? And its highest-paid employee is the basketball coach . . . ?"

But he couldn't resist taking swipes at "the fiasco of the lacrosse team . . . a sense of entitlement, a jockish beer-bust mentality and a parochial team in-bredness that can breed loutish behavior." And while preferential admissions for football players did have what Starn saw as a happy side effect—bringing in more black students—he clearly preferred basing admissions decisions on race, not on athletic talent.

Senior Wintta Woldemariam, president of the Black Student Alliance, complained at an April 12 meeting that "what disgusts me is the media is fram-ing the issue" as "a black woman versus white male issue." She seemed obliv-ious to the fact that her own professors had done more than anyone but Nifong to racialize the case.

Had Nifong harbored any doubt that he needed to bring charges against lacrosse players to have much hope of winning the May 2 primary, it was dis-pelled the morning after he received the damaging DNA news from Dr. Mee-han. In an April 11 forum at NCCU, ostensibly addressing the issue of violence against women, the mostly black crowd of seven hundred was seething with anger, clamoring for arrests, and overflowing with conspiracy theories about the DNA.

Nifong arrived with several aides, "strutting" to the stage, one witness re-called. In his opening remarks, he reveled in the spotlight, saying, "I'm some-body who probably most of you didn't know before a few weeks ago, and now everywhere I go, I've got newspapermen following me around, and television cameras." He mentioned the defense attorneys' press conference on the DNA test results, only to dismiss it: "I hope that you will understand by the fact that I am here this morning that my presence here means that this [case] is not go-ing away." The crowd erupted in applause, and Nifong reiterated his pledge that "this case is not over."

On the other hand, the crowd booed lustily when Duke student govern-ment president Jesse Longoria cautioned that people needed to "allow the justice system to find the truth." Nifong kept the audience clapping when he restated "my conviction that a sexual assault actually took place," based on "the examination that was done at Duke Hospital." He hinted that the ac-cuser had identified one or more rapists. And he deprecated the DNA tests, while suggesting that there would be more. "For most of the years I've been doing this, we had to deal with sexual assault cases the good old-fashioned way," Nifong declared. "Witnesses got on the stand and told what happened to them." Nifong did not mention the fact that "for most of the years [he'd] been doing this," sophisticated DNA testing did not exist; neither did he mention the expert consensus that the kind of assault described by the accuser would have had to leave her DNA in the bathroom and lacrosse-player DNA on and in her.

"Anytime you have a victim who can identify her assailant, then what you have is a case that must go to the jury," Nifong added. The false implication was that as a matter of law the he had no choice but to bring charges, no matter how strong the evidence of innocence. In fact, while North Carolina law makes it hard for a *judge* to dismiss such a rape case without a jury trial, *the district attorney always* has the option of not bringing charges or dropping them if discredited. Indeed, Nifong's office had dropped more rape charges (thirteen) than it had taken to trial (twelve) over the previous year.

But while these remarks all triggered applause, the crowd was not satisfied. Shawn Cunningham, an NCCU senior, accused the press of having "disrespected this young lady"—even of going so far as to suggest that she "deserves to be assaulted, sodomized, raped, abused, or beaten." (Given the almost uniformly pro-Nifong coverage at this time, it remains unclear to which publication Cunningham was referring.) Two other NCCU students asked why Duke hadn't immediately expelled the entire lacrosse team, as Houston Baker had demanded. Another NCCU senior, Tolulope Omokaiye, said, "This isn't the first incident of racial acts with the lacrosse team," since "it's a privilege sport and there's power and all that and Duke, and . . . the racial comments they've made to other people and things of that nature."

Omokaiye further charged that "we all know if this happened at Central and the young lady was from another school or another persuasion the outcome would have been different." When Nifong denied the claim—"there has never been a case under me where the decision was made based on race"—the crowd started to murmur. Another NCCU student, Chris Bridge, mocked Nifong: "It strikes me as funny how we can say let's just wait for justice to play its part and clearly justice hasn't been served and isn't going to be served anytime soon." Pastor John Bennett, who two days before had led a protest outside 610 North Buchanan, announced that "the moment that they were accused" the lacrosse players "should have been handcuffed; they should have been arrested; and then bail should have been set."

Then NCCU graduate Victoria Peterson arrived at the microphone. A perennial, unsuccessful political candidate, Peterson was best known for her far-right crusades against gay rights and abortion rights. Now she adopted race-baiting conspiracy theories. The reason for the negative DNA results, she declared, was that people at Duke University Hospital had "tampered" with the evidence. The crowd cheered. The lacrosse players "should be in jail." More applause. Nifong defended the integrity of the investigation, explaining that "Duke University Hospital is the best trauma center in the area," and he lectured Peterson "that your comments are exactly what this case does not need right now." The crowd hissed at the DA.

In the audience, Tricia Dowd shook her head as she heard Peterson's remarks. Sitting next to five female students from NCCU, she said she was a friend of the lacrosse team, and asked them whether they believed Peterson's wild claims. All five nodded yes. Dowd asked them why. One replied, "Because he [pointing to Nifong] told us they did it."

The final questioner offered an even more extreme position than had Peterson. Harris Johnson, a longtime official in the Durham Democratic Party, noted that, in the past, black students who had fit a profile had been mistakenly arrested. He fumed, "Those lacrosse players met the profile; why weren't they arrested?" Applause. "Is there a double standard of justice law and order without justice?" More applause.

Nifong, visibly taken aback, asked whether, because innocent black men were wrongly arrested, Johnson wanted the forty-three white nonrapists on the team arrested as well. The DA maintained, "I want to convict the right person and I don't want anybody who did not commit a crime to be arrested or put on trial." This remark met with catcalls and screams from the crowd, and the forum then ended. As members of the crowd surged toward him, Nifong required a police escort to exit the building.

NCCU junior Chan Hall, an elected member of the student government who later would narrowly fall short of being elected its speaker, made explicit what appeared to be widespread sentiment at the forum. He told *Newsweek* that Duke students should be prosecuted "whether it happened or not. It would be justice for things that happened in the past."

"That meeting was like a political pep rally for an indictment," Bill Thomas later observed. "It was the worst thing that I've ever seen in a criminal case. Politics and law simply do not mix."

Dave Evans had started to watch this production on television, but after a while, he later recalled, "I had to turn it off. Nifong would say this case isn't going away and the crowd would roar. People were up there screaming. This man was an out-of-control freight train. At no cost was he ever going to slow down."

Joe Cheshire, meanwhile, saw the reactions of many black Durham leaders during this time as "a reverse O. J. Simpson in which truth matters nothing and we have a chance to get these rich white boys no matter what the facts." A man who takes pride that "my family has been involved for generations and generations in trying to help lift the black race," Cheshire was seeing race relations more strained than in years. He deplored "the dark underside of both black and white racism and of a number of black leaders who do little for their people but whenever something goes wrong or simply does not go as they wish become demagogues playing the race card and blaming everything on white people irrespective of the truth. As a result they push white moderates further and further away from the real issues confronting our nation about race."

Cheshire added: "I can't walk down the street without white people coming up to me and saying that this is the worst injustice in forty years in the South. I've never seen people so angry about a criminal case, and I wonder if they would feel the same if the defendants were black kids."

As the police escorted the district attorney though the angry NCCU crowd, Nifong learned that his "victim" seemed to be getting cold feet. She had called Himan a few hours after the defense lawyers' televised DNA news conference. "She stated that she felt bad (not wanting to hurt herself but depressed about what has been going on)," Himan later wrote. "She stated she thought it would be easier. She stated she wanted to talk with some [sic] but did not want to think that she was crazy. She asked for counselor's number. I gave her number for rape crisis counselor. Amy Wilkinson."

Nifong needed to keep Crystal Mangum on the team. He met her for the first time hours after the NCCU forum—and twenty-eight days after the alleged rape. Gottlieb, Himan, and police lieutenant Mike Ripberger were there, too. "She probably did not speak fifteen words," Nifong was later to claim in court. "She had trouble making eye contact. She looked like she was going to cry."

Nifong did not discuss the case with her at all, he said, because she was "still so traumatized from this offense." Never mind that she had *not* been too traumatized a week before to play her part in the rigged photo-ID process on which Nifong was relying to target two players for indictment despite a mass of evidence that they were innocent. Nor did Nifong *ever* interview his "victim"—an almost unheard-of aloofness from the facts.

Nifong's version of events contradicted Gottlieb's subsequent statement in a thirty-two-page memo that on April 11 "the victim and District Attorney Nifong met one another and discussed the case." Not to mention the "traumatized" Crystal's acrobatics at the Platinum Club on March 23, 24, 25, and 26, or her March 18 boast that "I'm going to be paid by the white boys."

Nifong played the racial demagogue at another campaign forum on April 12, declaring: "The reason that I took this case is because this case says something about Durham that I'm not going to let be said. I'm not going to allow Durham's view in the minds of the world to be a bunch of lacrosse players at Duke raping a black girl from Durham."

After these remarks, his two opponents, Freda Black and Keith Bishop, who had generally avoided public comment on the Duke case, finally started criticizing Nifong's behavior. Bishop, the only black candidate in the race, suggested that Nifong had oversold his case to woo black voters. "Do you want to live over the next four years with what we have endured over the last three weeks?" he asked voters. "It's no wonder this community is as fragile as it is and is able to break like a twig under the unsteady hand of the incumbent." Turning to Nifong, he said, "Don't put the public through this kind of discord. You should have some compassion both for those who are accused and for the victim. I would have done things a lot differently—with integrity."

Black, who had been the front-runner, tried to use the April 12 forum to regain her footing after weeks of Nifong dominating the news. She charged that his demonizing of the lacrosse players had crossed ethical lines, risked a change of venue, and divided the community. "Perhaps," Black said, the DA "thought he landed a case that would save his prosecutorial career. Now the damage has already been done. Some of the damage is most likely irreversible. Durham has been portrayed in a negative light nationally. When the cameras leave, who will pick up the pieces?"

According to subsequent testimony given by Ben Himan, he asked a simpler question when told by superiors that despite the lack of evidence and the procedurally flawed April 4 lineup, Nifong planned to seek indictments. "With what?" Himan asked.

12. BLIND INJUSTICE:

INDICTED AFTER PROVEN INNOCENT

NIFONG'S FAILURE TO ARREST Collin Finnerty and Reade Seligmann for two full weeks after April 4, when Crystal Mangum identified them as assailants, was all the more striking given the loud demands from the Durhamites whose votes he wanted that he lock up the "rapists."

Why had he not arrested them as soon as he decided to charge them? In the previous year, Nifong's office had gotten alleged rapists off the streets of Durham as quickly as it could. Even in the thirteen rape cases where Nifong ultimately agreed to dismiss the charge, the defendant was arrested.

Nifong appears to have followed a different course in this case to exploit a loophole in North Carolina law. In the Tarheel State, as in most, the main judicial check to a prosecutor's arresting a demonstrably innocent defendant and forcing him to trial is the so-called "probable cause hearing," a sort of truncated minitrial.

In this case, of course, Nifong had no serious evidence at all except for Mangum's inconsistent and wildly incredible succession of stories. At a probable cause hearing, defense lawyers could have destroyed her credibility, especially if she showed up to testify. In attacking probable cause, they could have also demonstrated the unreliability of Nifong's rigged April 4 photo-ID process and any in-court identification Crystal might be asked to make thereafter. And they could have sought to introduce the DNA results and any other evidence of innocence already in their hands.

Such a hearing would have been a disaster for Nifong. His claim-to-fame case would probably not have been dismissed—not with a friendly judge presiding. But Nifong would have been humiliated and his case torn to shreds in open court. This alone might very well have cost him the primary election.

Fortunately for Nifong, North Carolina prosecutors routinely avoid probable cause hearings by submitting cases to a county grand jury, which, under North Carolina law, is a secret proceeding where only the state can present evidence, where the defense is not entitled to be present or challenge evidence or present its own evidence, where the proceedings are not recorded, and where the law prohibits anyone from discussing what goes on inside the grand jury room. And that's exactly what Nifong did in this case, in the process leaving the alleged rapists at large for two weeks until the Durham County grand jury's next regular meeting, on April 17.

Nifong also moved on April 12 for Judge Stephens's permission to seal indictments of Reade Seligmann and Collin Finnerty that he would have the grand jury issue at its regular meeting the day after Easter. Sealing the indictments, a tactic regularly used when the accused is a flight risk, was another way for Nifong to imply the players' guilt. The next day, while preparing to indict two innocent young men to win his election, he said on the campaign trail: "The reason you should vote for me for DA is I would rather do the right thing than win this election."

Nifong was evidently still worried about a loose end: What if either or both of the two players he was about to indict could quickly show that he (or they) had not been at the stripper party at all? Such a development might be devastating to Nifong's case, his career, and his pension. So on the night of April 13, Himan, Gottlieb, and other police went without warrants into the dorm where Reade Seligmann and Collin Finnerty lived.

Duke campus cops let the Durham officers into a locked dorm—illegally, perhaps—in what the Brodhead administration would later call a low-level blunder. The Durham officers spent seventy-five minutes asking lacrosse players which team members had *not* been at the party. Since Nifong was personally directing the investigation, this move seemed to be a clear violation of the state bar's ethics code provision prohibiting a district attorney or someone representing him from questioning people known to be represented by counsel without obtaining the lawyers' permission. Most players refused to answer the cops' questions. One or two did respond.

"We're on your side," one cop sweet-talked sophomore Rob Wellington, a close friend of Reade Seligmann's. "We're fighting for you guys. Can you tell us what happened that night?" Wellington sensed that his questioner was deceitful.

The next day, Himan tried pumping Ekstrand, saying at one point that he thought Seligmann had never been at the party.

Such was the background when defense lawyer Bill Cotter told Ron Stephens during a preindictment session that he thought Nifong might charge someone who wasn't even at the party. "Bill, in your wildest dreams," the judge responded, with a knowing look over his glasses. One of the lawyers wondered whether the judge had been getting private briefings from the DA.

During this preindictment period, "All of the lawyers sat in my conference room talking about who it was going to be," recalled Bill Thomas. "We always thought, 'Well, she's going to pick the guys who lived in the house, who met her and talked to her.' Collin and Reade we never even considered because they never spoke to her or had anything to do with her. She was throwing darts and we just didn't know where they were going to land."

But as Easter weekend approached, the word started spreading through the lawyers that Nifong had indicated it would not be any of the captains. Suddenly everyone else on the team felt more exposed. Ekstrand told his clients that any one, two, or three of them could be indicted and that they should be ready to turn over their passports and to post bond if arrested. One of the retired New York firefighters came to Durham with the deed to his house in case he might need it to post bond.

It "felt like Russian Roulette," Seligmann was later to tell Ed Bradley on 60 *Minutes*. "It could have been any single one of us. Kids were even calculating their chance . . . the percentage . . . that you would get picked."

Bill Thomas decided to make one last effort to show Nifong that he was about to make a horrible mistake. He called Butch Williams, another Durham defense lawyer (for Dan Flannery) who had also known Nifong for many years, and Wade M. Smith of Raleigh, the universally respected, courtly, sixty-nine-year-old dean of the state's criminal defense bar. Nifong himself was later to say of Smith: "I don't know of an attorney in North Carolina that would question Wade Smith's integrity."

If he will listen to anyone, thought Thomas, he will listen to us. The three went to see Nifong on Friday, April 14. They asked him not to rush indictments on April 17, when the grand jury was scheduled to meet, and instead proposed a dialogue in which they would disclose their own evidence, including the photos taken at the party and interviews of the lacrosse players. This material, they said, would reinforce the proof of innocence provided by the DNA evidence that Nifong already had.

"He looked at us," Thomas later recalled, "and said, 'Gentlemen, I know a lot more about this case than you do. Thank you for coming down.' I was astounded at his refusal to discuss the evidence with us. I have never seen anything like that in my professional experience."

As Nifong walked the three defense lawyers to the door, he started to say—in a voice suddenly laced with anger—something like, "And you can tell that Joe Cheshire"—when Butch Williams cut the DA off before he finished the sentence. They did not want to hear him venting against Cheshire. This, too, mystified Bill Thomas. He thought of Cheshire as a wonderful person and lawyer, a straight shooter, honest and forthright. He later asked Cheshire what Nifong might have against him. Cheshire said he had no idea.

That same Friday, Nifong called Richard Brodhead to notify him confidentially that two Duke lacrosse players would be indicted on Monday. This was the only conversation that the two men ever had.

"That Easter weekend was one of the worst moments in my life, as it was for forty-six other families," Larry Lamade later recalled. "Nifong had indicated that he was going to indict at least three lacrosse players the week after Easter. All the lacrosse families knew the allegations were false, but all had to retain attorneys. We felt like the men of the USS *Indianapolis* in World War II after their ship was sunk. They bobbed hopelessly in the waters of the Pacific for days while the sharks indiscriminately picked them off. Innocence did not mean that the boys were not vulnerable. It was a Kafkaesque moment. Your son could be indiscriminately indicted. Multiple choice—no wrong answers. Were you praying that your son not be indicted? Of course. Would there be any relief if he were not indicted? No. Collin, Reade, and David could just as easily have been Peter, Ned, and Matt. We were all in this together. The truth had been trampled."

The inevitable Jesse Jackson—claiming that "something happened"—recited a host of factually incorrect "facts" (that Mangum had never before danced at a party, that Devon Sherwood didn't attend the party). He vowed that his Rainbow/PUSH Coalition would pay Crystal's college tuition even if she were proven to have lied.

"My son is being pursued by a pack of wolves," MaryEllen Finnerty had felt for weeks. Over Easter weekend, Collin learned that he was on the short list of possible defendants. But still nothing was definite. Was it a list of three? Of thirty? The next few days were an emotional roller coaster. Collin canceled a planned trip to a Mets game Friday night to hang out with his longtime girlfriend, Jess. He spent a relatively carefree Saturday with friends from his high school, Chaminade, in Minneola, Long Island. Then came trouble sleeping and nightmares about being indicted. He and Jess went to Manhattan's Chelsea Piers and talked about how this might be their last normal night together.

On Easter Sunday, MaryEllen and Kevin Finnerty took their son and fled their home in Garden City, Long Island, for fear that Nifong might put on a show for the media by having Collin dragged away in handcuffs. On this, the holiest of days in the Christian calendar, the devoutly Roman Catholic Finnertys could not go to their own church. They hid out in a New York City hotel, leaving Collin's two younger sisters, Molly and Emily, with friends.

That morning's *Los Angeles Times* kept the media bandwagon rolling with a long piece headlined: "Lax Environment; Duke Lacrosse Scandal Reinforces a Growing Sense That College Sports Are Out of Control, Fueled by Pampered Athletes with a Sense of Entitlement."

CNN's Paula Zahn came on that night, sounding like a paid mouthpiece for Nifong. She dripped with arch incredulity at defense lawyer Joe Cheshire's assertion that no assault had occurred. How, Zahn wondered, could Cheshire explain the accuser's "internal injuries"? Why would she have "made up this story"? The truth was that no "internal injuries" had been found and that Crystal had claimed rape to get out of being locked up in a mental facility. But Cheshire could not yet be sure of that, because Nifong had not yet turned over this evidence. Zahn also asserted confidently that Nifong "would not be proceeding with this case if he didn't believe that this alleged victim had been raped" and that he must have the evidence to prove it. Wrong again.

The Finnertys spent Monday morning, April 17, waiting for Collin's lawyer in Durham to tell them who had been indicted under seal by Nifong's grand jury. Finally the phone rang. Kevin answered and scribbled, Collin sat on the bed reading over his shoulder: "If there are indictments, Collin will be one . . . 90 percent sure there will be indictments." The big kid fell back on the bed. It was the first time he had cried since a friend's murder by terrorists on September 11, 2001.

"How can this happen in the country we live in?" MaryEllen Finnerty asked herself. Her son had never been contacted for questioning by police or prosecutors. Never been asked to testify to the grand jury. Never given a chance to show that he had left before any rape could have occurred.

It could happen because grand juries are rubber stamps. The notion that they protect defendants—*any* defendants—against prosecutorial abuse is a fraud. The old adage that any prosecutor could get a grand jury to indict a ham sandwich—for the murder of the pig, in a longer variant—is valid in most states and especially in North Carolina, which does not even transcribe or tape-record witnesses' testimony.

As in most states and the federal system, prosecutors choose the only evidence that grand jurors hear. They use hearsay and other evidence inadmissible in trial. They need not tell the jurors about evidence of innocence, no matter how strong. Not surprisingly, it is very rare for any grand jury in North Carolina or anywhere else to turn down a prosecutor who asks for indictments. This is well known to every lawyer and every sentient journalist who spends any time covering criminal justice in this country. But that did not stop dozens of TV lawyers and journalists from citing the grand jury indictments as showing that Nifong must have strong evidence that Finnerty and Seligmann were guilty of rape.

Writing in the *Baltimore Sun*, Rick Maese asserted, "I know that a grand jury indictment means the prosecutor feels like he has the case, like he's ready to stand in front of a jury the very next day and get a guilty verdict." On Fox, USC law professor Susan Estrich—who would later come to a very different view of the case—accused defense lawyers of trashing the "victim" with "a vigor I have never before seen in the 25 years I've been writing about and teaching rape law" rather than operating "the way things are supposed to work." The defense, she wrote, "should have presented its evidence to the District Attorney before he went to the Grand Jury seeking indictments; did they?" Of course, they had tried to do so, and Nifong had refused to see them. Nancy Grace hailed the grand jury as a critical check on the prosecutor, noting that "the grand jury can actually open up the floor to questions to, say, the detective or the victim, the alleged victim herself." She brought on a defense attorney, Nicole Deborde, who noted that "one of the things that the prosecution potentially could have done is actually bring her into the grand jury to testify. They could have subpoenaed additional people from that house to testify in that grand jury . . . and those records would then be available not only for the defense but for the prosecution, as well, and future use in trial."

In reality, the Durham grand jury heard no testimony from Crystal Mangum, Kim Roberts, any lacrosse player, any doctor or nurse, or anyone else with firsthand knowledge of what had happened. The only witnesses were two cops who had already lied repeatedly to the players and the court about the case: Gottlieb and Himan. According to North Carolina law, no record remains of what they were told—despite what Grace and her guest informed television viewers. The grand jurors, evenly divided along racial lines, even though the county is only 38 percent African American, indicted eighty-one people in the space of a few hours that day. They obviously had no time to do anything but approve without serious deliberation all of the indictments drafted for them by Nifong's office.

Months later, after the fraudulence of the case and Nifong's conduct had become a national scandal, one of the grand jurors who had indicted Finnerty and Seligmann told Chris Cuomo of ABC News: "Knowing what I know now and all that has been broadcast on the news and the media, I think I would've definitely made a different decision. I don't think I could've made a decision to go forward with the charges that were put before us. I don't think those charges would've been the proper charges based on what I know now."

That same morning, which happened to be Richard Brodhead's fifty-ninth birthday, Joe Alleva and Tallman Trask echoed Nifong's trashing of Collin, Reade, and their teammates. The Duke officials did not quite call them "a bunch of hooligans." But they were quoted expatiating on the team's "boorish behavior" in the April 17 *Herald-Sun* and *Chronicle*. Dean Sue made similar comments. Trask added that lacrosse players had been "caught hitting golf balls onto East Campus." The article did not mention that this had happened *in 2002.*

After learning of Collin's indictment on charges of first-degree rape, first-degree sex offense, and kidnapping, the Finnertys flew to Raleigh-Durham and checked into the Washington Duke Inn under an assumed name.

Phil and Reade Seligmann were already in Durham. What with Phil's post-9/11 business misfortunes and Reade's run of injuries at Duke, Kathy worried that Reade might also be unlucky in what some called the "Crystal lottery." Phil thought that he would be in the clear because he had left the party so early.

Reade and Phil were sitting around at a lawyer's office that Monday with Reade's roommate Jay Jennison, his father George, and Rob Wellington, killing time by playing video games and reading newspapers while awaiting word of who had been indicted. "It was like waiting for a sword of Damocles to cut you in half," Phil later recalled. A phone call brought the bad news. Crystal had picked Reade. It was the first time the son had ever seen his father cry.

Reade called Kathy. It was her birthday. She was at a lacrosse game, watching her twin boys Maxwell and Cameron, both Delbarton juniors, following in their big brother's athletic footsteps. "Mom," he said, "she picked me." Kathy was in shock. Reade made her promise not to watch him being arrested the next morning on TV.

Phil and Reade immediately got moving to nail down Reade's alibi evidence. First they picked up records of the ATM withdrawal that Reade had made as his first stop after leaving the party. Then they tracked down Moezeldin Elmostafa, the cabbie who had picked Reade up at 12:19 A.M., while the alleged thirty-minute rape had to have taken place. The cabbie remembered the young athlete and his generous tip and signed a hastily drafted statement for Phil.

Meanwhile, Joe Cheshire had recommended that the Seligmanns retain Kirk Osborn, a seasoned, widely respected defense lawyer and onetime public defender from nearby Chapel Hill. "We needed someone who was not going to be afraid," Cheshire later recalled, "because this is going to be a war. He was very smart and a good lawyer with a lot of courage. This was a war against someone we both knew to be evil." Osborn, a six-foot-four, three-year letterman on the University of Colorado football team, who at age sixty-four was still as fit as most twenty-five-year-olds, had defended more than a dozen capital murder defendants and saved them all from being sent to death row. He was known for fighting clean but very hard.

That night from seven to ten, Reade and Phil had their first meeting with Osborn. "They're absolutely innocent," Phil had declared in a preliminary phone conversation. "Well," thought Osborn, who had represented more than fifty murder defendants, "I've heard that before." But it didn't take much time with Reade for the lawyer to become a believer.

"I love Reade," Osborn said months later, after the sole practitioner and his friend and fellow lawyer Ernest L. "Buddy" Conner Jr., had yielded the lead role in Reade's defense—and a grateful client—to a larger law firm from Charlotte, North Carolina's biggest city. "I was immediately attracted to him. I was awed by him, really. He was such an exemplary guy. He had never done anything wrong. When things started to go bad at the party he had had the good sense to get out of there. I didn't know what to believe at first. But after talking to him I believed that nothing had happened, just as Joe Cheshire had told me."

Reade and Collin encountered each other at five the next morning, April 18, in a Durham parking lot. That was the appointed time and place to surrender to Durham police. Then came the jail cell, the fingerprinting, plus some patter from Sergeant Gottlieb, who seemed a nice guy at the time. He even asked Collin if there was anyone in Durham whom they wanted the police to look after on their behalf. Reade, asked the same question by Himan, said yes: the other lacrosse players.

To avoid the media siege, Kathy Seligmann had moved out of her own home and taken refuge at a friend's house with the twins and fourteen-year-old Benjamin. The morning of the arrests, she found Ben sobbing in the basement TV room. "Why are they doing this to him, Mom?" the boy asked. Kathy looked over at the TV. There was Reade—a hero to his little brother—in handcuffs, being led to jail.

Reade was not sobbing. He was angry. He carried himself with pride, ramrod straight, while handcuffed. And he approached his indictment as a challenge. The Seligmanns' pride in their oldest son burned brightly through the fears and hardship. "The kid is a rock," Phil said months later, when asked how Reade was handling the pressure. "I'm not half the man that kid is—he is so courageous and tough. From the start, he told me, 'Dad, it's a no-brainer. The truth is on our side.'"

But having the truth on your side only goes so far, the defendants and their families were learning, when the district attorney, the cops, and many in academia and the media are bent on destroying you.

Collin found himself waiting his turn in a courtroom while a convicted child molester was sentenced. This was the worst day of his life. A mob of photographers burst through the door, surging within inches of his face. He tried to remain expressionless. In that atmosphere, if he had smiled the media would have called it a smirk; if he had frowned they would have called it an angry glare.

Reade and Collin were both released after a few hours on $400,000 bond, a sum set far higher than the bond for most murder defendants in Durham. Judge Stephens said they were "flight risks" because they were from out of state. That might have been more convincing had the judge bothered to have them turn in their passports. Nifong understood that Finnerty and Seligmann weren't flight risks; he wanted a large bail to suggest to Durham voters that he had apprehended dangerous criminals. Kirk Osborn and Julian Mack, Reade's first lawyer, hustled him out the back door of the courthouse to a car so that they could escape most of the media mob. Someone stuck a microphone in Osborn's face. He said his client was totally innocent.

Then Osborn and Mack went to Nifong's office to urge him to look at their alibi evidence, which they said would show that it was impossible for Reade to have been part of any rape. But Nifong, who had known Osborn for twenty-five years, refused to see them or look at the evidence. Instead, he sent an aide with this message: "Mr. Nifong says that he saw you on TV declaring your client is absolutely innocent, so what is there to talk about?"

There was plenty to talk about. Unlike most alibis, Reade's did not depend on the testimony of friends or family. There were time-stamped photos showing that the dancing had stopped at 12:04 A.M. There were phone company records of Reade's eight cell calls between 12:05 and 12:14, the last being to a taxi service. There was the cabbie's matching phone record, plus his written statement that he had picked up Reade and Rob Wellington at 12:19, a block from the party house, and had taken them to an ATM machine five minutes away, where Reade got cash. There was a bank record of Reade withdrawing cash from the same ATM at 12:24. And later, Osborn also tracked down the security video showing Reade at the ATM from 12:24 to 12:25, and got a more detailed, signed affidavit from the cabbie showing that he had also taken Reade and Rob from the ATM to the Cookout Restaurant, where they bought food to go, and then back to their dorms, where an electronic record showed Reade swiping into his dorm at 12:46.

During this same period, in photos time-stamped from 12:30:12 through 12:31:12, Mangum was smiling and unmussed on the back stoop of the house, trying to get back in; in a 12:37:58 photo she was passed out on the back stoop; and in the 12:41:32 photo she was being helped into Roberts's car by an unindicted player. At 12:31, a lacrosse player also captured a brief video of Mangum exclaiming, "I am a cop."

When could Reade have fit a thirty-minute gang rape into this schedule?

The Seligmanns went from the courthouse to Bob Ekstrand's office, where Reade, his dad, Osborn, Ekstrand, and Stef Sparks spent much of the next two days attacking Reade's alibi from every angle, as they debated whether they could risk making it public.

When Tricia Dowd saw Reade and Collin get out of the police car in handcuffs, she thought to herself, "Oh my God, what has this man done?" Later in the day, Dowd dropped by Ekstrand's office to say good-bye before returning to Long Island. When she saw Reade, she started to cry. He came over and hugged her, saying, "Mrs. Dowd, don't worry. I have an alibi; I can take the bullet for the team. If they were going to pick anyone, I'm glad they picked me." Dowd stayed in the office for an hour and a half: Reade remained upbeat throughout.

Reade's alibi evidence was made public in stages, which may have diluted its impact on public opinion. Lawyers for other players dribbled some of it out on the day of the arrests. The cab driver, Moezeldin Ahmad Elmostafa, a Sudanese immigrant, confirmed what Reade had said about his role on an April 20 CNN program. Osborn made most of the rest of the alibi evidence public on May 1, as an attachment to a court motion.

From that point forward, no serious student of the case had any doubt: Seligmann was innocent of rape. He was innocent of standing by while others raped. He was also, it would soon became clear, innocent of abusing women. Innocent of racism. Innocent of thuggishness. Innocent, even, of hiring strippers, a decision in which Seligmann—and, for that matter, Finnerty—had no part and for which they had had no enthusiasm.

But Nifong continued to assert Reade's guilt. Duke continued to treat him like an outcast. And many a journalist and professor continued to call for his head. The inimitable Wendy Murphy, for one, dismissed the photographs establishing that the rape could not have occurred before Reade left. "All the photographs . . . were doctored, where the date stamp was actually fraudulent," Murphy speculated without a shred of evidence. Even Nifong had made no such claim. And experts hired by defense lawyers confirmed the accuracy of the time stamps by digging into the underlying metadata, which are almost tamper-proof.

All this kept a possible thirty-year prison term hanging over Reade, ruined his college experience, and drained his family's savings. Reade later told Ed Bradley of 60 Minutes what it was like:

> To see my face on TV, and that, you know, in those little mug shots, and above it saying, you know, "Alleged rapists." You don't know what that does to me and to my family and to the people that care about me. . . . Your whole life, you try to, you know, stay on the right path, and to do the right things. And someone can come along and take it all away, just by going like that. [He pointed a finger.] Just by pointing their finger. That's all it takes.

Even so, Reade told more than one teammate: "I'm glad they picked me. I can prove I was not there."

Collin was not glad they picked him. He took it very hard, worried about the effects on his family. He, too, had a good alibi: He had never been near Crystal after the dancing had stopped. Nor had he ever been in the bathroom where the attack allegedly occurred. Finnerty's legal team fingerprinted the bathroom, from top to bottom, and found no prints from Collin. That result came as no surprise: Finnerty never set foot in that bathroom — either on March 13–14 or at any other occasion in his life. From 12:10 until 12:20, as Roberts and Mangum went to the back of the house, Finnerty and several other members of the team milled around for a brief period in the living room. At no point during this period was Collin ever alone; several members of the team recalled seeing him leave through the *front* door. At 12:22 A.M., in the first of a series of eight cell-phone calls, Finnerty called another member of the team and asked whether he wanted to get something to eat. Five minutes later, he received a call from a different member of the team; they talked about where and what to eat. By this point, Collin had gone to the house around the corner rented by William Wolcott and K. J. Sauer — he had to pick up his Playstation, which he had left there. Finnerty's legal team had later used technical means ("triangulation") to prove how his eight calls were made "on the move" and in different zones away from Buchanan house.

In short, as of 12:27 A.M. on March 14, 2006, Finnerty had unimpeachable electronic evidence to prove that he was not at 610 North Buchanan. For the next half hour, he made several more calls and then walked across East Campus to pick up food at Cosmic Cantina, a Mexican restaurant. A credit card receipt showed Jay Jennison, one of the team members with Collin, paying Cosmic Cantina at 12:56 A.M. Finnerty then took a cab back to his dorm. And, of course, even more than Reade, the six-foot-five, rail-thin, freckle-faced Collin looked nothing like the three "plump," far shorter assailants whom Crystal had described to police on March 16.

But in those days nobody would take the word of any Duke lacrosse player, or any of his friends, for anything. And Nifong had not revealed such evidence of innocence as Crystal's March 16 descriptions. It was also clear from Kirk Osborn's experience that Nifong was bent on prosecuting Collin and Reade no matter what the evidence; he would (and later did) simply change his allegations to get around the alibis. So Wade Smith, Collin's cagey, conservative lawyer, kept his cards close to the vest. The details of Collin's alibi would remain secret until any trial.

After the release of Reade and Collin on bond, the Finnertys returned north. (One consequence of being charged with a violent felony was suspension from Duke.) They found their home besieged by TV trucks. Kevin Finnerty parked some distance away and got close enough on foot to see cameramen trespassing in his yard to shoot through the windows of his home. A helicopter buzzed overhead. The Finnertys drove east, to their vacation home in Westhampton Beach. The media had not yet found it. They would. The Seligmanns arranged to stay at a friend's house in Connecticut.

The media mob was in full cry. One of the very few guests who tried to speak up for the presumption of innocence, Stephen Miller, of the Duke Conservative Union, was worrying "that two innocent people may have possibly—" when Nancy Grace, his host, impatiently cut him off: "Oh, good lord! . . . I assume you've got a mother. I mean, your first concern is that somebody is falsely accused?"

Conservative MSNBC host Joe Scarborough, showing the versatility of cable news at spewing venom from the right as well as the left, announced: "The ax falls at Duke as two star athletes are busted on rape charges adding to an ugly all-star team of accused rapists, wife beaters and murderers who have filled the ranks of college and professional sports teams over the past several years."

On Fox, Wendy Murphy declared that "we are all being spun by a group of defense attorneys" claiming to have evidence of innocence. "Why didn't he go to the DA with this information?" she demanded. The answer of course, was that defense lawyers *had* gone to the DA with powerful evidence of innocence, and the DA had refused to look.

And in cnnsi.com interviews, the outrageously biased Lester Munson, identified by *Sports Illustrated* as its "legal expert," displayed how ready some liberals were to throw the presumption of innocence into the trash for all practical purposes in their zeal to dump vitriol on the lacrosse players. Munson dismissed DNA evidence—which has cleared many an innocent poor defendant—as virtually irrelevant except to prove guilt: "There are hundreds of convicted rapists in prison even though there was no sign of their DNA in the examinations of their victims . . . the absence of DNA is not conclusive by itself." He also falsely implied that the team had a history of "previous predatory conduct."

The next day, the better to slime Reade Seligmann, Munson went to astonishing lengths to convict *all* defendants who say they have alibi evidence: "You don't see many alibis in criminal cases—it's a very rare thing. Ordinarily, 99 times out of 100, the police have the right guy, and you'll find that most people arrested were involved in something. Getting the wrong guy is very unusual."

So why not just send all defendants straight to prison, or to the execution chamber in capital cases, without trial? Munson did not explain. Ironically, in Munson *Sports Illustrated* had hired a "legal analyst" who had forfeited his license to practice law in Illinois. In 1991, the Illinois Attorney Registration and Disciplinary Commission moved to disbar him because of his continued misconduct while on probation for "neglect of three client matters as well as misstatements regarding the status of two of the client matters." He entered into a plea bargain to voluntarily give up his license.

"The media," MaryEllen Finnerty said later, "are disgusting."

One of the very few journalists who leaned against the pack was Chris Cuomo of ABC News. He interviewed Brian Loftus, who had two sons on the Duke team, on *Good Morning America* on April 18. "This man and his family come from Syosset, New York, they're working class," Cuomo said by way of introduction. "He's a former fireman and a veteran of 9/11. He speaks to us about how sending his kids to Duke University, let alone to play on the lacrosse team, was a dream, and that now all of these families are dealing with almost unimaginable pain."

> CUOMO: *"Two young men that you knew are now known at least to the system as potential felons. How do you deal with that?"*

> LOFTUS: *"You know, Chris, when I got word today that my kids weren't two of the kids being indicted, it, you know, . . . it was a relief. But right now, I'm sick to my stomach. Like I told you, I'm not an emotional person, but I started crying earlier today because those two kids' lives are ruined, I mean, just totally ruined. For the next six to nine months they're going to be scrutinized and looked at as criminals. I know these kids. And—it's the furthest thing from that. . . . I heard about this was when one of my sons was going to the precinct to give DNA. I asked him 10 times, I said, 'Did anything happen? Both my sons vehemently, all they ever told me, that, Dad, nothing happened, nobody did anything.' "*

> CUOMO: *"We hear about the 'Blue Wall of Silence,' not talking about the police, but the Duke Blue Devil lacrosse players. Do you think that's fair?"*

> LOFTUS: *"It's not fair. These kids were willing to take polygraphs, these kids were willing to take blood tests, they were willing to come down and give statements. They did everything. They gave their DNA. We thought that once we give that, we—thought it was going to be over. . . . But every night, every day, all we see on the TV is that we're hiding something. Obviously,*

there's nothing to hide. . . . I feel like the world has been pulled from under-neath my feet. My kids—when you hear them sobbing on the phone that, that their lives are like destroyed and you hear other people saying the same thing to you, you just wonder what went wrong? We know nothing went wrong. I cannot stress that any more. Nothing happened that night."

Nobody who knew Collin or Reade well ever believed for a second that they were capable of such a crime. Yani Newton, a friend of both, learned of their indictments when a weeping friend came down the hallway waking every-body up. The sophomore women sat in their pajamas watching TV in disbelief. "If you had to pick two people from my class, those would be two of the last you'd pick," Yani recalled. "I thought, no way this could have happened. This is bullshit." Kertsin Kimel, the women's lacrosse coach, called to check on how Yani was bearing up. She could no longer hold back the tears. She didn't un-derstand how this could be happening, she told the coach.

Yani and some other women made a banner saying WE SUPPORT DUKE LACROSSE and hung it out their window for the camera crews to film. Every day from then on she proudly wore Duke lacrosse insignia. "I was like a walking billboard," she said later. "I felt that there was some power in me saying this. . . . I understand the power of me not being white." Yani has African-American, Native American, English, Irish, and Italian blood. This ancestry, she later said, "is at the end of the list of characteristics or attributes that describe me." But if she could use it to help her friends a little bit, she would.

A "Support for Reade Seligmann" petition soon circulated at Duke and elsewhere. "I met Reade in high school and ever since then he has stuck out in my mind as the most caring and honorable individual I have ever met," wrote a young woman. "He's the most amazing person I have ever met, with the biggest heart." Others wrote: "Everyone that knows Reade loves him"; "one of the most kind and gentle people I know"; "one of the least violent people I know"; "the nicest person I have ever met."

Collin's friends and family also rallied around him, for many long months. "He is such a gentle soul," mused Eileen Cornacchia, MaryEllen Finnerty's sister and best friend, "that it is a knife in the gut to think that someone could try to mess with his life the way they did." A well-known figure in Palm Beach, Cornacchia described the effect on the family in an e-mail to a friend:

Kevin has been working 28 hours a day—8 days a week—to clear his son.This, while trying to get his fledgling Hedge Fund Company off the ground.This is my family's defining moment. Everything is designated as either before or after the Collin thing. We are all different people than before this happened. I used to enjoy the Palm Beach social thing, the black tie charity galas, chaired several of them myself. All that is over—seems empty now. We have circled the wagons—kept our real friends—keeping family close—cherishing all of the children in our large family—creating events to gather us all together whenever possible. We are strong Irish stock— overachievers—and extremely close. Talk about a slap across the face wake- up call as to what really matters—this was it. Now we talk about things like The Innocence Project, the judicial system, academia in America, the press, judges, injustices of all kinds. It's all different now. Nothing petty anymore, lots of grace and empathy and positive action when necessary. Time with Collin is so precious.

The day after the indictments, Bo Carrington talked things over with his Spanish instructor, a graduate student. She started out very hostile, saying that she lived in the Trinity Park neighborhood and feared that Duke students were committing rapes there. Then Carrington mentioned that Reade Seligmann was one of the two students indicted. The instructor had taught Seligmann in a course the previous semester. "All of a sudden," Carrington later recalled, "she went from an accusatory position to being so sad that Reade was being caught up in a big lie. She started talking about how sad it was that Reade's picture was all over the news. She knew Reade and therefore *knew* he was innocent. That's all it took, knowing Reade, Collin, or Dave."

Taylor Price, then a twenty-year-old Georgetown freshman, had known both Collin and Reade for years. He had spent some fifteen summers playing tennis and golf with Collin in Westhampton Beach, on Long Island, where the Prices and the Finnertys vacationed, becoming very close friends. Taylor and Reade had been classmates at Delbarton, a high-quality, all-male school in Morristown, New Jersey, run by Benedictine monks.

Taylor loved them both like brothers. He saw Collin as a big, gentle, lov- able kid who never wanted to say or do the wrong thing. Reade was one of the nation's most accomplished high school athletes as well as a quiet leader off the field. Not the type to run for class president, but he was a guy "who would do anything for you."

A loud shriek woke Taylor up the morning of April 18. It was his mother, reacting to the television image of Reade and Collin getting out of a police car in handcuffs. Taylor went through the day in shock. Spending much of it at the funeral of yet another friend's father only made it worse. For weeks he had thought it possible that some lacrosse players had done something to the accuser. But the instant he learned that Collin and Reade could be targets, he became 100 percent certain that nothing could have happened. These were decent, gentlemanly guys, and the allegations went against everything Taylor knew about their characters. Not to mention the fact that both were in serious relationships with their girlfriends.

Talking through the situation with others, Taylor came to what to some seemed a startling conclusion: "What they're going through," he told people, "is a whole lot worse than what I'm going through."

What Taylor was going through was the aftermath of spinal cord injury that had left him a quadriplegic, from a freak accident while diving under a wave off the same Long Island beach that he and Collin had frequented for so many summers. It happened in July 2004. After Taylor was helicoptered to Stony Brook Hospital, the Finnertys and Seligmanns were among the first people at his bedside. Later, Kevin and MaryEllen Finnerty led the charge in organizing a charity golf tournament to raise money for Taylor's long-term medical expenses. After many months of therapy, Taylor entered Georgetown University a year later than planned. He maneuvers around campus in a motorized wheelchair. For the foreseeable future, he has no fine motor skills and will need a full-time attendant. Friends marvel at his upbeat attitude and determination to recover.

How could anyone think that what had befallen Reade and Collin, whom Taylor was confident would be found innocent, was worse than Taylor's own misfortune? "People say, 'Oh, come on Taylor, how can you say that?'" he explained. "But I've had a lot of time to think about it. Some of my physical abilities and the way I move around in life are different. But I'm still Taylor, the same person I always was, and my accident didn't affect my credibility, my reputation, or the way people think about me. For all I know, medical science may change my situation in the future.

"Look at their situation. They have all the same abilities they had, but the way they could be perceived will be different. This changes their reputations. This will always follow them. Twenty years from now, if you Google Reade Seligmann or Collin Finnerty, this will probably come up. Any time they go sign a job application, this is there, and unfortunately forever stays with them. If they walk into a bar, someone might say, 'Aren't you that guy?' And if it's dismissed without going to trial, well, people can think, 'They're white and they're rich and that got them off.'"

Indeed, the media reveled in portraying the Finnertys and Seligmanns as stinking rich. "They came from a world of hushed golf greens and suburban homes with price tags that cross the million-dollar line [and] exclusive, all-boys Catholic prep schools," *The News & Observer* gushed the day after their arrests.

In fact, Phil Seligmann, an intense, self-made man boiling with rage at the treatment of his son, had lost much of his money due to his business setbacks related to the terrorist attacks of September 11, 2001. Raising Reade's $400,000 bond was a tremendous hardship for the family. And the legal costs to come— about $90,000 a month, with the total expected to rise to well over a million dollars—would be especially onerous for a family that had three other sons to put through college. Twins Cameron and Max, both high school juniors when Nifong filed his charges, were also lacrosse stars.

As the media were playing up his supposed wealth, Phil commented wryly to friends: "I live near three country clubs; I can't afford any of them and two wouldn't have me as a member." He especially resented the "racism" smear. Born a Jew, he had endured anti-Semitic slurs growing up. And he had been raised largely by an African-American woman after his mother was killed by a falling tree that had nearly killed seven-year-old Phil, too. Reade's mother, or-phaned at fifteen, was born Protestant. The parents sent their sons to a Roman Catholic school. But nobody was giving the Seligmanns points for multicultur-alism, or for enduring hardships, in that spring of 2006.

When Phil and Reade were starting the long drive home to New Jersey two or three days after Reade's arrest, Phil pulled into a Durham car wash. Waiting outside for their Ford Explorer to go through the machinery, Reade, wearing a hat and sunglasses, tried not to look like the six-foot, one-inch, 225-pound jock whose face had been on millions of TV screens.

It didn't work. "Dad," Reade said with some urgency, "it's time for us to leave." Four black car-wash workers were buzzing among themselves and one was making gun-to-head and other menacing gestures with his finger at Reade. Would they attack the defendant accused of a racially motivated rape of a black Durham woman? The Seligmanns did not want to find out. They pulled away and headed north, toward home, leaving Duke and Durham be-hind them as fast as they could.

Kevin Finnerty, one of five boys from a close-knit family of modest ori-gins, was another self-made man, and rich in more ways than the media imag-ined. He had worked to support himself from age fifteen and started college on a swimming scholarship. It took ten years to pay off the loans. He had bor-rowed money to buy an engagement ring for MaryEllen, his longtime girl-friend. Then Kevin had made it big on Wall Street in a succession of financial jobs. He had an extraordinarily loving family. He was also an exceptionally generous and self-effacing donor to charities, especially to a mission in Tan-zania run by a childhood friend who became a priest.

Kevin and MaryEllen, granddaughter of a New York City fireman and of Irish immigrants, had five children, all good athletes. They were very religious

Catholics, and she devoted herself to her kids, who called her "the strictest mother in America." "This is an incredibly tight family who are happiest when they are sitting around the family room after dinner sharing stories and laughing," said a close relative. "They adore each other." Kevin, the relative said, "has told me personally on many occasions that he is the most surprised of anyone at his financial success and the great blessing of his family and he knows that God is watching what he does with what he has. He is truly the most generous person I have ever met."

Collin and Reade and their families were not the only ones being slimed in the media. The whole team had been smeared from coast to coast as a bunch of thugs who stood by and watched while a defenseless woman was being raped by their friends. But at least they weren't looking at thirty years in prison. Dave Evans would later admit a surge of relief on learning that he had not been one of those indicted. "But you hate yourself," he later said. It felt bad to feel good when teammates were in such peril.

Dave's peril would come. Within days it became clear that Nifong was still gunning for him as his third defendant. "We knew for weeks that he was coming after us," Dave later recalled. "Every day you wake up and you never know when it's coming. You're walking down the street and you never know when it could happen. We were stuck on the tracks and could see the train coming." Added his father: "Every day was a bad day because every day he could be arrested and of course at the same time he's studying for his final exams—and doing real well on them, by the way."

"That someone such as Crystal Mangum could come forward and tell these wild and outrageous stories, someone who is either disturbed or making up stories for some other reason," Bill Thomas later reflected, "and can hold Duke University hostage, hold Durham hostage, destroy a national championship caliber lacrosse team, and put three young men in danger of thirty years in prison is just an incredible, complete failure of the justice system."

And of the media system. And of the higher education system. And of the political system. Quite apart from Nifong, all have been deeply infected by the brand of racial politics practiced by many of today's black leaders and embraced by politically correct journalists and academics. And all share responsibility for trashing the lives of Collin Finnerty and Reade Seligmann.

Richard Brodhead certainly did his part. Two days after the arrests of Reade and Collin, he drew applause while telling the Durham Chamber of Commerce: "If our students did what is alleged, it is appalling to the worst degree. If they didn't do it, whatever they did is bad enough." While Brodhead mentioned the need to avoid "a rush to judge," he seemed oblivious to the fact that by this time, the evidence pouring into the public record was making it ever clearer to careful students of the case that the rape charge was very probably a fraud. It also was becoming perfectly clear that even if a rape occurred, Reade Seligmann was not there.

Nor did Brodhead say what Reade and Collin had done, apart from the rape charge, that was "bad enough." Such language struck many as an innuendo that they had done something terrible to the accuser even if it was not rape. The facts, on the other hand, show that Reade and Collin had attended a team party organized by their captains; had watched with polite distaste the strippers whom the captains had hired; and had probably engaged in underage beer drinking. If every Duke student who had ever done something like that were suspended, the place would be almost empty.

That same evening Brodhead participated in the first Campus Culture Initiative discussion of the lacrosse scandal in the Duke chapel. This "Conversation on Campus Culture" was designed in part, said Dean Sue, to make a start at improving Duke students' "culture of crassness." Brodhead called it "a moment to look at things and ask if those things are what we want for ourselves."

The nine-member panel included students, the university chaplain, and one faculty member. That was Group of 88 member Mark Anthony Neal, who pressed for curricular changes to "allow our students to engage one another in a progressive manner." He was joined by student Dinushika Mohottige, whose admission to distributing wanted posters earned her no rebuke.

Soon thereafter, Neal was to describe himself as devoted to "intellectual thuggery." Calling himself a "thugniggaintellectual," he said in *Duke Magazine*, the journal the university publishes and sends six times a year to its alumni, that this meant a "figure that comes into intellectual spaces like a thug, who literally is fearful [*sic*] and menacing. I wanted to use this idea of this intellectual persona to do some real kind of 'gangster' scholarship, if you will. All right, just hard, hard-core intellectual thuggery."

Neal also termed the strip club the "new church" for African-American women in an interview with Duke's alumni magazine. "In some ways this is legitimate labor, and we need to be clear about that," the professor explained. "I don't want to get into the business of policing black women's sexuality."

In the previous days, Neal had been active in campus protests against the lacrosse players. In a statement posted to his blog on April 13, he clearly implied (though with the qualifier "alleged") that this was one of many incidents of "sexual violence related to a college campus" and that it had "racist implications." He added, "Regardless of what happened inside of 610 N. Buchanan Blvd, the young men were hoping to consume something that they felt that a black woman uniquely possessed. If these young men did in fact rape, sodomize, rob, and beat this young women [*sic*], it wasn't simply because she was a women [*sic*], but because she was a black woman." Neal was also apparently unaware that the players never believed the agency would send over black strippers, nor had they desired that the agency do so.

Meanwhile, Kim Roberts received an $1,875 favor from Nifong—and started telling reporters that she thought the lacrosse players had probably raped Mangum and maybe given her a "date-rape" drug, too. This assertion contradicted Roberts's March 20 statement to Detective Himan that the rape claim was "a crock," as well as her March 22 statement to police. But the reporters did not know about that. Nifong and the police had kept it secret.

On April 17, the day of the lacrosse indictments, Nifong helped reduce Roberts's bond on a charge of violating her probation on a 2001 conviction for embezzling $25,000 from her employer. This saved Roberts the 15 percent fee that she would otherwise have had to pay a bondsman. Nifong made this move at the request of his new friend Mark Simeon, who represented Roberts and aspired to represent Magnum, too. Simeon was open about his hope of collecting big bucks in a civil lawsuit against lacrosse players. He thus had a financial stake in seeing them convicted.

The very day that she got her favor from Nifong, Roberts dramatically changed her tune about the rape charge. In an article headlined "Involuntary Intoxication," *Newsweek* reported that even as the grand jury was meeting to consider indictments, "the second dancer has come out in support of the accuser, and offers details that suggest the alleged victim may have been drugged."

Simeon, said *Newsweek*, had told the magazine that the accuser was "clearly sober" when she arrived at the party but "appeared to be under the influence of some substance" when she left. *Newsweek* added that "Nifong told *Newsweek* several weeks ago that her impaired state was not necessarily voluntary." The DA had hinted that the lacrosse players had drugged the accuser by putting something into her drink.

Simeon also disputed defense lawyers' assertions that Roberts had never been alone in the house for more than about ten minutes. Perhaps he was unaware that Roberts had told Detective Himan it had been "less than five minutes." That's why she had been so sure that the rape claim was a fraud.

Newsweek later reported Roberts's account of her dealings with Durham lawyer James D. "Butch" Williams. After learning of the rape claim, she had gone to Williams for advice. He told her that he represented one of the Duke lacrosse players (Dan Flannery). When Williams asked if she believed there had been a rape, Roberts had said no. According to Williams, who had not yet seen her statement to Himan, the words that Roberts had used were "a crock of shit."

"But when Williams tried to get her to sign an affidavit," *Newsweek* reported, "she balked. She said she later became livid when she heard that Williams had shared her story with other attorneys. Seeing Williams's face appear on a TV during her interview with *Newsweek*, she stood up and began punching the air in anger at him. 'I feel like he preyed on my naïveté,' she told *Newsweek*. 'I don't want someone to play me like I'm stupid.'"

No naïf, Roberts sent an e-mail on April 19 to 5W Public Relations, in New York City. The agency represents rappers, including Lil' Kim, of whom Roberts said she was a huge fan. Her e-mail said: "Hi! My name is Kim and I am involved in the Duke Lacrosse scandal. . . . Although I am no celebrity and just an average citizen, I've found myself at the center of one of the biggest stories in the country. I'm worried about letting this opportunity pass me by without making the best of it and was wondering if you had any advice as to how to spin this to my advantage."

Dozens of experts on spinning the event to one's personal advantage were close at hand, of course, sitting on the Duke arts and sciences faculty. But Roberts didn't know about them.

The agency shared the Roberts e-mail with the Associated Press. When this revelation spurred questions about whether she was trying to profit from the case, Roberts retorted: "Why shouldn't I profit from it? I didn't ask to be in this position. . . . I would like to feed my daughter. . . . Don't forget that they called me a damn nigger. She [the accuser] was passed out in the car. She doesn't know what she was called. I was called that. I can never forget that." Roberts did forget something else during her AP interview: that (as she was later to admit to Ed Bradley) she had provoked the lacrosse player's use of the N word by shouting a racial taunt at him while walking to her car.

"In all honesty, I think they're guilty," Roberts told the AP reporter. While "I was not in the bathroom when it happened, so I can't say a rape occurred and I never will," she explained, "I have to wonder about their character." Why so? Because she was upset that defense lawyers had released information about both dancers' criminal records and photos taken of the women at the party.

Apart from this animus against defense lawyers, Roberts said nothing that confirmed significant details of Mangum's many accounts, which her statements to police had contradicted on multiple key points. Duff Wilson of *The New York Times* nonetheless reported that Roberts had "corroborated some of the accuser's details." In fact the contradictions between the two dancers' accounts to police were both numerous and stark.

Meanwhile, the Nifong-led police investigation veered from farce to malevolence. The long-delayed, postindictment search of Seligmann's and

Finnerty's rooms was a Keystone Kops production. Himan, searching Selig-mann's room, began tearing through the belongings of Reade's roommate, Jay Jennison. "Bingo!" Himan exclaimed, when he came across Jennison's car-toon of Reeve Huston saying, "Ejaculation has occurred." Jennison had to call Bob Ekstrand to remind Himan that the warrant gave police no legal au-thority to search through Jennison's belongings.

Meanwhile, Gottlieb, who was downstairs coordinating the search of Finnerty's room, had his own "Eureka!" moment when he spotted a storage space in the ceiling. Hoping to find evidence he could use against Collin, the rotund sergeant tried doing a pull-up to open the hatch. He got stuck, causing the ceiling to sag slightly. The yield from the search? Some coursework, a lacrosse scouting report, and an iPod.

There was nothing farcical about the April 21 meeting at which Nifong, Gottlieb, and Himan got a more detailed oral report from Dr. Brian Meehan of DNA Security. He told them that the DNA of multiple males had now been found on the pubic hair comb as well as the rectal swabs and panties from the rape kit, and that none of it matched Collin Finnerty, Reade Selig-mann, or any other lacrosse player. Nifong and Meehan agreed that Mee-han's report would omit this stunning evidence of innocence and thereby conceal it from defense lawyers and the court.

Who were the criminals now?

13. NIFONG DEFEATS THE EVIDENCE

DURING THE TWO WEEKS between the indictments and the May 2 primary election, more and more previously secret evidence of Mike Nifong's probable ethical violations and the probable fraudulence of his case poured into the public record. At the same time, the district attorney gained momentum politically, especially in the black community.

How could both developments occur simultaneously? One explanation was that most of the national and local media downplayed or ignored the evidence and continued to produce misleading, pro-Nifong coverage and commentary. In particular, the egregiously slanted coverage of *The Herald-Sun*, the only newspaper with substantial circulation in Durham, misled many a primary voter about the facts. Nifong also got a boost from the North Carolina NAACP, some other key black leaders, and, of course, the Duke faculty and administration, which continued to demonize the lacrosse players.

In mid-to-late April, a mountain of other evidence of both prosecutorial misconduct and innocence came to light:

- Time-stamped photos taken at the party, released by defense lawyers to *Newsweek* and others in mid-April, established a time line that did not leave even a seven-minute interval during which Mangum could have been raped, let alone the thirty-minute ordeal that she had repeatedly described.

- Photos taken between midnight and 12:04, while the women were performing, showed bruises and cuts on the accuser. These appear to have been the same injuries that Nifong had claimed were evidence of rape.

- In mid-April, Durham police released the audio of Sergeant Shelton's call from the Kroger parking lot about Crystal's condition thirty minutes after leaving the stripper party: "She's just passed out drunk." It also became known that Crystal had first claimed rape at a time when she was facing the prospect of involuntary confinement.

• Reports of the highly suggestive and unreliable nature of the April 4 photo-ID process in which Crystal had picked Reade and Collin leaked out on April 21. As *The News & Observer* reported in late April: "The accuser picked out her alleged attackers in a process that violated the Durham Police Department's own policy on identification line-ups," most importantly its requirement of five "fillers" for each suspect.

• The same article described Nifong's unheard-of refusal on several occasions to look at evidence offered by respected defense lawyers hoping to persuade him that their lacrosse-player clients were innocent. The article also cited Nifong's failure to ask or subpoena defense lawyers for copies of the highly informative photos taken at the party—another sign of the DA's striking lack of interest in finding out what had really happened.

• The accuser's credibility was further battered by multiple public revelations in late April. Among them: Her report accusing three other men of gang rape in 1996, in Granville County, plus her failure to pursue the charges, which (her father told reporters) were false. And her statement "under oath in '98 that her husband took her into the woods and threatened to kill her," which MSNBC's Dan Abrams reported on May 1. She had not pursued that case, either.

• *Essence*, meanwhile, revealed Mangum's involuntary hospitalization in 2005 and in several articles in late April described her behavior in ways that could be seen as evidence that she might be having a relapse. The black-oriented magazine quoted her aunt saying: "She needs some help. That girl needs some professional help." Crystal had "started screaming at the sight of White men in the streets." This not long after she had been seen pole dancing at the Platinum Pleasures Club. *Essence* also reported claims by Crystal and her father that they had seen flyers with "KKK" scrawled on them strewn across their front yard, only to see them vanish "because the police came by so fast and put them in bags."

The *Essence* reporter also wrote:

Racing back and forth to undisclosed locations with her two small children in tow, the young woman has not spoken to anyone from the press and will only call her parents. Sometimes, said the aunt, she doesn't even talk to her mother and father when she calls, but simply blurts out, "I'm okay, Mama," before quickly hanging up. . . .

Although the parents say their daughter drives by the family home on occasion—as she did early Thursday afternoon when this reporter was present—she does not stop. "She looked me straight in the face," her mother told Essence. *"But she saw you were here, so she kept on going."*

Readers who got all their news from *The New York Times* would have learned nothing about the highly exculpatory revelations concerning the April 4 photo-ID process; nothing about Nifong's repeated refusals to look at exculpatory evidence; nothing about the accuser's prior gang rape claim; nothing about her prior accusation against her husband; and, for that matter, nothing about her 2002 cab theft and car chase.

Perhaps these revelations also escaped the attention of Byron Calame, the newspaper's "public editor," or ombudsman. In an April 23 piece rejecting complaints of bias against the lacrosse players, Calame pronounced his newspaper's coverage "basically fair, I think, with a few miscues mainly related to the placement and the space given articles." He defended as close enough to being true the completely false claims of sports columnist Selena Roberts that the team had observed a "code of silence" with police. He clucked indulgently at the fact that the *Times* had published barely a hint that Nifong had been using the case to court the black vote in a close primary election.

The politically correct Calame had one suggestion for future coverage "in case the rape and kidnapping charges do not hold up." It was not that the *Times* should apologize for rushing to its all-but-explicit judgment of guilt. Nor was it that the newspaper should scrutinize the Duke faculty's rush to judgment, or Nifong's conduct, or any of the others who had been so eager to railroad innocent students into long prison terms. No, Calame suggested that the *Times* should redouble its efforts to examine "the racial insults voiced by various players"—all two of them, presumably—and "the lacrosse team's seemingly flawed culture."

Two days later, on April 25, readers of *The Washington Post* were treated to a cliché-crammed op-ed by regular columnist Eugene Robinson. He took the by-then-standard swipe at "privileged white kids who play lacrosse" and repeated the by-then-standard mantra that "it's impossible to avoid thinking of all the black women who were violated by drunken white men in the American South over the centuries."

Perhaps, before likening the lacrosse players to slavemasters, Robinson should have taken a peek at the mountain of evidence of innocence already in the public record. And perhaps, before painting modern America as a place where black women are regularly terrorized by white rapists, he should have checked the statistics on how extremely rare white-on-black rapes are today.

Also on April 25, Mangum called Officer Michele Soucie and gave this account: Three cars had followed her, with occupants taking her picture. She turned into a dead-end road and been trapped. She then escaped. She did not explain how she had been able to drive through the three cars. But this tale did ring a bell for those familiar with her 2002 arrest after she had stolen a cab, led police on a high-speed chase, and rammed a police car that had blocked her, while laughing.

Crystal also told Soucie that "she had no one she could trust because everyone (including her family) was talking to the media." The next day, Himan and a representative from the North Carolina Coalition for Rape contacted a woman who found a place for Crystal to stay. As long as the charges remained on the books, the "victim" would have food, shelter, and privacy.

That last week in April, Dave Evans was working long hours at Ronald McDonald House, a charity providing a home away from home for families of sick children. He was cooking meals, cleaning up, hanging out with the kids, answering phones, and the like to do the community service he had earlier agreed to do, to avoid a trial and possible conviction on his January 15 noise citation and a charge of having an open beer in the backseat of a car driven by Kyle Dowd the previous August. Nifong, meanwhile, was in the process of revoking the deal, Dave later recalled, "because he wanted me to have a criminal record" to be used in his expected rape trial.

Dave's father called to tell him to get out of Durham. Word had come from Joe Cheshire that Nifong's private lab had supposedly found some DNA that might possibly be Dave's under one of Mangum's plastic fingernails.

Nifong, meanwhile, dismissed the succession of blows to the credibility of himself and the woman he called "my victim" by trying to erase from memory his unprecedented media campaign and accusing the defense lawyers of doing what he had done. "It's not me who is trying this case in the media," he said on April 25. "The defense is trying this case in the media. Maybe they want us to move it to Aruba or someplace like that." This last bit was calculated to further inflame Durhamites by suggesting that the defense was trying to deny them the chance to sit in judgment by forcing a change of venue.

In fact, the defense lawyers' public comments were well within the state bar's pretrial publicity rules. In 2003, the rules had been revised specifically to allow lawyers to make public comments when reasonably "required to protect a client from the substantial undue prejudicial effect of recent publicity" generated by others. And in this case the need to counter Nifong's unprecedented, falsehood-filled media offensive was quite obvious.

But the defense lawyers were not having much success in focusing the media on the evidence. In late April the Seligmanns, Kirk Osborn, and Bob Ekstrand debated whether to mount a stronger counterattack. The question was whether to file a battery of motions, with attachments exposing Nifong's misconduct and showing Reade's innocence, including an almost unheard-of request that the court kick Nifong out of the case.

It was a tricky strategic decision. Such a move would be a bold step for any defense lawyer to take, let alone one as experienced and respected as Osborn. The other defense lawyers were not planning any such move. The defense was still in the dark about what Nifong might have up his sleeve. The motions would be certain to infuriate Nifong. The pro-prosecution Judge Stephens was unlikely to be receptive. And making all details of Reade's alibi public would allow Nifong and Mangum to change her story to work around it—as in fact they would later do. On the other hand, the legal and factual grounds for the motions were strong, if not yet fully developed. It was clearly going to take something bigger than scattered defense-lawyer statements to counter the torrent of false and misleading publicity and grab the attention of the media and the judiciary. And if one of the defendants was to go after Nifong, Reade, with his airtight alibi, was the logical choice.

Kirk Osborn was initially reluctant to take such an unorthodox and lonely step. But "I pressed him to do it," Phil Seligmann later recalled. "He did exactly what I asked. I said, 'Kirk, this man is perpetrating a hoax and we've got to point it out.'" So they charged ahead.

On May 1, the day before the primary election, Osborn and cocounsel Buddy Connor filed six motions totaling eighty-nine pages. The motion for recusal of the district attorney included a blistering account of Nifong's conduct, charging that he had "neglected his duties as a prosecutor to seek the truth and a fair prosecution [and] ignored the actual facts of the case which demonstrate the defendant [Seligmann] could not have committed this crime." The lawyers accused the DA of persecuting innocent defendants to further his "personal, vested interest in getting elected" and his "zeal to make national headlines." They excoriated Nifong's publicity offensive as that of a man "willing to prostitute the truth and fair prosecution for personal gain." Attached to the motion was Reade's alibi evidence, stunning in its detail and comprehensiveness.

In a separate motion to suppress identification testimony, Osborn sought an order barring Nifong from using the rigged April 4 photo-ID process. He also attached a previously nonpublic transcript that graphically illustrated the improper nature of the ID process. More boldly still, Osborn urged the court to bar the accuser from identifying the defendants in court unless Nifong could show that any in-court identification was not derivative from the April 4 ID—which Nifong could not have done. Nor could he have connected the defendants to the alleged rape in any other way. So this motion, if granted, would end the case.

Nifong was predictably enraged. He railed against Osborn's effort to "try cases in the media by filing motions containing outrageous and false statements." Not that Nifong had read the motions with any care, by his own account: He told reporters, "I just don't have as much time for reading fiction right now." Nifong also taunted Osborn, boasting that "if I was him, I wouldn't want to try a case against me either," and mocking him as having been "the best-dressed public defender in North Carolina."

More important, the judge presiding over the case, Ronald Stephens, was also furious. He seemed to see Osborn's motions as a frontal attack on Durham justice. He put a news article about Osborn's motions on top of his desk. "I'm going to keep that right there," the judge had told a visiting lawyer. It was unclear whether the judge had ever read Osborn's motions carefully. It was clear that the defense lawyers would get no sympathy from Ron Stephens.

Some other defense lawyers doubted the strategic wisdom of the Seligmann team's counterattack, and not only because it had offended the judge. Wade Smith, Collin Finnerty's lawyer, was not one to go after any district attorney hammer and tongs. Osborn's request for a speedy trial, ahead of cases filed earlier, had no chance of success. "I had to defend Kirk and his pleadings against numerous judges who were calling me and saying, what the hell were we doing, attacking the district attorney in this manner?" Joe Cheshire recalled later. And while it was in Reade's interest to convince the world that he had an airtight alibi—perhaps even forcing Nifong to drop him from the case—that would not necessarily help Collin, who had the additional burden of the false reports that he had engaged in violent "gay bashing." Nor would it get other possible defendants, among whom Dave Evans seemed in greatest danger, off the hook.

But as Osborn and Phil Seligmann saw it, the motions would benefit Collin and the other lacrosse players as well as Reade. They were the best hope for focusing the media as well as the judiciary not only on Reade's alibi but also on the ample evidence that the whole case was a big lie. "It was those motions," Phil recalled later, "that got people all over the country to say, 'What the hell is going on down there?'"

Osborn's motions in fact were effective in putting Nifong on the defensive. On the night before the May 2 primary, the eleven o'clock newscasts on all three television stations in the Raleigh-Durham area led with the time-stamped, video image of Reade at the ATM at the time when, supposedly, he was more than a mile away raping the accuser. Even *The Herald-Sun* covered the Osborn motions in an impartial fashion, publishing a front-page article that mentioned allegations of the procedurally flawed lineup and detailed Seligmann's alibi.

Wendy Murphy, of course, dismissed Osborn's motions, stating on MSNBC's *The Situation* that "defense attorneys lie with impunity." Most of the media ignored the motions.

If too aggressive for the taste of some other defense lawyers, Osborn's May 1 motions were ultimately vindicated. It would take a long time.

After the case was dismissed, Jim Cooney, who had become the Seligmanns' lead lawyer, explained: "Conventional wisdom is to hold an alibi back until you absolutely have to produce it. The theory behind this is that no alibi is perfect (with a few exceptions) and that you do not want the DA to shift the time line to get around the alibi. However, Kirk and Buddy [Conner] made the exactly correct decision (though it would have scared the hell out of me to do it) by filing their notice of alibi early and laying out much of the alibi. This was a masterstroke by Kirk that helped to continue to change the atmospherics of the case, and suddenly raised serious questions about Nifong, his motives and his witness."

Osborn never entertained any illusion that his motions would swing the May 2 primary election against Nifong. Keith Bishop and Freda Black were weak challengers. Bishop had raised less than $3,000 for the campaign, compared to Nifong's $62,000, and had almost no campaign apparatus. He never had a realistic chance of winning. And Nifong cut deeply into Bishop's base by pursuing the black vote by indicting young men of whose innocence there was overwhelming evidence.

Black was a more serious contender. In 2003, she had joined then-DA Hardin in prosecuting Michael Peterson, a former mayoral candidate convicted of murdering his wife. The trial attracted extensive local attention, making her a well-known figure in Durham. But she was not much of a campaigner. She would take questions only through her spokesman, Brad Dixon, of Campaign Connections in Raleigh, and would grant interviews only if written questions were submitted in advance. "We've got a sound strategy," Dixon said. "We're going straight to the people."

The lacrosse case also forced Black off message. Her initial campaign pitch had been that she would be tougher than Nifong on crime, especially gangs, and in plea bargaining. But while she promised to prosecute the lacrosse case "to the fullest extent of the law," it would have been impossible to outpander Nifong. He was the obvious choice of those voters who wanted to see lacrosse players prosecuted no matter what the evidence.

The most forceful challenge to Nifong came not from his primary opponents but from N&O investigative reporter Joseph Neff, especially in a front-page exposé on April 22, four days after the Seligmann and Finnerty arrests. In 2002 and thereafter, Neff had taken the lead in exposing the egregious prosecutorial misconduct in the Alan Gell case. He was to play a similar role in the lacrosse case, offering the first serious scrutiny of Nifong's conduct in the local media.

N&O news editor Melanie Sill initially assigned Neff to the case in late March, with a specific task—to determine the identity of the second dancer. Neff didn't track down Kim Roberts's name before it became public knowledge. But Sill sensed the possibility that Nifong's actions were improper, and she kept Neff on the story. He missed few other scoops in the case. In his April 22 article, Neff showed the gravity of Nifong's seeming violations of the ethical rules against publicly trashing targets by quoting independent experts who seconded the defense lawyers' complaints. UNC law professor Ken Broun urged a state bar investigation of Nifong's public attacks. Forsyth County district attorney Tom Keith broke the unspoken taboo against criticizing fellow DAs by telling Neff that "he would never have made such statements, especially before criminal indictments had been filed."

David Rudolf, who had been a defense lawyer in the sensational Michael Peterson murder case, predicted that the "state bar would have to be concerned" when "a district attorney talks to the local and national media about his personal belief that certain people are guilty and are 'a bunch of hooligans,' about how horrified he is by the allegation, that 'a bunch of lacrosse players from Duke . . . raped a Black girl from Durham,' or how alleged racial slurs 'make what is already an extremely reprehensible attack even more reprehensible.'"

Neff also elicited a revealing answer when he asked Nifong whether he had made any mistakes in the Duke case: "I wouldn't say I regret anything I've said. I think what I have learned, basically, is that if you cooperate with the media out of a sense of duty to public truth, you make yourself a victim." Defiance plus self-pity—a combination that would recur.

Another Neff question, about Nifong's refusal to look at the evidence of innocence that defense lawyers had tried to show him, elicited another revealing answer: "Lawyers are always saying that people are innocent." Nifong had reason to know, however, that these lawyers were not just saying it. They could prove it.

Any chance that the Neff article might turn voters against Nifong ended on April 27, when Darrell Luster, Freda Black's campaign manager and main link to the African-American community, resigned after revelations that he was facing charges of holding a knife to his estranged wife's throat and threatening to kill her. That Luster's attorney was Black benefactor Jerry Clayton intensified the political damage by reinforcing perceptions that Clayton was trying to install Black as DA to get sweetheart deals for his clients.

Meanwhile, Nifong worked the race-class angle hard. Asked before the primary by *The Herald-Sun* to name his favorite book, he cited *To Kill a Mockingbird.* In Harper Lee's story, small-town Southern lawyer Atticus Finch stands up to racial prejudice (which Nifong was fanning) and a rush-to-judgment atmosphere (ditto) by defending a black man falsely accused of rape (as two white men were falsely accused by Nifong). At the final candidates' forum, on April 27, Nifong vowed to use the lacrosse case to rectify the facts that "blacks and whites have not always gotten equal justice" and that wealth also "creates a disparity in justice."

Bishop had the endorsement of the normally all-powerful Durham Committee on the Affairs of Black People. And Black had established an aggressive outreach effort to rural black voters. But neither could deliver the lacrosse players' heads on a platter. Nifong's handling of the lacrosse case made him a hero to many black voters despite his weak ties to the African-American community before the case arose. Most had no way of knowing that he was pressing bogus charges. *The Herald-Sun* and most other news organs available to them were ignoring or distorting the most probative evidence. "As I would go through the black community before the election," Nifong told *The News & Observer* afterward, "people would stop me and say, 'Keep your head up. We're with you.'"

Nifong ended up edging Black by 883 votes in the May 2 primary, with just fewer than 25 percent of registered Democrats turning out. Nifong's share of the total vote was 45 percent; Black's was 42 percent; Bishop's 13 percent. Both anecdotal and statistical evidence strongly suggest that Nifong's indictments of Seligmann and Finnerty, and his rhetorical attacks on them and their teammates, won enough black votes to give him the edge over Freda Black. Had there been no lacrosse case, Black would probably have won. She would also have fired Nifong as soon as she took office.

"The Duke lacrosse case was the overwhelming issue," County Commissioner Philip Cousin, a Durham minister and member of the Durham Committee on the Affairs of Black People, told *The N&O.* "When Nifong came through with the indictments, that indicated to the black community he would be fair." Lacrosse developments also made Nifong the fallback choice for Bishop supporters who saw that he could not win. "I wanted to vote for Bishop, but I knew he didn't have a chance, so I voted for Nifong," one black woman told *The N&O*.

Before Nifong had latched onto the lacrosse case, NCCU professor Irving Joyner had stated that "within the African-American community, none of the three running are widely known. African Americans, in large part, rely on what the Durham Committee decides." But on primary day, Nifong decisively carried all eight of the Durham precincts in which at least 93.4 percent of the registered voters were black. In these eight precincts combined, the district attorney captured 46.6 percent of the vote, with Bishop tallying 28.6 percent and Black just less than 25 percent. With a black candidate in the race who had the endorsement of the city's normally all-powerful black political action committee, this result was extraordinary. Nifong also won by overwhelming margins in the handful of precincts controlled by the far-left People's Alliance.

Nifong claimed after his win that "we would have ended up with the same outcome" had there been no lacrosse case, saying that it had cost him "among conservative white voters" as well as winning black votes. So it had. But 55 percent of the registered Democrats in overwhelmingly Democratic Durham were black; the other 45 percent included few conservatives. In Durham, as in most of the South, conservative white voters had drifted out of the Democratic Party and were ineligible to vote in the primary. With nobody seeking the Republican nomination, "We had a lot of irate, irate Republicans who couldn't vote for district attorney," Mike Ashe, director of the Durham County Board of Elections noted the day after the primary.

Nifong rejoiced at the results. "I really felt like I was the best candidate all along," he told *The News & Observer*. "I am satisfied I did the [lacrosse] case as it should be done."

The paper's editorial board disagreed, but waited to say so until the day after the primary. Nifong, it asserted then, had "doubtless" won "in part on the strength of publicity over the rape case." In a blistering editorial, *The N&O* said that prosecutors' "methods are supposed to be controlled by standards of fairness," or else "suspects or defendants who may well be innocent can be crushed by the power of the state." The liberal-leaning page found it "disturbing" that Nifong had ordered the police to violate lineup procedures and refused to meet with defense attorneys. Now that Nifong had won the primary, it hoped, "perhaps he'll be more open-minded."

A much stronger commentary came the next day from Jason Whitlock, an African-American sportswriter for *The Kansas City Star* who was also then a regular panelist on ESPN's *Sports Reporters*. "If the Duke lacrosse players were black and the accuser were white," wrote Whitlock, "everyone would easily see the similarities between this case and the alleged crimes that often left black men hanging from trees in the early 1900s. . . . If this were 1940, an angry white lynch mob would then gather at the scene of the alleged crime and promise to dole out justice to anyone they suspected of playing a role in the crime. In 2006, mixed-race prayer vigils and protests were held, and black community activists pressured the district attorney."

Whitlock admitted that he did not know what had happened at the stripper party but asserted that the heroes of the civil rights movement did not battle apartheid and injustice "so that the poor, black and oppressed could surrender the moral high ground and attempt to inflict injustice on the privileged." Whitlock urged African Americans in Durham to start demanding that the authorities "pursue justice in the Duke lacrosse case regardless of where that pursuit leads." Those lonely pleas fell on deaf ears.

Throughout April and early May, the lacrosse case continued to generate intense interest in cable news legal affairs programs. But with the wheels visibly coming off of Nifong's case, a few were breaking from the pack. The astute Dan Abrams of MSNBC's *The Abrams Report* and his frequent guest Yale Galanter, a defense lawyer, plus Sean Hannity of Fox's *Hannity & Colmes*, grew outspokenly skeptical of Nifong's claims. On the other hand, CNN's *Nancy Grace* show and its ilk kept up a stunning series of distortions and falsehoods. But after the April 10 defense DNA press conference, serious lawyers became increasingly unwilling to put their credibility on the line defending the district attorney. Wendy Murphy was always available to spew out vitriol, of course. But she could not be everywhere at once. So the shows—including *The Abrams Report*, whose format required bringing people on to defend views that Dan Abrams knew to be indefensible—turned to people like Georgia Goslee. Her stock rose as Nifong's credibility fell.

Goslee lacked even the meager paper credentials boasted by Murphy, who at least had prosecuted sex crimes and taught a law school course. With a law degree from the University of Maryland, Goslee specialized as a sole practitioner in facilitating racially preferential contract awards. She was a certified health and fitness instructor and personal trainer. She had appeared on TV in Baltimore in a diet workshop series and been an occasional guest on *The Montel Williams Show*. She knew next to nothing about the Duke case, and although she was a licensed member of the North Carolina bar, she admitted on *The Abrams Report* that "I'm not familiar with the North Carolina statutes."

Goslee made her first appearance in mid-April, when revelations of Nifong's questionable conduct and evidence of the players' innocence were starting to pile up. Her indifference to facts, eagerness to presume guilt, and status as an African-American woman made her a hot commodity.

Asked by Dan Abrams on April 27 about the conflict between the time-stamped photos from the party and the accuser's allegations, Goslee said: "The victim in this case, I mean she has been brutally assaulted. And to hold her testimony even at this time to hard and fast specific time periods I think is a little unfair. . . . For God's sakes this poor woman may still be wallowing under a cloud."

An incredulous Abrams asked whether she really meant to say that the accuser's specific allegations need not be consistent with the established facts. "You know," responded Goslee, "one of the problems you guys attach is consistency and inconsistency. . . . If you can't call her a liar, then maybe there's some credibility . . . to what she's saying even though she's inconsistent." She seemed oblivious to the fact that the time-stamped photos and other evidence meant that you *could* call Crystal Mangum a liar. Indeed, they proved it.

When fellow guest Yale Galanter noted that the kind of phone company call records and bank transaction reports that underpinned Reade Seligmann's alibi "do not lie," Goslee shot back: "I'm not so sure about that." Later she explained away the negative DNA results by adopting the wild conspiracy theory that Duke Hospital had tampered with the evidence. Even Nifong, whom Goslee credited with "doing a great job," had never suggested that.

Consistency? In early May Goslee said that the accuser had "been obviously brutally beaten and there were obvious bruises on her." When this claim was belied by the news that the hospital had reported no injuries besides small, nonbleeding scratches on the heel and knee, Goslee switched to the theory that all of the doctors and nurses were incapable of detecting bruises on "a dark complected African-American woman."

That a figure such as Goslee—who admitted she knew nothing of North Carolina law—was the most credible lawyer the TV bookers could find to take a pro-Nifong view provided a revealing insight into the weakness of the DA's case. Yet in the weeks following his primary victory, Nifong was riding high, seemingly on his way to an unopposed election triumph and the maximum pension that would result. And no one in Durham, it appeared, could stop him.

14. EXPERTS VINDICATE LAXERS, DUKE HARASSES THEM

W HILE THE PROFESSORS and the media continued demonizing the lacrosse team through April, the most important of the five committees that Brodhead had announced on April 5 was actually interviewing people who knew something about the team. This was the seven-member committee that the president had named to review the team's pre-March 13 conduct. The members included professors of sociology, political science, psychology, art and art history, the environment, and engineering. The chair was James E. Coleman Jr., a Duke law professor.

Coleman, among the most widely respected members of the Duke faculty, had impeccable civil libertarian credentials. A former member of North Carolina's Actual Innocence Commission, he had also chaired the American Bar Association's Section of Individual Rights and Responsibilities (1999–2000) and Death Penalty Moratorium Implementation Project (2001–2006). Coleman was also a former Democratic chief counsel to the House Ethics Committee and well known within national NAACP circles.

The Coleman Committee included no members of the Group of 88. But some lacrosse parents feared that its secret process was rigged against the lacrosse players. Their behavior was on trial, but they could not speak to committee members or have a representative cross-examine or even hear witnesses, the better to point out any inaccuracies. And after most of the faculty's left-wing African Americans had already rushed to judgment against the players, some parents worried that their sons might not get a fair shake from Coleman, a liberal African American, and six other mostly liberal professors.

They did not worry for long. Jim Coleman was known for a decency and judiciousness that commanded respect across the political spectrum. And it soon became clear that he was determined to conduct a fair and thorough inquiry. A few years before, Coleman had chaired a committee dealing with the university's response to reports of steroid abuse in the baseball program.

Unlike many Duke professors, he had a reputation for fairness in the Athletic Department.

Coleman provided structure by preparing a dossier of facts for each member of committee, so all would be operating from the same premises. He tried to schedule interviews when all members of the committee could be present. He did his best to track down all rumors, but to base reports solely on facts. He scheduled interviews to establish baseline facts first, the better to test later witnesses' credibility; he deliberately scheduled Pressler toward the end for this reason. And he went out of his way to interview anyone who might have bad things to say about lacrosse players and their racial attitudes or behavior. When a member of the city council asked to testify about the lacrosse players' behavior, Coleman obliged. It turned out that the complaints were about Duke students who were not on the team.

All committee members agreed not to comment on the lacrosse case for the duration of the inquiry. Among others, the committee interviewed Trask, Moneta, Wasiolek, Associate Dean for Judicial Affairs Stephen Bryan, Alleva, Kathleen Smith, Chris Kennedy, Pressler, and representatives of the Duke and Durham police departments.

Coleman also went out of his way to create the appearance of fairness to the lacrosse players and their parents. On April 24 at 7:00 in the evening, the committee heard from four lacrosse parents—Thom Mayer, his wife, Maureen, Brian Loftus, and Melinda Wilson—along with three sophomore women who movingly described their lacrosse-team friends as gentlemen who treated women with respect. Coleman told them up front that it was unlikely that much of what they said would illuminate the committee's examination of the team's disciplinary records. But they could speak for as long as they wanted and provide the committee with any information they deemed relevant.

"I have given over five thousand speeches in my life," Thom Mayer, a prominent Northern Virginia physician, told his son Kevin before going in, "but I'm about to give my best one." Brian Loftus, a retired New York City firefighter, encountered Brodhead and Moneta on campus while en route. He told them the same thing that he was about to tell the committee: "I spent thirty-six hours in the World Trade Center after the 9/11 attacks. I thought that was the worst day of my life. But seeing what is happening to my son and his friends is worse."

Speaking from the heart, without notes, Loftus also explained to the committee what a heavy blow to the players it would be to end the lacrosse program. He turned toward the art professor. You are an artist, Loftus said politely, and if you lost your arms, you would not be the same person. These boys are not just students. They are lacrosse players. If you take their sport away from them, they will not be the same. The woman "looked like she had been shot," said a parent who was there. "She got it." At the end of the meeting she came up to Loftus and spoke with him warmly.

"Jim Coleman was kind, gracious, and fair, as were all the members of the committee," Thom Mayer later recalled. Few if any Duke lacrosse parents or players would ever say that about Brodhead. Or Moneta. Or Alleva. Or the Group of 88.

The committee issued its twenty-five-page report on May 1, the first day of final exams. It demolished the negative stereotypes of the players that Nifong, much of the media, the Group of 88, and Duke administrators (less egregiously) had worked so hard to establish. But the media largely ignored the report's highly positive major findings. Those who reported on it at all triumphantly highlighted its conclusion that the laxers got drunk too often. Relying on statistics provided by Dean Bryan—and later challenged by parents as misleading—the report said that the lacrosse players drank more than most Duke students, or at least athletes, and had a disproportionate percentage of alcohol-related citations from Durham police. But it also noted that all of these alleged offenses were routine matters such as holding an open beer container, underage drinking, or making too much noise: "Their conduct has not been different in character than the conduct of the typical Duke student who abuses alcohol. [Durham Police Captain Ed] Sarvis said lacrosse players did not represent a special or unique problem . . . in fact, none of the houses rented by lacrosse players was . . . among the top 10 houses about which neighbors complained the most."

Alcohol aside, the Coleman Committee's portrayal of the lacrosse players could hardly have contrasted more dramatically with Nifong's ("hooligans") and Brodhead's ("racist language," "disorderly," allusions to slavemasters and sexism). The committee said the players had no record before March 13 of bullying, fighting, racist talk, hostility toward women, cheating, or other serious misconduct. (It did not look into Collin Finnerty's then-pending assault charge.)

"The committee has not heard evidence that the cohesiveness of this group is either sexist or racist," the report said. "On the contrary, the coach of the Duke Women's Lacrosse team has expressed her sense of camaraderie that exists between the men's and women's team; members of the men's team, for example, consistently come to the women's games. The current as well as former African American members of the team have been extremely positive about the support the team has provided them. . . .

"Their behavior on trips is described as exemplary. Players clean the team bus before disembarking. They obey the team's no alcohol rule before games. They are respectful of people who serve the team, including bus drivers, airline personnel, trainers, the equipment manager, the team manager [who was female], and the groundskeeper. . . . Both the groundskeeper and the equipment manager spoke about the players' respect and appreciation of their efforts for the team. They described the members of the team as the best or among the best group of athletes they have served in their long tenures with Duke athletics. Although they give Coach Pressler credit for instilling these values in his team, they emphasize that the players themselves are a 'special group of young men.' "

The committee interviewed ten Duke professors who had taught significant numbers of lacrosse team members. Nine offered positive comments. Several had not even realized that the lacrosse players—who acted like normal students—were on the team. One recalled that "the lacrosse players were willing to defend unpopular positions in class," presumably meaning positions unpopular with the overwhelmingly leftward tilt of Duke's faculty.

The tenth professor interviewed was the same Peter Wood who had spent the preceding five weeks trashing the lacrosse players in the local and national media. The Coleman Committee took his measure. It noted that Wood had given the committee (and the media) an account of lacrosse players' conduct in his class substantially harsher than anything that he had ever said before March 13. This included his 2004 letter criticizing team members for what he apparently saw as the mortal sin of missing a Friday class, with special permission from a dean, for a pregame practice.

Wood could not substantiate his new, harsher claims. Committee members even spoke to his teaching assistant. She reported that "she did not think the lacrosse players intentionally intimidated other students, but thought that they displayed aggressive body language in class." But she could not recall a single example. And she admitted that no other student had ever complained about any classroom "body language."

The report also found that Coach Pressler had done nothing wrong. Nothing at all. Coleman and his colleagues portrayed Pressler as a tough but fair disciplinarian who had responded appropriately to each and every notice from the administration about behavioral problems on his team. Pressler's effectiveness in this regard was compromised not by any fault of his, but by the Duke administration's failure to keep him informed about what he needed to know. The report also contextualized the players' behavior by noting that it was the rule, not the exception, for Duke students to ignore Duke's "arbitrary and often ineffective" alcohol rules.

This report closed the book on the Pressler era in Duke lacrosse. He was perhaps "the only one *who did nothing wrong* during this incident," noted William Gerrish, whose son captained the 2005 Duke lacrosse team, "and yet he ended up paying for it." The Coleman Committee concluded by recommending that

Brodhead reinstate the lacrosse team for the next academic year. It also urged adopting a new athletes' code of conduct, improving communications between the student affairs and athletics departments, and developing a more coherent alcohol policy for all Duke students.

How did the Coleman Committee's stunningly positive portrayal play in the media? Barely at all. The media displayed little interest in hearing anything that did not fit their chosen story line. The *Chicago Sun-Times* ran something under the headline "Pack men, alcohol a bad mix at Duke." Most newspapers and most television outlets outside the Durham area ignored it. *The New York Times* did run a summary on page 22. It began with the most negative aspect of the generally positive report: "Duke University lacrosse team members do things in 'packs' and often behave irresponsibly when they drink alcohol, but their conduct parallels a broader campuswide problem with drinking by students and should not cause the team to be disbanded, according to a review of the team culture conducted by members of the Duke faculty." But in general, the positive portrayal by the only people who had actually investigated the team was like the proverbial tree falling in a forest with nobody around to hear it.

This report was a bitter disappointment for the many professors who had rushed to judgment against the team. Houston Baker, for instance, lashed out at Coleman and his colleagues. In an interview with WRAL, Baker fumed that the report "says they are model academic citizens—they've been on the honor roll." He did not dispute any of the committee's factual findings but exuded rage that it had broken the pattern of demonizing the team. "Underage drinking!" thundered Baker, as if unaware that the vast majority of students at Duke and every other major university outside of those associated with the religious right had done that.

Brodhead ignored the Coleman Committee's highly favorable findings for more than a month, other than a perfunctory statement of thanks to the committee.

By the time of the Coleman Report, most Duke undergraduates, on the other hand, had long since decided that the rape charge was likely a fraud. Some women wore INNOCENT UNTIL PROVEN GUILTY T-shirts, tank tops, and baseball hats.

"Indeed," wrote Janet Reitman in *Rolling Stone*'s June issue, "with the exception of self-described 'feminists,' and African-American women, . . . there has been barely a peep out of the mainstream girls at Duke, unless it's to support the players." The possibility that this had something to do with the evidence, which Reitman barely mentioned, seemed not to occur to her. Instead, she deduced, Duke women have a "retro view of rape" and "are not overly concerned for the victim, who, many girls point out, was a stripper." Reitman displayed no doubt that "the victim" had been raped.

Yani Newton was certain that her friends Reade and Collin had never raped anyone. During that exam week she got a message from Reade on her voice mail. He said he was sorry that the high-flying women's team had lost to Virginia and wished her luck on her exams. He was going to do some yoga with his mom. But the loneliness and boredom of living in exile came through. "I'm sitting here talking to my imaginary friends," Reade said sadly. Yani saved the message. She kept it for months.

Exam week also featured a visit from the New Black Panthers, an antiwhite, anti-Semitic hate group. The organization's leader, Malik Zulu Shabazz, informed the press, "We are conducting an independent investigation, and we intend to enter the campus and interview lacrosse players." To the horror of many parents, the Brodhead administration initially seemed content to let the Panthers come onto the campus. "As an institution we support free speech," stated John Burness, "and we will treat them like any other group. But we do not permit weapons. We will take necessary steps to keep the campus safe."

Parents of lacrosse players and other Duke students learned of the Panthers' plans only through the media. Lacrosse parents who lived in Richmond and suburban Washington told their sons to round up members of the team; they drove to Duke, picked up the players, and got most members of the team out of Durham. A few had too much work to leave campus for a weekend just before finals. But their requests that the university put them up for a night in the Holiday Inn or take other measures to protect their safety were spurned. One player spent the weekend in his on-campus apartment with a sliding glass window as one of his walls, as about forty New Black Panthers, local sympathizers, and a handful of NCCU students descended on Durham demanding "justice" for Mangum. Some wore black berets, military fatigues, long knives in scabbards strapped to their legs, and ammunition belts.

In the end, Duke officials decided to keep the Panthers off campus. At a rally adjacent to the campus, Shabazz declared, "This is a hate crime, and we want a conviction. . . . We demand justice, and we will have justice, one way or the other." Shabazz also said that he had discussed the case at length with Nifong; the DA confirmed the conversation, but refused to reveal the details.

Victoria Peterson, last seen at the NCCU forum claiming that Duke Hospital had tampered with the DNA samples, shared the platform with Shabazz as he delivered his remarks. As the rally proceeded to 610 North Buchanan, Peterson urged the crowd to burn down the house. Duke police "quietly" asked her to refrain from such comments. Eventually Shabazz agreed to announce that he did not support burning the property.

Defense attorneys at their November 2006 retreat. From left to right: Joe Cheshire, Buddy Connor, Wade Smith, Jim Cooney, Brad Bannon, Doug Kingsbery, Bill Cotter, and Kirk Osborn. (Photo by Wade M. Smith.)

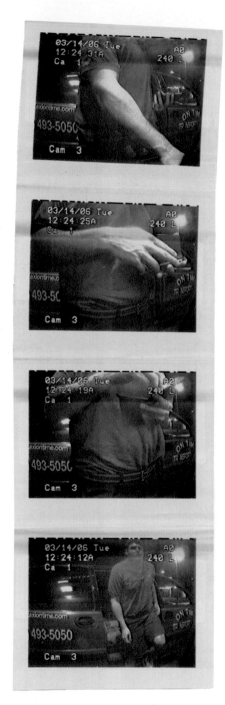

Reade Seligmann at a Durham Wachovia ATM. The photo, timestamped at 12:24 A.M., March 14, 2006, helped conclusively establish Seligmann's innocence. Kirk Osborn released it as part of a series of motions on May 1, 2006, the day before the Democratic primary. (Courtesy defense attorneys.)

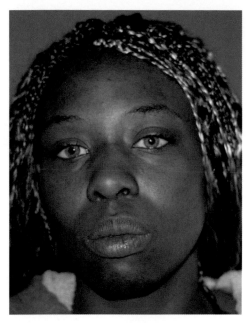

Crystal Mangum. One of a series of photos that police took of Mangum when they interviewed her on March 16, 2006. The case memorandum produced by Sgt. Mark Gottlieb would imply that this photo showed bruises on Mangum's face and neck. (Courtesy defense attorneys.)

Duke president Richard Brodhead and Athletic Director Joe Alleva announce the suspension of the lacrosse season, March 28, 2006. Eight days later, Brodhead would cancel the season and demand Coach Mike Pressler's resignation. (Photo by Chuck Liddy, courtesy *News & Observer*.)

We are listening to our students. We're also listening to the Durham community, to Duke staff, and to each other. Regardless of the results of the police investigation, what is apparent everyday now is the anger and fear of many students who know themselves to be objects of racism and sexism; who see illuminated in this moment's extraordinary spotlight what they live with everyday. They know that it isn't just Duke, it isn't everybody, and it isn't just individuals making this disaster.

But it is a disaster nonetheless.
These students are shouting and whispering about what happened to this young woman and to themselves.

. . . We want the absence of terror. But we don't really know what that means . . . We can't think. That's why we're so silent; we can't think about what's on the other side of this. Terror robs you of language and you need language for the healing to begin.

This is not a different experience for us here at Duke University. We go to class with racist classmates, we go to gym with people who are racists. . . . It's part of the experience.
[*Independent*, 29 March 2006]

If it turns out that these students are guilty, I want them expelled. But their expulsion will only bring resolution to this case and not the bigger problem. This is much bigger than them and throwing them out will not solve the the the problem. I want the administration to acknowledge what is going on and how bad it is.

Being a big, black man, it's hard to walk anywhere at night, and not have a campus police car slowly drive by me.

Everything seems up for grabs--I am only comfortable talking about this event in my room with close friends. I am actually afraid to even bring it up in public. But worse, I wonder now about everything. . . . If something like this happens to me . . . What would be used against me--my clothing? Where I was?

I was talking to a white woman student who was asking me "Why do people -- and she meant black people -- make race such a big issue?" They don't see race. They just don't see it.

What Does a Social Disaster Sound Like?

You go to a party, you get grabbed, you get propositioned, and then you start to question yourself.
[*Independent*, 29 March 2006]

... all you heard was "Black students just complain all the time, all you do is complain and self-segregate." And whenever we try to explain why we're offended, it's pushed back on us. Just the phrase "self-segregation": the blame is always put on us. [*Independent*, 29 March 2006]

. . . no one is really talking about how to keep the young woman herself central to this conversation, how to keep her humanity before us . . . she doesn't seem to be visible in this. Not for the university, not for us.

I can't help but think about the different attention given to what has happened from what it would have been if the guys had been not just black but participating in a different sport, like football, something that's not so upscale.

And this is what I'm thinking right now – Duke isn't really responding to this. Not really. And this, what has happened, is a disaster. **This is a social disaster.**

The students know that the disaster didn't begin on March 13th and won't end with what the police say or the court decides. Like all disasters, this one has a history. And what lies beneath what we're hearing from our students are questions about the future.

This ad, printed in the most easily seen venue on campus, is just one way for us to say that we're hearing what our students are saying.

Some of these things were said by a mixed (in every way possible) group of students on Wednesday, March 29th at an African & African American Studies Program forum, some were printed in an issue of the *Independent* that came out that same day, and some were said to us inside and outside of the classroom.

We're turning up the volume in a moment when some of the most vulnerable among us are being asked to quiet down while we wait. To the students speaking individually and to the protestors making collective noise, thank you for not waiting and for making yourselves heard.

We thank the following departments and programs for signing onto this ad with African & African American Studies: Romance Studies; Psychology: Social and Health Sciences; Franklin Humanities Institute; Critical U.S. Studies; Art, Art History, and Visual Studies; Classical Studies; Asian and African Languages and Literature; Women's Studies; Latino/a Studies; Latin American and Caribbean Studies; Medieval and Renaissance Studies; European Studies; and the Center for Documentary Studies. Because of space limitations, the names of individual faculty and staff who signed on in support may be read at the AAAS website:http://www.duke.edu/web/africanameric/

The Group of 88 ad. This full-page statement, signed by 88 members of Duke's arts and sciences faculty, appeared in the Duke *Chronicle* on April 6, 2006. Signatories committed themselves to "turning up the volume" and proclaimed, "To the protestors making collective noise, thank you for not waiting and for making yourselves heard." (Courtesy of Ekstrand & Ekstrand, LLP, with permissions, all rights reserved.)

Dave Evans, Collin Finnerty, and Reade Seligmann, at the press conference following the declaration of their innocence by Attorney General Roy Cooper, April 11, 2007. (Photo by Travis Long, courtesy *News & Observer*.)

Mike Nifong, during a press conference at the Durham Police Department, mid-October 2006. (Photo by Shaun Rocco, courtesy *News & Observer*.)

Taxi driver Moezeldin Elmostafa, who provided crucial alibi testimony for Reade Seligmann, at his bench trial, August 29, 2006. In the background were lacrosse case investigators Ben Himan and Richard Clayton. Nifong had asked to be notified immediately when police arrested Elmostafa on a 2-year-old misdemeanor warrant. (Photo by Chuck Liddy, courtesy *News & Observer*.)

Col. George Naylor of the Durham County Sheriff's Office is surrounded by journalists as he handed out mug shots of Reade Seligmann and Collin Finnerty, April 18, 2006. "The media," Kathy Seligmann later recalled, "were vultures." (Photo by Chuck Liddy, courtesy *News & Observer*.)

Dave Evans, flanked by his parents, seniors from the 2006 lacrosse team, and his attorneys, proclaiming his innocence, May 15, 2006. (Photo by Harry Lynch, courtesy *News & Observer.*)

Mike Nifong, on *The Abrams Report*, MSNBC, March 31, 2006. The district attorney demonstrated to a national television audience how Mangum allegedly was choked during the attack. No physical evidence existed to corroborate this claim, which Mangum didn't even make in most of her versions of events. (Courtesy MSNBC.)

PLEASE COME FORWARD.

"We're not saying that all 46 were involved. But we do know that some of the players inside that house on that evening knew what transpired and we need them to come forward."

- Durham Police Cpl. David Addison

ABCNews 3/26/2005

Please call Durham CrimeStoppers at 683-1200. Callers may remain anonymous.

Breck Archer — Bo Carrington — Casey Carroll

Mike Catallino — Tom Clute — Kevin Coleman — Josh Coveleski — Ned Crotty — Matt Danowski — Ed Douglass — Kyle Dowd

David Evans — Collin Finnerty — Dan Flannery — Gibbs Fogarty — Zack Greer — Erik Henkelman — Jay Jennison — Ben Koesterer

Fred Krom — Peter Lamade — Adam Langley — Chris Loftus — Dan Loftus — Kevin Mayer — Tony McDevitt — Ryan McFadyen

Glenn Nick — Nick O'hara — Dan Oppedisano — Sam Payton — Brad Ross — KJ Sauer — Steve Schoeffel — Rob Schroeder

Reade Seligmann — Dan Theodorisis — Bret Thompson — Chris Tkac — John Walsh — Michael Ward — Rob Wellington — Matt Wilson

NOTE: There are four more players that were not retrieved from the GoDuke.com website before Duke took down the lacrosse team's roster on Monday morning, March 27th.

The "vigilante" poster distributed around the Duke campus March 29, 2006. "What kind of society is this?" lacrosse player Tony McDevitt asked himself when he first saw a poster, nailed to a tree on East Campus. (Courtesy of Ekstrand & Ekstrand, LLP, with permissions, all rights reserved.)

In this atmosphere, the team's remaining members met with Brodhead on May 3, after a postponement due to the Black Panthers' visit. The players got fifteen minutes' notice that Brodhead would arrive: The administration feared that more advance notice might give lacrosse parents an opening to come to the meeting and confront the president. Team members clapped when Brodhead entered the room, accompanied by a Duke lawyer. Most expected little from the meeting. Some hoped that, behind closed doors, the president might apologize for the University's response.

"I'll tell you one of the things I said," Brodhead later recalled. "I said why I think it's inappropriate for boys in their late teens to have enough money to make a woman come take her clothes off and dance around for you for pleasure. You wouldn't have your sister do it, you wouldn't have your girlfriend do it; it's demeaning. That's the source of the ill. Is this the worst thing in the history of the world? I know it's not and so do you. But it doesn't mean I find it acceptable. When I was asked about this by the team and a person there brought up this idea of twenty-two other strippers, I said, 'You can take a stick of dynamite into a house twenty-one times, but the time it blows up is the time you realize that wasn't such a good idea.'" Broadhead also recalled expressing "my deep sympathy for them and recognition that they were going through an incredible and painful ordeal."

But the president's message seemed so uniformly harsh to the players that it stunned even the most pessimistic of them. He demanded that the team adopt a code of conduct and present it to him if it wanted a chance to play lacrosse in the future. And he stressed over and over again that everything that had happened was the team's fault and that the team needed to take collective responsibility publicly. This after the captains had already apologized abjectly in their March 28 statement as well as in their private meeting with Brodhead that day, and after he had punished them for holding a stripper party and drinking beer by firing their coach, canceling their season, and publicly associating them with racism and oppression of women.

Brodhead addressed the team as a group and insisted that all bore equal responsibility for the stripper party. This despite the well-known facts that a few of them, such as Brad Ross, had not even been in Durham the night of the party and that others, such as Bo Carrington, had nothing to drink and left before the strippers arrived. The president avoided eye contact throughout, looking often at the floor or ceiling. Various lacrosse players later used the words "scared," "intimidated," and "frightened" to describe his demeanor.

When Brodhead took questions, players later said, he seemed unable to give straight answers. Why had he shown no support for Seligmann and Finnerty? Brodhead said repeatedly that it was not his place to determine guilt or innocence. Why had he been silent about the dozens of Duke professors who had pronounced the team guilty in the media? Brodhead cited their First Amendment rights. What of the Coleman Committee's finding that Coach Pressler had been blameless? Brodhead said that Pressler had to go because he was the coach when the stripper party had been held. What of the mistreatment of Duke students by Durham police? Brodhead had nothing much to say. Would he, Dan Flannery asked, have done the same if Coach K's basketball team had had a stripper party? (In fact they had, two weeks before the lacrosse party.) "Absolutely," Brodhead responded. "No, honestly," Flannery pressed. Brodhead was silent. None of the players believed him.

By coincidence, Ryan McFadyen was in Durham that day to clean out his dorm room. He went to the meeting, stood and introduced himself, and said he was sorry for the pain that his e-mail had caused. Then he broke down in tears. Composing himself, McFadyen tried again to speak but broke down again. Brodhead appeared unmoved. Another player asked how Duke could have suspended McFadyen for sending an e-mail that was a sick joke while giving a pass to the student (Chauncey Nartey) who had sent the Presslers the e-mail that they considered a threat to their child. The president seemed baffled, and apparently ignorant of the Nartey e-mail.

"Brodhead could have made history; he could have stood by his students," Tony McDevitt later recalled. "Instead, he threw us under the bus." Added Bo Carrington: "Our confidence in anyone in the upper levels of the university was just trashed. We couldn't trust anyone."

Three days after the Coleman Committee report came another report that Houston Baker, Richard Brodhead, and the media must have found much more to their liking. The president had asked William G. Bowen, former president of Princeton University, and Julius Chambers, a civil rights lawyer who had been chancellor of North Carolina Central University, to examine his own administration's response to the allegations.

Instead of sticking to that assignment, the duo intruded on the Coleman Committee's terrain by going out of their way to attack the lacrosse players. They praised Brodhead's "eloquent" April 5 statements implicitly associating the lacrosse players with rape and "dehumanization," with "memories of systematic racial oppression," with "inequalities of wealth, privilege, and opportunity and the attitudes of superiority those inequalities breed."

Bowen and Chambers ignored the mass of favorable evidence about the team in the Coleman Committee's much better researched report, which was about three times as long and packed with facts. While admitting that "in the time available" they could not speak to all the people they wanted to in order to fulfill their assigned task (evaluating the administration's response), Bowen and Chambers did find time to interview Houston Baker, Karla Holloway, and Peter Wood about the lacrosse players. Wood, freshly discredited by the Coleman Committee, was the only faculty member quoted by name (with no sign of skepticism) in the Bowen-Chambers report. Bowen and Chambers never sought to interview Mike Pressler.

Taking their insights from the lacrosse team's most virulent and ignorant critics, Bowen and Chambers implied vaguely that team members did not show "respect for other people." They uncritically parroted the views of un-named "community members"—Houston Baker, perhaps?—that the team was "a manifestation of a white, elitist, arrogant subculture that was both in-dulged and self-indulgent."

Bowen and Chambers also faulted some of Brodhead's subordinates for inadequate "sensitivities" to minorities. These sins included giving credence to the Duke campus police report that Durham police did not consider the accuser credible because, among myriad other inconsistencies, she initially said she had been raped by twenty men and then revised it to three. Bowen and Chambers also rapped Larry Moneta for—of all things—his e-mail noti-fying students of the report by Durham police that drive-by shootings were a possibility. This e-mail, the duo judged, "was thought to be unnecessary, and to be a coded and gratuitous statement about race and violence that only made a difficult situation worse." Better to risk a student getting shot without warning, they seemed to suggest, than to ruffle the feathers of any hypersensi-tive African Americans.

For Brodhead himself, his two handpicked graders had only praise. And they hinted no disagreement with the Group of 88 or other professors and stu-dents who had led or joined the anti-lacrosse mob. Among the remedies that Bowen and Chambers prescribed was more "diversity" in doling out top ad-ministration jobs. That was a code word for ever-greater use of racial and gen-der preferences, a cause that both Bowen and Chambers had assiduously pursued for decades. What better occasion to put in another plug than an up-roar about a black woman's probably-false rape charge victimizing innocent white males?

In short, the Bowen-Chambers report read almost like a *Saturday Night Live* parody of the race-obsessed political correctness that is pervasive in higher education today. As such it helped illuminate why not one Duke pro-fessor or administrator had questioned Nifong's myriad apparent violations of legal ethics and established procedures to go after Duke students. The two gave no hint that Nifong's conduct had been other than admirable. They also gave short shrift to due process while stressing that "in the eyes of some faculty and others concerned with the intersecting issues of race, class, gender, and respect for people, the Athletic Department, and Duke more generally, just didn't seem to 'get it.' "

While Brodhead and the media had cause to celebrate the Bowen-Chambers report and similar stuff, some Duke professors were using their power over classroom discussions and grades to harass lacrosse players and other students who sympathized with them. John Walsh, one of the ACC academic honor roll members, missed a class to meet with his lawyer before it was clear who would be indicted. His instructor, Claire Ashton-James, gave him a bad grade on the makeup assignment. He went to her to discuss it. According to Walsh's subsequent account to *The Chronicle,* the woman opened the conference by claiming his team "wasn't right" and that Ryan McFadyen was "sick in the mind." Stunned, Walsh replied, "Well, I'd just hoped you'd have some sympathy, it's not the easiest time in the world right now." Ashton-James responded, "Yeah, well, if you guys really were innocent, I would feel sorry for you." Walsh heard many stories from teammates about other professors who "threw us in the guilt boat right away."

Even in this groupthink atmosphere, Kim Curtis stood out. Married to a tenured associate professor and Group of 88 member, Rom Coles, she was a longtime "visiting" professor of political science with thin scholarly credentials. Her courses were usually cross-listed by the politically drenched women's studies program. She had a reputation as an easy grader but also a paragon of political correctness.

Curtis had attended public rallies denouncing the players as rapists. She had signed the Group of 88's statement. She had e-mailed fellow Durham activists on March 29 expressing outrage at defense attorneys who had predicted—correctly—that no lacrosse player's DNA would be found on or in the accuser. This announcement "makes me wonder if we've gotten the full story about who was at the house that night," she wrote. "Were there others present who in fact carried out the rape and who are being protected by everyone else who was there? How do we know who was there?" The possibility that the lawyers' confidence reflected an evidence-based conviction that there had been no sexual assault at all seemed beyond Curtis's imagining.

With these words, Curtis had all but accused all of the lacrosse players, including two in her spring 2006 class, of being accomplices to rape. She took her most direct action against senior Kyle Dowd. Her politics and literature course required three papers. Dowd got a C+ on the first. The second was due on April 5, at the height of the media frenzy orchestrated by Nifong and the day before the Group of 88 published its statement. This time Curtis gave Dowd a C−, even though he had come to her to seek suggestions on how to do better. The other lacrosse player received an identical C−, down from a B+

on the first paper. In the third and final paper, Curtis gave both Dowd and the other lacrosse player F's. She also gave Dowd an F for the course.

This move would have blocked Dowd from graduating but for the extraordinary intercession of an administrator who arranged credit for a course that Dowd had taken at Johns Hopkins. When Dowd appealed the F's for the paper and course, Duke initially rebuffed him. Eventually it raised his course grade to a D. The official explanation was not that Curtis had used her grading power to punish a student for being on the lacrosse team. It was that Curtis had miscalculated. This was a bit like saying that a woman deemed qualified to teach at Duke did not know how to average 3.3, 2.7, and zero. Dowd and his parents eventually lost patience and filed a lawsuit against Duke and Curtis. Duke quickly settled, implicitly rebuking Curtis and changing Dowd's grade to a P (pass).

When asked about these and other reports over the summer, Brodhead spokesman John Burness told *The Chronicle*, "We did hear rumors early on, reports early on, that some faculty members were permitting a potentially hostile situation within a classroom environment." But he cited no evidence that the administration had ever actively investigated the matter or done anything to protect students against faculty harassment and punitive grading, other than April 3 e-mail to faculty sent by Dean Robert Thompson, urging caution in light of the "traumatic" campus climate.

In early May, Group of 88 member William Chafe, building on his March 31 association of the lacrosse players with the white mob that lynched Emmett Till, demanded that they be sanctioned for unspecified use of "racial stereotypes." In an essay published in *The Chronicle of Higher Education*, he railed against their drinking and complained that this team—less than one percent of the undergraduate body—was spoiling his vision of an ideal Duke. Somehow, it seemed, the lacrosse team had taken the joy out of "celebrating the 'playfulness' and pleasure that infuse the process of debating intellectual and spiritual issues over extended lunches after class," and "using some of our 'party time' to discuss the origins of the universe or existential ethics."

After more than six weeks of this rhetorical assault by Duke faculty on Duke students—broken only by the report of the one committee that had actually knew something about the team—a solitary dissenter stood up. That was Kerstin Kimel, the women's lacrosse coach, who as an undergraduate had been National Defensive Player of the Year. Kimel told a columnist on May 11 that the men's team had "made a very bad decision in hosting the party and hiring strippers. But I will tell you they are great kids. There is a strong camaraderie between our teams, and my players—being smart, savvy young women—would not associate with them if they felt on the whole, there was an issue of character." She added that "at an elite university, where every side of every issue is debated, my kids were shocked, disillusioned, and disappointed that their professors and the university community were so one-sided in their condemnation of the lacrosse players."

Kimel was, and would long remain, the only full-time Duke coach, professor, or administrator other than the Coleman Committee who had said anything positive in public about any member of the men's lacrosse team's character, academic performance, or athletic prowess. To Kimel, this was a basic part of her job. "I was speaking what I believed to be the truth," she recalled later, "and trying to give support to the players, the coaches, my colleagues, and friends—as no one was doing otherwise. I was not trying to send a message or politicize the incident. I felt the effect of having forty-plus kids have their names and faces plastered all over the mainstream media and having their character not just questioned but ripped apart would potentially have a devastating impact on them all. I'm in the business of developing kids, and so it was not all unnatural that I would have spoken about the men's team."

This attitude was in short supply on the Duke campus in the spring of 2006.

15. "FANTASTIC LIES"

A S THE MONTH OF MAY UNFOLDED, Nifong needed a third defendant. David Evans had been in his sights for a long time. Evans had avoided indictment in April only because Crystal Mangum had picked him with only "90 percent" confidence *if* he had a mustache.

Joe Cheshire tried one last time to get Nifong to look at the evidence of innocence the weekend of May 7–8. He offered to show photographs of Evans with no mustache the day before, the day of, and the day after the party. He offered to bring Evans in to be interviewed. He offered Nifong the results of an April 21 lie-detector test, administered by a leading former FBI polygrapher, that Evans had passed with flying colors.

But as in the past, the last thing Nifong would have been interested in was seeing proof of the innocence of the young men whom he was trying to send to prison for thirty years. The district attorney spurned Cheshire again.

Nifong did, however, have time to take a sudden and peculiar interest in whether a cab driver had knowingly helped a woman get away after shoplifting about five purses from a Hecht's store three years before. The DA told two of his Duke rape case detectives, Clayton and Himan, to hunt down the cabbie and bring him in under a warrant that could have been served at any point during the previous three years. "Mr. Nifong wanted to know when we picked him up," Himan wrote in his notes.

It was no coincidence that this same cabbie, Moezeldin Elmostafa, had signed an affidavit and gone on television supporting Reade Seligmann's alibi that he had left the party in Elmostafa's cab before the alleged rape could have occurred. Elmostafa, who had never met Seligmann before, was a disinterested and therefore especially credible witness. That made him especially dangerous to Nifong's case. And law enforcement officials have their ways of neutralizing dangerous witnesses.

Clayton and Himan picked up the Sudanese immigrant on May 10. "The detective asked if I had anything new to say about the lacrosse case," El-mostafa later testified. "When I said no, they took me to the magistrate." They also handcuffed him, locked him up, checked his record, and combed through his insurance and driving history and several years of job-related drug tests (all negative). Elmostafa, perhaps pondering the adage that no good deed goes unpunished, frantically called Kirk Osborn, who helped arrange bail and find him a lawyer, Thomas Loflin.

This high-level interest in a rinky-dink larceny case, Loflin later argued, showed that the real agenda was to pressure the cabbie to lie for the prosecution in the lacrosse case. It was flagrant witness intimidation, a crime far more serious than shoplifting. But again, there was no public objection from the Duke administration, the arts and sciences faculty, or most in the media.

Elmostafa didn't budge on the alibi. As to the shoplifting charge, he had always maintained that the woman had been a routine fare and that he had been unaware of any theft. His account was backed up by a Hecht security video that showed the woman hiding her loot behind her hip as she came out of the store and reentered the waiting cab. The woman herself later said the same.

The same day as the Elmostafa arrest the prosecution also managed to spin as incriminating—indeed, "a touchdown for the state," as Nancy Grace put it the next day—the virtually conclusive evidence of innocence that DNA Security had found.

Someone on the prosecution team leaked to Nifong's most faithful supporter, *The Herald-Sun*, and other outlets, including local station WRAL, ABC News and CBS News, a highly misleading account of the private lab's DNA test results. This information was known only to the prosecution and the lab. Nobody ever accused anyone at the lab of being the leaker.

The leak included none of the stunning new evidence of innocence. It omitted both the fact that the DNA of at least four males had been found in the accuser's rape kit and the fact that none of this DNA matched any of the lacrosse players.

Rather, *The Herald-Sun* reported that "tissue found under the [plastic] fingernail" left behind by the accuser, who said she had scratched at one of her assailants, might "partially" match the DNA of a third lacrosse player other than Finnerty or Seligmann. The DNA pattern of the tissue was incomplete, which precluded a definitive match.

In another prosecution leak, ABC News reported on the same day that the third player was the same one whom the accuser had supposedly identified with "90 percent certainty" during the photo ID session on April 4. Dave

Evans, his parents, and his lawyers knew what that meant: He would probably be indicted at the next meeting of the grand jury, on May 15, the day after his graduation from Duke.

CNN's Nancy Grace loved the news. She also distorted it, as usual. "Well," she said that night, "it all looked bleak for the prosecution of the Duke lacrosse team multiple rape case. At the eleventh hour, suddenly, a Hail Mary pass was thrown, and it's a touchdown for the state! Apparently, DNA matching one of these three lacrosse players has turned up under the nails of the student-turned-stripper." A few days later Grace changed it to "human flesh found under her fingernail."

To the contrary, even *The Herald-Sun* had not reported a DNA match. And it would later become clear, again contrary to all of the leaked news reports, that the DNA that might (or might not) have come from Evans had *not* necessarily been lodged "under" a plastic fingernail. Rather, the SBI had extracted and mixed together all the DNA taken from all surfaces of the three used plastic fingernails found in the wastebasket in Evans's bathroom.

The SBI had reported to Nifong that there were "multiple contributors" to the DNA mixture but that "no conclusion [could] be rendered" as to whether any of this fingernail DNA was even a possible partial match with any of the players. On Nifong's orders, DNA Security had subsequently obtained the same fingernail DNA mixture from the state lab, along with the rape kit items, to do its own tests.

Based on the same testing process that had led the state lab to find no basis for any conclusion at all, DNA Security offered a singularly weak conclusion: that 98 percent of the male population could be "excluded as a contributor to the mixture" and that David Evans was in the other 2 percent. At the same time, DNA matching that of another lacrosse player, who was never indicted, was found on another plastic fingernail that police had found on top of a computer unit in Evans's room.

The private lab did not address the possibility—indeed, the likelihood—that even if the DNA on the fingernails in the wastebasket came from Evans, it could have been transferred to the fingernails from used facial tissues, Q-tips, and other DNA-laden stuff that Evans had tossed into the same trash can during the three days before the house was searched.

Nifong, Gottlieb, and Himan had their third meeting with Meehan at his lab on May 12, after the highly misleading leaks about the DNA results had been reverberating through the media for two days. Meehan filled in his Durham visitors on the last of his tests (no help for Nifong), and then turned over to the trio his final report. The lab director gave Nifong what he wanted: a bare-bones, ten-page report that omitted all of the massive evidence of innocence, including the presence of the DNA of multiple non-lacrosse team males all over the rape kit.

Nor did the report mention a fact later dug up by defense lawyers: The male DNA found on the public hair comb included some that came from Dr. Meehan himself. This illustrated the fact that the Y-STR tests were so sensitive that despite standard laboratory precautions, even lab personnel could inadvertently contaminate rape kit items with tiny but detectable amounts of their own DNA.

This long-covered-up fact sheds especially interesting light on the evidence which Nifong—contrary to the SBI lab's analysis—found incriminating enough to justify indicting Dave Evans: The undisclosed match between Meehan and the DNA on the public hair comb was *more conclusive* than the so-called partial match between Evans and the DNA found in the fingernail extraction.

The May 12 Meehan report did make public another interesting lab finding: The sperm of Matthew Murchison, whom Crystal Mangum called her "boyfriend," had been found in the vaginal swab. While covering up the other "multiple males" whose DNA had turned up in the rape kit, Meehan's report included the Murchison match because police had provided his lab with Murchison's DNA profile.

The Murchison match should have told attentive journalists and academics this: Improbable as it is that a sexual assault such as the one alleged would leave none of the assailants' DNA on or in the accuser, it is still more far-fetched to imagine that leftover sperm from a prior encounter could be found in the same place where three rapists had somehow contrived to leave no trace of their own DNA.

Nifong delivered the ten-page Meehan report to defense lawyers after 5:00 P.M. that day. After looking through the document, Joe Cheshire decided that they had to have a press conference. Other defense lawyers were reluctant, in part out of concern that the defense team had not had time to get expert advice on this new, highly technical report. And, indeed, Cheshire describes himself as "a retard when it comes to DNA." Brad Bannon's efforts to get to an expert whom Bob Ekstrand had consulted failed. So just a few minutes before the press conference was to start, Bannon sat down at a computer, went to Google, and typed in: "Y-STR."

Meanwhile, Dave Evans had been calling from a parking garage after his graduation baccalaureate service. He wanted to know whether he would be indicted on Monday. The answer was yes, barring a miracle. His mother Rae, a strong, self-made woman, started crying when she heard that. She pulled herself together to go to Dave's favorite steak house to celebrate his graduation weekend.

Minutes before the press conference, while his clients were having dinner Cheshire was asking Bannon, "Is this good for us or bad for us?"

Bannon replied, "I think it's good."

"What is good about it?" Cheshire asked. Well, said Bannon, it appears that they were able to find DNA from one male in the rape kit, and it belonged to Crystal's boyfriend, *not* to any of the lacrosse players.

Cheshire thought that was pretty good. On the finer points, though, he had to wing it in front of the media. But his demeanor was confident and his facts were right. Cheshire led off by stressing that supposed findings had been "leaked by the district attorney's office, according to press people who have told me specifically that they leaked it to them," to create a "false impression" that there was an incriminating DNA match. While "there was DNA material from multiple different people on one plastic fingernail," including "some of the same characteristics as the genetic [profiles] of some of the Duke lacrosse players," Cheshire pointed out, there was "no conclusive match" between the wastebasket fingernail DNA and any lacrosse player. And even if one assumed that this DNA had come from a lacrosse player, the most logical explanation would be the plastic fingernails' proximity to "Q-tips, where people blew their nose, toilet paper" and other DNA-laden stuff in the trash can.

Much later, after digging out the evidence that Nifong had concealed on May 12 and for months thereafter, Bannon mused: "Imagine what the effect of that press conference would have been if we had been able to announce that DNA from at least four unidentified males, *in addition to the DNA from her boyfriend*, was all over that rape kit, and it did not match the lacrosse players."

At the lawyers' office in Raleigh the next morning, Saturday, Cheshire said to Dave, "I want to throw something out. Would you feel comfortable making a statement Monday? I've never suggested that to a client in thirty-five years but I think you can do it and I think it will have a real impact." Cheshire was knocking on an open door. Dave had already been thinking along the same lines. He wanted to speak out for his team, for Collin, for Reade, and for himself. Cheshire gave Dave about five talking points and left it to him to flesh out his statement.

Later in the day, Dave and David went to a mall to get haircuts. "Then," Dave later recalled, "I find myself in Nordstrom hanging shirts over my neck to find which ones would look good on TV after my indictment, like preparing for a wedding or a dance. It was surreal to be picking out clothing to talk to fifty million people about being accused of rape."

They decided that he should not wear a tie or blazer lest the preppy look send the wrong image to the people of Durham. Facial expressions also needed to be planned. "If you even crack a smile," Dave recalled later, "they say, 'Oh, he doesn't believe this is serious.' If you frown, they say, 'This guy looks evil.' So you sit there with this stoic, unnatural face because that's all you can do."

Dave Evans and his family went through his graduation that Sunday knowing that he would be indicted the next day. "It was a very long weekend," he later told Ed Bradley of CBS 60 *Minutes*.

BRADLEY: *"What was going through your mind at graduation?"*

EVANS: *"I didn't want to cry. I was surrounded by all these people who were so happy. If you remember, it was Mother's Day. So, this should have been one of the greatest days of my mom's life. The culmination of twenty-two years, twenty-three years, of schooling, all this work and she couldn't experience that. When I wanted to walk and get my diploma with all my friends but I couldn't. My dad had to go and get it because so many people in the press knew I was going to be indicted the next day and they wanted to take a picture of me with my diploma. And, I never got to get it."*

BRADLEY: *"You didn't feel comfortable walking up to there."*

EVANS: *"I didn't want to give them the satisfaction of that photo."*

That Monday morning, May 15, Nifong was seen storming out of his office, blowing past reporters gathered in the hallway, and rushing toward the judges' chambers. In the hallway he bumped into defense lawyer Kerry Sutton. She had been a friend and supporter of Nifong's election campaign. She also represented Matt Zash, had done some work for Dave Evans, and had been among the other lawyers standing behind Joe Cheshire at the press conference Friday evening.

In front of a judge's elderly secretary, Nifong lit into Sutton with a screaming succession of expletives, including liberal use of the familiar four-syllable insult that begins with "mother." He spewed spittle on her. He yelled something about what he would "ram up her" and something else about how "I'm going to cut Joe Cheshire's dick off and shove it down his throat." His voice carried across the sixth floor of the courthouse, causing a stir.

Cheshire came on the scene at 9:15 A.M., shortly after Nifong had stormed off. Sutton and the judge's secretary were shaken. "Mr. Nifong just attacked

Ms. Sutton, screaming and yelling at her," the secretary began. After hearing some details, Cheshire strode down the hall to the DA's office to have a little talk with Nifong. But Nifong would not come out to face the man whom he had just been cursing out behind his back. "He screamed, yelled, and cursed at a woman, but he won't face me," Cheshire later recalled. "He's a bully and a coward."

A bully and a coward with his own rubber-stamp grand jury. While concealing from the grand jury the overwhelming evidence that his entire case was a lie, Nifong rammed through the indictment of Dave Evans, Cheshire's client, that day. Evans's was one of eighty-three indictments the grand jury pushed through in its one-day session.

"I carry a little bit of a cross around," Cheshire confessed later, "because I sometimes feel that Dave might have been charged because I stepped out on Nifong. But somebody had to take the son of a bitch on."

With Kerry Sutton's help, the lawyers had worked out an arrangement that would give time to make his postindictment speech in front of a magistrate's office before being arrested, so that he would not be handcuffed like Reade and Collin were before the media saw them. As he walked down the hallway of the magistrates' building at about 2:00 P.M., it was full of teammates and defense lawyers giving him encouragement—as did some of the marshals. Dave later recalled the scene:

"I follow Joe and Brad out of building and there's this stand of microphones and press everywhere. And when they first saw me everyone just started sprinting, yelling, 'Down in front, down in front,' trying to get camera angles, putting cameras in my face. I was like a piece of meat with sharks coming at me. It was suffocating. It was one of those out-of-body experiences. I have no recollection of actually speaking."

It had been because his determination, grit, and maturity stood out that Dave Evans had been made cocaptain ahead of teammates with more athletic talent. Those qualities were on display in his speech outside the courthouse. "Dave just stepped right up there to the plate," his father later said. The speech was a model of controlled anger and eloquence. Facing the cameras with his parents and fellow lacrosse team seniors behind him, without glancing at notes, he began in a strong, confident voice:

"I want to thank you all for letting me speak to you today. My name is Dave Evans, and I'm the captain of the Duke University men's lacrosse team. I have to say that I'm very relieved to be the person who can come out and speak on behalf of my family and my team and let you know how we feel. First, I want to say that I'm absolutely innocent of all the charges that have been brought against me today, that Reade Seligmann and Collin Finnerty are innocent of all the charges that were brought against them. These allegations are lies, fabricated—fabricated, and they will be proven wrong."

The defendant went on to detail his and his two housemates' complete cooperation with police, their spurned offers to take police polygraph tests, his own success in passing the polygraph test arranged by his lawyers, his repeated offers to be interviewed by Nifong, and the DA's "apparent lack of interest in my story, the true story." He closed:

"I've always taken pride in my name. I take pride in my name today. And I'll gladly stand up to anything that comes up against me. I've never had my character questioned before. Anyone who's met me knows that this didn't happen. And I appreciate your support. As for my teammates, I love you all. I've never—The honor of being voted captain of all of you, the forty-six best guys you could ever meet, has been the greatest honor of my life.

"If I can clear things up and say this one more time, I am innocent. Reade Seligmann is innocent. Collin Finnerty is innocent. Every member of the Duke University lacrosse team is innocent. You have all been told some fantastic lies. And I look forward to watching them unravel in the weeks to come, as they already have in the weeks past, and the truth will come out. Thank you for your time."

Fantastic lies. It had a certain, memorable ring. As Dave turned to go inside and be booked, his dad leaned into his ear. "You nailed it, son," he said. "You nailed it."

Inside the magistrates' office, an unexpected scene unfolded as Sergeant Gottlieb was processing Dave in front of Brad Bannon. Gottlieb "shook my hand," Evans later recalled, and said, " 'You are in my prayers. I don't support what's going on here.' " Bannon was stunned. Never before had he heard a cop speak in such a way to a defendant accused of a heinous crime.

Dave Evans's speech marked a turning point in public perceptions of the case. Tens of millions of people heard and saw him. Few were unmoved by his passion, sincerity, and eloquence. An NBC reporter sought out Rae's eye and mouthed the words: "I'm so sorry." Television commentators effused about how sincere and truthful he seemed.

"That was an awesome thing he did that day," Joe Cheshire later recalled. "He was shaking like a leaf. But he stepped out there with his head up, standing in front of a massive bank of people, about to be arrested for rape. Dave's statement was an enormously important point in this case. You could see these people changing. You could hear their voices, the ones who had been strident. They felt the power of Dave's innocence from what Dave said, and they felt, 'Oh, my God, this boy didn't rape that woman.' Particularly women. Women just looked at him and knew that he didn't do it.

"That speech was a declaration of war [against Nifong]. It was saying, 'Fuck you and all your soldiers. We're going to kick your ass.'"

Others were equally proud of Dave. Sue Pressler: "He was a captain. He was saying, 'This is my job. I'm here to stand up for Collin and Reade and for my team. These are my guys. They didn't do it.' That's what captains do. It was his place to speak." Jim Cooney: "That was one of the most courageous acts that I have seen from a twenty-two-year-old outside the battlefield. Joe recognized that it was necessary for Dave not only to proclaim his innocence, but to do it personally—not through press release or his attorney—and do it right under Nifong's nose. Others on the defense side were strongly opposed to this; however, Joe rightly recognized that the atmosphere needed to be changed. While in the usual case, you would be crazy to do this, in this case it made perfect sense."

There were, of course, naysayers in the media determined to ignore everything but their own pet race-class-sex theories. Among them were the carnivorous tag team of CNN's Nancy Grace and her frequent guest Wendy Murphy. "How [would he] know whether the other two were guilty or innocent?" Grace declared. "What, were they all together, holding hands at a prayer meeting?" Murphy chimed in: "I don't buy it." Then Grace played clips of Richard Nixon saying "I am not a crook," O. J. Simpson saying, "Absolutely, hundred percent not guilty," and Michael Jackson saying, "If I were to hurt a child, I would slit my wrists."

Turning to Patti Wood, "our body language expert," Grace elicited the observation: "He said, 'It did not happen,' and then he had a significant eye close. Typically, that means he didn't believe that particular statement."

Then there was James Gordon Meek of the New York *Daily News*, whose chief contribution to public understanding, in a piece headlined "Duke Rape Suspect Is Son of Rich & Powerful," was to observe that "Evans' preppie-looking parents stood stiffly behind him."

"Preppie looking" was a deliberately snide way to describe Rae Forker Evans, strong, self-made professional woman who had mothered two children while making herself one of the top lobbyists in Washington and chairwoman of the Ladies Professional Golf Association; and David C. Evans, a self-made man who was the first in his family to graduate from college. A native of Savannah and graduate of Marymount College and George Washington University, both in the District of Columbia, Rae had risen through CBS News and CBS corporate to head the Washington office of Hallmark Cards for fifteen years before starting her own company. As cochair of the Duke lacrosse team's booster club for two years, she had close-up knowledge of the team's members.

Her husband, David, son of a Warsaw, Indiana, yellow pages advertising sales manager, won fourteen varsity letters (in football, basketball, baseball, and golf) at his Indiana high school, still a school record, and a four-year football scholarship at Indiana University; there, he was a member of the 1967 Rose Bowl team, won academic honors, and was president of his Indiana class of 5,400 students. He worked twenty-five hours a week to pay for Indiana University Law School. He arrived in Washington, D.C., to look for a job in 1971 in a used VW Bug with only a cot to sleep on, one sport coat, and a school loan to pay off. He found a job at Reed & Smith, which has since become one of the world's top law firms, with fifteen hundred lawyers, while Evans has become a senior partner specializing in representation of non-profit trade associations.

The Evanses had done well for themselves. That was reason enough for a reporter like Meek to evince distaste, at a time when Rae was "physically worried and physically sick" for fear of an attack by someone like the New Black Panthers on her son while he was speaking.

The same day as the Evans indictment, Nifong announced that he had no more targets on the Duke lacrosse team: "I believe it is important to state publicly today that none of the evidence that we have developed implicates any member of that team other than those three against whom indictments have been returned."

This was a dramatic, unexplained shift from Nifong's claims in late March and April that all of the thirty to forty lacrosse players in the house who failed to prevent the alleged rape or implicate their teammates could be charged with complicity in the alleged sexual assault.

Nifong's new stance contrasted even more dramatically with the statement, still not made public, that Crystal Mangum had written and signed on April 6. Had Nifong forgotten Mangum's claim that "three guys grabbed Nikki, and 'Brett,' 'Adam,' and Matt grabbed me [and] they separated us at the master bedroom door, while we tried to hold on to each other"? If Nifong believed "my victim," as he liked to call her, then why was he so willing to give a pass to these three accomplices who "grabbed Nikki"?

Whatever the answer, Nifong did not clear the forty-three unindicted white lacrosse players out of kindness or devotion to justice. He did it after a private request from the Brodhead administration, according to Duke sources. It saw such a Nifong announcement as a prerequisite to getting the scandal behind Duke and restarting the lacrosse program for the next season.

Why would Nifong do Duke a favor that would weaken his case? Defense lawyers could use the statement at trial to show that even the DA did not believe a central premise of his accuser's story. Was he grateful for Brodhead's acquiescence in the DA's public attacks on, and indictments of, three innocent Duke students? Was he hoping for future favors, such as continuing acquiescence in his behavior toward the three?

Brodhead did continue to acquiesce in this oppression without a murmur of disapproval for another seven months. All the while Nifong was coming under increasing harsh public criticism and was becoming a pariah even among his fellow North Carolina district attorneys. But as far as one could infer from Richard Brodhead's public remarks, Nifong was doing just fine.

On May 18, three days after Dave's indictment, the Evans family had an eighty-ninth-birthday lunch with Rae's father, Raymond Anthony Forker, in Savannah. The guest of honor gave Dave a little poke in the ribs and said, "Here—I made this for you." It was a makeshift button bearing the words: IN-NOCENT BUT STUPID. "Grandpa did not think that young men should drink beer," David Evans said later.

Also on May 18, Reade and Phil Seligmann returned to Durham for the first judicial hearing in his case. The damp Durham air hung heavy with danger. Adherents of the New Black Panthers were waiting when Reade, Phil, and Kirk Osborn walked through the gauntlet of cameras into the courthouse.

"Justice will be served, rapist!" a man screamed into Osborn's face. The rugged, onetime University of Colorado football lineman later told a friend: "I came within a quarter of a second of just taking my right hand with the briefcase in it and smashing it in his face." Phil Seligmann brought up the rear, scanning the crowd for anyone who might attack his son from behind. Inside the courtroom, one of the New Black Panther entourage glared at Reade and declared, "Dead man walking."

None of this bothered anyone in the Duke administration or among the Group of 88 enough to prompt them to say anything about protecting the rights of the demonstrably innocent Seligmann from the dishonest district attorney or the mob.

The hearing was short but not, for the defense, sweet. Judge Ronald Stephens, still apparently angry about Osborn's more aggressive motions, turned down a request for a speedy trial for Seligmann, who wanted to be cleared in time to go back to college in the fall. This "case is not going to jump ahead of the line and be handled any differently," the judge declared. He also demonstrated his apparent ignorance of the open discovery law by cautioning that defense lawyers may not "rummage through" the files of police officers in the case. Judge Stephens gave no indication of being even a little bit familiar with the evidence. If he had read Osborn's motions with any care, it did not show. The judge thinks they are guilty, Osborn thought.

"This was classic, small Southern city justice," another defense lawyer later recalled. "His attitude was, 'I'm going to take care of my boys and you guys coming in here and raising hell better watch out.'" Indeed, Judge Stephens not only denied motions to get copies of DNA documents to which the defense lawyers were clearly entitled; he took the almost-unheard-of step of refusing to put the documents in the record under seal for possible appellate review.

Viewed as the most pro-prosecution judge in Durham County, Stephens was due to rotate off the case as of July 1. Defense lawyers suspected that Nifong's plan to delay the trial until the following spring might be designed to stall until Judge Stephens might rotate back into the case.

Nifong chose the May 18 hearing date to begin to comply, belatedly and very selectively, with his obligations under North Carolina's 2004 open discovery law. It required that defense lawyers be given copies of *all* witness statements, hospital records, other documents, tapes, photos, videos, and other evidence in the DA's hands. Nifong gave them 1,278 pages of documents, two videotapes, and a compact disc containing photos.

Nifong claimed that these were all of the files created by his own office and the police during the first two months of the investigation. Many in the media had been explaining away the extraordinary weakness of the prosecution evidence made public thus far by speculating that the DA must have a smoking gun up his sleeve. If he did, it would have to be somewhere in that 1,278 pages.

Kirk Osborn began looking through them with some trepidation. After all, most criminal defendants are guilty. Discovery documents usually contain damning evidence against them. Osborn was confident of Reade's alibi but had not focused on whatever had happened at the party after Reade left. "As a criminal defense lawyer, you cringe when you get the discovery," Osborn later explained. "You think, 'Oh, my God, what am I going to see?' I was in a murder case where I had to stop reading, it was so horrible."

This time was different. As Osborn turned the pages, he later recalled, "I just could not believe it. Every document was good for our side"—and not only because they made Seligmann's alibi even more airtight than it was before. "The medical records," Osborn recalled, "just stunned me." They starkly belied Nifong's oft-repeated claims that the medical evidence supported the rape charge. They also belied the DA's claims that the rapists might have used condoms: The accuser had repeatedly told doctors and nurses that the alleged assailants had not used condoms and that at least two had ejaculated.

Defense lawyers learned for that first time that Kim Roberts had dismissed the rape claim as a "crock" in her initial police interview from Detective

Himan's forty-nine-page typed memo. They learned from other documents more about how wildly inconsistent each of the accuser's successive accounts had been with all of her own previous accounts as well as with Kim Roberts's and all of the lacrosse players'. They also learned from her "driver" Jarriel Johnson's police statement about her professional assignations with at least four men during the weekend before the party.

Osborn went to see Nifong five days later. "Please don't take this person-ally," he began. He told the DA that it would be clear to anybody reading these discovery documents that there was no rape and no case. Why don't you go to the accuser, get her to admit that her charge was false, announce it, and dismiss the case? "Everybody would win," said Osborn. "How will I win if I do that?" Nifong shot back. Osborn was tempted to respond: "At least you'll keep your job." But he bit his tongue as the angry DA launched into a tirade at-tacking the defense lawyer's handling of an unrelated murder case.

One of the authors got access to the 1,278 pages later that month. No Ni-fong smoking gun. No nothing.

Meanwhile, back home in New Jersey, Reade Seligmann was not one to go into hiding, despite being recognized everywhere as a Duke lacrosse rape de-fendant, dogged by photographers, and sometimes harassed. On May 20, two days after the "dead man walking" threat, two big lacrosse rivals, Reade's high school, Delbarton, and Collin's, Chaminade, were playing at Chaminade's field in Mineola, Long Island. Reade was there with his parents and youngest brother to cheer on their twin brothers, who were juniors at Delbarton.

Taylor Price was there, too, in his motorized wheelchair, with his dad. Taylor was glad to see Reade and not surprised. The big guy's attitude, Taylor later recalled, was: "You got something to say to me? Bring it on. You're not going to incite me and get me riled up."

When they started talking, Taylor recalled, "Reade was more interested in me than in his own problems. He would say, 'I keep hearing great things about you, that your year at Georgetown was great. How are you doing?' He was so into what was going on with me. That's just the type of guy Reade is."

Kevin Finnerty and a daughter were at the game, too. Afterward, the Prices went back to the Finnertys' nearby home "to give Collin a hug," as Tay-lor recalled. The usually animated, welcoming Collin came out looking tired and drained. "He was physically there, but he wasn't really there," Taylor re-called. "I think he was just tired of thinking about it all."

After a quiet reunion of about forty-five minutes, the door opened and in came the entire Seligmann family. Reade and Collin bear-hugged. It was the two friends' first moment together since they had climbed out of the police car in handcuffs thirty-two days before.

"It was one of the most special, emotional moments I've ever witnessed," Taylor recalled. "Collin was a totally different person, much more lively. He did a 360. For the first time I think he felt like he wasn't going through this alone. His parents are very close to him. But my parents can't know what it's like to be in a wheelchair and have your life changed, and it's impossible for Mr. and Mrs. Finnerty to know what it's like to be in Collin's shoes."

Reade and Collin went inside to spend some time alone together and watch an NCAA lacrosse tournament game on TV. Two months before they had dreamed that they would be the ones playing on TV, helping their team soar to a national championship. Now they could only watch, and wait for the next ugly headline.

And more ugly headlines there were. As evidence of innocence continued to pile up, many in the media and at Duke persisted in ignoring or burying it. Now they spent less space plugging the increasingly discredited rape charge and more depicting all of the lacrosse players as monsters based on the undisputed blunders and sins of a few, blunders and sins that were hardly atypical on any college campus in the country.

Ignoring the glowing findings of the Coleman Committee's report, these journalists and professors ranted about underage drinking, noisy parties, and hiring strippers as though they were rare, mortal sins. They also magnified two players' exchange of racial taunts with the departing Kim Roberts into an unprovoked barrage of racial epithets from multiple players.

Washington Post reporter Lynne Duke wrote a May 23 Style Section piece that did little more than echo her colleague Eugene Robinson's facile, fact-free April 25 op-ed. Both fed the myth that rapes of black women by white men are commonplace. "The Duke case," she wrote, "is in some ways reminiscent of a black woman's vulnerability to a white man during the days of slavery, reconstruction and Jim Crow, when sex was used as a tool of racial domination."

Most news organs chose not to report the revelations in May and June that the medical records belied Nifong's claims and that Kim Roberts had told police that the rape claim was "a crock." Defense lawyers, who got the discovery files on May 18, attached the most revealing documents to publicly filed motions in late May and June. Sean Hannity of Fox, one of the few journalists to question the rape charge, reported the medical evidence and the "crock" statement on May 22. But the big newspapers that had hyped both the DA's mischaracterization of the medical evidence and Roberts's guilt-presuming public statements in April were not interested.

It took *The New York Times* until June 9 to run a cursory report on page 18 of the defense assertions that Nifong had falsified the medical records. It took the *Times* until August 25 to report Kim Roberts's "crock" statement, in passing, deep in a very long article. *The Washington Post, USA Today,* and the *Los Angeles Times* were even slower.

By and large the media drifted away from covering the case as more and more facts came out that did not fit their politically correct morality play. But they still looked for chances to grind their axes. They pounced ravenously on the Duke women's lacrosse team in late May for the sin of standing up for their friends on the men's team and the presumption of innocence.

While the three defendants had been in exile, Yani Newton and her teammates had been advancing to the semifinals of the national championship. In the ACC tournament, all the players had worn blue shoelaces to show solidarity with the men's team. While preparing for the trip to the Final Four in Boston, Coach Kerstin Kimel mentioned to a *Herald-Sun* reporter, in an off-the-record conversation, that the players might wear "innocent" armbands. By the time the team got to Massachusetts, the tentative plan was all over the news—and was being assailed as scandalous.

The players and coaches discussed the issue before the May 26 semifinal game against Northwestern. Given all the attention, Kimel said, the players could wear the armbands if they wanted but should not if it would be a distraction from the game. Most players settled on armbands displaying the lacrosse-team numbers of Dave, Reade, and Collin: 6, 13, and 45, respectively. A few stuck with "Innocent." Midfielder Rachel Sanford wore that message on a headband right across her forehead.

The women lost a heartbreaker in the semifinal, 11–10, in overtime. But many in the media, and on Duke's faculty, were less interested in the game than in trashing the Duke women for having the gall to resist the media-faculty rush to judgment against their friends.

The New York Times again led the pack. Sports columnist Harvey Araton indignantly excoriated the Duke women on May 26 for "sanctimony." Oozing sexist and racist condescension to "the lacrosse gals, 30 of 31 of whom are white," Araton complained that they "are apparently free to martyr their male lax mates" and render "pre-judgment of the alleged victim, who is . . . African-American." Araton wondered how "cross-team friendship and university pride [could] negate common sense at a college as difficult to gain admission to as Duke." He turned to Kathy Redmond, of the National Coalition Against Violent Athletes, to call for censorship by Duke: "It's obvious that the women's team lacks maturity—and the school should have been quick to remedy that."

Jeff Schultz, of *The Atlanta Journal-Constitution,* quoted the same Redmond calling the Duke lacrosse women "stupid, spoiled little girls." Kevin

Sweeney of Salon.com raged that "by saying so clearly that the accused is a liar, the women of Duke's lacrosse team won't make it any easier for other women to step forward." Sweeney also whacked the women for the sin of inviting the fired, blameless Mike Pressler to speak at a team function.

"I never believed the day would come when we'd see an educational institution so flagrantly stupid, so selfish, so conspicuously aloof," Philadelphia *Inquirer* sports columnist Stephen A. Smith wrote two days later. Why so ballistic? He theorized that the Duke women must not understand that there are a lot of rapes in this world. Oblivious to the evidence of innocence on the public record, as were the others, Smith clucked: "How anyone who wasn't there [at the stripper party] could possibly think they know anything is beyond me. But that's why we call them kids."

Kimel was at her parents' home for a few days of postseason rest when Smith's article appeared in Philadelphia's major paper. Her whole family read the story in horror, around the dinner table. Smith never contacted Kimel for comment. Nor did Araton, Schultz, or Sweeney.

"Reporters didn't seem to think," Kimel observed later, "that we might have access to information [about innocence] that the media didn't. Members of the men's team had told my players what happened at the party—they knew there was no rape. Also, no one in the press seemed to think that we had our own experiences with sexual assault. I had coached players who were sexually assaulted, and a former George Mason lacrosse player who I knew, Aimee Willard, was raped and murdered in 1996. She was driving home from Philadelphia, was bumped from behind and pulled over on the side of the road. The guy dragged her out of the car; her body was found naked. I know the horrors of sexual assault."

Araton, Schultz, and Smith all exuded dismay that Duke had not censored the women lacrosse players. Of course, no journalist had ever suggested that Duke should censor—or even distance itself from—the 88-plus faculty members who had rushed to assume guilt.

Karla Holloway, in her distinctively opaque prose style, piled on. She denounced "the team-inspired and morally slender protestations of loyalty that brought the ethic from the field of play onto the field of legal and cultural and gendered battle as well." This from a professor who had previously rationalized signing the Group of 88 statement as an effort to "understand and encourage the free speech rights" of the Duke students who were clamorously presuming the lacrosse players guilty.

The implicit credo of Holloway, Araton, and their kind was familiar in the annals of censors and would-be censors: Free speech for me (and my allies), not for thee.

Amid the national print media commentariat, one *New York Times* columnist showed some class. That was David Brooks, who as an op-ed writer was independent of the paper's editor and management.

In a May 28 column headlined "The Duke Witch Hunt," Brooks wrote: "Now that we know more about the Duke lacrosse team, simple decency requires that we return to that scandal, if only to correct the slurs that were uttered by millions of people, including me." Summarizing the Coleman Committee report, which "stands out as the one carefully researched and intellectually honest piece of work in this whole mess," Brooks noted dryly: "Curiously, Nexis searches suggest that these facts have scarcely been reported in any newspaper or magazine." He also stressed the weakness of the evidence that the accuser had been raped. And in a fitting sketch of the "civil rights" activists and Duke professors who took such joy in trashing white, male, upper-middle-class lacrosse players: Brooks added: "For many on the tenured left, bashing people like that is all that's left of their once-great activism."

The widely respected columnist's salvo caught the attention of people around the country. (Brooks would teach a class at Duke that fall.) But inside *The New York Times*, it was widely shrugged off as of little interest. Why? Because Brooks's brand of conservatism—so moderate that he rooted for the Democrats to win control of Congress in 2006—still put him far to the right of almost every other writer and editor at the *Times*.

16. LACROSSE REINSTATED, WITH DISRESPECT

A s EVIDENCE IN FAVOR of the lacrosse players' innocence and good character mounted, the Brodhead administration continued sending disdainful messages about them. One was a long article sent to Duke alumni in the May–June issue of *Duke Magazine,* an official publication of the university overseen by the senior vice president for alumni affairs. The article, "A Spring of Sorrows," by Robert Bliwire, reached alumni in late May.

All but ignoring the Coleman Committee and its May 1 report, Bliwire quoted four professors: Paul Haagen, Peter Wood, the departing Houston Baker, and Orin Starn. All had previously denounced the lacrosse players. Starn had been the mildest: "Unlike at least some of the men's lacrosse players, most Duke athletes are smart, delightful and hard-working." The Bliwire article used an interview of Donna Lisker, head of the Duke Women's Center, as the centerpiece of a long discussion of male students' supposed sexual misconduct and some female students' dislike of the party scene.

Bliwire was even more selective in reporting on the views of students. Unlike the student-run *Chronicle,* his 6,200-word article ignored the groundswell of student support for the lacrosse players spurred by the April 10 release of the DNA results and other evidence of innocence. The *only* student whom Bliwase interviewed and quoted was Nick Shungu, an African-American senior who implausibly suggested that the rape allegation showed racism to be so pervasive at Duke that his friends felt "extremely vulnerable" there. He added that the university should issue "an acknowledgement of sympathy for the alleged victim."

At least Bliwise did not liken the players to Hitler. But Wendy Murphy did, while scoffing at the Coleman Committee's praise of the lacrosse team in a June 5 exchange on MSNBC's *The Situation with Tucker Carlson*:

> MURPHY: *"To suggest they were well behaved, Hitler never beat his wife either. So what?"*

CARLSON: *"You're comparing lacrosse players who have been, in most cases, accused of nothing. Nothing has been proved against any of them. You're . . . comparing them to Hitler now?"*

MURPHY: *"No. . . . They've all done very bad things. Maybe they've all not been convicted of rape, but they have a very ugly history of bad behavior."*

CARLSON: *"What the hell are you talking about? I honestly don't know what you're talking about."*

On June 5, with students and many professors off on their summer vacations, President Brodhead announced that he had decided to reinstate the lacrosse team for the next season. One of Pressler's assistants, Kevin Cassese, himself a former Duke lacrosse player (Class of 2003), would serve as interim head coach while the Athletic Department conducted a national search for a permanent coach. "As you probably know," he said, "initial reports circulated through the media advanced the case against the students; more recent reports have made the case in their favor."

This sentence was the closest Brodhead had ever come to hinting at disagreement with anything that Nifong had done. (He had also told Bliwise he deplored "prejudices against athletes.") But most of his statement continued to evince distrust of and distaste for the lacrosse players. He declared that he was "taking a risk" in reinstating the program. He avoided mention of Nifong's conduct and of the evidence of innocence, including the alibi that had convinced all open-minded observers that Reade Seligmann had not been there. And he distorted the thrust of the Coleman Committee report, stressing that "though it did not confirm the worst allegations against this team, [it] documents a history of irresponsible conduct that this university cannot allow to continue."

A reasonable reader would have assumed Brodhead's meaning to be that while leaving open the question of gang rape ("the worst allegations"), the Coleman Committee had said nothing good about the players. Could Brodhead, a former English professor who takes great pride in his skills as a wordsmith, have been unaware of this?

Brodhead also expressed gratitude to "the Durham leaders who have recognized that truth and justice are common values, things we must pursue and uphold together." Was he talking about Nifong—by far the most famous and consequential "Durham leader" of the day? Not so, Brodhead's spokesman later explained: His praise was aimed at (the unnamed) Mayor Bill Bell and NCCU chancellor James Ammons.

The president conditioned the team's reinstatement on its adoption of a new "behavior code" and "mission statement." Ed Douglas, soon to be named cocaptain of the 2007 squad, and Bo Carrington, who was on campus taking summer classes, took the lead for the lacrosse team in drafting the documents. They were understandably eager to see the team resume play, but also concerned about saying anything in the new code that Nifong could use against their teammates at a trial. In their back-and-forth with the administration, it seemed to them that Brodhead wanted a code that would constitute an implicit admission of wrongdoing by the players. The code went through several drafts, with Bob Steel behind the scenes suggesting language that might be acceptable to both sides. Unfortunately for the lacrosse players, it was exceptional for Steel to play such a role during the crisis, seeking behind-the-scenes compromise for the good of the institution, a function that might be expected of a board of trustees chairman.

The eventual wording proved vague enough to allow both Brodhead and the players to interpret the code and mission statement as each side pleased. The players promised to "promote pride, unity, and confidence in Duke University"; to place primacy on their academic endeavors; to "practice positive leadership and display the courage necessary to advocate just causes in the face of public or social pressures"; to treat everyone with "compassion, sensitivity, and respect"; and to hold themselves responsible and accountable for their "thoughts, feelings, and actions."

The final requirement was almost Orwellian. Should college students be held "accountable" for their "thoughts" or "feelings"? Should anyone? How would the disciplinary authorities read their minds? But Brodhead approved the language, clearing the final hurdle necessary to resume the program.

Brodhead's new rules inspired veteran journalist Sidney Zion, a former federal prosecutor who had been a *New York Times* reporter in the 1970s, to join the growing band of commentators to break from the media pack: "The fundamental rule he should have imposed was on himself and his college: Respect the presumption of innocence and never impose collective guilt."

The New York Times itself seemed to flirt with journalistic seriousness about the case in the first part of June. David Brooks's more liberal colleague, Nicholas Kristof, a man not afraid to tackle sacred cows, wrote a powerful June 11 column headlined "Jocks and Prejudice." Kristof wrote: "This has not been the finest hour of either the news media or academia: too many rushed to make the Duke case part of the 300-year-old narrative of white men brutalizing black women. That narrative is real, but any incident needs to be examined on its own merits rather than simply glimpsed through the prisms of race and class.

"Racism runs through American history—African-American men still risk arrest for the de facto offense of 'being black near a crime scene.' But the lesson of that wretched past should be to look beyond race and focus relentlessly on facts."

After reviewing evidence of innocence, Kristof told his readers about Nifong's political incentives, which they could hardly have gleaned from the more than twenty news articles that the *Times* had run: "Heavily outspent in a tough three-way election race, he was the lone white man on the ballot, and he needed both media attention and black votes to win. In the end, he got twice as many black votes as his closest opponent, and that put him over the top."

Kristof concluded: "Look, we have a shameful history in this country of racial prejudice. One of the low points came in the 1930's when the Scottsboro Boys were pulled off a train in Alabama and charged with rape because of the lies of two white women. The crowds and media began a witch hunt (one headline: 'Nine Black Fiends Committed Revolting Crime') because they could not see past the teenagers' skin color.

"So let's take a deep breath and step back. Black hobos shouldn't have been stereotyped then, and neither should white jocks today."

Kristof was taken more seriously than Brooks among the good liberals who populate the *Times*. And even news reporters Duff Wilson and Jonathan Glater departed from the paper's anti-lacrosse-team, pro-Nifong slant in a 1,600-word article on June 12, describing the "growing perception that the case was in trouble." But it was buried on page 13.

Then, on June 13, after three months of Duke professors joining Nifong in launching dozens of falsehood-filled attacks on Duke's lacrosse players, a lone professor raised a powerful dissenting voice. It was the same Jim Coleman who had chaired the committee that had so eloquently praised the players' characters (while criticizing them for drinking too much). To make clear that he was speaking only for himself in commenting on Nifong, Coleman waited until a few weeks after his committee's May 1 report.

In a letter to and subsequent interview with *The News & Observer*, he became the first Duke professor—and for four more months the only one—to criticize Nifong's handling of the case publicly. And a singularly devastating critique it was, including the most forceful public explanation from anyone unconnected with the defense as to why the April 4 photo-ID process so grossly violated due process:

"Up to now," Coleman asserted,

> *virtually everything that Nifong has done has undermined public confidence in the case. The circumstances under which the alleged victim identified the three defendants is typical. An assumption has been that Nifong*

*and the Durham police merely botched the procedures under which the al-
leged victim identified the three members of the lacrosse team whom she
claims raped her. According to the police account of the identification, however, the police officer who presided over the proceedings told the alleged victim at the outset that he wanted her to look at people the police had reason
to believe attended the party. Thus, the police not only failed to include people they knew were not suspects among the photographs shown the woman,
they told the witness in effect that there would be no such "fillers" among
the photographs she would see.*

*This strongly suggests that the purpose of the identification process was
to give the alleged victim an opportunity to pick three members of the
lacrosse team who could be charged. Any three students would do; there
could be no wrong choice. The prosecutor would not care if the pre-trial
identification was subsequently thrown out by the court. The accuser would
identify them at trial by pointing to the three defendants seated in front of
her as the three men who assaulted her. The prosecutor would argue that
she had an independent basis (independent of the identifications thrown
out) for doing so.*

Coleman called upon Nifong to remove himself and his office from the
case and ask the state attorney general to appoint a special prosecutor to take
over.

This letter should have commanded widespread attention, coming from
a figure of Coleman's legal and political weight. Yet his criticism of Nifong
was ignored by most of the national media, including *The New York Times*
(which as of June 13 had published more than fifty pieces about the case) and
The Washington Post. Locally, *The Herald-Sun* also made no mention of it.
On the Duke campus, no other professor seconded Coleman for more than
four months and no member of the Group of 88 reconsidered the wisdom of
their rush to judgment.

The *Times*, back to its old habits, did find room ten days later to publish an
attack on defense lawyer Joe Cheshire's credibility by Nifong's chief investigator, Linwood Wilson. Cheshire said at a June 22 news conference after a hearing in the case that a police report newly provided to the defense showed that
the accuser telling one cop hours after the alleged attack that five men had
raped her. At that point Wilson interrupted and challenged Cheshire's claim.
Cheshire stuck to his guns. ("You'd better be right about this," Cheshire said
privately to Brad Bannon, the defense team's document expert, as they walked
away.) The next day, the *Times* reported that "in an interview later, Mr. Wilson
said he had seen all the evidence and that the woman, a 27-year-old student

and stripper, had not changed her story." Cheshire then gave the lie to Wilson's claim by releasing the police document proving that he had been right. This the *Times* ignored.

Newsweek's Evan Thomas and Susannah Meadows, on the other hand, had paid careful attention to the massive evidence of innocence emerging since their April 24 article, which their editors had billboarded with mug shots of the indicted Reade Seligmann and Collin Finnerty on the cover. On June 19, they published a new piece with a different spin. The headline was "Doubts About Duke: The prosecutor insists his rape case is strong. One problem: the facts thus far." The article included a detailed review of the publicly available evidence and pulled no punches in its analysis: "It is possible, almost three months later, that the players are maintaining a conspiracy of silence. But it seems highly unlikely. Rather, court documents in the case increasingly suggest that Durham County District Attorney Mike Nifong had very little evidence upon which to indict three players for rape. Indeed, the available evidence is so thin or contradictory that it seems fair to ask what Nifong could have been thinking when he confidently told reporters that there was 'no doubt' in his mind that the woman had been raped at the party held by the lacrosse team."

Nifong was not used to being challenged by reporters. When Meadows e-mailed him skeptical questions while preparing the piece, he responded by accusing the national media of getting spun by "misleading" and "false" defense claims. (He did not identify a single such claim, then or ever.) Nifong asserted that the ethics rules barred him from commenting on the evidence. (He did not explain why the same had not been true at the time of his March-April media barrage.) And he dug in his heels by declaring: "None of the 'facts' that I know at this time, indeed none of the evidence that I have seen from any source, has changed the opinion that I expressed initially."

The *Newsweek* article's compelling review of the evidence was the first major break (other than the Brooks, Kristof, and Zion op-eds) in the national print media's generally pro-Nifong, guilt-presuming coverage. The rush-to-judgment crowd did not take this lying down. Washingtonpost.com columnist Andrew Cohen trashed the skeptics on June 27: "I suspect race and money and access to the media have a lot to do with it." The public, he lectured, had been denied the "privilege" of a trial; until then, criticism of Nifong's conduct was out of bounds. Most others simply ignored all the new evidence that had eventually dismantled the foundations of their coverage.

And others continued to pile on. Peter Wood, a leading unfair criticizer of the lacrosse players, resurfaced in the June 28 issue of the *Indy*, the Research Triangle's alternative weekly. Hal Crowther, the writer, asserted that the lacrosse players were "subhuman" and told Nifong's critics to "catch a glimpse of your inner racist in the mirror." Wood posed for a photo in front of the lacrosse field, his arms sternly across his chest, and revealed that he had taught two of the indicted players. (Reade Seligmann's transcript, which at that point was available online as part of a defense motion, confirmed he was one of the two. The other was Dave Evans.) He then characterized lacrosse players as "cynical, arrogant, callous, dismissive—you could almost say openly hostile."

Wood did not respond to five e-mail requests from KC Johnson, one of this book's authors, sent over a period of several months, requesting evidence to substantiate this portrayal. In the fall, Kathy Seligmann called the professor directly to ask for any evidence he had to justify his attack on her son. Wood explained that he liked Reade and thought him a good kid, and that perhaps Crowther had quoted him out of context about Reade but that Wood himself was under no obligation to clarify the issue. When Reade's mother pressed, Wood complained that she sounded "hostile"—the same word he had used in the *Indy* interview to describe lacrosse players—and hung up the phone.

Another professor, Karla Holloway, resurfaced in the June 29 *Herald-Sun*. She did not show any new awareness that the allegations underlying every attack that she had made on the lacrosse players had been discredited. Rather, she styled herself as a "victim" of the whole affair, because the appointment that she had accepted to the Campus Culture Initiative involved doing some work. "When you are serviced to fix a problem and you are also the victim," she said in an interview, "it's a double duty."

While many in the Duke arts and sciences faculty appeared stuck in time, unable to process any information that had emerged after April 5, Nifong's behavior was exposing fault lines in Durham politics. With no Republican nominee opposing him, Nifong had seemed shoo-in for a full four-year term. But, in early June, a challenger suddenly emerged. County Commissioner Lewis Cheek, a moderate Democrat, announced on June 11 that he was considering a petition drive to run for district attorney against Nifong. Cheek said he was embarrassed by Nifong's handling of the lacrosse case, and, if elected, would ask the attorney general to appoint a special prosecutor. North Carolina law puts on the ballot in a countywide race, as an "unaffiliated" candidate, anyone who can gather the signatures of 4 percent of voters. In Durham County that year, 6,303 would do it.

Later in June, Cheek authorized a signature drive while remaining undecided on whether to run. His law practice was in civil matters, not criminal cases. But he had an impressive political résumé: undefeated in races for city council and then county commissioner, plus a term as Durham's mayor pro tem. He also had influential, politically savvy backers. They included Jackie

Brown, the veteran Democratic campaign operative who had managed Nifong's primary bid but become disenchanted with his behavior; Roland Leary, another disenchanted primary supporter of Nifong, who had previously served as Durham County sheriff; insurance and banking executive Dan Hill, a prominent Duke supporter, who had served on the city council; and Ed Pope, a state juvenile justice official who had long been active in Durham politics.

Jackie Brown coordinated the petition effort, including a mailing to 25,000 registered Durham County voters at a cost of over $18,000, with all of the money raised from Durham and surrounding areas. In a matter of days, the Cheek team collected around 10,000 signatures, virtually all of which proved valid. This easily qualified Cheek for the ballot and showed that Nifong could conceivably find himself in real trouble. He had won the primary with only 11,206 votes.

With Cheek on the ballot, it seemed as if Nifong might finally pay the price for his handling of the lacrosse case. But during most of July and August, the district attorney would enjoy a run of good luck.

17. NIFONG DEFIES GRAVITY, WITH HELP FROM FRIENDS

O N JULY 10 AND 11 Collin Finnerty was tried and convicted in Washington, D.C., on a misdemeanor assault charge. Much of the media coverage before, during, and after the trial left many people around the country believing that Finnerty had beaten up a gay man in a homophobic rage.

In fact, Finnerty had beaten up nobody. And nobody involved in the incident was gay.

These facts were conceded even by Collin's prosecutors. They never claimed that he had so much as landed a punch during the scrap outside a Washington, D.C., bar. Nor did anyone claim that Finnerty had thought that either of the two twenty-seven-year-old men with whom he and two friends had tangled was gay.

Rather, the assault charge was based solely on allegations by the two twenty-seven-year-olds that Finnerty had pushed his six-foot, five-inch antagonist, Jeffrey Bloxsom, and thrown fake punches designed not to connect but to frighten. Finnerty and his friends, on the other hand, consistently said that Bloxsom's friend Scott Herndon had knocked Collin down with a punch to the head from behind. Then (all agreed) one of Collin's friends had rushed in and knocked Bloxsom down with a punch to the face.

The arrival of a police cruiser broke up the brief brawl, at about 2:30 A.M. on November 5, 2005. Collin and his friends started running toward the Georgetown University campus, where one was a student. Bloxsom and Herndon stood their ground, telling the officer "they went thataway," or words to that effect. He gave chase in his car. Collin and his friends stopped. They were arrested and charged with assault based solely on the Bloxsom-Herndon report to police.

Prosecutors initially treated the case as standard, beer-soaked, chest-thumping, college-kid stuff. "It was an argument between two young guys who were sizing each other up," in the words of the spokeswoman for the U.S.

Attorney's Office. "Both sides had an equal portion of discussion." Finnerty and friends were channeled into a "youth diversion" program. By admitting responsibility and doing twenty-five hours of community service, they could get the charges dismissed with no criminal record. Finnerty wanted to plead not guilty and fight the assault charge but yielded to his friends' desire to take the deal.

These details (excepting Finnerty's preference for pleading not guilty) were clear long before the trial to any reporter who consulted public police and court records. But this would hardly have been clear from much of the media coverage.

It began with an accurate April 4 *New York Times* report about the charge against Collin. The article quoted a Bloxsom statement to police that someone had punched him in the face and body because he had told Finnerty's group "to stop calling him gay and other derogatory names."

That phrase — "calling him gay" — launched dozens of inaccurate news reports, although not, this once, in the *Times*. A widely carried Associated Press dispatch and articles in *USA Today*, the Houston *Chronicle*, the Philadelphia *Daily News*, the *Baltimore Sun*, *Newsday*, CNN, MSNBC, and elsewhere all reported erroneously that Collin had been accused of "gay bashing."

Wendy Murphy, the lacrosse-player-bashing ex-prosecutor, accused Finnerty on MSNBC's *Rita Cosby Show* of a "demonstrated history of picking on disenfranchised people, whether it's race, gender or sexuality." She added: "Obviously this is a guy who thinks wealthy white boys are better than the rest of the world." Duke professors spread similar distortions.

Finnerty's April 18 rape indictment turned up the volume. It also ended his eligibility for the D.C. diversion program. Prosecutors reopened the assault charge, refusing to defer it until after the rape case had been resolved. D.C. Superior Court Judge John H. Bayly Jr. put Finnerty under a pretrial curfew amounting to virtual house arrest from 9:00 P.M. to 6:00 A.M., seven days a week, and barred him from going anywhere that alcohol was sold or served; in Garden City, Long Island, where the Finnertys lived, this provision included delis, gas stations, restaurants, and even the trains into New York City.

The bow-tied, fastidious Judge Bayly also displayed a peculiar penchant for erroneously accusing Finnerty of violating the terms of his curfew. In June, the judge complained that the defendant had not answered a nighttime phone call from a pretrial services officer to check on curfew compliance. But Judge Bayly himself, it turned out, had authorized Finnerty to spend that night in North Carolina while seeing his lawyers in the rape case.

Bayly embarrassed himself again during the trial. At the end of the first day, he warned Finnerty's lawyers in ominous tones that he had heard tell of a report on "something called Wonkette" that the defendant had recently been seen at a drinking party in Washington. Finnerty's lawyer said this was false. "I want you to know that I'm going to get the bottom of it," harrumphed the judge.

Wrong again. The rumor about Finnerty had been floated by a reader in an online forum on Wonkette, a well-known Washington blog billing itself as "Politics for People with Dirty Minds." This rumor was quickly proven false. And Wonkette herself lectured Bayly online that judges should not be jumping to conclusions based on Internet rumors published with "very, very little editing and no fact-checking."

The media crowded in force into the standing-room-only courtroom to see Finnerty's misdemeanor trial before Judge Bayly, with no jury. A reporter was pushing her way into an elevator already crowded with Finnertys when one of them asked her to let them have some time to themselves and Collin's older brother Sean moved to block the door. Snarled the reporter: "Maybe you want to go up on an assault charge, too."

The trial testimony raised grave questions of why the case ever went to court. Undisputed testimony showed that one of Finnerty's friends had gotten into an angry argument of disputed origin with Scott Herndon and Jeffrey Bloxsom outside the Third Edition, a bar on Wisconsin Avenue in Georgetown. Finnerty came on the scene and backed up his friend.

The two groups spent half an hour yelling at each other while slowly walking up Wisconsin Avenue. There was some shoving back and forth. Finnerty, who was described as "fired up" by a third friend watching from a distance, was chest-to-chest with Bloxsom. Finally fists flew. Herndon (according to Collin's friends) knocked Finnerty down from behind. One of his friends then charged in and punched Bloxsom in the face, knocking him down, too. Then came the police car and arrests.

The most hotly disputed question was who had been the aggressors. Collin's three friends blamed Bloxsom and Herndon. The defendant did not take the stand.

Bloxsom, testifying in a languid, almost bored manner, and Herndon claimed that Collin's group had attacked them without provocation. Finnerty in particular had repeatedly pushed Bloxsom and thrown fake punches while screaming ugly homophobic slurs, they said. The whole time, claimed Bloxsom and Herndon, they had been passive, peaceful, and punctilious in avoiding even bad language.

Right.

Many judges would have been skeptical of this self-serving tale of completely unprovoked aggression against virtuous victims patiently petitioning for peace. Especially after hearing an admission by the hotheaded Herndon during cross-examination by Collin's lawyer, Steven McCool: Herndon had told a police officer who had put a hand on his shoulder one night in 2004, when Herndon was extremely drunk, at a bar, accompanied by Bloxsom, "Get your fucking hands off me." And especially since both Herndon and Bloxsom had consulted lawyers about filing a suit for money damages against Collin. (They decided not to sue.) Most judges might at least have concluded that neither side had been proved the aggressor beyond a reasonable doubt because the witnesses were all interested parties whose testimony was in hopeless conflict.

But Judge Bayly pronounced himself impressed by Bloxsom. He accepted the smooth-talking young professional's version of events—except for his sworn testimony that Finnerty had punched and kicked Herndon, which inconveniently contradicted a prosecution admission that Finnerty had not assaulted Herndon. The judge also disregarded the three witnesses who contradicted Bloxsom and the two character witnesses who had vouched for Collin's nonviolent nature. On this basis, the judge found Finnerty guilty of assault, not by hitting anyone but by "shadow boxing" so that "Bloxsom said he was in fear of being struck."

Then Bayly pronounced a sentence of six months probation with conditions that unintentionally suggested this had all been for show: The judge removed both Collin's curfew and the community-service requirement, which remained in effect for his two unconvicted friends. If this had been a serious proceeding, wouldn't the postconviction sentence have been tougher on the defendant than the pretrial conditions imposed by the same judge? What, exactly, had been the point of spending tax dollars to put the defendant through a two-day trial with two prosecutors, two defense lawyers, a court reporter, bailiffs, and the judge himself, while summoning witnesses from near and far?

Long after it had become clear to anyone interested in facts that this episode involved no gay people, *The Herald-Sun* editorialists (on October 17) kept writing that Collin had been convicted of an assault "with strong homophobic overtones, against a gay man on a Washington, D.C., street." And Professor Houston Baker, now at Vanderbilt, kept accusing the lacrosse team of having "beat up a gay man in Georgetown."

(A few months later, on December 28, Bayly would quietly set aside the assault conviction itself, leaving Collin with no criminal record.)

Despite its inconsequential facts, the Finnerty trial proved a serious public relations blow to the defense. *Washington Post* columnist Marc Fisher helped set the tone of the coverage. Under the headline "Wolves in Blazers and Khakis," Fisher accused Finnerty of "find[ing] fun in tormenting the innocent," called his two character witnesses "arrogant" for praising his character, and sneered at his Georgetown friends for attending "the finest of schools."

With the Georgetown trial concluded, the focus returned to Durham, where the defense team had another bad day in court. On July 17, Judge Kenneth Titus, to whom the lacrosse case had passed from Judge Stephens under routine North Carolina procedure, presided over his first (and, ultimately, only) hearing of the case. Titus, a UNC law graduate, had worked in Durham as a defense lawyer before winning election to the bench in 2002. But in what defense lawyers took to be an ominous sign, he disclosed that he hadn't even read all the motions in the seventeen days since he had taken over the biggest case in North Carolina history. These included Kirk Osborn's May 1 motions cataloguing the misconduct on which he based his request to have Nifong removed from the case and seeking suppression of the rigged April 4 photo lineup. Titus also had on his desk defense motions complaining that Nifong appeared not to be complying with his obligations under the state's open discovery law.

Nifong, accusing unnamed defense lawyers of seeking publicity, said to the judge at the July 17 hearing: "It looked sometimes over the course of the last few months that some of these attorneys were almost disappointed that their clients didn't get indicted so they could be a part of this spectacle here in Durham." Judge Titus silently tolerated this unfounded attack on highly respected lawyers. Nifong also trashed the forty-three unindicted white lacrosse players as "a lot of witnesses who haven't cooperated with police." Titus remained silent then, too.

The judge threw one bone to the defense, quashing Nifong's months-belated subpoenas of the dorm keycard records of the unindicted players. A prosecutor interested in the truth would have sought this information before indicting anyone; it would show when each party attendee who lived on campus had arrived back at his dorms and could have helped reconstruct what had happened. But Nifong had never shown the slightest interest in reconstructing what had happened. And by July, with the DA having said on May 15 that the other forty-three players had done nothing wrong, even Judge Titus could not come up with a constitutional justification to grant Nifong's request.

The keycard records were completely consistent with the defense position that no rape had occurred. But the unindicted players stood on their privacy rights because they had reason to fear that, given the opportunity, Nifong would find ways to distort the records and limit the damage they would do to his case at any trial.

Titus issued two more important rulings, both bad for the three defendants. He refused to act on a request by Kirk Osborn to impose a deadline for Nifong to turn over all evidence as required by the state's open discovery statute, so that substantive motions could be heard. Osborn wanted the case resolved in time for Reade Seligmann to return to school in August. But Titus was in no rush to find out how weak Nifong's case really was.

More important, citing the extensive publicity to date and the need for "a jury free of partiality, bias or prejudice," Titus announced that he would rigorously enforce the bar's rules against public comments about the evidence. Indeed, he would enforce them against all potential witnesses—including the defendants, their forty-four teammates, and Coach Pressler—as well as the defense lawyers and Nifong. Titus did not explain how he could enforce against nonlawyers state bar rules that apply only to lawyers. And while the constitutionality of censoring speech by defendants and other witnesses is questionable, appealing would have been futile; appellate courts almost never intervene in criminal cases at the pretrial stage.

Defense lawyers minimized the scope of Titus's statement, noting that the ethics rules still allowed them to respond to Nifong's early, misleading statements. But the judge's statement amounted to a de facto gag order on the defendants, their families, and their teammates. They could not afford to take a chance on speaking out and perhaps being held in contempt if the judge were to decide after the fact that they had shown too little deference to his vague warning. "We were making Nifong look bad and making the local system look bad, and we were making some headway," a defense lawyer later recalled. "That was an effort to stop us."

Titus's de facto gag order was extraordinary in another respect: Neither the prosecution nor the defense had requested it. Nifong could not credibly have asked for a gag order given his preprimary publicity barrage. The defense attorneys wanted to be free to continue speaking out to counter the effect of Nifong's poisoning of the prospective jury pool in March and April.

It was, rather, the North Carolina NAACP that had been pushing since May for a gag order. The organization represented a constituency vital to the reelection of Judge Titus and other Durham County judges. It also had acted as cheerleader for the prosecution throughout the case. "Praise God," remarked William Barber, president of the state NAACP, when informed of Titus's action. Incredibly, Al McSurely, chairman of the group's Legal Redress Committee, used the occasion to lecture the *defense* lawyers: "Most other lawyers, including myself, just don't feel right challenging other lawyers and their tactics. But here, it was clearly over the edge what they were doing. As an attorney, there are supposed to be professional standards which you abide by. I'm glad someone in authority has reminded them of that." Irving Joyner, an NCCU law professor chosen by the state NAACP to "monitor" the case, accused Cheshire, Smith, and Osborn of fostering "prejudice" with their "grandstanding" on the case.

The push for a gag order was one of a succession of statements and actions by NAACP representatives throughout the lacrosse case that dramatically contrasted with the group's traditional positions.

The organization had been a strong voice both for the freedom of speech and for jealous protection of the rights of criminal defendants. But in the Duke case, with white defendants accused of raping a black woman, the rules changed for the NAACP. Suddenly it stood for denying free speech to criminal defendants and many others. It also endorsed denying the defendants the basic elements of due process and fair trials. A brief compendium:

Free Speech

From the time when NAACP leader and justice-to-be Thurgood Marshall was laying the groundwork for the great 1954 desegregation decision, *Brown v. Board of Education*, until the group's abrupt about-face in the lacrosse case, the NAACP had taken the lead in winning some of the most important First Amendment decisions ever issued by the Supreme Court. In the civil-rights era, cases it won or helped win included the 1958 decision in *NAACP v. Alabama* and the 1964 decision in *New York Times v. Sullivan*. During the Clinton administration, the organization had assailed a politically popular proposed "victims' rights" amendment to the Constitution because it would tilt trials against defendants. In an April 2000 letter to Senate leaders opposing the amendment, and stressing that "people of color have . . . historically been wrongly accused in this nation of crimes varying from the very minor to the most heinous," the NAACP leadership declared "our deeply held belief in the need to protect the innocent and allow every American the right to a fair trial."

But in the Duke case, McSurely called for a gag order to ban the defendants, their lawyers, and witnesses (as well as the prosecution) from speaking feely about the case. He euphemistically called this a request for a "quiet zone/let's let justice work" motion. His justification, according to *The Herald-Sun*, was that "media coverage of the alleged rape may deprive the alleged victim of her legal rights to a fair trial."

The NAACP had not asked for a "quiet zone" when Nifong was trashing the lacrosse players every day of the week of March 27; it was the evidence of innocence that McSurely wanted withheld from the public. And the Constitution does not confer upon any accuser any "legal rights to a fair trial." It is *defendants* whose fair-trial rights are protected; accusers with solid evidence have the power of the state on their side. Indeed, McSurely went beyond what even the most ardent victims' rights advocates on the national scene have endorsed.

Change of Venue

In criminal cases, the NAACP and its allies had repeatedly supported defendants' rights to a change of venue if they would have difficulty getting a fair trial where the alleged crime occurred. In 2000, a change of venue supported by the NAACP Legal Defense & Educational Fund, Inc. (which is allied but no longer affiliated with the NAACP) made possible the eventual release from prison of Wilbert Rideau, a Louisiana black man who served forty-four years in prison after being thrice convicted of murder by all-white, all-male juries. After the Fifth Circuit threw out his third conviction in 2000, the retrial was held with jurors from Monroe, a racially mixed university city, rather than overwhelmingly white Lake Charles. The Monroe jury convicted Rideau of manslaughter, which allowed him to be immediately released for time served.

But in the Duke case, the state NAACP furiously opposed any change of venue even before any defense lawyer suggested it. The reason was clear: to increase the chance of conviction, no matter how much Nifong had poisoned the jury pool against the lacrosse players. Nifong "still has a viable shot at victory before a jury in Durham," Irving Joyner told *Sports Illustrated* in June. Asked why, Joyner explained, "The Durham jury will probably have more African-Americans on it than would be involved in most other counties in North Carolina." Joyner stressed that "this case originated in Durham and should be tried here." Never mind the massive, almost unprecedented attacks on the defendants in Durham by the district attorney, the cops, their own professors, some black leaders, and the local and national media. Never mind that the case was the central issue in both the spring primary campaign and the fall general election campaign, or that it had polarized the community more than any event in recent memory, heightening the difficulty of choosing open-minded jurors.

Eyewitness Identification Rules

Working alongside the Innocence Project, the NAACP had been at the forefront of demanding greater procedural protections in eyewitness identifications.

And the state NAACP had strongly endorsed the work of North Carolina's Actual Innocence Commission, which had recommended strict lineup and photoidentification procedures, including seven filler photos per suspect.

But in the Duke case, the NAACP's Joyner and McSurely gave a pass to the same April 4, Nifong-Gottlieb photo-ID process that Jim Coleman had eloquently denounced as deliberately designed to get the accuser to pick "any three" lacrosse players. Joyner, declining to find any fault with the Nifong-Gottlieb process, asserted: "Based on case law from the U.S. Supreme Court and our North Carolina appellate courts, it is very easy for an identification procedure to pass constitutional muster and the written procedure which was adopted at some point by the Durham Police Department is not constitutionally required. Whether a jury will accept its validity is another question, but that has nothing to do with constitutional infirmities." McSurely said simply: "Mr. Nifong is an experienced prosecutor, and he can defend his decisions before the Court."

Not content merely to support procedures rigged against the lacrosse players, McSurely did his best to add his own poison to the jury pool. He posted on the state NAACP Web site (on August 9) a falsehood-filled, eighty-two-point memorandum of law entitled "Duke Lacrosse Update: Crimes and Torts Committed by Duke Lacrosse Team Players on 3/13 and 3/14 as Reported in the Press, Mainly from the Three Players' Defense Attorneys." Among McSurely's claims:

"The only Black [lacrosse] player, a freshman, left the party before the dancers arrived." False. "After about three minutes of dancing . . . there were racial remarks made." False. "Other men noticed Ms. M seemed quite vulnerable after drinking the clear liquid." False. "Around 12:20, some men who saw the vulnerable Ms. M returning to the house called their friends who had taken cabs and gone to get some cash from an ATM. Some returned." False. "The Sexual Assault Nurse Examiner (SANE) at Duke Hospital confirmed [the accuser's] injuries matched her reports when she was examined about 2 hours later." False. "Theresa Arico, the SANE coordinator at Duke Hospital said 'there was a certain amount of blunt force trauma present to create injury' and that the injuries the victim suffered were 'consistent with the story she told.'" False; Arico's comments referred to a generic definition of blunt force trauma, not to this specific case. "The ER doctor on duty that night also has reported that Ms. M. suffered trauma consistent with her story." False; Dr. Manly had made no such claim and found no physical evidence of rape.

McSurely subsequently defended the memorandum as embodying the NAACP's commitment to fairness for "both sides."

Beyond helping sustain the prosecution of three innocent men, the state

NAACP also undermined the interests of the minority and poor defendants whom the organization claims to represent, people who are disproportionately victimized by overzealous prosecutors and police misconduct in cases every year that draw zero publicity. The Duke case, as Jim Coleman pointed out, provided a "chance to engage" groups that ordinarily are little concerned with the rights of defendants and civil liberties, and perhaps create a multiracial coalition across ideological lines to seek fundamental reforms of North Carolina's criminal justice system. McSurely, Joyner, and their allies discarded the opportunity. Instead, they showed that they are indifferent to injustice—and even applaud it—when the victims are innocent white kids falsely accused by a black person. This decision not only set back race relations. It will make it harder ever to get the prosecutorial-misconduct boot off the necks of innocent black kids.

As if to prove this point, the state NAACP made no objection when on July 20 an African-American cook named Rene Thomas said he had been victimized in a brawl by two white, off-duty Durham police officers, one of whom used a racial epithet, while at least four other officers, including Sergeant Gottlieb and Officer Clayton, looked on. The incident happened after an exchange of words outside a Raleigh bar and restaurant named Blinco's, where Thomas worked. The Durham Police Department placed all five officers on administrative leave, promising an internal affairs investigation after Raleigh police filed charges. Yet when the charges came against two officers uninvolved in the lacrosse case, Police Chief Steve Chalmers, in a rare public appearance, fired them but did nothing to rebuke Gottlieb, Clayton, or the other officer for the racial epithets. That was fine with the NAACP.

With traditional defenders of due process and civil liberties such as the NAACP actively supporting Nifong's behavior, or at best keeping silent, new groups stepped into the breach. Perhaps the most influential was Friends of Duke University. FODU sought to give voice to the many, but scattered, Duke alumni and supporters concerned that Brodhead and much of the faculty had thrown the lacrosse players to the wolves.

The group's spokesperson, Jason Trumpbour, had earned his undergraduate (1988), master's (1991), and law (1991) degrees at Duke. He then took a Ph.D. in law from Cambridge, where he focused on the development of the court of exchequer in the fourteenth century. He spent three years as a prosecutor in the Maryland attorney general's office and then moved to teach courses including legal ethics at the University of Maryland Law School and the University of Baltimore.

Soon after its creation in May, FODU had established itself as a presence on the Web, offering relatively temperate criticism designed to appeal to the better angels of the Duke administration's nature. On July 19, it published as a full-page ad in the Duke *Chronicle* an open letter urging Brodhead to uphold due process protections and Duke's reputation. FODU conceded that Brodhead could not publicly attest to the accused students' innocence. But it criticized as excessively "passive" Duke's response to Nifong's improper statements, rigged lineup, refusals to look at exculpatory evidence, and sending of police into Duke dorms to interview players outside the presence of their counsel. "We believe," the open letter continued, "that the Duke administration has a positive obligation to ensure that Duke students are not singled out for unjust treatment by local authorities." FODU also lamented how "Duke cowered in the face of media pressure engineered by the unethical and possibly illegal conduct" of the district attorney.

Trumpbour's group asked Brodhead for two things. First, Duke should "use all its influence and moral suasion to ensure that these three Duke students receive justice through a fair process." Second, the university should "call attention to the larger, more positive, context the [Coleman] committee found. A resolution to look at oneself, warts and all, should not omit the 'all.'" FODU also asked members of the Group of 88 to reconsider their position and "count themselves among those victimized by this spring's false accusations."

The letter received extensive coverage from the Associated Press, the North Carolina print media, and Raleigh-Durham television stations. Brodhead responded a week later. He stressed a need "to move forward," not to debate what he or anyone else at Duke had done in the past. Studiously skirting what FODU had asked him to do, Brodhead added that "the University does not have direct access to the full truth of the case now any more than we did earlier, and we can't speak with certainty of matters that only the criminal justice system can resolve." But the FODU letter had been carefully worded to avoid asking him to comment on guilt or innocence; it had asked him to say something about Nifong's misconduct.

When Brodhead was offered direct access to "the full truth of the case," he declined to look. On July 27, Kevin and MaryEllen Finnerty flew to Durham to meet with the president. Given the mounting evidence of innocence and Nifong's questionable conduct, they urged the president to lift the suspensions of Reade and Collin. Brodhead wouldn't budge, and again mentioned the difficulty of making decisions without access to all the evidence. Kevin Finnerty then offered to allow Brodhead or anyone from the Duke legal office to meet with Wade Smith and review the entire discovery file that Nifong had turned over to the defense. He and his son had nothing to hide, Finnerty said, and anyone who looked through the prosecution's own files could see that, or at least make more confident decisions. The president wasn't interested.

Asked in an interview by one of the authors why he had declined the Finnertys' offer to show all of the of discovery documents to him or his designee, Brodhead responded: "I'll tell you why. . . . Because that would have made me be the court. It is not because I was indifferent to the students or the families. I was fully aware of the pain they were suffering and was very sympathetic to them. But the notion that I was the appropriate judge and cen- ter of certainty was something I tried to defend against because I was aware that my direct involvement could undermine the legal system and jeopardize the chance for a satisfactory outcome. . . . Our country and our culture work better if you have a process with its own rules and discipline to take these is- sues away from private parties. But I was also conscious that if Duke had used its institutional power to attack the case the DA might have complained of outside pressure and folded his hand, leaving an ambiguous, equivocal result. We could only ever have got to a satisfactory outcome through the workings of the legal process."

So it was that the university president deliberately cultivated ignorance of the overwhelming documentary evidence of innocence and of Nifong's abuse that were offered him while continuing to defer to the district attorney in all public statements. The students, as he stated in his response to the FODU letter, could wait for a trial at which they would have an opportunity to be "proved innocent."

Meanwhile, in Durham, the Lewis Cheek campaign against Nifong in the DA election was flagging. Cheek held a July 12 press conference to an- nounce that he hadn't made up his mind because of his obligations to his cur- rent clients and his three-year-old law firm, intensifying doubts that he would run at all. On July 27, he announced once and for all that he would not cam- paign and would not serve if elected. But his name would remain on the bal- lot; he would vote for himself; and he invited others unhappy with Nifong's performance to do the same. If Cheek won, Nifong would be out. And with Cheek declining to serve, Governor Mike Easley would need to appoint a new district attorney

Hours after Cheek's announcement, a posting appeared on a newly cre- ated blog called Liestoppers. It had begun a few weeks before as a private fo- rum of around twenty people. Some were from Durham, some not; none had any connection to the lacrosse team or defense lawyers. But they all had fol- lowed the case closely and were outraged by Nifong's behavior. They had met each other online as participants in Court TV forums commenting on the case. When the forum's moderator grew open in her pro-Nifong bias—even removing comments critical of the DA—these Nifong critics set up their own discussion board. One of their first plans was to use Cheek's line on the ballot to convert the campaign into an effort to recall Nifong.

Beth Brewer, a Durham resident and Verizon employee who had never before been active in a political campaign, agreed to serve as the group's spokesperson if others would help behind the scenes. She got in touch with Jackie Brown, who discussed the logistics of a successful campaign (forming a political action committee, raising money, distributing signs). Brown said she would support the effort but would initially stay behind the scenes, citing the need for a fresh face, someone unconnected with petition drive, to lead the charge against Nifong. Brown also cautioned Brewer to examine her personal record and that of her family, since if she had any skeletons in closet, they would come out in the campaign. When Brewer said she was perfectly clean—"not even a traffic ticket"—the Recall Nifong campaign began. And the Liestoppers blog was born.

Liestoppers took Cheek's July 27 move as its cue to start the recall-Nifong effort in earnest. The blog explained that regardless of Cheek's decision not to run, his presence on the ballot meant that "the people of Durham do have an option of voting against Mr. Nifong, if not a choice of voting for a specific candidate." It framed the issues for the fall campaign by saying: "A vote for Mr. Nifong will be a confirmation that the practices he has exercised in recent months are acceptable to the community," and also a public indication "that the citizens feel comfortable with a District Attorney willing to prejudge guilt, personally and in the media, prior to the completion of a complete police investigation." A vote to recall Nifong, on the other hand, "would serve as an expression of the unwillingness to accept the deception created by hinting at evidence which does not exist or by expressing theories of the case that are belied by what is known."

Nifong gave his one and only press conference of the general election campaign the next day. As to the lacrosse case, he admitted: "Obviously there were some things that we hoped we would have in terms of evidence that we ended up not having." But he nonetheless insisted without explanation that no evidence had emerged to change his opinion since March 27, when he had first asserted that lacrosse players had certainly raped the accuser with racist motives. Nifong also said he had underestimated the media attention the case would receive and had spoken out so aggressively only to assure people "that the community was in good hands with respect to this case, and they did not need to worry about it."

The district attorney dismissed the calls of Lewis Cheek, Jim Coleman, and others for a special prosecutor. Defiantly proclaiming that the case "remains a

Durham problem, and it demands a Durham solution," Nifong promised: "At the end of the day, this [lacrosse] case, like every criminal case, will be decided by a jury of twelve Durham citizens sworn to base their decision not on prejudice or emotion, but on the facts presented and the rule of law. I intend to be the prosecutor who presents those facts and argues that law."

Nifong lashed out at the now-withdrawn Cheek by claiming that he had joined with Ed Pope and Roland Leary in an attempt to buy the office. Ignoring the difficulty that they would have controlling an office in which Cheek had announced he would not serve, Nifong said: "I realized that their concern had not been with the concept of a small group of people owning the District Attorney's Office but with the concept of it being owned by someone other than them." This wording was almost identical to what Nifong had said during the primary campaign about Jerry Clayton, a key Freda Black backer. Nifong also implied that Cheek, Pope, and Leary had effectively blackmailed him by visiting his office to threaten a challenge in the election unless he would accept their advice on an unspecified political matter. Cheek, Pope, and Leary all told journalists the next day that they had no idea what Nifong was talking about. The DA never offered a public explanation.

Nifong also showed a stunning obliviousness to his own personal history by ridiculing the Liestoppers idea of an "Anybody but Nifong" campaign and declaring that "Durham's district attorney should be selected by the voters of Durham, not by the governor." Everybody knew, of course, that Nifong himself had been selected by the governor.

Nifong was behaving even more strangely in private. As district attorney, he was an ex officio member of the Durham Animal Control Advisory Committee, a volunteer body that oversees the county's animal control office. Two of the board's eight members had signed the petitions to place Cheek's name on the ballot. This, Nifong wrote in a July 28 e-mail to all board members, "truly dismayed" him: "Since it is apparent that many of you do not have confidence in me, I intend to reassess the position of my office with respect to representation on the board." His e-mail spurred wide ridicule after *The News & Observer* made it public two days later. Other board members expressed bafflement. Cheek observed, "I don't really understand how whether somebody signed my petition or not reflects on their confidence in Mr. Nifong's service on that board." Nifong stayed on the board.

After *The N&O* broke the animal control story, *The Herald-Sun* contained no mention of Nifong's e-mail in a follow-up piece the next day. This was par for the course. By early August, Durham residents who read both papers might have wondered whether they were covering the same case. *The Herald-Sun* editorial board had sought to bolster the DA no matter how egregious his conduct.

It dismissed criticisms and expressed confidence in early July that "the 25-year veteran of the prosecutor's office must have some evidence, or he would have dropped the case long ago." A July 30 editorial claimed that the Recall Nifong–Vote Cheek effort would "cheapen and demean the seriousness of the political process." An August 1 editorial praised Nifong's strange press conference, saying that "for Nifong's supporters, his words are sure to give them a boost of confidence."

The Herald-Sun's news coverage was dependably biased. The editor was Bob Ashley, a Duke graduate installed in 2005 when Kentucky-based Paxton media bought the newspaper. Soon dubbed the "Duke of Paducah" by staffers, Ashley promptly fired nearly 25 percent of them. He promised that the new, leaner workforce would focus intensively on Durham issues. Yet he seemed to rule certain Durham issues off limits. While regularly quoting the flaccid pro-Nifong commentary of the NAACP's Irving Joyner, the paper waited five months before mentioning the devastating anti-Nifong analysis of the far more respected Duke law professor Jim Coleman. *The Herald-Sun* also ignored complaints about police misconduct and the political agendas of Trinity Park neighbors who had led protests against the lacrosse players. Ashley would later plead that he lacked the resources to explore these issues.

In a July 23 column, Ashley enthusiastically endorsed an argument by Washingtonpost.com columnist Andrew Cohen suggesting that a type of "insanity" infected Nifong's critics. Portraying the mass of evidence of innocence and of false statements by Nifong as mere bumps in the road, Ashley claimed that "it is possible that a savage rape occurred" and that the truth could emerge only at a trial. He also stressed that "all the facts aren't out, and that the defense attorneys are releasing just what fragments of the total evidence they choose to make public."

The paper's crime reporter, John Stevenson, put his own bias on display in an August 1 story claiming to report the "previously undisclosed" news that "semen found in the house where three Duke lacrosse players allegedly raped an exotic dancer matches the DNA of two team members."

But in fact this was very old news. And even Nifong had never claimed that it supported his case. In mid-April, both *The News & Observer* and WRAL had reported that semen of Matt Zash (whom Nifong cleared on May 15) had been found on the bathroom floor and that semen of Dave Evans and another person unrelated to the case had been found on a white towel in the hallway. In the words of blogger John in Carolina, a sharp critic of the local media's handling of the case, the August 1 Stevenson article was "a sham repackaging of material previously disclosed."

The Stevenson article offset quotes from defense lawyers Bill Thomas and

Kerry Sutton dismissing these semen findings as insignificant against quotes of two other local attorneys who were misleadingly described as neutral about Nifong's behavior. One was the NAACP's Irving Joyner. He said: "It would tend to support the prosecution's case. . . . There are still some hurdles, but this will help the prosecutor. The defense will have to go some lengths to explain it." The other was John Fitzpatrick, a Nifong friend who had donated to his campaign. He said: "I think it's crucial. . . . It gives more credence to the prosecution's theory that something happened. It is a potential link to a crime. It is a big thing." The paper did not disclose these connections, which gave both men a vested interest in seeing the case go to trial.

Heavily tilting the news in Nifong's favor in this manner might have seemed like a good business idea to the circulation-starved *Herald-Sun*. Few Duke students, after all, were subscribers, and Ashley had made a big effort to increase the paper's visibility in the African-American community. But perhaps the paper's bias was so obvious that it turned off readers. In the six months after Nifong's nomination, the paper experienced the greatest decline of *any* of North Carolina's largest newspapers, seeing its circulation plunge 7.3 percent daily and 10.5 percent on Sunday.

The N&O, on the other hand, distinguished itself after its lamentable first few articles in late March—and saw its circulation rate outperform that of every other North Carolina newspaper of comparable size. While the paper's left-leaning editorial board virtually ignored the case, reporters Joseph Neff and Benjamin Niolet produced by far the best news coverage of any newspaper in the country. And columnist Ruth Sheehan produced some of the sharpest commentary. Herself a survivor of rape, Sheehan had penned the March 27 "we know you know" column, condemning all members of the team for conspiring to cover up a three-man gang rape. But unlike legions of other journalists around the country, who had participated in the rush to judgment only to fall silent as Nifong's case imploded, the liberal Sheehan revisited her assumptions as the facts emerged.

Sheehan called on June 19 for removing Nifong from the case, in the first of a series of columns that would make her one of Nifong's most passionate and influential critics. While conceding what she still saw as the possibilities that a rape had occurred and that Nifong had a "stash of evidence" hidden away, she asserted that "the prosecutor's case appears to be unraveling" and wondered whether Nifong's "over-the-top remarks don't violate the bar's admonition against prosecutors 'heightening public condemnation of the accused.'" (The state bar would make exactly that charge six months later.) Sheehan was most troubled by "what the district attorney appears to have known, compared with what he said" about condoms, the medical evidence, the 911 caller's identity, and the supposed racial motivations of the alleged rapists.

The most thorough exposé yet of the phoniness of Nifong's case and of his abuses came in an August 6 article by Joe Neff, who had gotten access before Judge Titus's de facto gag order to the 1,813 pages of discovery documents that the DA had turned over to the defense by late June. This appeared to be all the evidence that Nifong had—given his June 22 claim that he had turned everything over the defense.

Document after document, Neff reported, contradicted the authorities' claims. "To get warrants, police made statements that weren't supported by information in their files," Neff reported. "The district attorney commented publicly about the strength of the medical evidence before he had seen it. He promised DNA evidence that has not materialized. He suggested that police conduct lineups in a way that conflicted with department policy."

Neff also reported an April 4 memo by Office Michele Soucie revealing that Brian Meehan of the DNA Security had been so eager to get Nifong's business that he had quickly offered to lower his company's usual price. Neff later had to publish a correction because he misreported the date of this memo at the top of his article. Critics used this conspicuous but not very significant error to try to discredit the rest of Neff's article, which proved accurate.

With *Newsweek* and now Neff suggesting that the initial storyline had been completely off base, *The New York Times* decided to revisit the case. Duff Wilson had been very much part of the journalistic pack committed to the now increasingly discredited presumption-of-guilt approach. But his editors kept him on the case and in effect assigned him to reassess, among other things, his own work.

Wilson had one new piece of information with which to work. He had obtained a thirty-three-page document entitled "Supplemental Case Notes for: Sergeant M. D. Gottlieb." It included eighteen previously nonpublic typed pages purporting to describe Gottlieb's case-related actions before and after the April 4 photo-ID process as well as fifteen more already-public pages reproducing the transcript of the April 4 photo-ID process. Because the eighteen pages had not been given to defense attorneys until July 17, when Judge Titus had imposed his de facto gag order, whoever leaked the memo risked being accused of violating the order.

This memo appeared to have been typed from memory months after most of the events it described. And Gottlieb said he had no contemporaneous notes of witness interviews or other investigative tasks, excepting two pages about his work on an insignificant matter one April afternoon. This was a shocking departure from standard police practice. Competent officers always take notes of witness interviews and other matters on which they need a reliable record to document their work and refresh their recollection.

"This is a pristine white document that fell out of the sky four months later," observed Wade Smith, Collin Finnerty's lawyer. "Where are his notes? How can you interview the most important witness you've ever interviewed in your life and not take notes?"

Gottlieb also admitted that he had consulted the notes of other officers in preparing his memorandum, another violation of standard police practice. Even so, his memorandum contained no fewer than eleven contradictions of the contemporaneous, handwritten notes of Detective Himan, Officer Soucie, Officer R. A. Reid, SANE trainee Tara Levicy, and the UNC doctors who saw Crystal Mangum the day after the alleged attack. In *each and every case*, Gottlieb's version of events was more favorable to the prosecution.

It could hardly have been coincidental that these contradictions purported to paper over many of the holes that defense motions had exposed in Nifong's case. Perhaps the most blatant contradiction was between Gottlieb's memo and Himan's handwritten notes—which defense attorneys had already released to the public—of Mangum's vague descriptions of her alleged attackers during their March 16 joint interview. According to Himan's notes, she described her three "attackers" as a "white male, short, red cheeks fluffy hair chubby face, brn" (Adam); "heavy set short haircut 260–270" (Matt); and "chubby" (Brett). None of these descriptions even remotely resembled the six-foot, five-inch, rail-thin, freckled, baby-faced, light-haired Collin Finnerty. The six-foot, one-inch, 215-pound Reade Seligmann was neither short, nor chubby, nor anywhere near 260 pounds. Nor did any of these descriptions closely match the five-foot, ten-inch, 190-pound, superbly fit Dave Evans.

According to Gottlieb's memo, on the other hand, Crystal gave almost dead-on descriptions of Finnerty, Evans, and Seligmann, respectively: "1) W/M, young, blonde hair, baby faced, tall and lean, 2) W/M, medium height (5' 8"+ with Himan's build) dark hair medium build and had red (rose colored) cheeks, and the third suspect as being a W/M, 6+ feet, large build with dark hair." According to Gottlieb, she did not specify which description applied to "Adam," "Matt," or "Brett." Neither in his memorandum nor subsequently did Gottlieb ever explain why, if his memo was honest in stating that Crystal had given a precise description of Collin Finnerty on March 16, the police did not show her Finnerty's photo in either the March 16 or March 21 photo arrays. Indeed, it is inconceivable that the police would have omitted Finnerty's photo if Mangum had given those descriptions on March 16. This omission, a bit like Sherlock Holmes's dog that didn't bark in the night, proves that the descriptions in Gottlieb's memo were contrived after the indictments to match the defendants.

Another contradiction from the March 16 interview involved Officer R. A. Reid. Her photos of Crystal's face and neck showed no bruises despite Mangum's sometime story of being hit in the face, strangled, and having her head smashed against a sink. And Reid's written report of the session indicated that Crystal's only injuries were a cut heel, a cut toe, and bandages on both knees. The Gottlieb memorandum, on the other hand, claimed that "Reid stated [Mangum] had the onset of new bruises present." Gottlieb did not explain their absence from the photos, from Reid's own report, and from the many reports created to record Mangum's frequent hospital visits.

Gottlieb's memorandum also contradicted the medical records created by Tara Levicy on multiple points. Her notes of her March 14 interview with Crystal recounted the accuser's claim that Kim Roberts had stolen her money.

Gottlieb, however, had Crystal telling an entirely different story: that "after the men raped her, one of the men took her purse from her." No other officer or medical official involved in the case ever recorded any such claim by Crystal that the lacrosse players stole her money.

Levicy's March 14 report also showed that Crystal had no rectal injuries, as would have been expected based on her claim of anal (as well as vaginal and oral) rape, and listed nonbleeding scratches on the knee, anterior patella, and right heel as the only "signs of physical trauma."

Gottlieb, on the other hand, claimed that in a March 21 conversation Levicy had described Crystal's injuries in a dramatically different fashion and had recalled seeing physical evidence of rape. According to the sergeant, Levicy "stated the victim had edema *and* tenderness to palpitation both *anally* and especially *vaginally*." [Emphasis added.] Gottlieb also wrote: "I asked [Levicy] if the exam was consistent with blunt force trauma, and she replied yes. . . . I asked her if the blunt force trauma was consistent with the sexual assault that was alleged by the victim. She stated the trauma was consistent with the victim's allegation."

If Levicy—who did not even perform the physical exam (Dr. Manly did)—said any of those things, she thereby contradicted all of the hospital records, including her own.

Even if Gottlieb accurately reported what Levicy said, it would not mean much. That's because "consistent with" is a medically ambiguous phrase, especially when threaded through two interrelated leading questions. "Consistent with the sexual assault alleged" might be interpreted to mean only that the exam *did not rule out* (or support) Crystal's claim that she had been sexually assaulted. It could also mean that the exam found some far from conclusive evidence that she *may* have been sexually assaulted. The one thing that Levicy's supposed March 21 statement to Gottlieb could not mean to any serious physician, nurse, or lawyer was that the exam *proved* that Crystal had been sexually assaulted.

A good reporter reading the Gottlieb's memo would have smelled a rat, or a bunch of rats. And Gottlieb's claim that he took contemporaneous notes on only one afternoon during the four months of investigating the case establishes either that he was incompetent or that he was lying. But Duff Wilson and his colleague Jonathan Glater found Gottlieb's memo so credible—or perhaps so convenient—that they used it as the spine of the long-awaited *Times* reassessment. While blandly mentioning some of the contradictions between Gottlieb's memo and other, harder evidence, the *Times* proceeded as though the possibility that Gottlieb was lying had not crossed its collective mind.

Late in the afternoon of August 24, Wilson called Brad Bannon for comment—hoping, Bannon later suspected, to catch the attorney's voice mail so *The Times* could say that defense attorneys had not returned a call. But Bannon was at his desk, and when Wilson laid out the article's pro-Nifong thesis, he was horrified.

Bannon and Cheshire spent hours on the phone with Wilson that afternoon. When the reporter suggested that Mangum was bruised, Bannon sent along the March 16 photos showing no bruising. The lawyers painstakingly walked Wilson through the evidentiary holes in Nifong's case. Wilson thanked them for their help; that evening, he sent Bannon a peculiar request for a full copy of the discovery file, so he could engage in a "more careful" and "re-reviewing" of the material—*after* the huge article was published. Wouldn't that be a bit late? While Bannon and Cheshire got some (not all) factual errors removed, it was clear that the article's pro-Nifong slant was set in stone.

The big piece ran on August 25, jumping from the front page to a full page inside the paper and totaling 5,600 words. The headline was: "Files in Duke Case Give Details but No Answers."

Wilson and Glater led the piece with Gottlieb's claim that Levicy had found evidence of "blunt force trauma . . . consistent with the sexual assault that was alleged by the victim." Then a reference to the newspaper's favorite theme, the "tangled American opera of race, sex and privilege." Then came their main message: "By disclosing pieces of evidence favorable to the defendants, the defense has created an image of a case heading for the rocks. But an examination of the entire 1,850 pages of evidence gathered by the prosecution in the four months after the accusation yields a more ambiguous picture. It shows that while there are big weaknesses in Mr. Nifong's case, there is also a body of evidence to support his decision to take the matter to a jury. . . .

"In several important areas, the full files, reviewed by *The New York Times,* contain evidence stronger than that highlighted by the defense."

Most ludicrously, the reporters claimed that "aside from two brief early conversations with the police, [Mangum] gave largely consistent accounts of being raped by three men in a bathroom." This in the face of the mass of contradictions between her accounts to various police on March 14, and between all those accounts and the story she had told Tara Levicy the same day, and between all of her March 14 stories and her April 6 signed statement. The *Times* glossed over these contradictions. The reporters shrugged off as "misunderstandings" the reports by Sergeant Shelton (of Crystal recanting her rape claim) and Duke police officer Day (of Durham police saying that she claimed she was raped by twenty men). As for Officer Sutton's report of Crystal claiming she was penetrated by five men, that "has not been explained." The reporters attempted neither to explain it nor to reconcile it with their own "largely consistent" claim. Nor did they mention that after telling the SANE trainee that Kim Roberts had helped a guy drag her back into the party house to be raped and "took all my money and everything," Crystal had claimed in her April 6 written statement that "three guys grabbed" Roberts and "separated us . . . while we tried to hold on to each other."

Throughout, Wilson and Glater presented a superficially neutral tone. They conceded that "major problems" existed with the case, including the lack of DNA evidence linking any charged player to the accuser; the procedure followed in the April 4 photo lineup; Seligmann's apparently "powerful alibi, based on a cellphone log and other records"; and Kim Roberts's failure to corroborate the rape charge. While mentioning this and other exculpatory evidence, they understated its cumulative weight and gave unwarranted credence to contrary evidence of dubious credibility, such as the Gottlieb memo.

The article was littered with inaccuracies, such as its claim that, just after midnight, "the dancers stopped. An argument ensued. Using a racial epithet, someone yelled that they had asked for white dancers, not black ones. That much is agreed. It was 12:04 A.M. March 14." In fact, far from "agreed," the *Times* claim that a racial epithet was hurled at the women inside the house was clearly false. Kim Roberts—who had a strong motive to report any such epithet—as well as every other person at the party had contradicted Crystal Mangum's account that racial epithets were used inside the house. The *Times* never corrected this or its other factual errors.

But the most misleading aspects of the article were its selective presentation of evidence and omissions. Examples:

Time Line

Wilson and Glater suggested that no strong evidence existed of what occurred between 12:04 and 12:53, while ignoring highly probative evidence that there was no rape—such as the post-12:30 A.M. time-stamped photographs showing Magnum smiling, banging on the door, and passed out on the back stoop.

Duke Hospital

Aside from swallowing Gottlieb's far-from-credible account of what Tara Levicy had supposedly said about "blunt force trauma," the article touted his claim that she told him that Crystal "began to scream hysterically" when an unidentified male nurse entered her room. But Levicy had recorded no such event in her written report. That did not stop Wilson and Glater from assuming that Crystal "had reacted in a way that sexual-assault experts say is not uncommon among rape victims."

UNC Hospital

Wilson and Glater portrayed the March 15 UNC medical report as a big asset for Nifong's case, saying it showed that a day after the alleged attack, "the woman's condition appeared worse," with doctors observing "a limping gait" and confirming "muscle tenderness and that her head did not have the full range of motion." The reporters did not mention that such symptoms can easily be faked. They also downplayed the "puzzling" contradictions in various accounts of the woman's intoxication, which she had admitted to the UNC doctors. The article said with vast understatement that the accuser "has given slightly differing accounts of how much she drank that evening," while stressing police claims that whatever she drank, or however much Flexeril she used, "does not explain why the woman seemed so profoundly intoxicated."

March 16 Bruises

The reporters used Gottlieb's description of the March 16 interview to depict Crystal as a courageous victim in terrible pain: She "talked about her life" for about an hour before giving a detailed account of the party, when—according to Gottlieb—"tears ran down her face freely, and her nose began to run."

They reported Gottlieb's already-discredited claim that "she had the onset of new bruises present." While noting that "the female officer's report does not mention bruises," the reporters did not reveal that the photos, part of the 1,850 pages they had claimed to examine, showed no bruises.

March 16 Descriptions

Nor did the reporters seem skeptical of what they termed Crystal's "ambiguous" March 16 descriptions, which they said "closely correspond to the defendants." Noting the stark inconsistencies between that memo and Himan's note, they said again that the difference "could not be explained"—while adding that "Sergeant Gottlieb, 43, is by far the more experienced" of the two officers. The obvious implication: Himan had made a rookie mistake. Make that three rookie mistakes. *Big* mistakes.

April 4 Photo Lineup

Wilson and Glater never mentioned that Nifong had instructed police to violate their own procedures and show Mangum photos only of the forty-six them suspects. Instead, they marveled at how the "full transcript shows some precise recollections, three weeks after a relatively brief encounter with a large group of white strangers." What of Crystal misidentifying the player who made the broomstick comment? And confidently claiming that she saw Brad Ross in the front yard talking to Kim Roberts at a time when he was twenty miles away in Raleigh? Neither these nor her other errors were mentioned in the article. Instead, it made much of Crystal's "accurate" identification of Dan Flannery as the person who had paid her. The insinuation: Despite defense nitpicking about procedures, the accuser may well have correctly identified three rapists.

DNA

Wilson and Glater quoted half a sentence from Nifong's March 23 application for an order to obtain DNA samples from the forty-six white lacrosse players: "Mr. Nifong's office had written that the tests would 'show conclusive evidence as to who the suspect(s) are in the alleged violent attack upon this victim.'" But they curiously omitted the first half: "The DNA evidence requested will immediately rule out any innocent persons." Nor did the article explain how blatantly Nifong had contradicted this assurance after learning the DNA results. They added that "outside experts say it is possible for a rapist to leave no DNA evidence" without quoting any experts or discussing the views of many that the kind of rape and beating alleged by the accuser would have to have left DNA evidence all over the place.

Bogus DNA Connections

Mimicking the warmed-over August 1 *Herald-Sun* "news" article, the *Times* noted that "more DNA results have been made public in the case"—they had been public for more than four months—and suggested two connections that even Nifong had not attempted to exploit: Matt Zash's semen was in the bathroom at "about the same spot where the woman said she had spat out semen from someone who orally raped her." And Dave Evans's semen was on a bedroom towel, which the *Times* linked to the accuser's claim "that someone had wiped her vagina with a rag." Wilson and Glater neglected to mention that neither sample contained Crystal's DNA, which was presumably why Nifong had deemed them irrelevant. Nor did the article mention that Nifong had explicitly cleared Zash (and others) of participating in any assault.

Condoms

The *Times* cited Nifong's suggestion in early April that the reason no semen had been found might be the use of condoms. It failed to explain how deceptive this assertion was: Nifong's own files, which Wilson and Glater said they had thoroughly "reviewed," showed Crystal saying her rapists had not used condoms and that she had spat semen onto the floor.

Legal Ethics

Dismissing the DA's critics as "defense lawyers, amplified by Duke alumni and a group of bloggers who have closely followed the case," the reporters ignored Jim Coleman and the ethics experts who had accused Nifong of possible violations of the state bar's code of ethics. They noted Nifong's inexplicable refusal to look at evidence of innocence offered by defense lawyers, but treated it as inconsequential. [*]

Nifong's Political Motives

Wilson and Glater almost ignored the widespread view that Nifong had brought the rape charges to save his election campaign. Only 17 of their 5,600 words discussed the spring primary. They did not discuss the Cheek-Liestoppers challenge in the general election campaign at all.

Defense attorneys said that after the story appeared, Wilson told them that he and *Times* editors had led with the Gottlieb memorandum because it was "newsy." This came close to admitting that the *Times* valued its little scoop more than truthfulness or fairness—in an article three times as long as any other the *Times* published about the case. Wilson also conceded to defense attorneys that he had made some errors of fact in the article.

More astonishingly, Wilson claimed that he had not really meant to suggest that Mangum's (wildly contradictory) accounts were "largely consistent"— which is what his article said—but only that she had eventually settled on three as the number of attackers. Wilson was equally preposterous in telling defense attorneys that neither he nor his editors could tell whether Mangum's March 16 photos (including one in the photo insert for this book) showed bruises. Despite all this, *Times* editors seemed proud of Wilson's efforts.

"The thrust of this August story," *Times* standards editor Craig Whitney later explained, "is that there's more to the prosecution case than the defense would have you believe." Kurt Andersen of *New York* magazine offered a breezier summary: "It isn't a witch hunt, Nifong's not so bad, these aren't the Scottsboro Boys, the accuser may well have been raped, these Duke guys might have done it, the case deserves to go to trial."

With the nation's most influential newspaper effectively endorsing his handling of the case on its front page, Nifong was very much alive as August neared its end, despite all of the body blows to his case and his credulity. The Gottlieb memorandum, if believed, shored up weaknesses in his case. The misleading news coverage of Collin Finnerty's trial had reinforced the image of the lacrosse players as thugs. Cheek's halfhearted election challenge seemed beatable. The NAACP was pushing for trial of the lacrosse players and the Duke administration was treating Nifong with deference and respect as he oppressed Duke students.

18. TURNING THE TIDE

THE AUGUST 25 *New York Times* was a turning point in public perception, but not in the way *Times* editors might have hoped. Beginning three hours after the article's midnight publication, blogs deftly tore the piece to shreds, exposing the reporters' factual errors, their omission of critical evidence, and their overall pro-Nifong bias. The main blogs focusing on the Duke case thereby established their credibility as actors in the case.

Three factors had already made the case a natural focus for high-quality bloggers outraged by what they had seen of the case. The simplest was to provide an outlet for the natural curiosity that was frustrated by the refusal of the mainstream media either to name the accuser or to report much about her life or character. (The same media had no hesitation about naming and publicly dissecting the defendants.) Several blogs, notably the crime-oriented Johnsville News, named Crystal Mangum from the start.

Second, the extreme one-sidedness and inaccuracies of the media coverage, especially in the early weeks, left a vacuum to be filled by the two principal case-related blogs, Durham-in-Wonderland (published by KC Johnson, a coauthor of this book) and later Liestoppers. Finally, a steady diet of meaty new factual content—which kept the blogs engaged and interesting—was publicly available and accessible to an unusual degree. North Carolina's open discovery law gave defense attorneys physical possession of the state's files (such as the photo lineup transcript and statements of Mangum, her "driver," and Kim Roberts) much earlier in the process than in most states. When defense attorneys released key police documents, usually as attachments to motions, anyone with Internet access had the tools to provide informed commentary.

In the spring and early summer, the most widely read blog to focus on the case was Talk Left, run by Colorado criminal defense attorney Jeralyn Merritt. She became nationally known as a passionate and articulate defender of President Bill Clinton in the late 1990s, when she made hundreds of appearances on cable talk shows—especially MSNBC and CNBC—during his impeachment and trial. Shortly thereafter she started her blog, specializing in criminal defense and civil liberties issues, which had more than 15 million unique visitors between 2000 and the start of the lacrosse case in 2006.

For Merritt, the April 10 announcement of no DNA matches was definitive: "The DA should drop the case," she wrote the next day, citing her experience as a criminal defense attorney. "He can [keep doing] DNA testing till the cows come home. If there was none in or on the accuser, none under her fingernails and none on her belongings, how will he ever prove a rape?"

When Nifong continued to go forward, Merritt started looking harder at his publicity barrage and his rigged April 4 photo lineup. She ultimately wrote more than fifty posts on the case, in the process showing how, almost from day one, anyone sensitive to civil liberties and due process could detect the scope of Nifong's improprieties. Merritt also established an online forum, which attracted a number of impressive pseudonymous commenters into the summer. Then a self-described Nifong volunteer who lived in Trinity Park flooded the threads with tangential comments and drove most forum members away. By late August, the most serious online discussion of the case had migrated to the Liestoppers forums. And while most of the pro-defense commentary came from centrist and moderately liberal thinkers, conservative New York lawyer Michael Gaynor and others on the political right also pounded prolifically away with well-argued critiques of Nifong and his Duke and Durham enablers.

The Liestoppers blog took the lead in demolishing the *Times* story. In a 3,000-word post that went up at 3:20 A.M. on August 25, just over three hours after the 5,600-word Wilson-Glater article had hit the *Times* Web site, Liestoppers dissected what it termed "the unforgivable flaws and omissions in Duff Wilson's article." The blog stressed that Wilson's "bizarre" omission of Crystal Mangum's cellphone records and neighbor Jason Bissey's affidavit falsely suggested that there had been a fifty-minute period when a rape could have occurred; in fact, the longest period not ruled out by objective evidence was seven minutes (from 12:31 until 12:38 A.M.). Liestoppers ridiculed Wilson's claim that Crystal's stories were consistent, chastised the *Times* for its "incomplete" and "misleading" explanation of the DNA evidence, and wondered how Wilson could have treated the Gottlieb memorandum as credible.

Blog postings also quickly identified serious factual errors in the Wilson article—each of which framed the case in terms favorable to Nifong and each of which the *Times*, despite reader requests to the corrections page, subsequently refused to correct. The first was the false report (noted above) that a racial epithet had been uttered in the house as the women stopped dancing at 12:04 A.M. In addition, the article stated that on March 16, Crystal "identified four people she thought were at the party, including Mr. Seligmann." She did identify four people, but not Seligmann; she was only 70 percent sure she even saw him. (The *Times* did publish a correction on this item, but one that did not include the critical information that she was only 70 percent certain of seeing Seligmann, and therefore did not "identify" him.) The article stated, "The other dancer, Ms. Roberts, told the police that her partner had arrived 'clearly sober.'" That, too, was clearly false: Roberts's two statements to police contained no such remark, although she did make such a claim to reporters later—about the same time she asked a New York publicist for advice on how to "spin this to my advantage."

The blogs' dismantling of the *Times* piece soon spread to the mainstream media. Appearing on *The Situation* the evening that the *Times* piece ran, MSNBC general manager Dan Abrams, who had had earlier and better access to the discovery file than Wilson, described the "shameful" *Times* article as an "editorial on the front page of what is supposed to be the news division of the newspaper." A *Slate* column, published August 29 by Stuart Taylor Jr., a coauthor of this book, summarized a view shared even by many of those who had initially joined the *Times* in rushing to judgment:

> The Wilson-Glater piece highlights every superficially incriminating piece of evidence in the case, selectively omits important exculpatory evidence, and reports hotly disputed statements by not-very-credible police officers and the mentally unstable accuser as if they were established facts. With comical credulity, it features as its centerpiece a leaked, transparently contrived, 33-page police sergeant's memo that seeks to paper over some of the most obvious holes in the prosecution's evidence.

The blogs' critiques of Nifong and his enablers picked up more steam, and more readers, thanks to the August 29 trial of Moezeldin Elmostafa. He was the cab driver arrested and jailed by two of Nifong's rape-case investigators— on a two-and-one-half-year-old misdemeanor charge of aiding a shoplifter— after becoming a strong alibi witness for Reade Seligmann.

Bloggers including Johnsville News, Durham-based John in Carolina, and the Talk Left discussion forums portrayed Elmostafa's arrest as ill-concealed witness tampering. At first not even all critics of Nifong were persuaded. *The News & Observer*'s Ruth Sheehan called this attack on Nifong "a bit Grassy Knoll-ish" in an August 17 column. "This case boasts plenty of bizarre fodder that is actually true," wrote Sheehan, but "I warn you, there's plenty more online that isn't."

Then came Elmostafa's one-day trial, which made Sheehan a believer in the plausibility of the witness-tampering theory. That morning, defense attorney Tom Loflin, representing Elmostafa for free, asserted in a court filing that Nifong had used the shoplifting incident "to try to pressure [the cabbie] into changing his evidence to favor the prosecution in the lacrosse case."

Nifong's office had hinted to reporters that the convicted shoplifter would testify that Elmostafa knew that she was carrying stolen purses when he drove her away from a Hecht's department store in 2003. But the prosecution never called her to the stand. The reason, according to Kirk Osborn, who later interviewed the woman (as did Loflin), was that after Nifong's office had brought her from her prison cell to Durham to testify, she told the authorities that Elmostafa had been unwitting and innocent.

That revelation did not stop Nifong's office from proceeding with its effort to convict Elmostafa. The prosecution and a Hecht's security guard also claimed that a security video would show Elmostafa speeding off to escape before the shoplifter had even closed the car door. Instead, the tape showed the woman getting into the taxi and closing the door and the cabbie driving normally away. When Ruth Sheehan saw the video at the trial, she wrote, it reminded her of "going live with Geraldo Rivera when he opened Al Capone's vault: There was nothing there."

The evidence also exposed Nifong's extraordinary involvement in Elmostafa's arrest. Loflin disclosed that it was Nifong investigator and confidant Linwood Wilson, not the Durham Police, who had dug up the three-year-old Elmostafa misdemeanor warrant from files containing thousands of other unserved warrants. Loflin also introduced Detective Himan's notes stating: "Mr. Nifong wanted to know when we picked [Elmostafa] up."

As if to strip any remaining credibility from Nifong's repeated denials of any connection between Elmostafa's arrest and his role as a defense witness for Seligmann, Nifong rape-case investigators Himan and Clayton spent the entire day at Elmostafa's trial, in uniform. "Why are they here?" Loflin asked the court. "Supposedly they know zero about Hecht's, so why are they here?"

District Judge Ann McKown quickly rendered a not guilty verdict. Kirk Osborn, who had developed a warm relationship with Elmostafa, was in the courtroom to welcome the result.

Not coincidentally, some speculated, Elmostafa's reportedly reluctant trial prosecutor, Ashley Cannon, quit her job under Nifong in early November, complaining that she had been sexually harassed by another prosecutor and Nifong had ignored her complaint.

In her column on the Elmostafa trial, Ruth Sheehan recalled poking "a little fun at the bloggers in the black-helicopter-infested skies of cyberspace," but went on to add: "Darn if this isn't another case where the bloggers, with all their paranoid conspiracy theories, just might be right."

With Duke's students returning in late August for the fall 2006 semester, some of the many Nifong critics among them decided to mobilize fellow students to vote against him. The leaders included juniors Emily Wygod, a Democrat from San Diego majoring in psychology; Christiane Regelbrugge, a Republican from Charlotte majoring in economics; and Brooke Jandl, an independent from a small town in Kansas majoring in economics. With less than 20 percent of Duke students registered to vote in Durham, the three young women formed a nonpartisan political committee, Duke Students for an Ethical Durham, hoping to sign up at least two thousand more students.

The group's founding statement asserted that "principles of due process—and of basic fairness—mean that Duke students should be treated according to the same city procedures that apply to all residents of Durham" and that "Durham County residents and Duke students alike deserve a district attorney who rigorously follows all provisions of the North Carolina State Bar's Rules of Professional Conduct." The spokeswomen, Democrat Wygod and Republican Regelbrugge, also generated publicity. Within days of DSED's creation, both women appeared on a Fox segment with Greta Van Susteren. DSED also attracted notice from *The N&O* and *The Chronicle*.

In response, Nifong authorized formation of another citizens' committee, focused on registering NCCU students. The committee's leadership revealed a lot about Nifong and the extremist nature of his appeal to black voters. One cochair was Kim Brummell, who had written a 2005 book advocating greater use of DNA to free wrongly incarcerated minorities (but, she openly stated, only minorities); she did not even live in Durham County. The other was the same Victoria Peterson who had suggested at the April 11 NCCU forum that Duke University Hospital had "tampered with" the DNA samples; and who had urged a crowd to burn down 610 North Buchanan while sharing a platform with New Black Panther leader Malik Shabazz.

Nifong expressed elation that Peterson and Brummell had formed their committee, telling reporters, "I was very pleased. It made me feel good."

Beyond her anti-Duke conspiracy theories and her aligning with the New Black Panthers, Peterson had a background that made her an unusual choice for a high-profile position in a North Carolina Democrat's campaign. Before the Duke case, Peterson had been best known for her vitriolic opposition to gay rights. She had, for instance, opposed a statewide bill to ban discrimination against gay people on the ground that it would allow gays and lesbians to "come to work dressed one day looking like a female and two weeks later looking like a male."

Among Duke students, the anti-Nifong campaign was well received. "It was totally different in the fall," lacrosse player Michael Catalino recalled later. "Students that I didn't know went out of their way to show their support; it seemed like everyone on campus was 100 percent behind us. I also felt safer on campus. I didn't have to hide who I was." Not that the student activists who had been most vocal in attacking the lacrosse players that spring ever apologized. Senior Tony McDevitt occasionally crossed paths with some of them. "They know they were wrong, and we know they were wrong," he later recalled.

The Brodhead administration, meanwhile, continued to treat the lacrosse players as troublemakers on probation. Brodhead did not invite Reade Seligmann and Collin Finnerty back for the fall semester. Reade took a couple of classes at a local school, Caldwell College; Collin enrolled in a math class at Long Island's Hofstra University. Both also did volunteer work as their case inched forward. Seligmann spent several days a week working at a soup kitchen in nearby Morristown, New Jersey; Finnerty worked as a volunteer for a cystic fibrosis foundation.

Students who did return to campus were presented by the Brodhead administration with a new, supposedly improved behavior code, announced in a full-page ad in *The Chronicle*. The administration went out of its way to suggest that this was necessary to clamp controls on those lacrosse-team sinners. The motto it chose for the new code—that bad behavior was "Not fine by Duke"—was an obvious tweak of a slogan used by the springtime protesters: "Men's Lacrosse? Not fine by me."

The code's notions of bad behavior were an ideological mishmash, with many impossibly vague provisions that embodied the politically correct views of the faculty's left on sexual harassment, on suppressing politically incorrect speech, and much more. It amounted to an open invitation for selective enforcement against the students that faculty activists disliked, especially lacrosse players.

The "harassment" provisions in particular drew upon extreme versions of feminist theory, like the increasingly draconian codes at many other universities. At these institutions (including Duke), a student can be suspended from school, without a hearing, merely upon an *allegation* of sexual harassment. Given the malleability of the word "harassment," the new Duke code's sections were especially vague: "Harassment of any individual for any reason is not acceptable at Duke University," the code declared.

When student protesters had put lacrosse players' photos on "wanted" posters five months before, while joining with other potbangers to drive several players out of their rented homes, that was harassment by any reasonable definition. But the protesters would have nothing to worry about: The same Duke administration that had drawn up the code had made no objection to their protests and even mimicked their motto.

The extremely vague description of sexual harassment offenses, in particular, was an especially obvious formula for arbitrary enforcement. The section affirmed the importance of "honesty, trustworthiness, fairness, and—especially—respect for others"—thereby implying that the first three virtues were *less* "essential" than "respect," an odd hierarchy of values. The section also demanded "an environment free of personal affronts against individuals." Free speech? Forget it.

The sexual harassment section specified that prohibited "acts may *or may not* be accompanied by the use of coercion, intimidation, or advantage gained by the use of alcohol or other drugs." This language opens the door to punishing any speech deemed offensive by hypersensitive people, especially if they are not white males. Indeed, making the plan for selective enforcement almost explicit, the code specified that one of the "fundamental principles" underlying the policy was that "real or perceived power differentials between individuals may create an unintentional atmosphere of coercion." If one can be punished for *perceived* power differentials yielding an *unintentional* atmosphere of coercion, his "guilt" depends entirely on what the "victim" claims to "perceive." And who the "victim" is.

Other sections of the code cracked down hard on alcohol use. Incredibly, even students above the legal drinking age could not be served "spirituous liquor or fortified wines"—anywhere in the world. (This provision did not cover graduate students, but for undergraduates, the code's terms applied both on and off campus.) Why this throwback to Prohibition? Well, once all other charges against the lacrosse players had been discredited, many activist professors had turned for the first time in their lives to crusading against student drunkenness, with as much fervor as their counterparts on the extreme religious right. The code was especially tough on "groups"—such as athletic teams, fraternities, and sororities. They "will be held accountable if the "group" failed to take appropriate precautions" in holding an alcohol-related party. "Appropriate precautions must include . . . adequate and accessible non-alcoholic beverages and food."

These and other equally unclear code provisions could be enforced only by capriciously punishing random students caught doing forbidden things routinely done by most of their classmates. All forms of gambling other than the state lottery were banned, thereby outlawing (among other items) the NCAA basketball tournament pools that are ubiquitous on college campuses nationwide. Finally, on East and West Campuses, "quiet hours" were decreed for 133 of each week's 168 hours. The code's language could be interpreted as banning all speech louder than a whisper. As for the other 35 hours of each week, the code allowed "reasonable levels of noise," which was, of course, undefined.

Vague student behavior codes and arbitrary enforcement are a fact of life on most college campuses today. At Duke, however, there was particular danger for lacrosse players and their student allies, who had been targeted by powerful members of the faculty and administration. And *this* code's vague provisions would be enforced by two administrators—Larry Moneta and Dean of Judicial Affairs Stephen Bryan—who had long since made clear their contempt for the team.

But the new code's potential for selective enforcement against lacrosse players remained latent in the fall of 2006. And the team was buoyed by a newly supportive student body and a new head coach, John Danowski. He had been close to the team's trauma because his son Matt was on it; the returning senior was widely regarded as perhaps the best college lacrosse player in the country. John Danowski had had a successful career at Hofstra, in Hempstead, on Long Island. He took over from Kevin Cassese, the 2003 Duke grad who had done his best to hold the team together after the firing of Mike Pressler. Cassese returned to being an assistant coach.

Trying to use his own personal coaching style to help give the team a fresh start, Danowski instituted 6:00 A.M. practices and encouraged all-team events such as "date nights," when the entire team would attend a Duke volleyball game and bring dates. Still loaded with talent—if not as much as the year before—the Duke team was expected to be a contender for the national championship again.

But aftershocks of their ordeal the previous spring still dogged the players. Dave, Collin, and Reade were still being prosecuted for gang rape and all of the players (except freshmen) could be called as witnesses. The media that they had so many reasons to fear and distrust—as they did the Brodhead administration—were still watching them, and showed up in unusual numbers for the first workout and the first scrimmage.

Many players missed the four captains and six other now-graduated seniors. That kind of turnover happens every year, of course. But however much they liked Coach Danowski, most had chosen Duke because of the relationships they had forged with Mike and Sue Pressler during recruiting season. And only three of the seven high school seniors who had been offered lacrosse scholarships for the 2006–2007 season had come to Duke. Among the four who went elsewhere was Craig Dowd, who chose Georgetown after seeing what he viewed as the punitive grading of his brother, Kyle, by Group of 88 member Kim Curtis.

Most of all, perhaps, Devon Sherwood and others were haunted by the empty lockers that had belonged to "Reader" and "Finn-Man," who would have been juniors, and "Big Dave," who had graduated. Devon wished they were there with him.

As the summer was winding down and all of Collin's Lony Island friends were returning to school, the reality of his situation was taking a toll. His brothers, Sean and Kyle, wanted to do something to make him feel better. They spoke to all of his classmates on the team and suggested that they come surprise Collin for his twentieth birthday celebration. It was a huge undertaking, but they managed to get most of his peers to travel from North Carolina to Long Island. The team members arrived when Collin was not home, and hid in the Finnerty living room when he got home. When MaryEllen called him into the room, and all his friends jumped out and tackled him, Collin was stunned and thrilled. His parents watched with tears rolling down their faces, seeing firsthand the companionship that Nifong had taken away from their son. After everyone but Collin departed for Durham, MaryEllen Finnerty later recalled, the "house once again was enveloped in sadness"; she, Kevin, and their two oldest sons resolved to do everything they could to make the coming months bearable for Collin.

For the returning players, things were back to normal in class. Reports of faculty harassment of players stopped, in part because most members of the team exercised care in choosing professors. "Our response was that we all don't want to take classes with the Group of 88," Tony McDevitt later recalled. "It was clear that they had no respect for any of us." Indeed, *not one* of the eighty-eight, or of the other faculty members who had rushed to judgment against the lacrosse players, had publicly expressed any regret. So most players avoided the group members when they signed up for courses.

History major Ryan McFadyen and a few others took a different approach. The uncommonly intelligent McFadyen, whose suspension over the "kill and skin" e-mail had been lifted, enrolled in Peter Wood's fall semester course as an elective. Wood obviously knew who this six-foot, five-inch lacrosse player was. But Ryan introduced himself after the first class, without mentioning the professor's previous stream of denunciations of the team. McFadyen sat in the front row in every class, regularly participated, and ultimately received an A–. He said that upon his return to campus, he had been determined to go out of his way "to present a good image of lacrosse in everything I've done."

This sometimes required the patience of a saint. His adviser, assigned by the History Department, was the same Professor Reeve Huston who had provoked a walkout by McFadyen and four other lacrosse players in March by using class time to attack them while theorizing that "ejaculation had occurred." When McFadyen went to ask Huston to sign off on his fall classes, Huston suddenly started talking about McFadyen's infamous e-mail. The professor, who had no training in psychology and seemed unaware of the e-mail's well-known origins in *American Psycho*, absurdly theorized that it represented Ryan's own "deeply psychologized" fantasy. The student, aware that any retort could hurt his team's image, remained respectful.

The team's relations with the Brodhead administration remained frosty. The Duke president addressed the team for the first time since May a few weeks into its fall practices. As in May, he arrived unannounced, during the last fifteen minutes of a morning conditioning workout. The president opened his remarks by saying that in deciding what to say to the team, he had consulted Alleva—a man despised by the lacrosse players as much as anyone at Duke.

When Brodhead opened the floor for questions, Reade Seligmann's former roommate, Jay Jennison, spoke up. He said that all of the team had learned much from the case, about the importance of representing Duke, and of teammates and family. "What have you and the administration learned?" Jennison asked Brodhead. Ducking the question, Brodhead responded, "What do you think I should have learned?" The team was stunned. They heard a more straightforward statement from Dean Sue Wasiolek. In a low voice, she said she knew that many of them "despise me."

While the 2006–2007 lacrosse team was trying to return to normal, the three defendants' lawyers resumed the battle for their freedom on September 22, at another in the succession of routine, roughly monthly court hearings to deal with discovery disputes and other pretrial issues. The case had a new judge: W. Osmond Smith III, the senior resident Superior Court judge for a judicial district in neighboring counties. His selection ended up being a great help for the defense, not because he was pro-defense but because he proved to be pro-truth.

Perhaps Nifong did not know this when he listed Judge Smith, along with three pro-prosecution stalwarts, in response to a request by Durham County Superior Court Judge Orlando Hudson for both Nifong and the defense to list judges they would consider acceptable to preside over the case to the end. Defense attorneys were pleased with the choice. Nifong was influenced by a recommendation from Finnerty attorney Bill Cotter, whom Nifong had known and trusted for years. Joe Cheshire later called Smith "a great judge" who "plays it right, straight down the middle. When we got him we knew we were on a level playing field. We knew we no longer need to worry about the possibility of home cooking" from judges who bend over to accommodate their friend Nifong.

They were less pleased to hear an amazing but not exactly surprising revelation by Nifong. For the first time, Nifong speculated that the entire sexual attack "probably took about five minutes, ten minutes at the outside." This, he claimed, negated Reade Seligmann's alibi. "If he can't account for every minute of his time" between 11:30 P.M. on March 13 and 12:55 A.M. the next morning, Nifong asserted, "he does not have an airtight alibi."

This argument had three fatal flaws. First, the time-stamped photos and other electronic evidence (not to mention Kim Roberts, the cab driver, and other eyewitnesses) made it clear that any rape had to have occurred after 12:04 A.M., when the performance stopped, and almost certainly between the 12:31 A.M. photo of Mangum and 12:38 A.M., when she was passed out on the back stoop and about to be helped into Kim Roberts's car (at 12:41). Second, Seligmann's cell calls, ATM video, restaurant receipt, and dorm swipe-in *did* account for almost every minute of that time. Third, in every prior statement Mangum, the police, and the DA's office had said that the alleged three-man, three-orifice, gang rape plus beating, kicking, and strangling had lasted thirty minutes. Nifong was now contradicting both of Mangum's statements to police (March 16 and April 6); her *N&O* interview (March 24); and sworn affidavits filed by Nifong's office and police on March 16, 23, 27, and April 18.

When Kirk Osborn noted these contradictions and accused the authorities of changing the facts "because they can't prove their case," Nifong brushed the contradictions aside. "When something really awful is happening to you," the district attorney speculated, "it seems to take a lot longer than the actual time." He did not explain why it had taken six months for him to decide that all prior statements by his office and police had been so wildly off base.

Nifong also dropped another bombshell that was overshadowed by his revised, instant-rape theory: his claim that during his April 11 meeting with the accuser, they had never discussed the facts of the case because she was still too traumatized, twenty-eight days after the alleged rape. This was the reason he gave for not having turned over any notes of the meeting to defense lawyers.

Nifong also complained about defense lawyers' insistence that he hand over the lab records underlying the brief May 12 DNA Security report, and their questions about what else DNA Security had told him beyond what he had disclosed to the defense. From the first time that Nifong had handed over discovery material in May, the Finnerty legal team had suspected that the district attorney's disclosures had not been complete. They consulted with outside

DNA experts, who guided them on drawing up an all-encompassing discovery request that would include all underlying data from the DNA Security lab.

With the Finnerty discovery motion having asked for everything, Nifong was trapped. Supplying the data would cost too much (around $5,000), the district attorney said. Such a disclosure might cause unspecified privacy concerns. And he had been told nothing beyond the report, Nifong asserted. Judge Smith pressed for a specific answer: "So his report encompasses it all? . . . So you represent that there are no other statements?" Nifong responded, "No other statements made to me." This claim would later be exposed as a lie, thanks to aggressive defense lawyering and an order by Judge Smith that the foot-dragging DA hand over the DNA data by October 20.

The poker-faced Judge Smith presided in an even-handed manner seen by most defense lawyers as a marked improvement on Judges Stephens and Titus. Smith denied Osborn's motion to force Nifong to specify the time or date of the alleged assault. This ruling disappointed Osborn but was consistent with the thrust of the relevant legal precedents. At the same time, the judge handed the defense its first important victories, ruling that Nifong needed to hand over the DNA records and lifting Judge Titus's de facto gag order on the defendants and witnesses.

Nifong's demeanor during the hearing was noteworthy, reported Ben Niolet in the next day's N&O: "When defense lawyers spoke, Nifong occasionally sighed, rolled his eyes, laughed quietly or rubbed his temples."

Perhaps he was thinking about the fall campaign, which was heating up. By late September, the Cheek campaign had brought together Beth Brewer and the Liestoppers bloggers; Jackie Brown and her local political allies; and the DSED students who were focused on getting Duke students registered to vote. But with an October 13 deadline looming for voter registration, DSED was well short of its target figure of two thousand new voters.

Brooke Jandl and Christiane Regelbrugge had asked members of the lacrosse team from the start to help out with the voter registration drive. Nearly fifty well-networked students could sign up a lot of people. But the players' lawyers had cautioned them not to get involved. As the campaign wore on, Bo Carrington "just said screw it and started to work." More and more players joined him. Tony McDevitt later explained that "registering voters and working in the campaign were the only tangible things we could do for our teammates." The players' legal defense fund sold blue wristbands, with "Duke Lacrosse 2006" and "Innocent! #6, #13, #45" in white, for a dollar. An outside donor purchased six thousand wristbands and asked Michael Catalino's mother, Gail, to coordinate their distribution. She sent them down to her son, who managed to give out 5,600 of them by Election Day.

The entire team was helping the DSED effort by the end of September. They decided on a major push outside Duke's football stadium during the September 30 homecoming game. Stef Sparks, the Ekstrands' paralegal, called the Athletic Department several times in the week before the game to let them know of the plan. And Coach Danowski scheduled an early morning practice so the lacrosse players could devote their day to registering voters. McDevitt coordinated the effort, making up T-shirts with the (magic marker) slogan "Voice Your Choice" on the front. He bought fifty clipboards and distributed them to every member of the team, along with thirty or so registration forms apiece. The players had a "coaching" session on how to register people—what to say, what not to say, and how to answer common questions. To avoid unnecessary double registrations, McDevitt also got a list of already-registered students from the county board of elections. The goal was for every member of the team to register at least fifteen voters on homecoming day.

They assembled in groups of five at 11:00 A.M. to head out to the stadium parking lot. But as the first group started to register people, a Duke security officer came up and ordered them to stop. The officer also ordered Jennison to turn his "Voice your Choice" T-shirt inside out.

Then Mike Sobb, assistant athletic director for marketing, approached the team in the locker room, accompanied by another Duke police officer. He said that players registering students outside the stadium would constitute partisan political action on campus. Such activity, Sobb continued, could not be allowed, because there would be so many people around at the football game. If lacrosse players were allowed to register voters, Sobb asked rhetorically, "do we allow Nifong to come and put his head on the plasma TV [in the stadium]?" McDevitt and Michael Catalino pointed out that the players were seeking only to register people to vote, not tell them whom to vote for. Catalino also noted that the Athletic Department traditionally exercised no jurisdiction outside the stadium. Sobb refused to budge. Catalino went back to his dorm room, grabbed some wristbands, and handed out five hundred that day. Most other players dispersed.

Registering students to vote *outside* the stadium had nothing to do with broadcasting a candidate's political advertisement *inside*. Indeed, Sobb had violated at least the spirit of federal law. The 1998 Higher Education Act requires all colleges and universities that receive federal funds, such as Duke, to make a "good faith effort" to encourage students to register to vote. The U.S. Department of Education has never issued clear guidelines on exactly what constitutes a "good faith effort." But here we had a federally funded university actively *suppressing* an effort to register students.

In the days after Duke's voter-suppression move, John Burness (inaccurately) told reporters that the registration effort had caught Duke officials by surprise. Behind the scenes, the university worked to contain the public relations damage. Athletic Department officials conducted a review and determined that Sobb had erred. A second DSED event, a barbecue on campus in early October, went off without a hitch. Duke insisted that the organizers post notices that the university was in no way affiliated with the activity; the students complied.

While Duke was thus effectively assisting Nifong's political-survival effort, wittingly or not, the media tide was turning harder against him. Joe Neff published another bombshell exposé in the October 8 *News & Observer*. For the first time, he made public the highly exculpatory details of the March 16, March 21, and April 4 photo lineups, in the process demonstrating how flawed procedures beget flawed results.

Neff's revelations included that Nifong had gone forward with indictments despite knowing that the only player Crystal Mangum had twice identified as attending the party (Brad Ross) had been in Raleigh that night, that she had incorrectly identified the player who made the broomstick comment, and that virtually every ID she made in the transcript was flawed. With Nifong's entire case hanging from the frayed thread of that April 4 photo lineup, careful readers of Neff's article could hardly miss the inference that emperor Nifong had no clothes.

Meanwhile, the biggest cannon in the entire national media—CBS News's *60 Minutes*—had been spending months of exhaustive research putting together a program about the lacrosse case. As the program would make clear, neither the producers nor the anchor, Ed Bradley, had any doubt that the rape claim was a fraud and Nifong was guilty of outrageous misconduct. Word had spread among the lacrosse families that *60 Minutes* would blow what was left of Nifong out of the water and, they hoped, bring the case to an early end.

That scenario overestimated Durham's voters and North Carolina's governor, attorney general, and newspapers. But when the special, thirty-five-minute segment—twice the length of most *60 Minutes* segments—finally aired on October 15, after several delays, it hit Nifong hard and for the first time showed the most dramatic evidence of innocence to a national audience.

Among the highlights of the program—Ed Bradley's last before his death of leukemia—were interviews with the three defendants, who convincingly denounced the charges as lies and came across as appealing young men, and Kim Roberts.

The prospect of "going to trial for something you never did is very scary,"

Collin Finnerty said. "It's changed my life forever, no matter what happens from here on out. It's probably gonna be something that defines me my whole life."

The slippery Roberts, who in April had won much publicity by pretending that she thought Mangum might be telling the truth, moved back toward her original March 20 statement to police that the rape charge was a "crock." Referring to the accuser's claim that six lacrosse players had pulled the two women apart and dragged the accuser into a bathroom to rape her, Bradley asked, "Were you holding on to each other? Were you pulled apart?" The answer: "Nope."

Jim Coleman, interviewed at length, accused Nifong directly of prosecutorial misconduct: "He pandered to the community. . . . What are you to conclude about a prosecutor who says to you, 'I'll do whatever it takes to get this set of defendants'? What does it say about what he's willing to do to get poor black defendants?"

Richard Brodhead, also interviewed by Bradley, sounded his usual refrain by casting aspersions on the lacrosse players' characters while seeming agnostic about whether they were rapists. "This was an evening of highly unacceptable behavior whether or not the rape took place," Brodhead said. This after overwhelming evidence that no rape took place had poured into the public record. Brodhead also intimated incorrectly that several (or more) players had uttered racial slurs. This on the same program that featured an admission by Roberts—the stripper whose false 911 call about being pelted with racial slurs the Duke president had so credulously embraced—that she had heard only one slur and had "obviously provoked" that one.

A few media critics of the case also turned their attention to the Duke faculty. In a cutting October 22 op-ed focusing on "the people whose profession is dedicated, supposedly, to the search for truth," the *Arizona Republic*'s Doug MacEachern said that "whatever the ultimate judgment in this case, the Duke faculty has acted monstrously. Duke faculty members rendered instant judgments of guilt on their students in a lot of ways. But the actions of 'The Group of 88' were the worst. [The Group] wasn't indulging its inflated sense of personal morality for the sake of eager students. . . . In service of their personal, hyperpolitical judgments about social oppression, the faculty members proclaimed their indifference to the real guilt or innocence of their own students."

Then, after almost seven months of faculty gang-trashing of the lacrosse players, came the very first public dissent by any professor in any of the thirty arts and sciences departments. And a powerful dissent it was. Professors should speak up for their students, not engage in "mean-spirited, petty and unprofessional" denunciations to advance their own political agendas, wrote Chemistry's

Steve Baldwin. "These kids were abandoned by their university. They were denied the presumption of innocence, despite the mounting evidence that the case against them is made of smoke and mirrors and is fatally flawed procedurally. They have been pilloried by their faculty and scorned by the administration. They are pariahs. . . . Their treatment has been shameful."

Baldwin concluded with a rhetorical flourish: "The faculty who publicly savaged the character and reputations of specific men's lacrosse players last spring should be ashamed of themselves. They should be tarred and feathered, ridden out of town on a rail and removed from the academy. Their comments were despicable."

Baldwin's column ignited a faculty firestorm. Political science professor Kerry L. Haynie, codirector of the Center for Study of Race, Ethnicity, and Gender in the Social Sciences, sent a nasty e-mail implicitly challenging Baldwin to settle their disagreement by violence. And in an allegation that reflected either ignorance or malice, Robyn Weigman, director of Duke's women's studies program, publicly denounced Baldwin for using "the language of lynching." This assertion was false. It's true that some black people, as well as many more whites, have been tarred and feathered, as some have been punched, kicked, robbed, shot, and stabbed. But the practice originated in England and Ireland and has never been identified with lynching or carried any tinge of racism.

Nonetheless, living in a world dominated by political correctness, Baldwin found it necessary to apologize for "insensitive and inappropriate language [that] caused pain for some members of our community." Caused them pain? Or gave the PC police an opening?

19. NIFONG'S PYRRHIC VICTORY

BRAD BANNON, whose encyclopedic command of the facts made him invaluable as the mild-mannered junior member of the Evans defense, thought he had achieved the rare feat of working constructively with Mike Nifong as they neared the end of a phone call just after 4 P.M. on October 20, 2006. The subject was Judge Smith's order that Nifong turn over all DNA Security files to each of the three defense teams by the end of that day. When the district attorney complained about the large volume of documents, Bannon offered to relieve him of his responsibility to make copies for the Evans and Finnerty teams. Their chat seemed to be ending cordially.

Then Nifong's demeanor swung suddenly from sunny to dark tornado. Raising his voice, he started denouncing various defense tactics and complaints about the slow pace of his compliance with discovery orders. He reiterated that he had never discussed the case with Mangum. His voice continuing to rise, he ridiculed defense attorneys for always thinking that prosecutors were lying or hiding material from them and claimed that Bannon and Cheshire had not acted in good faith. Nifong ended this harangue with: "OK, Brad, good-bye," and hung up.

"He's hiding something," Kathy Seligmann told a friend that night, after learning of this Nifong meltdown.

Meanwhile, the Seligmanns were in the process of bringing new blood into the defense team. Amazed at how their son could still be a defendant months after Kirk Osborn had presented his airtight alibi to the court and the public, Kathy and Phil had pushed Osborn so hard to go on the attack that—however justified and powerfully argued his motions—the pro-prosecution Judges Stephens and Titus (not to mention Nifong) had set their faces against him. A new lawyer might have better luck. And while the hard-driving Osborn did the work of three men, he himself recognized that a large law firm would be better equipped than a solo practitioner like him for a three-front war against the abusive district attorney and the academic and journalistic mobs.

In late October, Jim Cooney, of Charlotte, North Carolina's largest city, became Reade's lead counsel. Cooney was widely seen as one of the state's finest lawyers; he had the state's largest law firm behind him; and he could work with Osborn on the basis of mutual respect. A Duke graduate, Cooney had played lacrosse his freshman year before a knee injury permanently side-lined him. He had majored in history, had taken several courses from William Chafe, and had written his thesis—on seventeenth-century Puritanism—under Peter Wood. The two professors had been "everything you'd want in a teacher," Cooney recalled; but in their zeal to exploit the lacrosse case, they had "thrown out the window everything they taught me" about dispassionately evaluating evidence, digging into primary materials, and challenging people in power.

Watching from Charlotte, some 145 miles away from the Duke campus, Cooney had been inclined to believe the allegations against the lacrosse team at first, based on Nifong's apparent certitude that a rape had occurred, and had been outraged at the thought of Duke lacrosse players committing such crimes. But Joe Cheshire's confident assertions at his March 30 press conference that no DNA matches would be found changed Cooney's mind. He had worked with Cheshire and knew him too well to imagine that he would ever risk such a statement unless he had powerful reasons to believe it. Then Cooney had seen Mike Nifong's March 31 "chokehold" television interview, which struck him as a preview of a "bad closing argument by a two-bit lawyer." And once he had gone through the discovery file in October, he was "horrified at the utter lack of evidence" linking any of the three defendants to any crime.

In Cheshire's view, Cooney's arrival reenergized the defense team and gave it "additional intellectual work product momentum" at a time when the lawyers needed to draw up compellingly documented and argued pretrial motions attacking Nifong's case. Cooney proved a particularly effective complement for Brad Bannon, who had immersed himself in mastering the discovery and forensic evidence. They had worked closely with one another in the second Alan Gell trial and were both detail-oriented, brilliant legal minds with tremendous work ethics.

On November 2 and 3, the defense team gathered for what was billed as a retreat to plot strategy. The locale was what Brad Bannon called "some fancy-ass golf club outside Chapel Hill with bungalows and stuff" where "they wouldn't even let a couple of us eat lunch because we had jeans on." Bannon thought that "a conference room in Raleigh, where most of us worked, would have been just fine," rather than driving an hour to sit in a fancier conference room. But the meetings were productive.

The first day, the attorneys reviewed every potentially harmful fact, with large Post-it notes, putting together a better case for the state than Nifong could ever have done. The defense attorneys anticipated that Nifong would lead by putting Detective Himan, Tara Levicy, the Durham Access Center nurse, and rape crisis counselors on the stand to testify that they believed Mangum's story; this could divert the jury's attention from the internal contradictions and inherent incredibility of her tale. Mangum would be the state's final witness.

The defense team worked out a plan for countering the expected Nifong strategy and allocated the work of trying to get Nifong's case thrown out or crippled before any trial. Cooney would handle the motions on suppressing the April 4 photo lineup—the best hope for getting the case dismissed—and for change of venue. Bannon would focus on DNA. The Finnerty team would concentrate on the medical evidence. And Cheshire would coordinate what would be Ground Zero at any trial: destroying the credibility of Crystal Mangum.

Nifong continued to stall on turning over the DNA files until the next scheduled hearing, on October 27. Judge Smith stated then that he had "accepted Mr. Nifong's representation" that "Dr. Meehan said nothing during [their] meetings beyond what was encompassed in the final report of DNA Security, dated May 12, 2006." Nifong's lies to the court about the DNA evidence had ensured that defense lawyers would have no opportunity to discuss the contents of the files in open court or make them public until after the November 7 election. The next hearing would not be until December 15.

Even so, the October 27 hearing was a public relations disaster for Nifong. His first problem was an October 11 letter in which Joe Cheshire had pointed out that Nifong himself had twice publicly contradicted his own oft-repeated (but little-publicized) claim that he had not spoken with Mangum about any of the facts of the case. In a September 20 motion, Nifong had said that Mangum had told him she never taken the drug Ecstasy; that claim would be an issue at any trial. And in seeking the endorsement of a political action committee called Friends of Durham in early October, according to the chairman of the group, Nifong had boasted that he was the only candidate "that's interviewed this victim."

Nifong opened the October 27 hearing by asserting a point of personal privilege to complain about Cheshire's letter. Claiming to be a man of "integrity," he asserted that Crystal Mangum had still been too "traumatized" to have any "meaningful discussion" during their April 11 meeting. "No matter how many times they ask the question, that will still be the answer," Nifong told Judge Smith.

Nifong's April 11 meeting with Mangum had, of course, come a week after she had spent an hour viewing the photo display of the forty-six white players and giving Nifong the answers he used to indict three of them. More dramatically, the meeting had come two weeks after she had been captured on videotape pole dancing. But defense lawyers did not have that fact nailed down in time for the October 27 hearing.

Bannon then pointed out that Nifong had "put himself in the position of being a factual investigator in this case." In that role, he had meetings with witnesses. What did Crystal say to Nifong on April 11 or any other day? The response was that she had been "on the verge of tears" that day, barely speaking fifteen words and struggling to establish eye contact. Thereafter, the only fact relating to the case that Nifong had discussed with her was whether she used ecstasy. He assessed her credibility, Nifong explained, in conversations about her children and other matters. This account, Bannon replied, "stretched credulity." Judge Smith maintained his usual poker face.

The national media, having been jolted awake by 60 Minutes, played the DA's admission that he had never interviewed his alleged victim and most important witness as a bombshell casting grave doubt on Nifong's handling of the entire case. So it was. But new information, in the strict sense, it was not. The N&O's Ben Niolet had reported this item weeks before, in a scoop that got relatively little attention in the national media. Nifong's in-court declaration, on the other hand, was a big national story. The Drudge Report picked it up within hours; ABC, CBS, Fox, MSNBC, and CNN soon followed. Linda Fairstein, perhaps the nation's leading expert on rape prosecutions after heading the Manhattan District Attorney's Sex Crimes Unit for more than two decades, spoke for many when she said that Nifong's approach "belies anything a prosecutor would do before making charges" and was "just against the progress that's been made in this very specialized field."

Nifong ran into more trouble when he tried to justify his refusal to consider the exculpatory evidence repeatedly offered to him by defense lawyers. These offers, he asserted, were a defense plot to make him a witness and thus block him from personally trying the case. "Any prosecutor with any sense" would refuse to talk to suspects, he said. Besides, he had received no "reciprocal discovery" from any of the three defendants.

Joe Cheshire rose to correct the record. He had initially asked Nifong to meet with Dave Evans's lawyers, not to interview the defendant himself. "Other than a very rude response," Cheshire noted, Nifong had ignored his entreaties.

Kirk Osborn, who had gone to Nifong's office after his client's April 18 arrest to tell the DA about Reade's alibi, termed it "rather stunning" to hear Nifong stand up and "piously" defend his refusal to meet by making such a claim.

The hearing also revealed that Sergeant Gottlieb, who had been the top cop on the case from the start, had been reassigned. Nifong cited lack of workload as the reason. Hardly anyone believed that. By this time, Gottlieb was very damaged goods. He had been involved in the midsummer Blinco's incident in which two police officers had hit a black cook and one had used a racial epithet. His seemingly fictionalized account of many aspects of the investigation in his typed "notes" had drawn widespread ridicule. And *The N&O* and *The Chronicle* had detailed in early September his record of disproportionately arresting and abusing Duke students.

Gottlieb's departure also allowed Nifong to give his close confidant and investigator, Linwood Wilson, an official, day-to-day role in the lacrosse case, with Himan remaining as the number-two investigator. Wilson also got a 66 percent raise, from $23,453 to $39,000.

Wilson's record was not much better than Gottlieb's. He was hired in 2005 to oversee a program in the DA's office that tracked down bounced checks. In 1998, he had relinquished his license as a private investigator. The previous year, the state licensing board had reprimanded him for charging a client for work he had not done. Wilson's record also included another formal reprimand and seven additional formal inquiries into his conduct during sixteen years as a private investigator. Yet he presented himself as a deeply moral man. He boasted on his singing group's Web site that his "ministry through gospel music is where God wants him to be and has been blessed for the past 38 years of seeing many souls won to Christ as a result of this ministry."

Nifong refused to comment when asked in February 2007 by *The N&O* when he had first learned of Wilson's ethical issues and what qualifications he had to be a chief investigator for a district attorney.

While Nifong's case was being exposed more and more as a monstrous hoax, lacrosse team supporters documented a number of instances in which both John Burness and Bob Steel, Duke's chairman, privately defended Duke's actions in the face of mounting criticism by making disparaging comments about the still-beleaguered defendants and their teammates. Burness repeatedly stressed to reporters that the players "were not choirboys" and cautioned against portraying them in an unduly favorable light. Steel repeatedly—and without apparent factual foundation—told people that lacrosse players at the party had done "terrible" things that were not yet publicly known.

Jason Trumpbour, FODU's spokesman, sent a memo to other lacrosse-team sympathizers describing a late September meeting with Bob Steel.

Trumpbour had sought the meeting in the hope of persuading the Duke administration to speak out against Nifong's unfair treatment of the Duke student defendants. (He did not ask Steel to take a position on innocence or guilt.) Steel responded that (in Trumpbour's words) "if Nifong were corrupt, why had nothing been done to stop him by the North Carolina bar." The board chairman added that it would not be that big a problem if the accused players were convicted because the appeals courts could eventually straighten out any problems.

Steel also defended the firing of Pressler and everything else that Duke had done, while telling Trumpbour (as he had told Peter Boyer of *The New Yorker*) that "even though it is not fair, people have to be sacrificed for the good of the organization." When pressed about Nifong's abuses, Trumpbour later recalled, "Steel's fallback position was that the lacrosse players did not deserve help from the University. He . . . affected an air of gravitas while telling me about the 'terrible, terrible' things that happened at the party."

Asked to respond to Trumpbour's account, Steel said: "I met with Mr. Trumpbour at his request. I found it an informative meeting, I think I was respectful to him and I appreciate his interest and passion about these issues. We have different recollections of some things that were said at the meeting. I did my best to describe the issues and choices that had characterized the university's path." Steel also stressed that he had discussed the lacrosse players with very few people outside the Duke community.

Meanwhile, the growing criticism of the Duke's Group of 88 professors by journalists like Doug MacEachern, *Chronicle* columnist Stephen Miller, and several bloggers provoked self-revealing counterattacks from professors, including Alex Rosenberg, Karla Holloway, and Grant Farred.

Rosenberg, the R. Taylor Cole Professor of Philosophy, told *The New York Sun* on October 27 that he had signed the Group of 88's statement to protest the role of alcohol on campus and "affluent kids violating the law to get exploited women to take their clothes off when they could get as much hookup as they wanted from rich and attractive Duke coeds." Nice try, Professor. But the statement signed by Rosenberg had mentioned neither alcohol nor the hookup culture.

Karla Holloway vowed that she would sign the Group of 88's statement again "in a heartbeat" and decried critics for supposedly misrepresenting what it had said; the statement had, of course, conveniently been removed from her department's Web site so that people could not see for themselves. Alice Kaplan, professor of literature and Romance studies, announced that "I signed the statement because I care about Duke and I care about the students and the experiences they're having." This assertion, observed engineering professor Michael Gustafson, one of the two faculty publicly critical of the eighty-eight, would have been more plausible if Kaplan or "any one of the people who signed that document had spoken out against the death threats hurled at our students, against calls for our students to be 'prosecuted whether it happened or not.'"

In an October 29 *Herald-Sun* op-ed that gave Nifong a boost at the polls if any voters took it seriously, Grant Farred denounced the "secret racism" that he saw underlying the lacrosse case. The Group of 88 member was not referring to Chan Hall or the state NAACP, but to Duke students who wanted to exercise their right to vote and to support the innocent lacrosse players. The "proliferation of Blue Devil blue armbands . . . inscribed with the numbers of the three indicted players and the defiant proclamation, 'Innocent' (in bold white)," Farred wrote, had been "too visible on campus early in the fall semester."

How dare Duke students register "in unprecedented numbers" to vote in Durham, fumed Farred. Such a move would "displace the problem of racism from the lacrosse team and the university to Durham's political system." Farred accused Duke Students for an Ethical Durham—whose leadership consisted of three female undergraduates—of seeking to "repair the damage done to historic white male privilege" by the case.

Without saying whether he believed a rape had occurred, Farred suggested it was racist to deny Mangum's allegations. "The vulnerability of black bodies," he asserted, "now assumes a different guise, but its political realities remain unchanged, especially in this instance, as it applies to black and minority women." After all, he suggested, didn't the lacrosse players shout all kinds of racist taunts? Well, no. There were two, both provoked by Kim Roberts's prior racial taunt, as she had admitted. That was deplorable, but noncriminal. And none of the three rape defendants was ever accused of uttering a racist remark. Not then. Not ever.

Then Farred came to what he really wanted: a human sacrifice to atone for "historic white privilege." The voter registration drive, he indicated, "does little more than obscure what is really at stake"—an analysis of the team's "reputed tendency toward arrogant sexual prowess" (he cited no evidence for this claim), among the "proclivities" that illuminated the "ongoing racism in the not-so-New South." Farred accused Duke students of "closing ranks against Durham" and demanded that they get out of the way of the mob of which he was so proud to be a part.

Farred's op-ed was the final public statement by any member of the Duke arts and sciences faculty before the November 7 election.

Two other African Americans provided a telling counterpoint to Farred's ravings about racism in interviews with Chris Cuomo of ABC's *Good Morning America*.

First, on October 30, came Kim Roberts, in her second big national TV appearance that month. She drove yet another nail into the coffin of Crystal Mangum's credibility with her story about how Mangum "chilled me to the bone" when "she said plain as day, 'Go ahead, put marks on me. That's what I want. Go ahead.'"

Then, the next day, came Devon Sherwood, still the only black Duke lacrosse player and now a sophomore. Of his teammates, Devon said: "We know we have a bond for life that no one else has. I came in this fall, I had one brother. Now, I have 47. Forty-six of them happen to be white. But I have, I have 46 guys that I can truly say they are my friends."

He added that the media and others had stereotyped him as well as his teammates: "I've even been stereotyped for being rich, being on full scholarship, [being] not in touch with my own black community at Duke. . . . It's terrible to find yourself being stereotyped. And you're like, 'Hold on. This couldn't be much further from the truth.' You know? So it's just amazing that the things you see and that [were] going on in this case and how the reversal from black stereotype to now rich white, privileged stereotype."

By this time the campaign for district attorney was in full swing. Nifong, buoyed by his solid base in the black vote and on the white left, eschewed public campaign appearances for weeks. He even refused an invitation to go on local television to be interviewed about the campaign. The DA had the endorsement of the Durham Committee on the Affairs of Black People, presenting the spectacle of a figure now nationally notorious for prosecutorial misconduct and trampling on civil liberties winning the backing of a group traditionally associated with protecting the rights of the accused. Nifong also kept the support of the People's Alliance. The radical, pro–gay rights group thus chose to boost the candidate who was "very pleased" to have homophobe Victoria Peterson leading his citizens' committee. Nifong could also count on fawning coverage from *The Herald-Sun*, Durham's only general-circulation newspaper and thus a pillar of the local establishment.

In the only media poll on the race, *The News & Observer* reported Nifong comfortably ahead as of October 25, with the support of 46 percent of those polled. Twenty-eight percent were for Lewis Cheek (despite his declaration that he would not serve), 24 percent were undecided, and 2 percent were for Steve Monks, chairman of the Durham County Republican Party. Black respondents favored Nifong over Cheek by 62 to 9 percent, with the rest undecided.

Monks, a write-in candidate, ludicrously claimed at an October 27 press conference that polling data showed that *he* was the only candidate who could beat Nifong. Few took him seriously, except as a threat to split the anti-Nifong vote. Some suspected that this was Monks's undisclosed goal; he confined his campaigning to the Duke campus and other areas where Cheek was strongest.

The Nifong campaign talked out of both sides of its mouth, depending on the audience. Nifong's message to black voters had long been that he alone would force the lacrosse players to stand trial in "a case that talks about what this community stands for." But his campaign's pitch to other voters was that they should forget about the lacrosse case because no DA should be evaluated on just one matter. "Nifong may have made mistakes concerning the lacrosse case, but he has done his job as an administrator by gathering around him people who do good work," said Lee Castle, a local attorney. It was a bit as if the 1972 Nixon campaign had urged voters to ignore his scandals because the president did lots of other things besides orchestrating the criminal cover-up of the Watergate burglary and secretly bombing Cambodia.

But as Election Day neared, Nifong seemed to be losing ground. The Cheek campaign-with-no-candidate, Recall-Nifong effort, initially short of cash, had started accepting out-of-state donations and outraised the DA by more than $5,000 in the final three months of the campaign. Despite Nifong's advantages, and despite Cheek's I-won't-serve posture and Monks's mischief, there seemed to be an outside chance that the DSED campaign to register Duke students could carry the day. More than two thousand Duke students registered to vote in Durham for the first time by the mid-October deadline, thanks to the work of DSED and lacrosse players such as Catalino, Carrington, McDevitt, and Wellington.

In the Duke *Chronicle*, two eloquent student op-ed columnists made the case against Nifong. Kristin Butler wrote that Nifong was "not fit to be our district attorney" because his "highly unethical and unprofessional conduct is as serious as it is systematic." Butler reminded campus readers that "it was Mike Nifong's mouth—at least as much as Durham's racial or socioeconomic tensions—that blew this case out of proportion." She also reminded students that they were all seen by Nifong (not to mention their own administration) as second-class citizens in Durham: "Whether or not it was true that 'there's been a feeling in the past that Duke students are treated differently by the court system,' Nifong has made sure that we are today."

Stephen Miller, an activist in the Duke Conservative Union and Students for Academic Freedom who was perhaps the most prominent conservative voice on campus, was even blunter. Accusing Nifong of an "assault on our peers, our community and the core values of our nation" that amounted to "a moral, social and legal outrage," Miller concluded: "Our D.A. has managed to go against criminal procedure, legal precedent, constitutional protections, hundreds of years of common law and thousands of years of ethics tracing back to the Old Testament. Nifong must have confused America with a police state."

A *Chronicle* editorial recapitulated Nifong's multiple abuses and argued that this appeared to be "a D.A. who will do anything to get a conviction and gain political favor." On the Web, Duke Basketball Report, a private site which did as much as any Web site to keep Nifong's misconduct in the public eye, departed from its standard practice to endorse Cheek. The lacrosse players were not being "treated equally under the law," the DBR said, and Nifong's "disgraceful" behavior was that of "a bully . . . no more interested in justice than the kid who used to take your lunch money."

Off campus, meanwhile, the alliance between political rookie Beth Brewer and veteran Jackie Brown was paying dividends. Their Recall Nifong effort received extensive, and fair, coverage in *The News & Observer*. (For most of the campaign, on the other hand, *The Herald-Sun*'s Web site described Nifong as running unopposed.) The group raised enough money from people outraged at Nifong to flood the county with blue-and-red yard signs, giving Cheek crucial on-the-ground visibility, and to buy newspaper (though not TV) ads. In the campaign's closing days, Cheek himself made several public appearances critical of Nifong. And Freda Black started campaigning for Cheek.

A poll released five days before the election by pro-Cheek PAC Ethical Durham showed the race as almost a dead heat. Nifong was down to 33 percent of respondents; Cheek was up to 32 percent; and a whopping 30 percent were undecided. The poll probably understated Nifong's lead because only 30 percent of the sample were black, compared to 38 percent in the earlier N&O poll. Even so, this was an enormous shift since Nifong's embarrassments at the October 27 hearing. In the N&O poll, taken before the hearing, Nifong led Cheek by 12 points among independents. In the Cheek poll, in early November, Cheek led Nifong by 27 points among independents, 42 to 15 percent, with the rest scattered or undecided.

The Recall Nifong effort also obtained the endorsement of Ruth Sheehan, who urged Durham voters in her October 30 N&O column to remove Nifong from office by voting the Cheek line. Calling the race "a referendum on the Duke lacrosse case," she urged voters to say no to "prosecutors with tunnel vision, who press forward with flawed cases at any cost." Sheehan also worried that if Nifong won, he would see it as a mandate to take the case to trial in the face of the evidence of innocence.

But the liberal editorial page made no endorsement. This despite the fact that by then the paper's devastating news coverage and exposés had made Nifong's unfitness for the office blindingly obvious. *The Herald-Sun* had an official no-endorsement policy but effectively backed Nifong in its news coverage and by publishing editorials attacking the lacrosse players' character.

As opposition to Nifong grew, he showed signs of panic, making a succession of statements that would horrify any ethical prosecutor. "If a case is of such significance that people in the community are divided or up in arms over the existence of that case, then that in and of itself is an indication that a case needs to be tried," he said at a late October luncheon of Rotary and Kiwanis club members. The implication was that public passions should trump facts, evidence, and truth. The American tradition, of course, is quite the opposite. Indeed, strong community passions and divisions are reasons not to put demonstrably innocent defendants on trial, but to grant them a change of venue, which Nifong steadfastly opposed.

"The future of Durham's in the balance," the DA declared apocalyptically on October 30 to the Associated Press. He added that dismissing the case would do "nothing to address the underlying divisions that have been revealed. My personal feeling is the first step to addressing those divisions is addressing this case."

Nifong stooped to thinly veiled racial appeals in an e-mail sent to his supporters the weekend before the election. He said that his opponents saw him as "a threat to their sense of entitlement" and that "they do not trust a jury of Durham citizens" to decide the case. His concoction tapped into memories of voter suppression by Southern segregationists by accusing the Cheek forces, without evidence, of seeking "to discourage my supporters from voting." And the DA celebrated his experience at the North Carolina Central Homecoming Parade, where he claimed "thousands of people responded to our positive message of equal treatment and access to justice for all of our citizens." So *that* was the message sent by trying to put three now obviously innocent young men in prison for decades?

Election Day 2006 dawned chilly and rainy in Durham. Students on East Campus awoke to a giant banner posted over the night reading END TYRANNY, RECALL NIFONG. DSED activists, lacrosse players, and Duke mothers fanned out around the city to polling places designated by Brown. Michael Catalino—on crutches while recovering from hip surgery—taped CHEEK signs to both crutches, wore a Cheek T-shirt, and stood in the rain at the bus stop where Duke students could catch a shuttle to their polling place, waving the crutches at students, urging them to vote. Bo Carrington addressed a man wearing an NCCU basketball T-shirt and urged a vote for Cheek, thinking at the same time that the T-shirt suggested this man might be a lost cause. "We'll see if we can get Nifong out," the man responded. It was the highlight of Bo's day.

Nifong, on the other hand, told a local reporter that when he had gone to the polls early that morning, "There was one guy who came by with a lacrosse T-shirt. I didn't talk to him. I might have prejudged him." The district attorney laughed awkwardly. Later, just before 5:00 P.M., with TV cameras running, Nifong aggressively confronted Bob Harris, radio announcer for Duke sports, as Harris got out of his car to head to the polling station. Harris turned away. "You've got to be nicer than that," lectured Nifong. "Get out of here," Harris said. "Don't pull this crap." Replied Nifong, "This isn't about Duke. This isn't about Duke at all." "No," retorted Harris. "It's about honesty. You're not honest."

Cheek and Nifong partisans gathered at the courthouse to await the results of this, the only closely contested race in Durham. It became clear that Nifong had won when more than 80 percent of the precincts' numbers became available all at once. Nifong had 49 percent to Cheek's 40 percent.

Nifong partisans erupted in cheers. A few taunted the three lacrosse players (Carrington, Catalino, and Wellington) at the courthouse. "Hope you lacrosse players get what you deserve," said one. An assistant district attorney wandered over and laughed at how the "poor little Duke kids didn't get your way." Many Duke mothers were in tears.

As many Nifong opponents had feared, and warned, Monks split the anti-Nifong vote, enabling the DA to win without majority support. In the end, Nifong's two opponents totaled 532 more votes than Nifong, who had 26,606, with Cheek at 21,211 and Monks at 5927.

Exultant at this limp victory, Harris Johnson, a former state Democratic party official and Durham resident for fifty-six years, told reporters, "This goes to show that justice can't be bought by a bunch of rich white boys from New York." And at a postelection press conference, Nifong made what sounded to some like a veiled threat of retribution. "I don't know if I've learned who my friends are," the district attorney told reporters, "but I have learned who my friends aren't. Which in some ways is more valuable."

How did Nifong win?

The precinct-by-precinct statistics show starkly the effectiveness of Nifong's race-baiting campaign strategy. He captured around 95 percent of the African-American vote and between 20 and 25 percent of the white vote. He swept the eight Durham precincts where African Americans comprised more than 90 percent of the electorate with between 91.2 percent and 96 percent of the votes. (One of these precincts was the NCCU campus, where the 8.9 percent voter turnout was by far the lowest in the county.) Nifong also did very well in a handful of precincts dominated by the left-wing People's Alliance PAC. Elsewhere he struggled. In his home precinct, he managed to win only 32 percent of the vote, trailing far behind Cheek.

Indeed, with the help of his enablers, Nifong's actions and rhetoric had recreated in Durham a mirror image of the legal and political cultures of the Deep South in the late 1950s, when racial appeals by segregationists such as George Wallace and Ross Barnett persuaded poor and working-class white voters to elect demagogues.

Similarly, racial appeals by Nifong persuaded poor and working-class black voters to elect a demagogue whose trashing of fair procedures for defendants could be turned against those same voters in many other cases. Criminal defendants, including innocent defendants, are very disproportionately black, in North Carolina and most other states. Electing Nifong would be a green light for him and other overzealous (and worse) prosecutors to offer the same treatment, and the same unfair procedures, that he gave the lacrosse players to black defendants and witnesses. Witness the wrongful prosecution of Sudanese cabbie Moezeldin Elmostafa.

Nifong's eagerness to play the race-baiting demagogue exceeded his skill at the game. But he only needed this one win; he had said upon announcing his candidacy that he would only serve one term, without mentioning that this would bring about his heart's desire of qualifying for the maximum possible pension.

Nifong's helpers in this enterprise included *The Herald-Sun*, with editor Bob Ashley overseeing the one-sided articles of John Stevenson and the fact-mangling, grossly misleading pro-Nifong editorials. Ashley's performance makes one wonder whether, had he been a local editor in the 1930s, he would have been cheering on the persecutors of the Scottsboro Boys. Some of Duke's Group of 88 radical professors resembled the white racists of old in their eagerness to join a mob driven by racial stereotypes. And the NAACP's demands for race-based justice in the Duke case echoed those of the old White Citizens' Councils in countless black-defendant cases.

Nifong's victory got a welcome, if a bit lukewarm, greeting from the editorial page of *The News & Observer*, as well as of *The Herald-Sun*. Evincing no sign that they had even read their own paper's devastating coverage, the *N&O*'s editors opined that Nifong should drop the rape charges "if at any time he loses confidence that he can prove guilt beyond a reasonable doubt." No acknowledgment that massive evidence now in the public record had already proved *innocence* beyond a reasonable doubt, as well as Nifong's monstrous unfairness. Against this background, the comments assumed with equanimity that Nifong would press the case to trial, in words reminiscent of the American journalists who had insisted that the Stalinist show trials were fair.

N&O editorial page editor Steve Ford also explained why he had not endorsed the Recall Nifong campaign before the election: That, he said, would "have had the effect of substituting the judgment of voters for the judgment of jurors." False. It would have had the effect of prompting Governor Easley to appoint a new district attorney, who would then decide whether the rape case should go to trial.

Ford added, "What we don't do in this country is decide the merit of criminal charges at the polls," since "the mix of politics and criminal justice can be volatile, verging on toxic." So it can. Nifong was the paradigm of mixing politics and criminal justice. Somebody should have told Ford.

The Herald-Sun conceded that "many more voters than we suspected, and perhaps more than Nifong suspected, have taken issue with the way he has handled the case." But this proof that the paper had been out of step with a majority in its community did not change its approach. Instead, *The Herald-Sun* presumed to preach to Evans, Seligmann, and Finnerty that Nifong's victory and a widely covered trial would *be good for them*. In a remarkable inversion of the principle that defendants are innocent until proven guilty, the paper said: "It would be better for the players to have an opportunity to prove their innocence at trial." Not that anyone had asked them if they thought they could get a fair trial in a community whose voters manifested a deep animus against them, nurtured by the deeply dishonest coverage of *The Herald-Sun* itself.

In this company it once again took a Duke student journalist, Kristin Butler, to talk sense. She was "shocked and dismayed" that 49 percent of Durhamites would vote for a man "who has disgraced this community before a national audience." And she called on Duke students to stand up for their rights and "continue to reject the ignorant, counterfactual and deeply offensive logic embraced by many of his proponents." Butler had no sympathy for the many Durham residents (and Duke professors) supporting a DA who "thinks it's acceptable to target Duke students because our 'rich daddies' can buy us 'expensive lawyers'"; a police force that openly discriminated against Duke students by arresting them for alleged petty infractions while not arresting nonstudents for much more serious alleged crimes; and a show trial for "three of our classmates [facing] a politically motivated prosecution . . . despite overwhelming evidence suggesting their innocence."

Butler reflected majority opinion among students, as suggested by *The Chronicle*'s unequivocal endorsement of Cheek and the ability of the DSED activists to register thousands of new student voters in the anti-Nifong effort. But the Brodhead administration had a very different view. It was moving to reward the faculty group that had charged most eagerly to the head of the rush-to-judgment mob.

On Brodhead's recommendation, the board of trustees formally elevated the African and African American Studies (AAAS) Program to academic-department status on December 4. This decision would allow AAAS to set up a doctoral program and start formally training the next generation of professors.

The AAAS vote came at the first board meeting since Steel had accepted appointment by President Bush as under secretary of the treasury for domestic finance, at the behest of Steel's old Goldman Sachs boss, Treasury Secretary Henry Paulson. He took office in mid-October. But still he held on to his position as chairman of Duke's board. This highly unusual combination of simultaneous heavyweight roles in both public and private sectors raised some eyebrows in Washington and among public interest groups (ranging from the right-leaning Judicial Watch to the left-of-center Citizens for Responsibility and Ethics in Washington), but not, apparently, at Duke.

In recommending this promotion of the AAAS in status, the Academic Programs Committee praised the AAAS faculty for their "admirable commitment to advanced research, teaching and outreach activities that deserves recognition." This despite the failure of AAAS teachings to attract the interest of very many students and most professors' conspicuous failure to produce much (if any) serious scholarship.

Teaching? The thirteen core faculty members (2.2 percent of the arts and sciences faculty) had attracted only thirty-three AAAS majors (0.5 percent of Duke's undergraduates). Advanced research? Did the committee read (or could they find) Wahneema Lubiano's scholarship? Or Houston Baker's pretentious prattle? Or the insights of Mark Anthony ("thugniggaintellectual") Neal? And what kind of "outreach" was the signing of the Group of 88's statement by 80 percent of the AAAS faculty?

Agitation for elevating the AAAS predated the lacrosse case, but the key decisions at Duke occurred well after the conduct of AAAS faculty was public knowledge. The vote of the Academic Programs Committee—with its praise of AAAS outreach activities—occurred on October 25, more than six months after the AAAS-organized Group of 88 statement appeared. The timing of the final decision, meanwhile, presented the Brodhead administration with an opportunity to distance itself from the professors who had led the campus rush to judgment. At the very least, it could have delayed the vote for a year or two or coupled it with a statement that the AAAS brand of outreach activities did not represent Duke's values.

Instead, Steel and Brodhead awarded those professors a big trophy, with a unanimous vote from the board. Even as the case to which they had attached their cause imploded, the power of the AAAS faculty on campus continued to increase.

20. THE CONSPIRACY UNRAVELS

O N DECEMBER 5, Jim Cooney met privately with Mike Nifong to ask for a fresh start for Reade Seligmann, hoping to get past the bitterness between Nifong and Kirk Osborn. As a conciliatory gesture, Cooney even withdrew Osborn's motion requesting Nifong's recusal from the case. Cooney also urged Nifong, logically enough, that the state would have a better chance of convicting Evans and Finnerty if Nifong would drop the charges against Seligmann: Since Reade's alibi showed that no rape involving him could possibly have occurred, Nifong's whole case was doomed as long as Seligmann remained a defendant. While Cooney was sure that there should be no case at all because there had been no rape, his first duty was to get his own client out of the case if he could.

Nifong's response: "There is no such thing as an airtight alibi." Cooney offered to open his whole file to Nifong and even bring in his client for an interview. "There is nothing you can show me that will change my mind," retorted the district attorney. He added that as long as his "victim" wanted to proceed, "we're going forward."

Thus did Cooney learn for himself that on the lacrosse case, the person effectively setting the district attorney's course was a mentally unbalanced woman who had never told the same story twice. Cooney was "frankly stunned"; any good prosecutor would have jumped at his offer to bring Reade in for questioning, if only to test the strength of the alibi. But Nifong continued his pattern of blinding himself to any evidence that might contradict his preferred version of events.

The district attorney had no idea what was about to hit him. Knowing that Nifong would try to convict Dave Evans by mischaracterizing the results of the tests by Dr. Meehan's DNA Security lab, Brad Bannon had spent endless hours studying the nearly two thousand pages of raw data that he had finally forced Nifong to cough up at the October 27 hearing. There were also hundreds of pages more from the state's DNA lab. Knowing nothing about DNA when he started, Bannon—who had not even taken a college math course—taught himself from a text entitled *Forensic DNA Typing*, by John Butler.

Along the way, Bannon had consulted confidentially with Rob Cary and Chris Manning, both partners at Williams & Connolly, an elite Washington law firm. Its most senior partner, the famed criminal defense lawyer Brendan Sullivan, a friend of Rae and David Evans, had offered the firm's services for free, on a confidential basis. Manning, like Dave Evans, had been a lacrosse player both at Duke and at Landon, a private boys' school outside Washington. Cary, like Bannon, became a self-taught DNA expert. The big firm retained Hal Deadman, who as former director of the FBI's DNA lab was one of the world's leading experts.

But mostly, Bannon spread out all the documents on the big conference room table at his law firm and worked feverishly to figure out where the bodies were buried. Joe Cheshire would find him there when he came in the morning and still there when he left at night. Bannon pulled a couple of all-nighters. Finally he thought he had it figured out, and wrote a long, internal defense memo. To make sure he had it right, Bannon sent the November 30 memo to Cary and Manning, and they relayed it to Deadman. Bannon flew to Washington to meet with the Williams & Connolly lawyers and Hal Deadman on December 8.

Meeting Bannon for the first time, the DNA expert shook his hand and asked where he had gotten his degree in science. "I am sure it was a joke," Bannon later recalled, "but it was an enormous compliment, because I am the most thick-skulled person you know when it comes to science or math, and I got my undergraduate degree in English without taking any math classes and, I think, only one biology class about marine life." Deadman confirmed the correctness of the analysis in Bannon's memo and the lawyer flew home to convert it into a motion.

Meanwhile, on December 12, U.S. Congressman Walter Jones, a Republican from eastern North Carolina, dramatized the extreme nature of Nifong's misconduct by calling upon the U.S. Justice Department to open an investigation of Nifong's behavior. Federal law makes it a felony for any state official to "willfully subject . . . any person in any state . . . to the deprivation" of his or her constitutional rights, or to conspire to do so. Cataloguing some of Nifong's best-known abuses—his procedurally improper preprimary statements and his ordering the police to violate their own procedures in the rigged April 4 lineup—Jones asserted that "if the American people cannot trust those who they've empowered to pursue justice fairly, then hope for this democracy is lost."

It is unheard of for the Justice Department to go after a state prosecutor. But Attorney General Alberto Gonzales did not immediately rule out that possibility. And seven other House members, along with Democratic senators Bob Menendez and Barack Obama, would later join Jones in calling for a Justice Department investigation of Nifong. Conspicuously absent from this list was Durham's congressman, David Price. He said through a spokesperson that it "would be premature and inappropriate" to comment on the matter. A Democrat on leave from a Duke professorship in political science, Price had depended on the African-American vote to win his seat.

Then the defense team pounded Nifong's case and credibility to bits in front of the world in a carefully prepared crescendo of four hammer blows on December 13, 14, and 15, 2006.

December 13

In a sixteen-page joint motion, the defense attorneys unveiled the staggeringly conclusive evidence of innocence, and of probable Nifong misconduct, that Brad Bannon had found hidden in the nearly two thousand pages of complex and highly technical data from Dr. Brian Meehan's DNA Securities lab.

Bannon's most stunning discovery was that Meehan's tests had found the DNA of several unidentified males in Mangum's panties, rectal swabs, and pubic hair comb. All of this DNA had to have come from sexual activities predating the stripper party, from which she had departed without a single cell of lacrosse-player DNA on or in her. And these males did not include three men (her "boyfriend" and two "drivers") with whom she had belatedly told authorities she might have had sex in the days before the party.

With tests so sensitive as to detect all that male DNA from before the party still lying around this apparently hospitable environment, how could anyone believe that three lacrosse players had pulled off a violent gang rape without leaving a trace of themselves on or in her?

"This is strong evidence of innocence," Bannon's explosive motion concluded, "in a case in which the accuser denied engaging in any sexual activity in the days before the alleged assault, told police she last had consensual sexual intercourse a week before the assault, and claimed that her attackers did not use condoms and ejaculated." Defense attorneys presented Judge Smith with a variety of options for possible relief, including a chance to question Meehan at some point.

Bannon's motion also stressed that the May 12 DNA Security report, with no mention of the unidentified males' DNA, was all that defense lawyers or the public would ever have known about the private lab's finding had Nifong had his way. This apparently violated both the lab's own policies and the state's open discovery statute.

Could Nifong deny guilty knowledge of these violations despite his three personal visits to meet with Meehan at his lab in Burlington just before and after the indictments of Seligmann and Finnerty, and just before the release of the highly misleading May 12 report?

December 14

The second hammer blow was a powerfully argued joint motion to suppress Mangum's rigged identifications of the three defendants. Prepared by Jim Cooney, the forty-two-page motion included a review of the succession of deeply flawed investigative moves by police and the DA culminating in the constitutionally flawed April 4 photo lineup and Mangum's April 6 signed statement. Flawed procedures, Cooney demonstrated, beget flawed results. To devastating effect, the motion cross-referenced all of Crystal's already contradictory stories with her still more inconsistent statements during the April 4 photo lineup.

To pick one of many possible examples: Crystal identified Reade Seligmann with 100 percent confidence on April 4 as the "Adam" who raped her; she said on April 6 that the same "Adam" had carried her from the bathroom to put her in the car. But the photos showed that she was put in the car 12:40 A.M. on March 14—more than twenty minutes after Seligmann had left the scene. So Crystal had lied on April 4 or 6 or—as was clear from many mutually corroborative pieces of evidence—on both dates. The motion also used photos of Dave Evans just before and after the party to belie Crystal's April 4 claim that she would be 90 percent sure he had raped her *if he had a mustache.*

The suppression motion argued compellingly that the only effective remedy for the violations of the defendants' due process rights by the April 4 "multiple choice test with no wrong answers" would be to bar Mangum from identifying Evans, Seligmann, or Finnerty during her trial testimony. If granted, this motion would effectively require dismissal of the entire case before trial, because Nifong had no other testimony linking any of the defendants to the supposed rape.

December 15

The third hammer blow came the next morning in yet another power-packed defense motion, this one arguing that the jury pool in Durham had been so poisoned against the defendants as to require a change of venue in the event of a trial. The motion began with quotes from more than a dozen of the attacks on the lacrosse players by Nifong, by their professors, by members of Durham's black community, and by the media. The quotes were so inflammatory and so false as to surprise even observers who had seen them all piecemeal before.

Anticipating a possible Nifong counterattack, defense attorneys withheld powerful statistical evidence on why the venue needed to be changed: survey data showing a polarized community. The September 2006 defense poll to which Nifong had so strongly objected at the September 22 hearing showed that more than half of Durham County's residents had already made up their minds, with 28.5 percent confident that Mangum had been raped and 31 percent confident that she had not been raped. Over 90 percent of Durham County respondents had heard of the case.

"There exists within this County among a significant percentage of residents so great a prejudice against the Defendants," the venue motion argued, "that they cannot obtain a fair and impartial trial and that a Jury selected from this County will be unable to deliberate on the evidence presented in the courtroom, free from outside influence." This atmosphere had been created, the motion said, by Nifong's improper March–April public attacks on the players; by the continuing attacks from many Duke professors; by the extreme bias of the only newspaper based in Durham, *The Herald-Sun*; and by the racial polarization evidenced by the rush to judgment of many in the local African-American community against the white defendants.

This appears to be the only case in American history in which a university's professors had spewed such vitriol against their students as to make it impossible, in the view of defense lawyers, for them to get a fair trial in the vicinity of the university.

The immediate media impact of these three blockbuster motions was blunted by the fact that many reporters don't take time to read such documents or the attached evidence carefully enough to separate wheat from chaff. Most of the media thus ignored the defense lawyers' devastating revelations, as did *The New York Times*, or glossed over them, reporting their arguments in such general terms as to suggest that this was just standard defense-lawyer stuff. In the print media, only *The News & Observer* gave the motions the attention they deserved, in consecutive front-page stories by Joe Neff.

But December 15 was also the date of a hearing that turned out to be the climatic court session of the case, a defense triumph with dramatic elements enough to capture the attention of most big media groups. (Not *The New York Times*.) The defendants—Seligmann, Finnerty, and Evans—and their parents were all in court together for what turned out to be the only time. The night before, the families and all the attorneys in the case had dined together at a Chapel Hill restaurant. Joe Cheshire concluded the evening by saying that whatever was to occur at the hearing, they needed to remember to hold their heads high as the three innocent men they were.

The courtroom was jammed by virtually everyone associated with the case—more than hundred in all—excepting Crystal Mangum (whose father, Travis, was there) and the heavily criticized Sergeant Gottlieb. The big show of support for the defendants included Tricia Dowd and other parents of unindicted players; women's lacrosse coach Kerstin Kimel, the first Duke employee to publicly defend the character of the men's team; Mike Pressler, the blameless fired coach, who said he had come because "it's all about being there for them"; his wife Sue; John Danowski, the new coach; Jackie Brown and Beth Brewer, leaders of the Recall Nifong campaign; and Brooke Jandl and Ekstrand paralegal Stef Sparks, leaders of Duke Students for an Ethical Durham. Shortly after the doors opened at 8:30 A.M., seven members of the 2007 men's lacrosse team also strode into the courtroom.

Michael Catalino said he probably should have been studying for a 7:00 P.M. final but wanted to see his buddies Collin and Reade. "I knew it could have been me," he recalled, "and if it had been, I would have wanted my teammates there to show support." The unindicted players sat in the first row of the jury box, within two feet of the district attorney's table. Bo Carrington and Ryan McFadyen stared at Nifong throughout the hearing. The DA avoided eye contact.

Then there were the reporters, from the local papers, the *Los Angeles Times*, *The Washington Post*, and *USA Today*, and every major network except CBS.

The courtroom crowd circulated and buzzed, with lots of reunions and hugs, while Judge Smith held a thirty-minute conference in his chambers with the lawyers. The issue at hand: Mangum's medical and mental health records. In the initial round of discovery, in May, the Finnerty lawyers had noticed scattered references to Mangum's psychological history; in an August meeting with Smith in chambers shortly after he came onto the case, they successfully urged that Mangum's medical records be subpoenaed. The ten-inch-thick file reached Judge Smith shortly before the October hearing. On November 9, Finnerty attorney Doug Kingsbery delivered a four-page letter to Smith contending that access to the records was critical both to impeach Mangum's credibility and to counter likely claims by Nifong that Mangum's behavior could be a product of "rape trauma syndrome." The argument persuaded Smith: in chambers, he made the extraordinary announcement to Nifong and the defense attorneys that he would release Mangum's *entire* medical file, under seal, to both sides. He had concluded, Smith said, that turning over Mangum's entire psychological history was critical for the proper administration of justice. The decision, Kingsbery later recalled, "was the first statement from the judge that he had begun to form an opinion as to the truth of the case."

Discussion then turned to the defense's DNA motion. The pressure was on Nifong to respond to the revelation that the highly exculpatory DNA of multiple males had been detected by DNA Security and withheld from the defense. In chambers, Nifong assured Judge Smith that he understood the seriousness of the defense's DNA motion and that he was wholly unaware of the issues it raised before he read it. He told the judge:

> I just, in terms of the discovery issues, frankly, you know, I got the report and I was, like, whoa. So I immediately faxed a copy to Dr. Meehan and said, "Read this, and I'll call you in the morning and get your opinions about this." And we discussed it and I said, "This is a major issue for the defense. They're entitled to hear about it, and I think it needs to be addressed right away. And so that's what we're going to try to do, okay."

The district attorney made a similar statement when the open session began, giving the first of what would become at least eleven separate explanations of his handling of the DNA Security test results. "The first that I heard of this particular situation," he assured Judge Smith, "was when I was served with these reports—this motion on Wednesday of this week." The implication seemed to be that Meehan had concealed the exculpatory test results even from Nifong. Then, in a grand gesture, Nifong announced that Meehan was present in the courtroom and prepared to testify.

This move took the defense lawyers by surprise, as Nifong had hoped it would. The standard procedure would have been for the district attorney to take a few weeks to file a written response—in which he would have to come to grips with the devastating details in the motion—and then schedule a hearing to argue the matter. So none of the defense lawyers had prepared for what would be a difficult cross-examination of the DA's expert witness on his own extremely arcane and complex scientific tests and documents. But it would be a big loss of momentum to pass on this chance to nail down the DNA motion's factual assertions and to explore questions still unanswered by the documents that Brad Bannon had deciphered.

As the attorneys debated, Cheshire made the decision: the defense had to take advantage of the immediate opportunity to question Meehan under oath. Bannon, the defense lawyer most steeped in the nearly two thousand pages of DNA documents, would handle the examination. The biggest question: What did Nifong know and when did he know it?

At the defense table, Bannon flipped nervously through the thick binders filled with the underlying data from Meehan's tests. "You could see Brad's pant legs were shaking," recalled David Evans. "He was really scared." A few minutes before the session began, Bannon told Cheshire he needed more time. Cheshire leaned over and said, "Listen, there's a difference between lawyers and great lawyers, and that difference is in moments like this. You are a great lawyer, Brad. I've always told you that, but you've never believed it. You can do this. You will do this. And you'll do great."

Expecting Nifong to ask a few questions of Meehan to warm things up, Bannon was surprised when the DA instead turned over the witness for immediate questioning from the defense. Then came an even bigger problem: When Bannon asked Meehan to confirm the accuracy of the defense motion's central assertions about the multiple males' DNA, the answer was "No."

Uh-oh. Had Bannon's analysis been wrong? Had he made mistakes? Was the scientific expert going to embarrass the defense or dance away on the strength of his superior knowledge? Every one of Bannon's improvised follow-up questions was based on the premise that Meehan's answer to this question would be "Yes."

Bannon thought to himself: "Wow, here we go. Not only am I about to fail, but I am about to fail *spectacularly*, in front of all of our clients, their families, these other lawyers, and dozens of other people. That question was my whole analysis."

Soldiering on, the young lawyer asked if Meehan had examined the attachments to the DNA motion. No, Meehan replied, Nifong had never sent them to him. Could this guy think he was going to bluff his way through a cross-examination without even reviewing the documents? Bannon took a deep breath, back on an even keel.

On the fly, he started asking much more specific questions, moving through each element of the rape kit evidence in succession, pulling exhibits out page by page, walking the witness through them one by one, speaking of "alleles" and other unfamiliar scientific terms. Courtroom spectators had trouble following all this. But Meehan's answers, once Bannon had him pinned and wriggling on the wall, were clear enough: Yes. Yes. Yes. Lots of yeses. And after well over an hour, Meehan had eaten every particle of that initial, evasive *no* many times over. Meehan kept looking expectantly at Nifong, as if for a rescue that never came.

Moving into new terrain, Bannon asked Meehan to discuss the concept of transference. Meehan could see where that might lead: toward exposing the insignificance of the *possible* Evans DNA found by his lab on the fake fingernail fished out of Evans's bathroom wastebasket. The lab director feigned ignorance. Bannon explained how the transference of one or two cells—between items intermingled in a wastebasket, or from a speck of dandruff falling onto something, for example—could lead to invalid conclusions.

Indeed, Bannon continued, had not Meehan's own DNA turned up on one of the items in the rape kit, despite all of his lab's precautions against such contamination? The answer was yes again. This discovery, Meehan admitted, undermined his lab's credibility. And this, too—though in the two thousand pages of documents that Bannon and Judge Smith had pried out of Nifong—had been left out of Meehan's May 12 report.

Watching Brad pull the truth out of Meehan page by page, exhibit by exhibit, fingernail by fingernail, with a surgeon's precision, until finally the witness was stripped naked, Dave Evans felt chills go down his back. Nifong is now exposed and caught, he thought. Bannon's masterly cross-examination, Joe Cheshire later recalled, "was one of the prouder moments of my life."

Meanwhile, the contrast between the teams at the defense and prosecution tables was striking. The defense table was all business, with Bannon regularly pausing to consult the fat binders of DNA Security documents spread out on the table or to whisper with others on the six-member defense team. The prosecution table looked like amateur hour.

Detective Himan, seated next to Nifong, did not consult with the DA, took no notes during Meehan's testimony, and barely moved for nearly two hours. To Himan's left, the tall, rotund Linwood Wilson sat with chair pushed back, legs spread out on the side, also taking no notes. The DA himself sat stonefaced through most of the hearing, occasionally yawning, rubbing his temples, or shuffling a few documents in front of him. He took few, if any, notes and rarely objected to Bannon's questioning. Behind Nifong sat Victoria Peterson, his conspiracy-theorizing, homophobic citizens' committee cochair. She chatted with Nifong during the break and brought in a bag of Lays potato chips and a soda, contrary to court rules.

Catalino, within feet of the DA and his expert alike, enjoyed "seeing Nifong's disorganization in person."

Bannon moved on to explore why Meehan had failed to report his lab's multiple-males finding and what he had told Nifong. The lab director offered an array of implausible answers. He spoke first of privacy concerns that he might have if he were a parent of an unindicted player. Bannon recognized the absurdity of this claim. "Let me ask you," the attorney stated, "whose privacy would it have violated if you had simply reported the male DNA characteristics found on multiple rape kit items from multiple different males who you didn't have reference swabs for? Whose privacy would it violate?"

Meehan's reply: "That . . . that wouldn't have violated anybody's privacy."

"Asked by a defense attorney how lab results clearing all 46 players would violate their privacy, Meehan fumbled for an answer as Nifong sat with his head lowered, staring at documents," reported David Zucchino of the *Los Angeles Times*. Joe Neff said that Nifong "looked ashen, resting his face in his hands or staring down at the table."

Meehan also claimed that he would have supplied additional information had it been requested by his "client" Nifong, and that his May 12 report was not a "final conclusive report on the case." Was Meehan planning to produce another report? asked Bannon. No, Meehan said sheepishly. Backed into a corner, he was forced to admit that his nondisclosure was contrary to state law and his own company's protocols, which called for reporting on all DNA examined. "I don't have a legal justification or a reason," he said, while insisting in apparent desperation that "I was just trying to do the right thing." Meehan went on: "By the letter of the law, by the letter of the wording of the standard," the defense was "absolutely correct" and so his report "might not hold any weight in your legal arena." But, of course, Meehan had been hired precisely to produce a report for the "legal arena."

Several times, Bannon came close to extracting an admission that Meehan and Nifong had agreed not to report the test results: "It is true that we did not release the full profiles of all the players in this case. And I did that after discussions with Mike Nifong because of concerns about getting those profiles out into the public media." Later: "Our client, Mr. Nifong, specifically wanted . . . to know . . . do any of the reference specimens [of lacrosse players] match any of the evidence? And that's the report that we gave him." Later still: "Mr. Nifong is our client and had he said, 'Listen, I want a report on everything,' that's what we would produce."

For Bo Carrington, "It was a redemptive feeling as Meehan testified and everyone saw what Nifong had done." Ryan McFadyen, staring at Nifong, thought, I can't believe you're ruining peoples' lives. Later he glanced over at the defense table and caught the eye of Collin Finnerty, who flashed a peace sign.

But Meehan had not yet explicitly confirmed that he and Nifong had reached a nondisclosure agreement—a freighted concept in the law because an agreement amounts to criminal conspiracy if its object is a criminal cover-up.

Having hit the cross-examination equivalent of a triple, but fatigued from fencing with the evasive expert, Brad Bannon sat down and left it to Jim Cooney to administer the coup de grace. Cooney asked Meehan to look at the six-inch-thick pile of documents of DNA test data in front of him on the witness stand. Wouldn't Reade Seligmann and Collin Finnerty have "needed to go through those six inches of paper to find" the results showing multiple males' DNA, none of it matching them? Yes, Meehan admitted. And wasn't there "more of your DNA than of Reade Seligmann's" in the rape kit? Yes again.

The hearing's Perry Mason moment went like this:

MR. COONEY: *"Did your report set forth the results of all of the tests and examinations that you conducted in this case?"*

DR. MEEHAN: *"No. It was limited to only some results."*

MR. COONEY: *"Okay. And that was an intentional limitation arrived at between you and representatives of the State of North Carolina not to report on the results of all examinations and tests that you did in this case?"*

DR. MEEHAN: *"Yes."*

Bingo. Nifong's own expert witness had just admitted that the two of them had agreed—or perhaps conspired—to hide extremely powerful evidence of innocence. In the process, Meehan had also exposed the falsity of Nifong's repeated assurances to the court, over many months, that Meehan had told him nothing about his findings beyond what was in the report given to defense lawyers on May 12.

Scattered applause erupted in the courtroom. Judge Smith looked momentarily stunned. Then he lowered his gavel to demand silence.

The hearing was adjourned a few minutes later, after Joe Cheshire persuaded Judge Smith (with Nifong unopposed) to order a paternity test as soon as the accuser gave birth to a baby that she was expecting in early February. Cheshire's goal was to make it clear that the father was not a Duke lacrosse player.

Shortly after the hearing, in an impromptu press conference in the courthouse corridor, Nifong admitted to the media that he had known that the DNA of multiple males had been found in the rape kit, contradicting the apparent implication of his statement to Judge Smith not two hours before. Now Nifong's excuse was that "we were trying to, just as Dr. Meehan said, trying to avoid dragging any names through the mud." Touching as it was to hear such concern for the privacy of the unindicted lacrosse players expressed by the same DA who had trashed them so loud and long as "hooligans," racists, and accomplices in rape, this did not wash. Disclosing the evidence of innocence would not have involved mentioning the name of a single unindicted lacrosse player.

The reaction to the December 15 revelations was swift, and marked the beginning of the end for Nifong and his case. "The more you hear about [Nifong's] missteps, the more you have to question whether it's purely a matter of incompetence or worse," Jim Coleman told *The News & Observer*. Congressman Jones issued a press release reiterating his call for a Justice Department inquiry. Brent Turvey, head of a private forensics lab and author of several forensics books, ridiculed Meehan's claim of not understanding how the "legal arena" worked. "What Dr. Meehan has admitted to, under oath, is that he personally conspired with prosecutors to conceal actual exculpatory findings from the defense. He has further testified that this is a violation of his own lab's policies—policies that he would have written. There is no good reason for such conduct, and there can be no excuses for such conduct." The American Society of Crime Laboratory Directors/Laboratory Accreditation Board announced that it planned to investigate the accreditation status of Meehan's lab.

The next evening, Nifong's case and the zeal of his enablers were subjected to biting mockery in a *Saturday Night Live* sketch from Amy Poehler. In "A Holiday Message from Nancy Grace," Poehler-as-Grace pronounced herself "saddened" by the DNA findings in the case of the "brave exotic dancer," the "heroic stripper" whose cause she had so championed on her television show. While support groups for real rape victims existed, Poehler's character said, "What about those whose claims of sexual assault are almost certainly false? Who's sticking up for them? Apart from me, and Durham County, North Carolina, D.A. Mike Nifong, nobody." And "that's a national disgrace."

But even this far into Nifong's public ignominy, as the December 15 hearing set legal ethics experts and commentators around the nation to clamoring about his abuses, another week went by with nary a word of explicit public criticism of the district attorney from Richard Brodhead or any other Duke official.

Asked later, by one of the authors, why he had made no criticism of Nifong even at this late date, Brodhead responded: "As the story turned, for consistency, and because I believe it was right, I had to continue to say, 'It's not mine to make the verdict here.' If people said, 'Yeah, but something's gone wrong with the legal process,' my view was, I do not believe the day ever comes when private individuals have the right to take public judgment back into their hands. You look for cures within the process. And you look for cures of faults of the process in a correction of the process."

Jim Coleman was later to second Brodhead's hands-off approach in an interview with the Duke *Chronicle*. "I'm not sure what more the University could have said that would have been supportive of the students and would not have appeared to be Duke trying to interfere in the judicial process," Coleman said. "Nifong had already basically attacked students as being wealthy, white, privileged students whose fathers could go out and buy them the best lawyers. I don't think the University could have asserted that the students were innocent under those circumstances."

Of course, with all respect for Coleman, most Brodhead critics had not been asking him to declare the defendants innocent. They had been asking him to speak out against Nifong's grotesque abuse of the legal process and of the students' rights to fair procedures and fair treatment. And they had been asking him to stop his succession of damaging and misleading public attacks on the characters of this group of generally admirable young men.

It was only because the Duke defendants had extraordinarily talented, hardworking, and expensive lawyers that the Nifong-Meehan DNA cover-up conspiracy was ever cracked. In this and other respects the lacrosse case opened a window into how helpless the vast majority of criminal defendants are when in the hands of unscrupulous or overzealous prosecutors.

"Most defendants cannot pay" for a full-court-press defense, observed one participant in the Liestoppers forum. "Accordingly the state hires these guys and if they say there's a match, you're guilty, and if they say there's not a match, well, then, you may be guilty anyway. Completely ludicrous. Who knows how many innocent people are sitting in jail because of this type of garbage. God help us all."

On December 20, the North Carolina State Bar, already secretly at work on a complaint seeking to discipline Nifong for multiple violations of pretrial publicity rules, informed the DA that it was considering still more ethics charges based on his withholding of exculpatory DNA evidence.

The very next day, Nifong moved to try to plug some of the gaping, newly apparent holes in his rapidly sinking ship. After nine months during which nobody in the DA's office had ever interviewed Crystal Mangum about her allegations, Nifong dispatched his faithful sidekick Linwood Wilson to interrogate her—alone. The duo didn't even tell the Police Department about Wilson's mission. The result was a new story, attributed to Crystal by the far-from-credible Wilson, that contradicted in numerous ways almost everything else in her myriad, mutually contradictory succession of stories and every other piece of evidence in the case.

According to Wilson's report of his December 21 interview of Crystal, she now supposedly could not recall whether her attackers had used their penises or some kind of object to penetrate her vagina. Not once before had Crystal even hinted at any such possibility. Nifong evidently hoped that the new version would reduce the apparent importance of the DNA evidence that he and Meehan had been caught trying to hide.

And now Crystal supposedly claimed for the first time that Evans had wiped her off with a white towel, which was also used to clean up the crime scene.

A January 11 defense motion made Wilson's interview report public and explained the absurdity of this tale: "To believe the accuser's present claim that her vagina was wiped with this towel, that her face was wiped with this towel, that Dave Evans was wiped with this towel, and that the floor was wiped with this towel, would require the belief that this towel could wipe away all DNA from her attackers on the accuser's body, but leave the DNA of other, unknown males. It further requires the belief that the accuser's face and vagina could be wiped with this towel, but leave no trace of her DNA on the towel. Further, it requires the belief that the floor could be wiped with this towel, but that it would only wipe Dave Evans' DNA, leaving Matt Zash's DNA behind on the floor. Finally, the towel, while apparently obliterating any DNA left behind by the alleged attackers on the accuser's body, somehow contained only one of her attackers' DNA, despite her multiple claims that two of her attackers penetrated her rectum and vagina with their penises."

The December 21 Mangum-Wilson story also purported, with similar implausibility, to paper over other big problems with Nifong's case exposed by the recent defense motions.

The Photo Lineup

Problems: The December 14 defense suppression motion showed the contradiction between Crystal's identification of Reade Seligmann as "Adam" and her claim that "Adam" carried her to Kim Roberts's car (at a time when Seligmann was in a cab en route to his dorm after a videotaped stop at an ATM machine). Another contradiction was the stark contrast between the tall, thin, baby-faced Finnerty and Crystal's March 16 descriptions of Brett, Matt, and Adam. A third was her April 6 mention of "Dan," a fourth attacker in what was alleged to be a three-man rape.

The revised story: In the December 21 version, Seligmann was still Adam—but now he sometimes was Matt, too. Dave Evans was still Matt—but now he sometimes was Adam, and Brett, and even Dan. And Collin Finnerty corresponded to none of the three aliases. Under the new tale, the "Adam" that carried Crystal to the car could have been Evans, not Seligmann. The March 16 descriptions failed to match Finnerty because he was neither Brett, nor Matt, nor Adam. The mystery of "Dan" was solved because Dave Evans was now Dan (except when he was Brett, Matt, or Adam—and, of course, Dave). Crystal had never previously claimed that any of her attackers had used more than one name or that one had used no name at all.

Seligmann's Alibi

Problem: The time-stamped photos, Seligmann's various electronic records, and the accounts of the cabbie and the neighbor had long made Seligmann's innocence redundantly evident to everyone except Nifong, Brodhead, and some of the Group of 88. This was also exculpatory evidence for Finnerty and Evans because it pointed to the fraudulence of the process by which all three defendants were picked.

The revised story: In the new, improved, December 21 version, Mangum and Wilson presented an entirely new time line, which contradicted every statement she had previously made and every item of electronic and eyewitness evidence. Never before had she mentioned specific times. Now, after more than nine months, she suddenly remembered that the supposed attack had happened at 11:40 P.M., before Seligmann's alibi kicked in. Nifong made no attempt to square this with the cell-phone records that showed Mangum had been on the phone frequently between 11:00 and 11:39 and that Seligmann had been on the phone from 11:50 until 11:52, not to mention the time-stamped photos of the women dancing for four minutes starting at midnight.

As the defense lawyers later explained this new absurdity: "According to the accuser's most recent telling, she apparently spoke with someone at her father's home for 7 minutes during the time that she was planning her nude dance routine, during the time that she was dancing, and then as she was fleeing to the car. In addition, the accuser was apparently talking with someone on her cell phone at the time that she was walking back into the house and being 'kidnapped' into the bathroom. She finished her last conversation at the time the rape was beginning. None of these facts has ever been mentioned in any statement that the accuser has given to date in this case . . . [while] at the height of the sexual attack now claimed by the accuser, Reade Seligmann was having a telephone conversation."

The Disappearing Mustache

Problem: The defense had clear proof that Evans had no mustache at the time of the alleged attack, discrediting Crystal's "identification" of him as a probable attacker *if he had a mustache.*

The revised story: Now, for the first time, Crystal supposedly recalled Evans having only a five o'clock shadow.

Nifong's apparent belief that these preposterous new yarns would improve his own now-perilous legal situation suggests that the DA was becoming increasingly detached from reality. Hoping to keep his case alive while dodging the wrath of the state bar, Nifong faxed a one-page form to the defense attorneys on December 22 at 11:37 A.M., notifying them that while pressing on with the extremely serious sexual assault and kidnapping charges, he was dropping the rape charges. "The victim in this case indicated that, while she initially believed that she had been vaginally penetrated by a male sex organ," Nifong wrote, "she cannot at this time testify with certainty [to that]. Therefore, the State is unable to meet its burden of proof with respect to this offense." Under state law, only unconsented vaginal penetration with a penis constitutes rape.

Nifong gave no advance notice of this bombshell to Mayor Bell, City Manager Baker, or Police Chief Chalmers. Reporters found the door to the district attorney's office locked, with a paper sign affixed reading, NO MEDIA. . . . . PLEASE!!!!!!!!!!!!!!

But try as he might, the man who so eagerly had cultivated the media in the spring could not silence observers as his case imploded. In *The Chronicle,* Jim Coleman, the voice of moral clarity throughout this affair, compared the Mangum-Wilson statement to "the end of a bad mystery novel where all the ends are tied up." The Duke law professor was even harsher in *The News & Observer,* suggesting that the time might have come to open a criminal inquiry into Nifong's behavior, since "Who would believe that a witness, nine months later, suddenly recalls facts that coincidentally negate evidence produced by the defense?" Coleman concluded, "It's like Nifong is mooning the system."

21. DEFENDANT NIFONG

A S THE NEWS THAT NIFONG had abandoned the rape charge careered around Durham and the nation, even erstwhile enablers like Richard Brodhead and steadfast supporters like the news sections of *The New York Times* began to abandon him. By the end of 2006 many had been forced to acknowledge implicitly what careful students of the record had known for many months: Nifong had engaged in grossly unethical—perhaps even criminal—misconduct, and the case against the lacrosse players was a travesty.

Brodhead ventured his first public criticism of Nifong on December 22, hours after the district attorney had dropped the rape charges. Apparently the day that never comes—when (to borrow Brodhead's words) "private individuals have the right to take public judgment back into their hands"—had come. "Given the certainty with which the district attorney made his many public statements regarding the rape allegation, his decision today to drop [the rape] charge must call into question the validity of the remaining charges," the Duke president said in a prepared statement. "The district attorney should now put this case in the hands of an independent party, who can restore confidence in the fairness of the process. Further, Mr. Nifong has an obligation to explain to all of us his conduct in this matter."

Brodhead also had some explaining to do, although he acknowledged no such need. Why had it taken him nine months to distance himself from the dishonest district attorney and speak out against his procedural misconduct? Why had Brodhead made so many harsh and misleading public comments about the lacrosse players? Could he be unaware that his voice had reinforced media and Duke faculty portrayals of the players as racist, sexist thugs?

The editors of the *Times*, meanwhile, were finally forced by events to pivot suddenly away from the steadfast pro-Nifong bias of the coverage that they had been happily running under Duff Wilson's byline. They had a long piece in the works as of the morning of December 22, seeking to recover from the embarrassing, near-total failure of the *Times* to cover the bombshell testimony of Brian Meehan on December 15 about his agreement with Nifong to hide exculpatory evidence. (The December 16 *Times* had carried a brief Associated Press item headlined "Duke Case Accuser Is Pregnant, and Test of Paternity Is Next"; it mentioned Meehan's testimony toward the end.)

A draft of the new *Times* piece, slated for the next day's paper, featured a three-hour, interview with Nifong on December 21—a remarkable favor from a grateful, now-beleaguered prosecutor who had spurned interview requests from other reporters for months, saying it would be improper for him to comment. This draft prominently featured a Nifong quote that he would press ahead with his case despite defense attacks and his recent setbacks, according to a source with knowledge of discussions among the reporters and editors.

Then, about midday on December 22, someone told the clueless *Times* editors and reporters that they had been overtaken by a big, breaking story: Nifong had just dismissed the rape charge that the *Times* had worked so long and hard to prop up. Editors scrambled. The initial result was posted that afternoon on the newspaper's Web site. For the first time the byline listed David Barstow, a seasoned national correspondent, along with Wilson, who had been widely ridiculed as a virtual Nifong PR agent. But it read like another Duff Wilson production.

The online article attributed to an anonymous source "close to the investigation" a supposedly neutral legal analysis strangely suggesting that the dismissal of the rape charge had made the rest of Nifong's case "stronger." This anonymous attribution was a violation of a declared *Times* policy against unexplained, unattributed analysis. It was an especially flagrant violation because the unnamed source turned out to be none other than Nifong himself, as the *Times* would inadvertently reveal a month later. The article also included a lengthy pro-Nifong quote from Victoria Peterson—without disclosing either her role in Nifong's campaign or her extremist views. It conspicuously failed to note the remarkable fact that the December 21 Linwood Wilson interview was the first discussion of the facts by any representative of Nifong's office with the accuser, ever. And while quoting defense lawyer Joe Cheshire, the *Times* mentioned none of the proliferating criticisms of Nifong by neutral legal ethics experts and others.

The *Times* did a much less embarrassing job in follow-up articles on December 23 and 24, now listing Barstow as lead reporter, with Wilson sharing the byline. For the first time, the nation's most influential newspaper told its readers on December 23 that Nifong had "faced relentless and rising criticism for his handling of the case," including from legal experts unconnected to the defense.

And for the first time the *Times* stressed a few of the reasons for these criticisms. These included the facts that the only lacrosse player twice identified by the accuser with 100 percent certainty had not even been in Durham the night of the party and that her identification of Dave Evans with 90 percent certainty as an attacker was discredited by her subsequently disproven claim that he had had a mustache that night. The December 23 article drew upon the three-hour Nifong interview but avoided the previous pro-Nifong spin. And Nifong unvarnished did not look good. *Times* readers learned that:

- The D.A. was unconcerned with the glaring flaws in the accuser's identifications during the April 4 photo lineup as long as she could claim many months later, in a courtroom, that she had been attacked by the three young men conveniently seated at the defense table: "You can't always tell from a photograph," he said, since "the only real time that you're able to say if you have a misidentification is to put the person in the courtroom with the other people."

- Nifong seemed almost to hint that he was indifferent to whether the accuser had been picking randomly among the forty-six white lacrosse players whose photos she had viewed (with no fillers) on April 4: "What is a lineup? What if I have no idea who did the assault?"

- Nifong promoted the accuser—"my victim"—to de facto Durham County DA for this case and himself as her obedient servant, with no discretion to end the prosecution even if the DNA and other evidence conclusively disproved her claims: "If she came in and said she could not identify her assailants, then we don't have a case," he said, but "if she says, yes, it's them, or one or two of them, I have an obligation to put that to a jury."

As the journalist Emily Bazelon commented in *Slate*, this last statement showed "so basic a misunderstanding of his own job that it raises questions about whether he is even qualified to hold it."

The December 24 Barstow-Wilson article led—better nine days after the fact than never—by focusing on "the moment that may have changed the course of the Duke lacrosse rape case": Meehan's December 15 testimony about his agreement with Nifong to hide exculpatory DNA evidence. The article detailed Nifong's repeated false assurances in court that he had disclosed to the defense all relevant DNA tests. It quoted a Nifong admission during the three-hour interview that he would later contradict: "Mr. Nifong conceded he erred in not providing all of Mr. Meehan's test results to defense lawyers months earlier than he did. 'Obviously, anything that is not DNA from the people who are charged is potentially exculpatory information,' he said."

At the same time, Nifong offered his third excuse for this "error": He was overworked. "You know," he explained, "it's not the only case I have right now. I have two. The other one's a quadruple homicide." He did not mention that the homicide case had not arrived in his office until mid-October, more than five months after the misleading May 12 DNA Security report. He also made a self-discrediting claim that "the whole point" of the defense attack on his effort to hide DNA evidence of innocence was "vilification of the district attorney" and intimidation of the "victim."

The unfailingly politically correct *Times* editorial page remained silent, however, while the nation's four other largest newspapers—*USA Today*, *The Wall Street Journal*, the *Los Angeles Times*, and the *Washington Post*—carried editorials or op-eds within six days of Nifong's dismissal of the rape charge demanding that other charges be dropped, too.

"What is clear is that Nifong, whose election campaign for a full term overlapped with the investigation, lost control of his tongue and participated in the transformation of this incident from a case into a cause—usually an ominous development for the administration of justice," asserted a December 26 *Los Angeles Times* editorial. It also urged an "examination of conscience" by "those who seized on this case as an emblem of a 'larger truth'—a racial double standard in rape prosecutions, the historical exploitation of black women by white men, the arrogance of adolescent privilege."

The first North Carolina publication to urge the DA's resignation was the *Wilmington Star*, the paper of record in Nifong's birthplace, in a December 27 editorial: "Mike Nifong has demonstrated that he is not ethically or professionally fit to prosecute a littering case, much less the sexual assault case involving three Duke lacrosse players." *The News & Observer* and *The Charlotte Observer* didn't go that far, but published editorials demanding that Nifong recuse himself from the case. Among major North Carolina papers, only *The Herald-Sun* remained in Nifong's corner, editorializing that "we want our law enforcement officials to be attentive to accusations of crime victims, no matter who the victim is or who is being accused. Yes, she may have changed her story in the days after the incident, but that is not uncommon with traumatized rape victims and is not in itself evidence of dishonesty."

With Nifong stubbornly hanging on to the case and blatantly manipulating the charges as his credibility and public support evaporated, the North Carolina State Bar—which had been investigating the district attorney for months—had seen enough. On December 28, it brought disciplinary charges that were supported by overwhelming evidence and aimed at forcing Nifong off the case. The bar dropped this bomb just after 5:00 P.M. by releasing a seventeen-page ethics complaint charging that he had "engaged in conduct involving dishonesty, fraud, deceit, or misrepresentation." And this was clearly just the first installment, with more charges to follow.

This initial complaint focused solely on Nifong's violations of the pretrial publicity rules, in particular Rule 3.8(f) of the Code of Professional Responsibility, which requires prosecutors to "refrain from making extrajudicial comments that have a substantial likelihood of heightening public condemnation of the accused." But unlike most complaints about prejudicial statements, this one alleged that Nifong *knew some of his comments were false when he uttered them.* The most damning allegation—"dishonesty, fraud, deceit, or misrepresentation"—focused on the DA's speculations that the alleged attackers might have used condoms despite the proof in his own files that Crystal Mangum had said repeatedly denied any use of condoms. The complaint also alleged that Nifong's many prejudicial attacks on the lacrosse players were of such magnitude that they amounted to "conduct that is prejudicial to the administration of justice."

One noteworthy aspect of the bar's complaint was that all of the Nifong attacks on the lacrosse players that the bar saw as self-evidently unethical under Rule 3.8(f) had been public statements, mostly made in the week of March 27. And it is common knowledge that such prejudicial pretrial statements are forbidden. So the egregious nature of Nifong's conduct should have been apparent from the start—to Duke president Richard Brodhead and all of the journalists, professors, and others who gave Nifong a free ride for so long.

The bar could have filed the complaint under seal and thereby deferred until after the lacrosse case both public disclosure and adjudication by the bar's Disciplinary Hearing Commission. By choosing instead to make the complaint public, the bar presented Nifong with an unavoidable conflict of interest. He was now known by all to be a defendant on ethics charges growing out of his conduct in the very case that he was trying to take to trial.

Meanwhile, on the same day, Nifong privately submitted his response to the even more serious charge that the bar was still secretly considering: hiding exculpatory DNA evidence. In a rambling, eight-page letter, improperly submitted on his official letterhead, the district attorney added four new rationalizations for his agreement with Meehan to the three excuses he had previously offered.

First, he claimed that the DNA evidence was irrelevant, contradicting his recent statement to the *Times*: "For me, this case was an eyewitness identification case, one in which I was looking for DNA evidence that either corroborated that evidence or refuted it." Of course, the undisclosed DNA evidence *did* refute Mangum's allegations and identifications. Indeed, just two weeks previously, Nifong had told Judge Smith that "the nature of the subject matter contained in this [DNA] motion is obviously very important," so much so that it needed to be addressed "right away."

Second, Nifong said that he had been distracted by his election campaign from complying with his obligations as a prosecutor: "Because I had never previously been involved in a political campaign, and because I was facing an unusually contentious challenge from an unprecedented number [two] of challengers, I was not always able to give the case my full attention." Third, it might have been his staff's fault: "Due to the volume of material to be copied for each defendant . . . several individuals, including both attorneys and support staff, were involved in the numbering and copying of pages, which was not supervised by me. These people were . . . [not] familiar enough with the facts of the case to have known whether anything was missing." Fourth, the bar should back off because Judge Smith hadn't sanctioned him immediately after the concealment of the DNA evidence had been exposed on December 15.

Nifong also tried his luck at insulting the people investigating him by complaining that for public relations reasons the State Bar was holding him to a different standard than others: "For some time now, the 'word on the street' in prosecutorial circles has been that the North Carolina State Bar, stung by the criticism resulting from past decisions involving former prosecutors with names like Hoke and Graves and Honeycutt and Brewer, is looking for a prosecutor of which to make an example."

Descending into blog paranoia, Nifong concluded by asserting:

"A well-connected and well-financed (but not, I would suggest, well-intentioned) group of individuals—most of whom are neither in nor from North Carolina—have taken it upon themselves to ensure that this case never reaches trial. (And if this seems like paranoid delusion to you, perhaps you should check out Web sites such as former Duke Law School graduate and current Maryland attorney Jason Trumpbour's www.friendsofdukeuniversity.blogspot.com, which has not only called for me to be investigated, removed from this case, and disbarred, but has also provided instructions on how to request such actions and to whom those requests should be sent.)"

Trumpbour responded by noting that the six-person Friends of Duke University board was entirely self-funded and that its members had all joined through its Web site.

It would have been hard for Nifong to come up with a less effective response had he been trying to get himself disbarred. His inability to keep his story straight on the DNA evidence made him look guilty. His potshots at the bar's motivations made him look unprofessional. And his lashing out at Friends of Duke and the gentlemanly Jason Trumpbour made him look delusional.

Still more dramatic proof of Nifong's isolation and disgrace came the very next morning: a vote of no confidence by his fellow district attorneys across the state. The North Carolina Conference of District Attorneys issued an unprecedented public letter demanding that Nifong recuse himself from the lacrosse case.

Repudiated by his peers, accused of unethical conduct by the bar, and scorned by virtually every editorial board except *The New York Times* and *The Herald-Sun*, the man who had ridiculed defense attorneys as "poultry" and a "bunch of chickens" seemed to be looking for some place to hide as 2007 began.

January 2 was the official date for Nifong to be sworn in for a full four-year term as district attorney, a traditionally pubic ceremony that in this case would attract a bunch of reporters and Nifong critics. But Nifong tried to keep them out by setting the ceremony for 8:00 A.M., half an hour before the Durham County Courthouse doors would open for business. As Nifong swore on the Bible to uphold the law, in the company of his wife, Cy Gurney, and their sixteen-year-old son, TV cameras showed dozens of people locked out of the courthouse in what Ruth Sheehan had jokingly termed the "People's Republic of Durham."

When reporters finally found a way into the building, Nifong gave an impromptu press conference, flanked by Gurney and their son, who seemed to shrink from the cameras. "I don't feel I'm part of the problem," Nifong asserted. "I feel that I have assisted in revealing the problem." He admitted that "Durham has some healing to do," adding that "I need to be part of that healing process." N&O columnist Jim Wise wrote that Nifong was like "the guy who set the barn on fire saying he'll go fetch the water hose," and wondered whether the DA thought he was "going to lead the quarter-million of us in a round of 'Kumbaya.'"

When asked why he had sought to exclude the public, Nifong initially suggested a scheduling snafu and said no one had informed him that people were waiting outside. But a sheriff's deputy then told a local TV station that Nifong had ordered him to exclude the public. Nifong then switched to claiming that he had done this so that he and his staff "could get back to work and do our jobs," and because "we're not here to basically help you guys sell newspapers or press coverage." Senior Resident Superior Court Judge Orlando Hudson was not impressed. Nifong, he told *The News & Observer*, had defied common sense.

The Brodhead administration took its second major step toward reversing its previous Nifong-enabling stance on the case the next day, January 3. Larry Moneta and Brodhead invited Collin Finnerty and Reade Seligmann to return for the spring term. The symbolism was obvious: Brodhead was strongly implying that he now found Nifong's allegations unworthy of belief and believed the defendants to be innocent.

Reade Seligmann's family replied with a carefully worded statement welcoming "the outpouring of support that we have received from Duke alumni" but making no comment on whether Reade would return to Duke. With charges still hanging over them and the danger of vigilante action—from the Durham police, Nifong's office, or self-appointed avengers—and perhaps classroom harassment or punitive grading by Duke professors, both Seligmann and Finnerty opted to stay home.

Meanwhile, the fear that had frozen into nearly unanimous silence those Duke professors who cared about truth and justice—a fear of being savaged by hate-filled colleagues—had begun to thaw. The clearest sign was a repudiation of the Group of 88 in a letter signed by seventeen economics professors and published on January 3 by both *The Chronicle* and *The News & Observer*. (*The Herald-Sun* predictably ignored the letter.)

Recognizing that the Group of 88's ad "was cited as prejudicial to the defendants in the defense motion to change the venue of the trial involving the three Duke lacrosse team members," the economics professors expressed their "regret that the Duke faculty is now seen as prejudiced against certain of its own students." They endorsed Brodhead's call for an investigation into Nifong's acts—which were "inimical to students at our university"—and welcomed "all members of the lacrosse team, and all student athletes, as we do all our students as fellow members of the Duke community, to the classes we teach and the activities we sponsor."

But the Group of 88 was not about to back off or tolerate dissent. On January 5, Karla Holloway ostentatiously resigned as race subgroup chair of the Campus Culture Initiative to protest Brodhead's decision to invite Seligmann and Finnerty back to Duke. "Especially just before a critical judicial decision on the case," Holloway asserted, this "is a clear use of corporate power, and a breach, I think, of ethical citizenship." This was a professor who had not recognized any need to defer to judicial decisions the previous summer, when she had written that "the seriousness of the matter cannot be finally or fully adjudicated in the courts" because "justice inevitably has an attendant social construction."

Holloway dramatized her resignation by circulating a baseless and scurrilous charge against the lacrosse players in a mass e-mail to dozens of colleagues. The previous March, she wrote, while in John Burness's office, she had overheard Burness taking a call from a Duke police official, to whom a Durham police official had passed along a tale of a never-identified witness supposedly reporting that lacrosse players used ugly racial epithets at the start of the stripper party, before the performance.

The allegation was false: No such witness statement existed, and none of the witnesses at the party—not Kim Roberts, not any lacrosse player, not even Crystal Mangum—had ever suggested any such thing. Yet the *Wilmington Journal*, a member of Black Press USA, printed this fifth-hand gossip. Holloway was never disciplined or criticized by the Duke administration for her unfounded attack on Duke students.

Another Group of 88 member, English professor Cathy Davidson, took to the pages of *The News & Observer*, also on January 5, to deliver an impassioned apologia for the group's April 6 ad. "The ad said that we faculty were listening to the anguish of students who felt demeaned by racist and sexist remarks swirling around in the media and on the campus quad in the aftermath of what happened on March 13 in the lacrosse house," Davidson claimed. "The insults, at that time, were rampant. It was as if defending David Evans, Collin Finnerty and Reade Seligmann necessitated reverting to pernicious stereotypes about African-Americans, especially poor black women."

What was Davidson talking about? Between March 29, when the idea for the ad originated, and April 6, when it appeared, hardly anybody "on the campus quad" was defending the players at all, much less using "pernicious stereotypes about African-Americans, especially poor black women." Rather, the campus had been dominated by activist students distributing the "wanted" poster and pressing Brodhead for more forceful action against the team. And Seligmann and Finnerty had not yet even been identified as targets of the investigation.

Davidson further contended that, before the ad appeared, "many black students at Duke disappeared into humiliation and rage as the lacrosse players were being elevated to the status of martyrs, innocent victims of reverse racism." This Orwellian exercise in lying or lunacy—it was hard to be sure which predominated—turned history on its head. In fact the lacrosse players had been viciously savaged during that period and for weeks thereafter by the likes of Cathy Davidson on campus and by the media across the country. The protesters to whom the Group of 88 ad had said thank you held signs reading: CASTRATE; SUNDAY MORNING; TIME TO CONFESS; and REAL MEN DON'T DEFEND RAPISTS.

Davidson made clear her disdain for lacrosse players she had never met, whose "sleazy" behavior brought her "shame," reflected America's "appalling power dynamics" and made Duke a worldwide symbol of "the most lurid and sexualized form of race privilege." She claimed to empathize with parents and friends of the defendants but exuded much deeper empathy for the "single mother who takes off her clothes for hire partly to pay for tuition at a distinguished historically black college." Indeed, it was almost as an afterthought that Davidson conceded near the end that Nifong "may well have acted unprofessionally, irresponsibly, and unethically, possibly from the most cynical political motives"—and might have "no evidence." This oblique reference to the mountain of evidence that the accuser's tale was a vicious lie aimed at ruining the lives of three innocent young men did not prevent Davidson from canonizing her.

The real victims of the affair, Davidson explained, were Cathy Davidson and the rest of the 88. Echoing Nifong's most notorious attack on the lacrosse players, she complained of criticisms of the 88 ad by unnamed "right-wing 'blog hooligans.'" This line delighted the Liestoppers crew, who began to bill themselves as "blog hooligans."

Privately, Davidson denounced the "borderline psychotic/dangerous" nature of the "aggressive blog," which was the province of "professional liberal-haters." (She cited no examples of her claim.) Meanwhile, she bizarrely contended that the Group of 88's ad had changed the campus attitude, forcing unnamed Duke administrators, professors, and undergraduates to stop treating black students "like criminals and rapists."

A few days later, engineering professor Michael Gustafson delivered a devastating reply in a letter to *The News & Observer*. Challenging Davidson's claim that she and others of the 88 had been "adamant about the necessity for fair and impartial legal proceedings" for the defendants, Gustafson reviewed their record:

"When Durham police entered a dorm to 'interview' lacrosse players without their legal representation present? Silence. When our students were threatened with taunts of 'You'll get yours, rapist' and 'Dead man walking!' Silence. When the committee tasked to examine the lacrosse team's behavior concluded that 'The committee has not heard evidence that the cohesiveness of this group is either racist or sexist' and 'The current as well as former African American members of the team have been extremely positive about the support the team provided them'? Silence. When Professor James Coleman stated 'the line-up ordered by the D.A. for the Duke lacrosse case violated local, state and federal guidelines'? Silence. When Moezeldin Elmostafa was arrested in connection with a crime he helped police to solve, shortly after coming forward with evidence of innocence for one of the students? Silence. When Mike Nifong refused to hear evidence from David, Collin, or Reade? Silence. When DNA evidence demonstrated just how fictional the district attorney's story was? Silence. Adamant silence."

Group of 88 antics could no longer do Nifong any good. He showed some appreciation of the gravity of his situation on January 10, when he belatedly hired Winston-Salem attorney David Freedman, a specialist in representing lawyers accused of ethics violations, to defend him in the bar's disciplinary proceeding. There was, however, one awkward little problem with this representation: Nine months before, the same Freedman had told *The Abrams Report* viewers that Nifong had made "potentially unethical statements, saying he believed a crime occurred"; that "he should not be commenting on the evidence"; and that "it's the D.A.'s job to make sure justice is done, to make the truth is found out . . . rather than rushing and doing indictments two weeks before the primary is held." After becoming Nifong's lawyer, Freedman parried questions about how he could represent a man whom he had called unethical by saying he had revised his opinion.

The same day, an increasingly desperate Nifong sent Linwood Wilson to meet with the ever-obliging Tara Levicy, hoping that the SANE nurse-in-training could salvage his case. She did her best.

In her report from the night of the alleged attack, Levicy had written without qualification that Mangum had said repeatedly said the rapists had used no condoms and that she was sure that at least one had ejaculated—*in her mouth*. But on January 10, according to Wilson, Levicy stated that Mangum "said 'no' but wasn't really sure" whether her attackers had used condoms and added that "victims can never be sure if condoms are used because if they can't see them how would they know for sure. You can't feel them so you have to realize there is always a possibility that a condom could have been used." Levicy then added a feminist cliché of no medical significance to explain the lack of DNA evidence: "I wasn't surprised when I heard no DNA was found because rape is not about passion or ejaculation but about power."

Levicy also changed her portrayal of Mangum's March 14, 2006, story regarding the attackers' names. Mangum, she now said, knew that her three attackers were using fake names at the beginning of the attack and changed their names during the attack. The SANE nurse had mentioned this item neither in her March 14 report nor in any other 2006 meeting with law enforcement officers or defense attorneys. In a late January interview with Levicy, defense attorney Doug Kingsbery pointed out this fact, adding that the police had based their March 16, 2006, lineup on the belief that the suspects were named Matt, Brett, and Adam. Levicy's sole response to this information? "Oh."

Levicy's assistance was too little, too late for Nifong. Late in the afternoon of Friday, January 12, seemingly acting on Freedman's advice, Nifong bowed out of the case by asking that Attorney General Roy Cooper's office take over. Hardly anyone lamented this except Nifong's wife, who complained to *The Herald-Sun* that she had only learned of it from the media, and Victoria Peterson, who convened a "rally for justice" on the courthouse steps—two people, in all—and declared that "we have a district attorney who is well able, qualified, to do his job."

The next day, Roy Cooper said that two of his senior prosecutors—James Coman and Mary Winstead—would reinterview all witnesses to determine whether to proceed. Among the new prosecutors' first moves was to review the evidence with defense attorneys, which Nifong had repeatedly refused to do.

The spreading media consensus that the entire case looked like a fraud spurred more and more Duke students, parents, and alumni to bombard the Group of 88 with mostly polite requests that they retract or apologize for their April 6 ad. A few seemed amenable. In late 2006, Group member Susan Thorne wrote to one of her old students, Danny Flannery, that she was considering a public apology for signing the statement. She even sent along a draft of a possible essay. "I have come to understand," she wrote, "through conversations with members of the lacrosse family why they were so upset by the ad's publication." The history professor added, "While our ad did not accuse the lacrosse team of anything, it did thank 'protesters making collective noise.' I regret and apologize for failing to make distinctions amongst that week's many protests. Some of the sentiments on display that week can only be described as vile and violent. They were wrong. And I was wrong not to condemn them. I also regret and apologize for our omission of the vital qualifier 'alleged' from the ad's reference to the victim." But, unlike Thorne, most responded to the collapse of their cherished myths by joining Karla Holloway and Wahneema Lubiano in escalating their endless war against empirical reality.

This took the form of an unrepentant letter that purported to "clarify" the April 6 Group of 88 ad by denying that it had meant what it seemed to say. The letter was posted to a newly established Web site on January 16 and signed by most of the 88, including Holloway, Lubiano, William Chafe, and Mark ("thugniggaintellectual") Neal. Alex Rosenberg signed on again even though the new statement was as devoid as the original of any mention of alcohol abuse, which was what the philosophy professor had claimed to be protesting. Abandoning her thought of publicly apologizing for joining the Group of 88, Susan Thorne explained to Flannery with coldhearted candor that she felt obliged to sign because otherwise "my voice won't count for much in my world."

A few of the original 88 refused to sign the new letter or no longer worked at Duke; all but one were replaced by new recruits. One of these, literature professor Kenneth Surin, said he had no worries about appearing hostile to athletes by signing the document, since no athletes enrolled in his courses: "I do not give quizzes . . . I give very hard reading." When asked by an author why he had signed the statement, another new signatory, Kerry Haynie, declined to answer, responding instead, "Get a freaking life! Quote me!"

This eighty-seven-professor "clarifying" letter, as it came to be called, categorically rejected all "public calls to the authors to retract the ad or apologize for it." The professors did say that "pain" was "generated" in connection with the ad—their own pain, at the indignity of being criticized for their attacks on the lacrosse players. The letter contained no criticism of Mike Nifong or the accuser, who had misled the Group of 88 and others into embracing a fraudulent rape claim. The real culprits, the letter said, were bloggers, journalists, and alumni who had criticized the Group of 88 ad. The letter also implicitly attacked Duke's student body by decrying an "atmosphere that allows sexism, racism, and sexual violence to be so prevalent on campus."

What evidence did the Group of (now) 87 supply for this breathtaking smear of their own students? None at all. Indeed, two signatories, Lee Baker and Mark Anthony Neal, subsequently conceded that race relations on the Duke campus were better than in society as a whole. As for "sexual violence," while no university is without some of it, less than one-fortieth of one percent of Duke's six thousand students per year were victims of any type of "sexual misconduct," which as defined by the campus Judicial Board is a far broader category than sexual violence.

One purpose of the "clarifying" letter seemed to be to reinvent the past to shield the Group of 88 from possible lawsuits, by suggesting that their ad had not prejudged the players' guilt, had not praised anyone who did, and had not even had anything to do with the lacrosse case at all. The Dowd lawsuit against Kim Curtis had sensitized the activist professors to the possibility that they could be financially liable for unsubstantiated public denunciations of students. Indeed, Cathy Davidson wrote that an attorney with whom she had consulted out of concern that she "may well end up being the subject of a civil suit" had advised that the "ambiguity of the language [in the Group of 88 ad] could be made, in a court of law, to seem as if we are saying things against the lacrosse team."

Trying to hide behind what little ambiguity there was in the ad, the "clarifying" statement declared that the 88 had made no "comment on the alleged rape" at all.

What of the ad's repeated references to the accuser's allegations, including its prominent assertion that something had "happened to this young woman"?

The "clarifying" letter simply ignored them. In a subsequent interview, Karla Holloway denied that the line referred to a rape: "Something did happen on Buchanan. . . . A party happened. Drunkenness happened."

"Drunkenness happened." So *that* was why eighty-eight professors had taken out an ad focusing on the woman who had sent shock waves through Duke and the country with her highly publicized allegations about being brutally gang-raped by Duke students. With "clarifications" like this, who needs obfuscation?

And what of the ad's "thank you for not waiting" to the protesters, its commitment to "turn up the volume," and its vow that the affair "won't end with what the police say or the court decides"? The Group of 87 explained that such language had *not* been a reference to the mobs of potbangers and other protesters who had branded the players guilty, plastered "wanted" posters around the campus, and received extensive media coverage both locally and nationally. Rather, the "clarifying" letter said, the 88 had had in mind other, still-unidentified protesters of somethingorother.

Mike Nifong made a similar effort to rewrite history in his second, January 16 reply to the State Bar's inquiry into the hiding of exculpatory DNA evidence. Denying that he had asked Brian Meehan to withhold evidence, the DA said that he had followed his standard operating procedure "in cases involving forensic testing": asking only for a listing of matches with suspects or others whose DNA samples were collected, or for a statement that there were no matches. While Meehan had also told Nifong that the DNA of multiple unidentified males had been found in the accuser, the omission of that information from the report that went to the defense on May 12 "failed to register with me at all at the time."

Such stuff seemed only to infuriate the State Bar. On January 25, it amended its December 28 ethics complaint by charging that Nifong had also withheld exculpatory evidence, in violation of three North Carolina laws as well as the ethics code; had lied repeatedly to the court about that; and had then lied to the bar itself in his initial response (also on December 28) to its DNA inquiry. The complaint traced a "systematic abuse of prosecutorial discretion in the underlying criminal cases" and accused Nifong of having "engaged in conduct prejudicial to the administration of justice." It painted a picture of a man flagrantly violating multiple rules of professional conduct over a period of many months without remorse.

The complaint reproduced Nifong's statements assuring Judge Stephens on May 18 and June 22 and Judge Smith on September 22 that he had turned over to the defense all exculpatory evidence relating to Meehan's DNA testing. As Judge Smith had summarized the DA's representations and his own reliance on them: "Mr. Nifong indicated that he did not discuss the facts of the case with Dr. Meehan and that Dr. Meehan said nothing during those meetings beyond what was encompassed in the final report of DNA Security, dated May 12, 2006. The Court accepted Mr. Nifong's representation about those meetings and held that there were no additional discoverable statements by Dr. Meehan for the state to produce."

The charge of lying to the State Bar's own investigators focused on Nifong's claims that his withholding of exculpatory DNA evidence reflected privacy concerns. These "were knowingly false statements of material fact," the bar pointed out, because Meehan's report had listed the names the names of all forty-six lacrosse players whose DNA had been tested and also the DNA profiles of two then-unindicted players (Dave Evans and Kevin Coleman).

Lying to state bar investigators is a very bad career move for a lawyer unless he succeeds in fooling them. And Nifong had not the slightest chance of fooling them, because his "privacy" dodge was not merely false but also *obviously* false. It was belied by public-record information well known to Nifong's adversaries. This dodge thus showed Nifong to be detached from reality as well as dishonest.

"If these allegations are true and if they don't justify disbarment, then I'm not sure what does," UNC law professor Joseph Kennedy told *The News & Observer*. "It's hard for me to imagine a more serious set of allegations against a prosecutor."

As February 2007 approached it looked like there would be a highly publicized trial in the lacrosse case after all. But it would not be the trial that people had been expecting. It would be District Attorney Mike Nifong in the dock before the Bar Disciplinary Hearing Commission. And the defense lawyers and their clients would all be potential witnesses against him, as would Nifong's DNA expert and, perhaps, any cops, assistants, or others on whom Nifong might seek to deflect responsibility.

22. DISGRACE AND EXONERATION

W ITH NIFONG NOW FACING POSSIBLE DISBARMENT, the coalition that had enabled him showed signs of fraying. Some local African-American leaders grew even more extreme; others turned on the district attorney.

The local and state NAACP doggedly continued to persecute the lacrosse players, no matter how clear the evidence of innocence. On January 26, 2007, Rev. Curtis Gatewood, president of the Durham NAACP from 1994 until 2002, denounced the State Bar for joining "the lynching mobs in Durham who have verbally lynched and sought to politically assassinate DA Mike Nifong." The State Bar's ethics charges, he claimed, formed part of a "conspiracy to disrupt justice in this Durham case." This conspiracy also included the media, since "it is unprecedented that the alleged criminals and/or their defense team will be given the luxury of such a high-media platform to repetitiously proclaim their 'innocence' and attack their prosecutor." All but abandoning any pretense that this racial-political crusade had much to do with whether anybody had done anything to the accuser, Gatewood blasted "the racist media and NC Bar Association who wrongfully used their influence to attack the integrity of a prosecutor at the rare time he prosecutes a case which profoundly has the potential to challenge racism, classism, and sexism simultaneously."

The *Wilmington Journal*, part of North Carolina's Black Press network, threatened state Attorney General Roy Cooper with political retaliation if he failed to hammer the lacrosse players. Again, the question of whether they had committed a sexual assault of any kind seemed quite secondary. In a January 18 open letter from "North Carolina's African-American community, and anyone else who believes true justice comes from the gavel of a judge, not the demands of a mob; or slick, race-baiting defense attorneys," the paper demanded a comprehensive review of "the team's drunken, perverted party last March." The editorial urged Cooper to consider charges of obstructing justice against every person who attended the party because they had refused to speak with Sgt. Mark Gottlieb before consulting with an attorney.

The editorial also demanded that the attorney general ignore public opinion, concluding with an implicit threat to seek political retribution against him: "After all, as a Democrat, just like Mike Nifong, you need the Black vote for any future political aspirations."

The current head of the state NAACP, Rev. William Barber, sounded the same tired, false theme more obliquely in preaching on January 29 at the Duke Chapel Sunday service. Barber spoke at the invitation of his good friend, Duke chaplain Sam Wells. The chaplain had smeared the lacrosse players in a sermon almost ten months before, associating their stripper party with "a disturbingly extensive experience of sexual violence, of abiding racism, of crimes rarely reported and perpetrators seldom named, confronted, or convicted, of lives deeply scarred, of hurt and pain long suppressed."

Amid copious references to Martin Luther King Jr., Barber urged listeners to "set aside the criminal charges for a moment, set aside what the courts will do about various things," and dwell on "having parties with strippers and drunkenness, and reports of racial slandering." Without mentioning Kim Roberts's admission that she had started the brief exchange of racial taunts, Barber apocalyptically summed up: "If we deny God's call to face reality, to change reality, then we sin, and the blood is on our hands." Several listeners walked out of the chapel in disgust.

Some other local African-American leaders showed more sense and decency. On January 27, Nifong's former citizens' committee cochair, Kim Brummell, told *The Herald-Sun* that "Nifong owes the alleged victim, his supporters and all who voted for him a public apology for his missteps in this case." She couldn't understand why "a district attorney with nearly 30 years of experience [would] withhold DNA evidence," and she recognized that the case was going nowhere. "How much can you really do," Brummell asked, "with a case riddled with bullet holes? Usually it's dead."

Brummell's change of heart appeared to reflect a broader shift among Durham blacks. Indeed, *Newsday* ran a story headlined, "Duke DA backlash: Year after rape charges, little support for Nifong or accuser among those in her Durham neighborhood." Finally, the article reported, many in the black neighborhoods that had provided Nifong his margin of victory in the election had come to the view expressed by seventy-six-year-old William Ragland: "It was a cover-up. He had evidence that those boys did not rape her."

The swiftness of Nifong's fall was stunning. In early February, the *Greensboro News-Record* noted that local prosecutors were saying, "I don't want to be a Nifong." This phenomenon, reporter Jonathan Jones asked, "raises the question: Is Nifong's legacy going to be his name as euphemism?" Quite possibly yes, according to Peter Sokolowski, a *Merriam-Webster's* associate editor, who noted that "Nifonged"—meaning "railroaded"—"is starting to get used. And that's how it happens that a word ends up in the dictionary."

Two federal judges also cited the district attorney as an example of a runaway prosecutor. In a February 2 dissent arguing that a defendant's conviction was the product of "a prosecution run amok," Judge Jerry E. Smith of the U.S. Court of Appeals for the Fifth Circuit added that "Mike Nifong, another prosecutor apparently familiar with the 'win at any cost' mantra, almost surely would approve." On the same day, a Sixth Circuit majority opinion cited one of the ethics charges against Nifong as an example of how "the desire to pander to public opinion has apparently become a 'higher authority' for some prosecutors than their duty to follow their code of professional responsibility."

With Nifong a pariah in legal circles, Governor Mike Easley belatedly distanced himself from the embattled prosecutor. In an address at NYU Law School in late January and then in discussions with North Carolina reporters, the governor revealed for the first time that he had appointed Nifong interim DA in 2005 only after extracting a promise that Nifong would not run for election in 2006. Easley said that Nifong was "probably [his] poorest appointment." He did not say, however, why he had waited more than a year after Nifong had broken his word to share this information with the voters.

Political figures who continued to attack the innocent lacrosse players now paid a price. One was leftist blogger Amanda Marcotte, who was hired in January by former North Carolina senator and Democratic presidential aspirant John Edwards to be his campaign's chief blogger.

This move was popular on the left. But Marcotte was in trouble within hours of her selection. James Taranto's OpinionJournal blog and then several other blogs quickly zeroed in on Marcotte's ugly rhetoric branding the lacrosse players guilty. "The rapists were making jokes about slavery and picking cotton to the victim, which is to say reminding her of their racial privilege by referencing the history that created it," she had written on April 9, 2006—before the indictments of three players who had never made a racist remark. A month later, she wrote that "there's just something about this Duke rape case that's inspiring to rape apologists." As Nifong's case imploded, Marcotte lashed out with increasing malice. She complained on January 21 about a CNN broadcast reporting Nifong's recusal, writing, "I had to listen to how the poor dear lacrosse players at Duke are being persecuted just because they held someone down and fucked her against her will—not rape, of course, because the charges have been thrown out. Can't a few white boys sexually assault a black woman anymore without people getting all wound up about it? So unfair."

Then, when Taranto and others criticized the post, Marcotte deleted it, explaining that it had received attention from "some anti-feminist" bloggers.

The controversy led to the unearthing of equally vile Marcotte rhetoric about other groups and causes she hated. The Roman Catholic Church, for example: "What if Mary had taken Plan B after the Lord filled her with his hot, white, sticky Holy Spirit? You'd have to justify your misogyny with another ancient mythology."

The publicity about such stuff put candidate Edwards on the spot. Firing Marcotte would enrage her fellow leftist bloggers. Keeping her would cost him Catholic votes. Edwards chose an awkward straddle, declining to dump Marcotte openly while criticizing her previous posts. It was as if nobody in his campaign had actually looked at her writings before hiring her. (She resigned a few days later.) But Edwards himself had to know how outrageous Nifong's conduct had been and how bogus the case was. The candidate has made his tens of millions as a civil plaintiffs' attorney in the law firm of the venerated Wade Smith, Collin Finnerty's lead defense attorney. Yet Edwards had said nothing about the lacrosse case, apparently to avoid offending the African Americans and leftist whites whose support he needed in Democratic primaries. His stance came in dramatic contrast to that of a main challenger for the nomination, Illinois senator Barack Obama, who in early March 2007 endorsed a Justice Department inquiry into Nifong's misconduct.

While mainstream politicians and honest journalists could no longer get away with pretending that the lacrosse players were villains, Duke's Group of 88 and their allies were immune to reality therapy. They "will continue to enjoy their aristocratic installment in Durham," predicted John Podhoretz in the *New York Post*. With heavy irony, he explained: "They're fighting the white patriarchy. They're on the side of the dispossessed and oppressed. They're giving voice to the voiceless. They're giving hope to the hopeless. They're fools at best and monsters at worst—and neither fools nor monsters are much troubled by attacks of conscience."

Indeed, after Nifong was forced out of the case, more than nine hundred Duke students were signing a petition (authored by Stephen Miller) demanding that the Group of 88 apologize. The Group's behavior became even more extreme—and their power on campus continued to grow. Jason Trumpbour, of Friends of Duke University, explained the former development. "They are used to controlling the scope and terms of debate on campus," he wrote in early February, "and are truly out of their element dealing with people from the real world."

FODU tried to get some of the 88 on record. Noting the clarifying-letter signers' purported interest in dialogue, FODU published a February 10 open letter in *The Chronicle* with ten questions for Group of 88 members. One was whether they believed "that Mike Nifong acted properly when he went to the grand jury on April 17 to seek indictments against Reade Seligmann and Collin Finnerty." The open letter also wondered about the wording of the original April 6, 2006, Group of 88 ad:

> [The ad] explicitly thanked "students speaking individually" and "protestors making collective noise" for not waiting. The fundamental question is what was not worthy of being awaited. Time for reason to assist emotion? Time for evidence to be gathered and assessed? Time for a defense to be made? If you were so attuned to due process, why did you fail to mention it in your April 6 ad?

The response? Silence. *Chronicle* reporter Lysa Chen contacted each of the "clarifying" faculty for their responses to the FODU advertisement. Every single one declined to answer any of FODU's questions.

Unhinged by the looming prospect of a dismissal of all charges, the activist professors lashed out at critics, real and imagined. In a March 2007 interview with *The Chronicle*, professors Diane Nelson and Pedro Lasch suggested that the outpouring of anger from Duke alumni and students was engineered by some kind of "conspiracy" against them. Their evidence? Group members had received anonymous, occasionally vile e-mails.

Meanwhile, on February 17, five Group of 88 members—Nelson, Lasch, Wahneema Lubiano, Maurice Wallace, and Mark Anthony Neal—joined "clarifying" signatory Charles Piot in a two-hour event entitled "Shut Up and Teach," ostensibly designed to counteract "the current of criticism and attempts at intimidation directed against faculty who comment on larger social and political issues . . . following the events of last spring." The flyer for the event invoked the specter of McCarthyism to symbolize the speakers' plight.

Economics professor E. Roy Weintraub could take such ravings no longer. He had experienced the original brand of McCarthyism firsthand: His father, a Keynesian economist, had been attacked in newspaper editorials for teaching "communism" in his classes at St. John's University. Weintraub penned a letter to *The Chronicle* noting that he had "read with astonishment the recent panelists' invocation of McCarthyism as their characterization of the criticism they have received for their public statements or writings." It was, he noted, time for the Group of 88 "to understand that for various Duke faculty, staff, administrators, students, parents and alumni to disagree with them in public or in private is neither McCarthyism nor an academic travesty and betrayal of the values of our institution, but is rather an expression of their believing otherwise."

Weintraub's words fell on deaf ears. At the February 17 forum, ironically billed as a teach-in, the six professors banned media audio and video recorders and refused to take questions from the media. It was a shame there was no video recording; it would have been wonderfully educational for parents thinking of sending their children to Duke or, for that matter, most other elite schools.

Lead speaker Lubiano, looking forward to the day when "we'll all get along together after the revolution's over," promised to run to the barricades—to save her job, at least—if the university adopted policies she opposed. Lasch handed out a set of questions entitled, "game scenario: knowledge/power/violence vs. knowledge/power/social justice." Nelson passed around a string, which a student then cut to symbolize disconnectedness. As one commenter on the Liestoppers blog noted, all this seemed more appropriate for elementary school playtime than a serious academic presentation.

To rationalize the presenters' positions on the lacrosse case, Lasch repeated the feminist fiction that on campus, "women live in an environment of constant sexual violence." Director of Women's Studies Robyn Weigman averred: "It's not a crime to assume an alleged victim of sexual violence is telling the truth." (Nobody had ever said it was a *crime* to presume guilt.) But Piot, denying that he and his fellow 88'ers were anti-athlete, claimed that "hundreds of athletes [had] enrolled" in African and African-American Studies courses. This despite the program's pathetic total of thirty-three majors. Piot devoted most of his presentation to wild-eyed attacks on Internet critics. He compared them fantastically to unnamed West African dictators. He slammed bloggers for publicizing the syllabi of Duke professors, some of whom had found it expedient to shield their course content from public view. Piot's AAAS colleague, Lee Baker, likened people scanning his syllabi to white supremacist groups sending him hate mail.

These professors twinned their invocations of academic freedom with refusals to engage critics in intellectual debate. Lasch said that it was not "worth responding to the bloggers' e-mails because they wanted [the discussion] to stop. They wanted all those questions, all those debates, all those discussions to stop right there. 'It was all a fabrication, you are making it all up,' they say. It's not true! And to say that is just utter self-deception."

Such babble confirmed Duke graduate student Richard Bertrand Spencer's observation in a February 2007 essay: "It is through [their] inarticulateness that the Group seeks to stake out a position that cannot be criticized or even rationally assessed."

By the end of the night, it became clear that, shorn of inflammatory rhetoric, the professors' position was: (1) Faculty critics of the Group of 88 should "shut up and teach," as Charles Piot declared; and (2) It was McCarthyism to criticize the 88 either for signing a statement so inflammatory as to be cited in a defense motion for change of venue or for their inconsistent and demonstrably untenable efforts to explain away what they had signed.

Yet even as their conduct grew more farcical, the activist professors' power on campus increased. They tightened their control of campus governance when the Academic Council voted on February 22 for a new chair to succeed Paul Haagen, whose two-year term was coming to an end. The most distinguished candidate academically was Craig Henriquez, a professor of biomedical engineering who had received his B.A. (summa cum laude) and Ph.D. degrees from Duke. He had taken no outspoken positions one way or the other on the lacrosse case. But Academic Council members instead elected, by a one-vote margin, political science professor Paula McClain, a Howard B.A. and Ph.D. who had come to Duke only in 2000, as part of a wave of "diversity" hires championed by the then dean, William Chafe. Typifying the Group of 88's metronomic pedagogical interests, McClain offered three undergraduate classes: "Race and American Politics"; "Introduction to Racial and Ethnic Minorities in American Politics"; and "Race in Comparative Perspective."

A signatory to both the Group of 88 and the "clarifying" statements, McClain had given a blunt answer—"no"—when asked in a July 2006 e-mail if she was willing to publicly urge due process for the Duke students targeted by Nifong. When queried about Haagen's proposal to pair individual professors with athletic teams to give the faculty a better sense of athletic life for Duke students, she told *The N&O* that "people are just aghast that it's being considered." And, in a summer 2006 interview with *The Chronicle*, McClain incorrectly asserted that black faculty members never got to meet with a top administrator to discuss the lacrosse case. In fact, a university-prepared timeline of the administration's actions indicated that President Brodhead himself met with black faculty on April 3 to discuss the case.

McClain's extraordinary sensitivity to imagined racial slights from the desperately politically correct Brodhead administration contrasted with her indifference to—if not approval of—the many very real racially inflammatory statements by her Group of 88 colleagues. She had indicated no disagreement when Houston Baker had stressed the players' whiteness, in a derogatory fashion, no fewer than ten times in his March 29, 2006, public letter. She had registered no dissent when Grant Farred had preposterously alleged that a "secret racism" was rampant among white Duke students. She had no objection when Karla Holloway had circulated unsubstantiated, fifth-hand, scurrilous allegations against the lacrosse players.

In one of her first acts as newly elected chairwoman, McClain celebrated the findings of the Campus Culture Initiative while dismissing the concerns of many Duke alumni: "If Duke wants to remain competitive and remain a top-notch institution, it's got to change with the times. Change is very difficult, especially for people who came through Duke years ago."

The CCI's twenty-five-page report, released on February 27, fully reflected the leading roles of lacrosse-player-bashing Peter Wood; Group of 88 members Karla Holloway and Anne Allison; and student members including Chauncey Nartey, who had sent the e-mail that Mike and Sue Pressler saw as a threat to their daughter. Three weeks before the report appeared, Brodhead had invited Nartey to be one of two Duke students to accompany him to "A Duke Conversation" event in Charlotte. The write-up for the event celebrated, among other items, Nartey's work as president of his fraternity—which by that point had been suspended by the national organization for a hazing incident.

When asked why the statements of Peter Wood and Karla Holloway appearing to slander some Duke students hadn't disqualified them for leadership positions in an initiative designed to produce a more tolerant campus, CCI chairman Robert Thompson replied that these comments had been taken "out of context." He added that he had heard "innumerable positive comments made about Duke students by both Professor Wood and Professor Holloway." That the duo had good things to say about students of whose pedigrees and ideology they approved, of course, hardly qualified them for such prominent roles. Thompson claimed that he had never heard of the Nartey e-mail—though, of course, CCI vice chairman Moneta had been informed of the e-mail in April 2006, and the lacrosse team told Brodhead about it the following month.

The CCI report, the work mostly of tenured professors over ten months, was hardly what could be called careful scholarship, or even serious inquiry. It cited a grand total of two publications: William Bowen's screed against Division I athletics and Janet Reitman's widely disparaged *Rolling Stone* article—which, perhaps because it placed the Duke student body in the worst possible light, was also assigned reading in a spring semester class. The four campus groups with which CCI members said they had "connected" were far from representative of most of the student body: They were the Women's Center; the Center for Lesbian, Gay, Bisexual, and Transgender Life; the Council on Civic Engagement (devoted to supporting "community-based experiential pedagogy"); and the Mary Lou Williams Center for Black Culture.

In an Orwellian view of the lacrosse case, the CCI report implied that those who had *opposed* the potbangers or the Group of 88 had exercised "pressures for conformity," engaged in "uncivil speech and intolerance," and failed "to engage difference constructively." To remedy these upside-down "problems," the CCI recommended that all Duke students be forced to take a class that engaged "the reality of difference in American society and culture."

The overwhelming majority of these offerings were taught by the Group of 88 and its ideological allies.

Other sections of the CCI report exhibited the double standards embedded within higher education's "diversity" crusade. The report urged raising the "low end of admissions standards" to weed out "students who are not adequately prepared to benefit from, or contribute to, the work of the academic community [and whose admission] places Duke's admirable graduation rates at risk, reinforces negative stereotypes, and does not serve the best interests of these students themselves, their peers, or their faculty." There was a catch, however: The proposed raising of academic standards was only for student-athletes and relatives of Duke alumni. The CCI called for *lowering* the already dramatically less demanding academic standards for (some) minority races, who already comprised 41 percent of the Duke class of 2010.

The report also urged ending selective living groups—including fraternities—on the grounds that such housing arrangements encouraged exclusivity. Yet, at the same time, CCI authors praised campus organizations that encouraged self-segregation among minority students.

Brodhead, perhaps beginning to sense how deep into the ditch of PC pap he had already helped steer his university, was strikingly tepid in greeting the report, especially its suggestion that Duke alter the scheduling for its athletics teams to minimize weekday games; that proposal would effectively require withdrawing from the Atlantic Coast Conference. The president said that while he welcomed "knowledgeable faculty advice," all decisions on athletics rested with the administration and Trustees alone. He also appointed *another* committee—headed by Peter Lange, perhaps the only administration figure untainted by the cowardly response to the lacrosse affair—to consider the CCI's other recommendations.

Once again, the most intelligent and forthright assessments of the antics of the extremist professors came not from other faculty members but from Duke students. *The Chronicle* ran a six-part editorial series rebuking the CCI for excluding student viewpoints. Student Government president Elliot Wolf—himself a CCI member—recounted how he had "spent the last several months (literally) banging my head against a wall" expressing his concerns about both the CCI's process and its recommendations. And Kristin Butler dismissed the CCI as "an unmitigated disaster . . . a caricature of University governance, populated by agenda-driven individuals, operating under cover of secrecy and lacking meaningful student input or support." Given the prominence of Wood, Holloway, and Allison on the CCI (not to mention its vice chairman, Larry Moneta, and Chauncey Nartey, one of its student members), Butler wondered "whether President Brodhead intentionally stocked the committee with voices sure to be considered illegitimate by many in the Duke community."

Meanwhile, in the classroom, Group of 88 stalwart Anne Allison offered a new course that could have been mistaken as a parody of the insipidity of many professors—except that Allison was not joking. "Hook-Up Culture at Duke" claimed to illustrate what "the lacrosse scandal tell[s] us about power, difference, and raced, classed, gendered and sexed normativity in the U.S." As context for understanding the lacrosse players' conduct, Allison assigned the movie *Rules of Attraction.* Its plotline: "The incredibly spoiled and overprivi- leged students of Camden College are a backdrop for an unusual love trian- gle between a drug dealer, a virgin and a bisexual classmate." And the course's run-up to the lacrosse case began with a week spent on Peggy Sanday's *Frater- nity Gang Rape: Sex, Brotherhood, and Privilege on Campus.* A revised edi- tion, according to its publisher, NYU Press, "updates the incidences of fraternity gang rape on college campuses today, highlighting such recent cases as that of Duke University." For Group members, pretending that a rape had occurred was apparently preferable to facing the facts.

Allison asked students to complete six assignments involving interviewing and observing (some would say spying upon) other Duke students. The results were preordained. Specific assignments included students exploring "the links between eroticism, capital, bodies, and identities at Duke." Or examining sports teams "in terms of the themes covered so far in class: gender, race, het- eronormativity, power, everyday culture, image and prestige of Duke. Con- sider the role of alcohol in these cultures." And finally, "Hook-Up Culture at Duke" had students look into the role "played by race, gender, sexual prefer- ence, class, drinking, and selective groups (Greeks, sports teams)." Students were told to "do participant observation"—though it's not quite clear how.

Sometimes, in the course of human events, something happens that lays bare the hypocrisy of a whole swath of people the way a big wind strips dead leaves from a tree in late autumn. Such was the nature of *another* claim of interra- cial rape, at another party attended by more than forty people, in another off- campus house rented by Duke students, where another group of hosts were serving alcohol to minors. But this party, held on February 11, 2007, was hosted by a black Duke fraternity, Phi Beta Sigma. There were no strippers. But according to a subsequent police report, there was marijuana, cocaine, and Oxycontin in the house—each of which, unlike strippers, was illegal. At about 3 A.M., a white Duke undergraduate entered the bathroom; a black male allegedly followed her and then raped her. The woman went to the po- lice the next day.

The similarities were striking. The disparate reactions—of the police, neighbors, professors, Brodhead administration, media, NAACP, and others who had rushed to judgment the previous spring—were stark, if unsurprising.

The Police

In the 2007 rape case, the police conducted the investigation, as was usual under the Durham Police chain of command. When asked by *The N&O* whether Nifong was directing the investigation, Maj. L. A. Russ replied, "We haven't made any arrests or anything yet. He would not get involved this early." But in the lacrosse case, of course, Nifong had assumed command of the police investigation twenty-five days before the first arrest. Also, the police did a far fairer and more accurate photo lineup in the 2007 case, using seven fillers per suspect, conducted by an officer unconnected to the case, in contrast to the rigged, forty-six-white-lacrosse-players-only photo lineup conducted by Gottlieb on April 4, 2006.

The Neighbors

In March and April 2006, the Trinity Park Listserv was a hotbed of radicalism and support for the potbangers. This March 25 posting typified the reaction: "It will be an unmitigated outrage if all of the students who refused to co-operate with the police (i.e., the wall of silence) are not expelled directly." In the 2007 case, the Trinity Park Listserv contained not a single item about the alleged rape in the ten days after *The N&O* reported it.

The Faculty

In their apologia for the Group of 88, the "clarifying" faculty had spoken without evidence of an "atmosphere that allows sexism, racism, and sexual violence to be so prevalent on campus." Yet not one Duke professor issued a statement condemning the 2007 fraternity party in which rape allegedly occurred. No jeremiads about the moral evils of underage drinking, either.

Why the double standard? To use Wahneema Lubiano's phrase, the lacrosse players were "perfect offenders." Those faculty who worship at the altar of the race/class/gender trinity leaped at the chance to exploit a poor black woman's accusations against white male athletes in a sport associated with the upper class. The 2007 case, on the other hand, was dangerous in terms of academic politics. Ultrafeminists such as Duke women's studies director Robyn Weigman could contend that women who claim rape never lie. But the woman in the 2007 case was white and came from a more privileged background than the black suspect. "Gender" pointed to presuming guilt; "race" and "class" pointed the other way. So the Group of 88 remained silent, even though in this case the alleged victim was a Duke student.

The Media

In the lacrosse case, the vast publicity in both local and national media almost always reported the race of the accused students. In the 2007 case, the national media did not report the alleged rape at all and the local media, chiefly *The N&O*, bent over backwards *not* to report the race of the suspect. This policy left readers trying to decipher code, such as the *N&O* report that the suspect was "wearing a black do-rag." The rationale for this decision was PC bosh. According to *N&O* public editor Ted Vaden, managing editor John Drescher "makes the case that in an increasingly multi-ethnic community, race is less useful as a description. . . . How do you distinguish between black, brown, white, dark complexion, light complexion and other? He pointed to photographs of Barack Obama and North Carolina U.S. Rep. G. K. Butterfield. Not knowing their ethnicity, would a reader describe them as black or white?" But a suspect in the 2007 rape case, Michael Burch, was a dark-skinned black man.

The University

Vice President for Student Affairs Larry Moneta assumed the point position in the 2007 case. In one of his first comments, he appeared to shift blame to the accuser, describing her situation as "part of the reality of collegiate life and of experimentation and some of the consequences of students not necessarily always being in the right place at the right time. This happens around the country. Duke is no different in that respect." The administration, obviously, adopted a far less forgiving attitude regarding the lacrosse incident.

Nifong, still the DA, was at least technically in charge of the prosecution of Michael Burch. Yet as February moved into March, his hold on power grew ever more tenuous. In two installments, on February 27 and March 16, Nifong's attorneys, David Freedman and Dudley Witt, filed a response to the Bar. They demanded dismissal of the most serious charge against their client (conspiring to withhold exculpatory DNA evidence) and contended that the other allegations (improper public statements and lying to the court) resulted from unintentional error.

As to the facts, Nifong made two particularly odd assertions about his dealings with Dr. Brian Meehan. First, he claimed to have no memory of the April 10 meeting among himself, Dr. Meehan, Sgt. Gottlieb, and Det. Ben Himan. Therefore, he asserted that he had obtained the indictments of Reade Seligmann and Collin Finnerty without knowing the results of any of Meehan's tests. But the record contained conclusive evidence that Nifong had met with Meehan on April 10, including the notes of both Gottlieb and Himan; Meehan's December 15 testimony; and Nifong's own statements in at least two hearings (in June and September).

Second, the Nifong team suggested that even if Meehan did mention the exculpatory DNA evidence in the April and May meetings, Nifong had failed to appreciate its significance, since he was only looking only for matches to lacrosse players. This claim seemed to reveal a profound misunderstanding of every prosecutor's solemn duty never to turn a blind eye to evidence suggesting the possibility of innocence.

Nifong and his attorneys also made four principal arguments of law to counter the Bar's DNA charges; each of them was strained on its face, at best, and each was shredded in the Bar's response: (1) his actions didn't violate the state's open discovery statute because the defense had received the relevant information before a trial date had been set; (2) while state law requires prosecutors to give the defense all witness "statements," there was no violation in the case of Meehan because the statute "failed to specifically define what the term 'statement' encompassed"; (3) neither Judge Stephens nor Judge Smith had ordered Nifong to turn over any Meehan statements (of course, this was because he had falsely assured them that Meehan had made no statements of consequence); (4) the overlapping state law requirement that the DA provide all forty-six subjects of the order to give DNA samples with copies of the resulting DNA tests "does not set out any specific format in which the 'report' must be," and in this case the "report" was Nifong's eventual compliance (which turned out to be incomplete) with Judge Smith's order to turn over the underlying Meehan data.

As to his March–April 2006 media attacks on the lacrosse players, Nifong admitted making all but one of the comments attributed to him by the Bar. But he contended that these comments didn't violate the ethics rule against heightening "public condemnation of the accused" because the forty-six white lacrosse players—who had been identified as suspects by him personally, his office, the Durham Police, and even Durham CrimeStoppers—weren't really accused within the meaning of the State Bar's rule. Nifong added that in his media campaign he was only passing along information provided him by Meehan, Gottlieb, Himan, and Soucie, so any inaccuracies were their fault, not his.

The State Bar dismissed Nifong's arguments as "semantic hair-splitting" in a March 16 memorandum of law. Nifong's conduct regarding the DNA evidence (along with the arguments presented in his defense), it said, violated the plain language of North Carolina law. Under the statute, the Bar's memorandum observed, "the issue is not whether a defendant is able to surmise — from a massive amount of raw data — whether the expert uncovered potentially exculpatory evidence, but whether a 'report of the results' was furnished to the defendant by the State."

The Bar also ridiculed Nifong's proposed bright-line rule that because no trial date had been set, he didn't have to turn over the exculpatory evidence. Such a rule, it said, would mean that in the vast majority of cases, which end in plea bargains, the defense would *never* receive exculpatory evidence. The Bar also took strong issue with Nifong's argument that because no judge had ordered him to memorialize his conversations with Dr. Meehan, he was under no obligation to do so. "It is worth noting," the Bar's response recalled, "that the content of each Order was based on Nifong's misrepresentations to the Court as alleged in the Amended Complaint. Therefore, Nifong is effectively arguing that he can make false statements to a court which result in the entry of an order, and then use the order that is based on his misrepresentations to claim he committed no discovery violation."

Foreshadowing the difficulties that Nifong would have in retaining his license, the Bar concluded, with a touch of astonishment, that the district attorney was attempting to argue that it violated none of the Rules of Professional Conduct for him to:

> (1) *discuss and be keenly aware of potentially exculpatory DNA test results and direct or agree that those results would not be contained in a report provided to indicted defendants and other named suspects, and*
>
> (2) *successfully and repeatedly deceive courts into entering orders finding falsely that he had had no previous discussions about these potentially exculpatory DNA test results, because . . . over five months later and pursuant to a court order to compel, he ultimately provided the defendants almost 2,000 pages of underlying data without any report. In essence, Defendant argues that, court orders and very specific discovery requests notwithstanding, he had absolute discretion to withhold potentially exculpatory information of which he was fully aware until some unspecified time prior to trial without violating the Rules of Professional Conduct. Defendant's contention that he was under no obligation to provide the information because no trial date was set necessarily implies that he was also entitled to withhold and never disclose potentially exculpatory information*

in any case that settled prior to trial. These precepts, if accepted, would ap-
ply not only to Defendant but to all other prosecutors and must be rejected.

As Nifong continued to personify the darkest side of the legal profession, a heartbreaking turn of events ended the life of an attorney who "embodied the words honor and integrity," in the words of his client Reade Seligmann. Kirk Osborn, one of the heroes of the the Duke lacrosse case, who had defended Reade Seligmann and joined Joe Cheshire in making courageous counterattacks when District Attorney Nifong was riding high, fell down at his home from a sudden, severe heart attack on March 23, never to awake.

The former University of Colorado football player had just finished his usual 5 A.M., hour-long full-tilt ride on his exercise bike. He was a youthful sixty-four years old, tall, thin, athletic, and had been the picture of health. Fellow defense lawyers in the case wondered whether Nifong's vicious personal attacks on Osborn might have taken a toll on this man of honor, who was used to dealing with honorable prosecutors; one of those, former Orange County (Chapel Hill) district attorney Carl Fox, now a judge, was a eulogist at the funeral. Osborn was survived by his wife, Tania, and two teenage daughters, Michela and Jenna.

Osborn fell just after writing these last words in a leather journal that Tania had given him to record on a daily basis things for which he was thankful:

1. —*I have the freedom to choose my thoughts.*
2. —*That I can dare to choose better thoughts.*
3. —*I can create my own world.*
4. —*The beauty of our children.*
5. —*The joy in our new puppy, Bemus, when he greets us in the morning.*

Amidst a vast outpouring of grief and praise for Kirk, the Seligmann family issued a statement that said they were "heartbroken over the death of Kirk Osborn. Kirk stood up for Reade at great personal cost. He stood by Reade and together they faced the mob that was outside the Durham County Courthouse a year ago; Kirk never flinched and faced both that mob outside the courthouse and the bias within the courthouse with the courage that he showed throughout this case. He passionately believed that the truth would emerge and that the world would know of the injustice that was done that day and every day of this baseless prosecution."

"He was one of our warriors," said Joe Cheshire the day Osborn died. A warrior for justice, for rich and poor, for black and white, for the rights of innocent and guilty clients alike to a fair trial.

At the request of Tania Osborn, who feared a media circus, the three defendants' families did not attend Osborn's March 28 memorial service. But each member of the defense team was present in a packed University Methodist Church, in Chapel Hill, where Osborn's close friend, Rich Preyer Jr., said this in a celebration of Kirk's life:

> Kirk, you know that D.A. over in Durham? The one who called you 'the best dressed public defender in the state'? And, Kirk, I don't really think he meant it as a compliment. Well, he at least got ONE THING right—because you always looked good—always stylish—beautiful suits—never arrogant or showy or seeking publicity—never that—just always looking, feelin' good.
>
> And you were so damn handsome and big and strong. My friend, Tony, told me yesterday, a woman in his neighborhood was secretly, madly in love with you and, then, he said, on second thought, every woman he knew was secretly in love with you—but you know and I know, Tania was never going to let that go anywhere. Nor did you care except when working the jury box. I remember you saying to me in one of your hopelessly guilty defendant's murder trials, "Rich, I think I caught one of the ladies' eyes." Oh yes you did, Mr. Osborn. You, who in every case you ever tried, never allowed a defendant to be placed on Death Row. . . .
>
> And I remember late one night, long ago, you telling me after your twin brother, Steve, had killed himself, "Rich, I should have been there. I should have been there"—And not telling me you were on your way to see him after his last call to you. After Steve's death, you promised yourself—you vowed—if anyone ever needed help, you would drop everything that minute—and you would be there. You never failed your promise. Never.

As Nifong's career imploded and his facilitators among the Duke faculty blindly clung to their spring 2006 opinions, special prosecutors James Coman and Mary Winstead undertook the comprehensive investigation of Mangum's claims that Nifong and the Durham Police Department had never performed. Coman, the son of a New Jersey cop, was widely considered to be among the state's finest prosecutors and most powerful lawyers. Winstead, ironically, had served alongside Nifong when both were assistant district attorneys in Durham before she joined the attorney general's office.

The special prosecutors asked both the defense and the Durham district attorney's office to present to them all information relevant to their investigation. Defense lawyers responded with a twenty-seven-page letter laying out the faulty nature of the identification process used by Nifong; the highly exculpatory nature of the DNA tests; the unreliability of Mangum as a witness; and the failure of any forensic evidence to substantiate Mangum's claims.

Coman and Winstead then met with all the defense attorneys on February 7, 2007. The highlight of the meeting was a lengthy PowerPoint presentation by Jim Cooney (described by Joe Cheshire as the "finest PowerPoint attorney I have ever seen") previewing a closing argument in the event of a trial.

Entitled "Anatomy of a Hoax," the PowerPoint began with "Crystal's Checklist," showing in visual form the vast differences among Mangum's March 14, March 16, and April 6, 2006, versions of what "Adam," "Matt," and "Brett" had supposedly done to her. Cooney then moved to "Who's who," which again used visuals to demonstrate that unimpeachable electronic evidence contradicted Mangum's allegations of where Seligmann, Finnerty, and Evans were at the critical times. Cooney's "DNA" section went through each of the DNA alleles to show how each unidentified bit of male DNA matched neither any lacrosse player nor Mangum's acknowledged sexual partners. "Opportunity"—the time-line section—demonstrated how all cell-phone and photographic records belied Mangum's latest, December 21 story (as well as her previous versions). "Crystal's Work Schedule" featured copies of Platinum Club records showing Mangum signing in for work on March 18 and March 21—a period when (in Nifong's imagining) she was traumatized from the attack.

Documents, photos, electronic records—all showing that Mangum's stories were false. And in a powerful conclusion, Cooney targeted the real villains. Accompanying a quotation from Proverbs 11:29 ("He who troubles his own house will inherit wind, And the foolish will be servant to the wise-hearted") was a clip of Nifong bellowing, "I'm not going to let Durham's view in the minds of the world to be a bunch of lacrosse players from Duke raping a black girl in Durham." Cooney closed with "Shame": an image of the Group of 88's ad—including its thank-you to protesters "for not waiting and for making yourselves heard"—followed by a photograph of the protesters carrying their CASTRATE banner.

Nifong, by contrast, offered the special prosecutors a wild, previously unmentioned theory. The party, he reportedly now claimed, was a fraternity initiation event. Everyone on the team, in this version of events, knew that Seligmann and Finnerty were people of high character, and so Evans and other seniors planned the attack to bring the two sophomores into the ranks of lacrosse team "hooligans." What evidence did the district attorney have for this theory of the crime? Coman and Winstead asked. None, Nifong reportedly confessed. Meanwhile, Linwood Wilson admitted showing Mangum the

April 4 lineup photos, this time *including the players' real names*, on December 21, even as those photos were the subject of a pending suppression motion. This, the special prosecutors concluded, "provided the defense additional grounds to argue that the out of court and in court identification should be suppressed which would have effectively ended the case."

At this point, Coman and Winstead had clear grounds to dismiss the case immediately due to insufficiency of evidence and the likelihood that the judge would suppress Mangum's identifications as manifestly unreliable. But the two prosecutors decided that they owed the public—and the accused players—an investigation comprehensive enough to document the full truth of the matter. And so they proceeded, exhaustively:

Witnesses

Putting to rest all claims of a "wall of silence," the special prosecutors interviewed seventeen members of the 2006 lacrosse team, plus two other non-lacrosse Duke students who attended the party. These interviews were grueling, featuring detailed follow-up questions—especially from Winstead—as well as discussions between the players and State Bureau of Investigation agents. Thanks to Bob Ekstrand's painstaking work at the start of the case, all had verifiable, electronic data to corroborate their stories.

Mangum, on the other hand, proved a wholly unreliable witness. Coman and Winstead discovered that she "attempted to avoid the contradictions by changing her story, contradicting previous stories or alleging the evidence was fabricated." Now, for the first time, she said that she had been suspended in midair during the rape. And that all three of her attackers kicked her after the rape. And that ten other lacrosse players assaulted her in the backyard. And that she and Kim Roberts left the premises at 11:50 P.M. And that Finnerty and Evans carried her to Roberts's car after the attack. When shown time-stamped photographs that contradicted all of these assertions, Mangum claimed that someone at Duke had altered the photos.

Medical Evidence

In the weeks before the special prosecutors took over the case, Doug Kingsbery had conducted fruitful interviews with Dr. Julie Manly, who had performed the pelvic exam on Mangum at Duke Hospital—and had *never* been interviewed by Nifong's office or the Durham Police Department. Manly told Kingsbery that she initially believed that a rape occurred, in part because of Mangum's hysterical behavior in the E.R. and in part because Manly assumed that the whitish fluid in Mangum's vagina was semen. When Kingsbery told Manly of the DNA test results and the evidence that Mangum resumed her stripping career two days after the party, Manly reconsidered her opinions. She said that the whitish fluid might have been a yeast infection, which might also explain the diffuse edema in the vaginal walls, adding that she would testify that Mangum's behavior was *not* consistent with that of sexual assault victims she previously had examined.

Tara Levicy, meanwhile, clung to her belief that a rape had occurred in the face of the overwhelming evidence to the contrary. But Levicy had little credibility by this point because she—like Mangum—had shifted her story so many times. Coman and Winstead tartly observed, "The SANE based her opinion that the exam was consistent with what the accusing witness was reporting largely on the accusing witness's demeanor and complaints of pain rather than on objective evidence." Indeed, the special prosecutors concluded, "No medical evidence [confirmed] Mangum's stories." Nor did the DNA.

New Evidence

The special prosecutors established once and for all that Mangum arrived at the party around 11:40 P.M.—not, as Nifong had claimed in December, at 11:00 P.M. They obtained from Brian Taylor, Mangum's driver the night of the party, a credit card receipt from a nearby gas station, where he had purchased a drink at 11:43 P.M. after dropping Mangum off at 610 North Buchanan. The defense also turned over to Coman and Winstead the 12:31 A.M. video showing Mangum, on the back stoop saying with a slur that "I am a cop."

On April 4, Mangum showed up significantly impaired for her last meeting with the special prosecutors and admitted that before the meeting she had taken Ambien, methadone, Paxil and amitriptyline. After this reenactment of Mangum's condition on the night of the party, Coman and Winstead had seen enough. The attorney general needed not only to dismiss all charges but to declare Evans, Seligmann, and Finnerty innocent, they told him. But Cooper's political advisors cautioned that such an unequivocal proclamation could alienate some of the African Americans whose support he would need in future elections; perhaps he should just say that there was "insufficient evidence" and leave it ambiguous whether there had or had not been a rape.

As the attorney general pondered what to say in dismissing the charges, Duke took one more shot at the lacrosse players. In a lengthy interview with *Newsday*'s Steven Marcus that appeared on the paper's Web site Monday afternoon, April 9, John Burness and an unnamed senior administrator attacked the players' characters, implied that Mike Pressler had condoned bad behavior, and vowed that Duke would never apologize for its handling of the case. People had asked him, Burness noted, whether anyone at Duke would say they were sorry. "I said," Burness replied, "'For what?'" A senior administrator added that Evans, Finnerty, and Seligmann were "no choirboys." And Marcus added, approvingly, that "Duke as an institution has a reputation to repair and that is paramount over clearing the names of the players involved in last spring's party."

Former Duke professor Stuart Rojstaczer suspected the article's motive: To beat back potential lawsuits, "One public thing you do is have your p.r. guy call in a chit to an old buddy who happens to be a reporter for a newspaper in the neck of the woods where the lacrosse players' families live. You tell him your side of the story. The kids are bad apples. The coach was rotten. Duke did nothing wrong. It's your way of signaling to those families that this is a 'teachable moment.' They are about to be taught a lesson that when attacked, Duke fights back."

Unfortunately for Duke, as Rojstaczer further noted, "The timing couldn't have been worse; the article, designed to be a calculated attack, instead turned out to be a p.r. blunder." The contemptuous tone expressed by both Burness and the unnamed administrator went too far, and both Burness and Bob Steel were forced to issue apologies. Even worse for the administration, Attorney General Cooper's office put out word that he would announce his findings in a press conference scheduled for Wednesday, April 11. So just as the eyes of the nation returned to the lacrosse case, senior Duke administrators had resumed their campaign of character assassination against the three innocent students and their teammates.

Cooper was briefly hospitalized on April 10, complaining of chest pains. But it was a false alarm, and his announcement went on as planned. Early in the afternoon of April 11, the three families and a few friends gathered in a conference room at the Raleigh Sheraton to watch Cooper's announcement. Wade Smith asked for a moment of silence to remember Kirk Osborn. He also reminded them that the most important word to come out of Cooper's mouth would be "dismissal." But everyone gathered in the room knew that a dismissal was coming: they wanted to know if Cooper would use what Seligmann and Evans later termed the "i-word": Innocent.

Addressing a room jammed with some hundred journalists and nine big TV cameras, Cooper started slowly, describing the process under which his office took the case. Then he said: "The result of our review and investigation shows clearly that there is insufficient evidence to proceed on any of the charges. Today we are filing notices of dismissal for all charges against Reade

Seligmann, Collin Finnerty, and David Evans." Watching from the Raleigh Sheraton, the players and their families felt their spirits sag. "Insufficient evidence": It seemed as if, as so often had occurred in the case, a North Carolina officeholder was taking the politically convenient way out.

But the attorney general had more to say: "We believe that these cases were the result of a tragic rush to accuse and a failure to verify serious allegations. Based on the significant inconsistencies between the evidence and the various accounts given by the accusing witness, we believe these three individuals are innocent of these charges." With those words, the families burst into applause and tears, hugging each other. Their nightmare had finally had come to an end.

And Cooper was just getting warmed up. After reviewing Nifong's faulty procedures and nonexistent evidence base, he targeted the district attorney—and unnamed others—directly. "In this case," the attorney general declared,

> with the weight of the state behind him, the Durham district attorney pushed forward unchecked. There were many points in the case where caution would have served justice better than bravado. And in the rush to condemn, a community and a state lost the ability to see clearly. Regardless of the reasons this case was pushed forward, the result was wrong. Today, we need to learn from this and keep it from happening again to anybody. . . . This case shows the enormous consequences of overreaching by a prosecutor. What has been learned here is that the internal checks on a criminal charge—sworn statements, reasonable grounds, proper suspect photo lineups, accurate and fair discovery—all are critically important.

In a question-and-answer session with reporters, Cooper labeled Nifong a "rogue prosecutor," suggested that Nifong might have committed criminal activity, and announced that the state would not file criminal charges against Mangum because her mentally imbalanced state suggested that she might actually believe her myriad tales.

The defense attorneys and the three families followed with a press conference of their own later that afternoon at the Sheraton. Virtually every member of the men's and women's lacrosse team attended, along with Coaches Kimel and Danowski, their assistant coaches, and Sue Pressler, whose husband could not make it because of his coaching duties in his new job at Bryant University, in Rhode Island.

Evans, Finnerty, and Seligmann all spoke of the pain caused by the false accusations and their desire to make sure that no one else experienced what they had endured. Dave Evans urged North Carolina lawmakers to "address some issues that arose from our case, most notably, the grand jury procedures. They are a check on the power of the prosecutor and in this case, there are no records of what was used to secure indictments against the three of us. We have no idea . . . and how can we, as a country, in the legal system, control the people who are supposed to enforce it if they can simply say whatever they want to say, produce whatever they want to produce, and nobody else has an opportunity to see or ever question it?"

Collin Finnerty asked that viewers see "something important about these three families up here, the Seligmanns, the Evanses, and the Finnertys, that we have become one big family through all this. We have a bond that will last forever. It's been a very long and emotional year for me and for all of us."

Reade Seligmann expressed concern for "people who do not have the resources to defend themselves." He had pointed words for "everyone who chose to speak out against us before the facts were known," saying that he hoped they would never be put

> in a position where you experience the same pain and heartache that you have caused our families. While your hurtful words and outrageous lies will forever be associated with this tragedy, everyone will always remember that we told the truth, and in the words of Abraham Lincoln, "Truth is the best vindication against slander." If our case can bring to light some of the flaws in our judicial system as well as discourage people from rushing to judgment, then the hardships we have endured over this past year will not have been in vain.

The attorneys had powerful messages of their own. Jim Cooney praised the heroes of the case—namely Jim Coleman and Moez Elmostafa—before criticizing two groups of "cowards." First, he took to task *The Herald-Sun*, who, "if they had done what journalists were supposed to do and spoken truth to power, could have slowed this train down." Then he rebuked "a number of other people in Durham, some of whom teach for a living, who should have stood up and said, 'Wait a second. Civil rights means something. We have spent careers studying civil rights. We're not going to throw them down the drain simply because a district attorney tells us to.'" Such academics, including Cooney's former professors Peter Wood and Bill Chafe, had put aside their previous commitment to civil rights to pursue other agendas in the lacrosse case.

Joe Cheshire reminded the assembled media that

> on March the thirtieth of last year, when the press was completely out of control, when these boys were the guiltiest people on the face of the Earth,

when everyone in this country was pillorying them as hooligans and rapists,
I called a little press conference in my office and I looked at you national
media and you local media and I said—I was kind of scared when I said
it—but I said you all are wrong and when this case is over, you're going to
be embarrassed if you don't open your eyes and listen to what the truth is . . .
Well, Roy Cooper said a word today. The word is I-N-N-O-C-E-N-T. And I
want to make sure everybody has got that and knows how to spell it. These
young men were, are and always have been innocent.

Cheshire also went after some of Nifong's facilitators. The district attorney's acts, Cheshire observed, "tore his own city apart, in a racial/class divide, allowing people on both sides of the racial divide who live to exploit racial tension, for no other purpose than their own self-aggrandizement or personal advancement—allowed them a stage from which to spew their self-serving but pathetic hatred. And some of you in the media call them community activists."

The media portrayed the announcement in varied ways. True to the end as the best of the print media, *The N&O* and *The Chronicle* led with identical banner headlines: "INNOCENT." True to its own disgraceful coverage, *The Herald-Sun* avoided the word "innocent" in its headline and ran a lead editorial the following day saying: "Love yourself, Durham. You've got good reason." In the following days, as *The N&O*'s Joe Neff did a five-part series containing at least twenty previously unreported items about the case, *The Herald-Sun* ran a front-page, above-the-fold story falsely asserting that concerns about the racial divide had played a role in Cooper's decision to declare the players innocent. The next day, the paper was forced to run a retraction.

In the national media, Duff Wilson filed a report posted on the *New York Times* Web site that didn't get to the "innocent" proclamation until the second paragraph. The *Times* editorial page continued to avoid comment on the case. Other major media outlets amazingly continued to trash the three players' characters. *The Boston Globe* labeled Evans, Seligmann, and Finnerty "louts." Columnist Dan Shanoff of espn.com called them "douchebags." *The Washington Post* clucked that the three "were not paragons of virtue," and that "some of the players—though not necessarily the three accused students—made racially derogatory remarks to the accuser and the other dancer who accompanied her." (Of course, Kim Roberts had unequivocally stated that none of the three defendants had said anything derogatory to her and that she had provoked the two who did so with her own racial taunt.) And *Nightline* cohost Terry Moran told people not to "feel sorry for the Dukies," since they were from privileged backgrounds and "there are many, many cases of prosecutorial misconduct across our country every year."

Nifong himself waited a day to issue a halfhearted apology: "To the extent that I made judgments that ultimately proved to be incorrect, I apologize to the three students that were wrongly accused." Nifong blamed Mangum for lying to him, incorrectly implied that only the new evidence brought to light by the special prosecutors accounted for Cooper's decision to proclaim the players innocent, and suggested that some of his initial actions were correct.

"It may be an apology," Collin Finnerty observed in a third *60 Minutes* program on the case, on April 15, "but it doesn't make me feel any better . . . for what I've gone through. It was his actions more than anybody's that caused the harm."

Dave Evans welcomed the exonerations of him and his teammates but added a melancholy prediction: "You can try to move on, but rape will always be associated with my name. 'Innocent' might be a part of that, but when I die, they'll say, 'One of the three Duke lacrosse rape suspects died today.'"

Scott Campbell, a close family friend, sent Dave a note after watching this statement. He began by saying that Dave's prediction "unfortunately (unjustly, but such is life) is true if you lead an ordinary life." But Campbell went on:

I believe in the transforming power of such tragic incidents in a man's life. You were victimized but you were chosen to experience a transforming event, so now you must live an extraordinary life. History is full of such people.

I know you want to get back to normal but your life now requires much bigger thinking. You must think, envision, what you can do to write large your life's story. The gift is that it is all before you and you can have a large impact. Your notoriety can give you a bully pulpit and be transformed into respect and honor. For most men, we only wish we could find a way to change the world. Some of us repeat and repeat the timeworn words of the Episcopal prayer—"O God . . . grant us in all our doubts and uncertainties, the grace to ask what thou wouldest have us to do . . ." You can make this tragic year the beginning of a remarkable journey.

23. NO ISOLATED CASE:

FROM DUKE TO DEATH ROW

MIKE NIFONG'S POLITICALLY MOTIVATED PERSECUTION of Duke lacrosse players—whose innocence was manifested by evidence in the DA's hands for nearly all of the nine and one-half months he spent hounding them—may well be the most egregious abuse of prosecutorial power ever to unfold in plain view.

Never in recent memory has misconduct on this scale been exposed while the pretrial phase of a big case was still under way: demonizing innocent suspects in the media as rapists, racists, and hooligans; whipping up racial hatred against them to win an election; rigging a lineup to implicate them in a crime that never occurred; lying to the public, to the defense, to the court, and to the State Bar; hiding DNA test results that conclusively proved innocence; seeking (unsuccessfully) to bully and threaten defense lawyers into letting their clients be railroaded.

Unlike some rogue prosecutors, Nifong has not put any innocent people on death row. Nor did he succeed in putting innocent Duke lacrosse players in prison. But if he had had his way, they would have been locked up for thirty years.

And among the most frightening aspects of the case is that even after much of this misconduct became publicly known in the spring and summer of 2006, Duke faculty activists, media organizations led by *The New York Times*, the NAACP, and others continued for many months to look the other way or even facilitate his efforts. And Duke president Richard Brodhead and Chairman Robert Steel continued to treat Nifong with deference *for more than six months* after Duke Law School's Jim Coleman had raised his strong but lonely voice on June 13, 2006, against Nifong's abuse of Duke's own students.

Whether evil or deluded or both, Nifong is history; as of May 2007 he is, or should be, on his way to disbarment. But his breathtaking rampage leaves one wondering whether this case points to a more general problem of innocent people being oppressed in large numbers by abusive prosecutors and police. As Reade Seligmann stated at the press conference following the dismissal of all charges, "If police officers and a district attorney can systematically railroad us with absolutely no evidence whatsoever, I can't imagine what they would do to people who do not have the resources to defend themselves. So rather than relying on disparaging stereotypes and creating political and racial conflicts, all of us need to take a step back from this case and learn from it."

Many prosecutors are quick to dismiss Nifong's misconduct as aberrational. It could never happen here, they say. And it's true that Nifong's abuses were especially extreme. It's also true that most prosecutors are ethical most of the time, that many are admirable public servants, that it's extremely rare for a prosecutor to go after people he *knows* to be innocent, and that most people charged with crimes are guilty.

But power corrupts. Prosecutors as a group are as imperfect as the rest of the human race. So are police. And so are the scientific experts—such as Dr. Brian Meehan in the Duke case—who help prosecutors convince jurors of guilt, often by suppressing exculpatory evidence or presenting as conclusive so-called expert opinions that are in fact highly debatable or just plain wrong.

If Nifong's conduct was so aberrational, how was he able to find so many willing accomplices? Linwood Wilson, Sgt. Mark Gottlieb, Det. Ben Himan, and Dr. Meehan also had to know of the overwhelming evidence that they were oppressing innocent young men. That never slowed them down. Officer Clayton, other police officers, assistant district attorneys such as Tracey Cline, and others may or may not have had much guilty knowledge; that question should be explored in a criminal investigation of the roles of the Durham Police Department and the assistant DAs in Nifong's oppression of the lacrosse players.

It's also clear that numerous other people in the DA's office and the police department had reason to suspect that something was wrong. It's further clear that Judge Stephens did much to help the DA victimize the lacrosse players through his pro-Nifong rulings, his refusal to consider defense motions in a timely fashion, and his overt hostility to Kirk Osborn's courageous challenges to various Nifong abuses.

Governor Mike Easley silently condoned Nifong's flagrant public misconduct for far longer than he should have. The problems with the criminal justice systems in Durham and in North Carolina spread well beyond Mike Nifong.

Indeed, the outrageous misconduct by four North Carolina prosecutors (discussed in chapter 4) that put James Hoffman and the demonstrably innocent Alan Gell on death row for many years suggests a wider problem. And the failure of the North Carolina State Bar to take action against those prosecutors showed that it was not a reliable watchdog—not before the Duke lacrosse case, at least.

In 2004, after the State Bar had weakly gone through the motions in its disciplinary hearing on the Gell prosecutors, one of Gell's lawyers—the same Brad Bannon who was to play such an important role in the Duke lacrosse case—wrote an anguished protest to the State Bar:

> *I am writing this letter to memorialize how terribly wrong this whole case has been, and how bad this whole system can be, from beginning to end, especially for indigent defendants who are wronged by powerful people. . . . It was all wrong from the beginning: from the initial scenario where Mr. Gell went through five court-appointed attorneys over three years and suffered a death penalty because of unethical prosecutorial conduct and reckless law enforcement conduct; to the post-conviction process where the Attorney General's Office failed to concede obvious error by its own office and fought Mr. Gell's request for a new, fair trial; to the State Bar prosecution, which appeared to lack even the most rudimentary commitment to success. Especially when the challenged conduct put an innocent man on death row [and] threw North Carolina's entire criminal justice system into question.*

Nor are such problems confined to North Carolina. Rare as it is for a prosecutor to try to frame a defendant he knows to be innocent, it is less rare for prosecutors and (especially) police to frame innocent people whom they wrongly believe to be guilty, by dishonestly manipulating evidence. There is also a whole spectrum of less extreme forms of prosecutorial overzealousness that also harm innocent people. The myriad problems with Nifong's handling of the lacrosse case range across that spectrum. Some are quite commonplace, such as the indefensibly narrow notions of what amounts to exculpatory evidence used by a great many prosecutors to withhold from defense lawyers evidence that could go a long way toward convincing jurors to vote not guilty. Many overzealous prosecutors begin by being too reluctant to question shabby or dishonest investigative work by police. Many rush to judgment based on sketchy evidence; facing huge caseloads, such prosecutors become complacent or lazy after seeing twenty clearly guilty defendants in a row and wrongly presume the guilt of the twenty-first. Many explain away late-arriving evidence of innocence that would make any open-minded prosecutor doubt his initial theory. Some allow close (or not-so-close) judgment calls to be skewed by political ambition and play to the crowd, or to the media mob, in high-visibility cases.

"For many years," says Joe Cheshire, "the rule for some prosecutors has been that the end justifies the means—that I know this person is guilty and therefore I can do anything I need to convict him." And some indeterminate number of prosecutors are, like Mike Nifong, driven by ambition, greed, ego, arrogance, overzealousness, or fanaticism to ruin the lives of people whom they know or should know to be innocent.

Both petty and serious prosecutorial misconduct may well be more widespread in America's gonzo adversarial, win-at-all-costs legal culture than in, say, the United Kingdom. Criminal defense lawyers in America—including the best and most ethical of them—consider it their professional duty to get guilty clients off the hook by hiding or distorting the true facts, if they can. Indeed, under current legal ethics rules it would be unethical for them *not* to do so. And it is all too common for defense lawyers to cross the indistinct line from necessarily zealous representation within the bounds of the law into outright lying to the court or coaching clients and friendly witnesses to give misleading testimony. These tactics sometimes work.

It is hardly surprising that more than a few prosecutors—especially career prosecutors who have never known what it's like to be on the other side—come to believe that they must fight fire with fire and use dirty tricks of their own to insure conviction of the guilty. In addition, says a former prosecutor, "if you hear the defense lawyers in every case bashing you for alleged misconduct and insisting that every defendant is innocent, you are less likely to be keen to listen when the defense lawyers says, in effect, 'Wait, in this case my guy really is innocent.'"

So it is that the overly adversarial ethic inculcated into defense lawyers in this country probably produces more wrongful convictions than would occur in a system such as England's, which imposes a stronger obligation of forthrightness on lawyers and has trial lawyers (barristers) act both as prosecutors and as defense lawyers, from one week to the next, throughout their careers.

A disturbing amount of misconduct among local prosecutors was documented in a 2003 study by the Center for Public Integrity, a nonprofit that investigats the use and abuse of institutional power. The study, "Harmful Error: Investigating America's Local Prosecutors," begins:

> Local prosecutors in many of the 2,341 jurisdictions across the nation have stretched, bent or broken rules to win convictions, the Center has found. Since 1970, individual judges and appellate court panels cited prosecutorial misconduct as a factor when dismissing charges, reversing convictions or reducing sentences in over 2,000 cases. In another 500 cases, appellate judges

offered opinions—either dissents or concurrences—in which they found the misconduct warranted a reversal. In thousands more, judges labeled prosecutorial behavior inappropriate, but upheld convictions using a doctrine called harmless error.

Misconduct by prosecutors led to the conviction of innocent individuals who were later exonerated. Guilty defendants have also had their convictions overturned and are placed back on the street.

Prosecutors and police come under especially intense public pressure to quickly solve especially heinous and horrifying crimes. This leads some to target the first suspect to come up on their radar screens without taking the time or care to make sure that they have the right man. Innocent defendants are especially at risk in such cases because of what Scott Turow, in *The Ultimate Punishment,* calls "the propensity of juries to turn the burden of proof against defendants accused of monstrous crimes."

To be sure, in a nation with a prison population of over 2.1 million people, a few thousand cases of proven prosecutorial misconduct over more than thirty years may not seem like much. And not every victim of prosecutorial misconduct is innocent. But the vast majority of prosecutorial misconduct cases never come to light, the "Harmful Error" study notes, in part because "at least 95 percent of the cases that pour in from the police never reach a jury, which means any misconduct occurs away from public view. The only trial those defendants receive takes place in the prosecutor's office; the prosecutor becomes the judge and the jury. The prosecutor is the de facto law after an arrest, deciding whether to charge the suspect with committing a crime, what charge to file from a range of possibilities, whether to offer a pre-trial deal, and, if so, the terms of the deal."

If even 99 percent of all prisoners nationwide are guilty as charged, that other 1 percent includes more than twenty thousand innocent people. And the best available estimates suggest that the number is far higher.

Professor Samuel Gross of the University of Michigan has calculated that 2.3 percent of all prisoners sentenced to death between 1973 and 1989 have been exonerated and freed. Professor Michael Risinger of Seton Hall Law School estimates that between 3.3 percent and 5 percent of defendants sentenced to death for murders involving rape between 1982 and 1989 were innocent. Other innocents almost certainly remain on death row.

Because death-row inmates attract the most dedicated postconviction lawyers, and because DNA evidence has subjected rape convictions to especially exacting scrutiny, it seems probable that the error rates are higher in other cases—armed robbery, burglary, and gunshot murders, for example.

Misconduct is even more common among police officers than among prosecutors, numerous studies suggest. Indeed, the word "testilying," coined by Harvard Law School's Alan Dershowitz, has entered our vocabulary because it is so commonplace for police to lie under oath to help convict defendants they believe to be guilty. In the early 1990s, the Mollen Commission studied this problem in New York City and concluded that many otherwise honest police officers "commit falsification to serve what they perceive to be 'legitimate' law enforcement ends. In their view, regardless of the legality of the arrest, the defendant is in fact guilty and ought to be arrested. Officers reported a litany of manufactured tales."

Examples included justifying an illegal search by falsely claiming that the car in question had run a red light; falsely claiming to have seen illegal drugs change hands; pretending to have (nonexistent) informants, and the like. "Several former and current prosecutors acknowledged—off the record—that perjury and falsifications are serious problems in law enforcement that, though not condoned, are ignored," the Mollen Report added. Officers rationalize such lies as necessary to allow admission at trial of probative evidence of guilt that they obtain by violating judicial limitations on searches and seizures that many cops see as nettlesome technicalities. But police lying can become a habit, to the detriment of innocent as well as guilty defendants.

"Every objective study of police perjury has come to similar conclusions," Dershowitz wrote in a 1997 *Boston Globe* op-ed. Police perjury is pervasive in every major city in the country, he asserted. Dershowitz quoted Joseph Mc-Namara, the former police chief of San Jose and Kansas City, saying that he had "come to believe that hundreds of thousands of law enforcement officers commit felony perjury every year testifying about drug arrests."

"As McNamara explains," added Dershowitz, "these testiliars are otherwise law-abiding cops, not bribe takers or excessive force users. [McNamara says,] 'They don't feel lying under oath is wrong because politicians tell them they are engaged in a holy war fighting evil. Then, too, the enemy these mostly white cops are testifying against are poor blacks and Latinos.'"

Dershowitz is right about the politicians, or most of them. Law-and-order conservatives typically believe in increasing police and prosecutorial powers and show little concern for the plight of defendants—unless they happen to be friends, have friends in common, or share political allegiances, as in the cases of convicted obstructer-of-justice Martha Stewart and convicted perjurer I. Lewis "Scooter" Libby, Vice President Dick Cheney's former chief of staff. Liberal politicians often have more empathy for the mass of defendants who are poor and black, but these politicians are terrified of being called soft on crime. So politicians generally do little to curb abuses of prosecutorial and police powers.

The advent of DNA evidence, which since 1989 has exonerated more than two hundred prisoners, including fourteen innocent death-row inmates, has made it clearer than ever that many innocent defendants are convicted and sent to prison on a regular basis, all over the country. There is also evidence that a handful of men who may well have been innocent have been put to death in recent years, including Ruben Cantu, Carlos DeLuna, and Cameron Todd Willingham, all of Texas, and Larry Griffin, of Missouri.

Recoverable DNA evidence—or the absence of DNA where one would expect to find it if the accuser were truthful—is a factor in only a small fraction of all felony cases, most obviously those involving alleged sexual assaults and murders by stabbing or beating. But logical extrapolation from the substantial number of cases in which DNA has proved the innocence of convicted prisoners has cast new doubt on the reliability of criminal convictions generally.

Ironically, law-enforcement assurances that wrongful convictions are few and far between have been undermined by DNA even as the Supreme Court and Congress have been busily restricting prisoners' rights to use new evidence of innocence to challenge their convictions. "The strong presumption that verdicts are correct, one of the underpinnings of restrictions on post-conviction relief, has been weakened by the growing number of convictions that have been vacated by exclusionary DNA test results," the Justice Department's National Commission on the Future of DNA Evidence observed in 1999.

"DNA testing's unique qualities justify a completely different balance than the courts usually strike in addressing post-conviction challenges," wrote U.S. District Judge Nancy Gertner, of Massachusetts, in an August 2006 decision, *Wade v. Brady*. New evidence suggesting the possible innocence of convicted prisoners was usually quite debatable in the past, falling well short of compete exoneration. "But because DNA testing can exonerate the defendant," Judge Gertner explained, "the government may only legitimately deny access to testing if it has a compelling reason to do so. To hold otherwise would subordinate the pursuit of justice to an arid obsession with procedure. . . . For a limited set of cases, adjudication at trial is no longer the most reliable determination of guilt or innocence." The judge ruled that prisoners had a due-process right to DNA testing.

The two-hundred-plus cases of convicted prisoners definitively cleared by DNA tests can be found on the Web site of the Innocence Project, www. innocenceproject.org. This renowned group of lawyers was created in 1992 by

Barry Scheck and Peter Neufeld for the purpose of exonerating wrongfully convicted people through DNA testing and reforming the criminal justice system to prevent future injustices.

Police and/or prosecutorial misconduct appears to have been a major factor in at least half of the cases in which the Innocence Project has cleared convicted prisoners, although precise percentages have not been tabulated. The most common forms of such misconduct are deliberately suggestive lineups and other eyewitness identification procedures (mistaken identifications, in turn, are the most common cause of wrongful convictions); withholding exculpatory evidence from the defense; mishandling, destroying, or fabricating evidence; pressuring truthful witnesses to change their stories; bribing dishonest jailhouse informants to invent confessions by fellow prisoners; and coercing false confessions.

A sampling:

Oklahoma: Ron Williamson and Dennis Fritz

Ron Williamson and Dennis Fritz spent more than a decade in prison—on death row, in Williamson's case—for the grisly rape and murder of twenty-one-year-old Debbie Carter, a cocktail waitress in a raffish bar in the small Oklahoma town of Ada. As novelist John Grisham explained in his first nonfiction book, *The Innocent Man*, there were no eyewitnesses; there was intense pressure on the inept local cops and prosecutor to solve the crime. The most logical suspect, Glen Gore, who had been seen in heated conversation with the victim that night, was never fingerprinted or asked for hair or saliva samples—even after he confessed to the murder! Police suppressed his confession because it inconveniently pointed away from their chosen target, the twenty-eight-year-old Williamson. He was "an unemployed guitar picker who lived with his mother, drank too much, and acted strange," Grisham wrote. He also lived near the victim and had twice been acquitted of rape. Fritz was dragged in almost solely because he was a friend of Williamson's. No fingerprint from the scene matched either man—"a gaping hole in the theory that the two were there during a prolonged and violent attack," in Grisham's words.

But like Nifong, the police and prosecutor turned a blind eye to all evidence of innocence while putting the men on trial based on two inconclusive polygraph tests and patently unreliable testimony from jailhouse snitches and the real killer, Gore. The prosecutor and cops suppressed exculpatory evidence, including a two-hour videotaped statement in which Williamson credibly maintained his innocence. The defense lawyers were as inept as the cops. The jury was hot to sentence someone to death and unconcerned about the possibility of innocence. Williamson ended up with a death sentence and Fritz with life in prison. They were saved, and released in 1999, only because of the extraordinary work of a lawyer named Mark Barrett, who handled death-row appeals for indigents, and the Innocence Project, which used DNA testing to prove that Gore was the killer.

In a subsequent civil lawsuit, in 2002, a federal judge wrote: "The repeated omission of exculpatory evidence by investigators while including inculpatory evidence, inclusion of debatably fabricated evidence, failure to follow obvious and apparent leads which implicated other individuals, and the use of questionable forensic conclusions suggests that the prosecutor and police were acting deliberately toward the specific end result of prosecution of Williamson and Fritz without regard to the warning signs along the way that their end result was unjust and not supported by the facts of their investigation."

New York: Roy Brown

Roy Brown spent fifteen years in New York prisons for a 1991 murder that he did not commit. The prosecutorial misconduct that helped convict him included suppressing police reports that implicated another man and an exculpatory expert analysis of bite marks on the victim. She was beaten, strangled, bitten all over her body, and stabbed in 1991 near the upstate New York farmhouse where she lived. Brown became a suspect because of threatening calls he had made to the social service agency where the victim worked concerning its placement of his son. The prosecution's centerpiece was an inexpert local dentist's "expert" testimony that the seven bite marks on the victim were "entirely consistent" with Brown. The district attorney, Paul Carbonaro, also commissioned an analysis by Lowell Levine, the state's leading forensic dentist. But when Levine told Carbonaro that Roy Brown was not the biter, they agreed that Levine would prepare no report and the DA's office unethically hid Levine's powerfully exculpatory findings from the defense. Just before Brown's trial, when his lawyers approached Levine about becoming an expert witness for the defense, he turned them away without mentioning that he had already excluded Brown as the biter. Might this have been because Levine is regularly paid to be a prosecution expert?

Brown cracked his own case from prison by using Freedom of Information laws to get previously withheld documents implicating a man named Barry Bench. Brown mailed Bench a letter warning that he was going to use DNA testing to prove Bench's guilt. Five days later, Bench committed suicide by lying down in the path of an Amtrak train. The Innocence Project took

Brown's case and proved through DNA testing that the saliva stains left by the biter/killer excluded Brown and matched Bench. Brown was released from prison and exonerated in early 2007.

New York: Douglas Warney

Douglas Warney spent ten years in New York prisons for a murder he did not commit before being exonerated and released in May 2006. The victim, William Beason, of Rochester, was stabbed to death in his home, apparently during a burglary, in 1996. Warney, with an IQ of 68 and a history of mental-health issues and making false reports to police, was convicted based on a confession he gave police after hours of interrogation. The confession was riddled with inconsistencies, transparently bogus, and produced by coaching: Two Rochester police officers fed Warney nonpublic details of the crime; he repeated them; and the cops used this "confession" to justify targeting him as the killer and ignoring other leads. For two years after the Innocence Project took Warney's case, Monroe County district attorney Michael Green fought tooth and nail against requests for DNA testing of tissue found under the victim's fingernails and other evidence. When this DNA finally was tested, it excluded Warney and eventually led to the real killer, Eldred Johnson Jr. He had slashed the throats of two other men in Rochester, nearly killing them, while Warney was serving time for Johnson's murder of Beason. So gross was the misconduct in this case that the Innocence Project charged that the two officers had criminally "created a false confession and then lied to the prosecutor and jury, claming that all the details originated with Douglas." The defense also termed the case "a clarion call for every law enforcement agency in the state to begin recording police interrogations for serious crimes."

Illinois: Rolando Cruz and Alejandro Hernandez

Rolando Cruz, then a teenager, and Alejandro Hernandez were convicted and sentenced to death for the 1983 murder of ten-year-old Jeanine Nicarico in Illinois. Police, under pressure to solve the horrible crime, first picked up Hernandez, who in exchange for a cash reward and other favors pointed them to Cruz. The lead detective in the case resigned before Cruz's trial, saying that prosecutors were pursuing an innocent man. The two were convicted based on supposedly incriminating statements, including what police called "visions" reported by Cruz that resembled aspects of the crime. After Cruz's conviction, a sheriff's detective contradicted police testimony at the trial that while in Illinois the detective had received a key phone call incriminating Cruz; in fact he had been in Florida. And when Brian Dugan, a repeat sex offender who had committed a similar murder, confessed to the crime, with powerful corroborating evidence, the Illinois Supreme Court overturned Cruz's conviction. But prosecutors refused to accept that Cruz was innocent and retried him. Represented by the Innocence Project, both men were exonerated and released in 1995 after DNA tests showed that spermatozoa found near the crime scene could not have come from either of them. Their case was championed by Michael Radutzky, the same 60 *Minutes* producer who oversaw the show's Duke broadcasts.

The Cruz case was one of those that prompted Illinois governor George Ryan, a moderate Republican, to declare a moratorium in 2000 on all executions after finding that his state had a "shameful record of convicting innocent people and putting them on death row." Thirteen of the men condemned in Illinois since 1977 had ultimately been exonerated of murder and set free. That total was one more than the twelve who had been executed.

Then there is the race factor. In the Duke case, Nifong sought black votes by pursuing innocent white suspects. More often it is the other way around.

A classic example was the Stuart case in Massachusetts. Just after a birthing class that Charles Stuart and his wife attended, he told police, he was robbed by a black man who killed his pregnant wife and shot him as well. Judge Nancy Gertner, who before taking the bench had represented Charles Stuart's brother Matthew, recalled in a March 2007 speech what happened next:

> [Charles Stuart's] claims set off an extraordinary manhunt that ripped this city apart, that sent the police illegally stopping black men on the street, sweeping the African American neighborhoods and ultimately focusing on one black man who was not guilty. Willie Bennett was about to be indicted for a murder he did not commit.
>
> Stuart was guilty; he had shot his wife and turned the gun on himself to make it look good. Buried in the police files was the statement of a witness, a friend, to whom Charles Stuart had confessed to the crime. The friend told the police. But unlike the African American witnesses whom the police interrogated for hours, until they incriminated Bennett, the friend was never questioned—not even for a moment. Not one police officer followed up the lead. And for his part, Charles Stuart's brother, Matthew Stuart, had told 20 or 30 people of his suspicions about Charles. Again, no one followed up.
>
> Why? Charles Stuart's story fit the racial stereotypes of the public— black-on-white crime. The police and the public easily—too easily—ignored

the other credible stories—husband killing his wife, especially when she was pregnant. In fact, Chuck's story was the less probable one: most crime is not interracial. Whenever the police learned a fact inconsistent with their stereotypes, they rejected it. It was just a fortuity that the truth was finally told. Matthew finally went to the police; word got out that Charles was implicated and he committed suicide.

In another form of police misconduct, Judge Gertner added, "Stuart identified Willie Bennett as his assailant under circumstances that strongly suggested he was coached. While he could only describe the killer as 'African American,' wearing a running suit, just after the crime, by the time of the eyewitness ceremony, he, a white man, was able to discourse about skin color, and hair curl—and identify the wrong man."

The problem of wrongful convictions typically takes on a different aspect in federal cases. In the run of state cases, on charges such as murder, rape, robbery, and burglary, it is usually clear that a crime has been committed and the question is who did it. (The Duke lacrosse case and many acquaintance-rape cases are exceptional in this regard.) In many federal cases, on vague charges such as mail fraud and political corruption, it is often clear what the defendant did and the question is whether it was a crime. "Vague criminal statutes in the federal system account for what appears to be a new wave of false, or at least unjust convictions," according to Boston civil liberties lawyer Harvey Silverglate, who is writing a book on that subject.

Most affluent Americans little imagine how their own lives could be trashed by a dishonest or an overzealous prosecutor. But this can happen to the rich and prominent as well as to the poor and downtrodden. Indeed, ambitious prosecutors tend to target the rich and famous so that they can climb to higher office on publicity bonanzas having little to do with the strength of the evidence.

And contrary to popular myth, fat wallets and expensive lawyers are no guarantee that defendants—even innocent ones—will be acquitted. Prosecutorial distortions sometimes convict innocent defendants no matter how skilled their lawyers. So do the incomprehension or the racial, class, political, or simply pro-prosecution biases of some judges and jurors.

Nifong's orchestration of the Duke lacrosse rape fraud aroused the concerns of many well-off people who had not previously given much thought to the dangers of rogue prosecutors and police. On such issues, says Joe Cheshire, "A liberal is a conservative who has had his child charged with a crime."

The flaw in our criminal justice system exemplified most directly by the Duke case is the unchecked, almost absolute power of prosecutors such as

Nifong to force people to undergo the ordeal and expense of months under indictment and a criminal trial even in the face of proof that they are innocent. Almost everywhere in this country, if a prosecutor is determined to force you to stand trial for a crime that you can prove you did not commit, few obstacles to such a course exist. Certainly the media will not stop him, as journalists proved in the Duke case. "Reporters feed at the trough of prosecutors every day," notes Silverglate. "They will not readily cross a prosecutor."

Grand juries in most states, as in North Carolina, act as rubber stamps because they see only the evidence shown to them by the prosecutor, who— the U.S. Supreme Court has held—has no constitutional obligation to tell them about evidence of innocence, no matter how strong. Many states do not allow defense lawyers the broad access to prosecution evidence that North Carolina legislated in its 2004 open discovery statute. And many do not empower or encourage judges to dismiss before trial prosecutions based on manifestly bogus or insufficient evidence.

As a result, most judges—especially elected judges—do little or nothing either to curb prosecutorial misconduct or to bring to an end prosecutions of demonstrably innocent defendants. So the only thing standing between a defendant persecuted by a bad prosecutor and conviction is usually the hope of a jury acquittal after a full trial.

Well, some might say, why isn't such a jury trial an adequate remedy for any prosecutorial overreaching? Aren't criminal cases supposed to be decided by trials? And if the defendants are innocent, won't they be acquitted?

The answers: In the real world, most defendants do not get a very good defense at trial, and innocence is no guarantee of acquittal. In the real world, only a tiny fraction of criminal complaints lead to trials; prosecutors decline to pursue many weak claims (especially rape claims); and the vast majority of charged cases end in plea bargains. And those defendants who do stand trial— even if acquitted—are put through a harrowing and hugely expensive ordeal that should never be inflicted on any demonstrably innocent defendant.

"It's hard to explain what it's like to somebody who has not sat through a trial as a criminal defendant, if you're innocent," explains Joe Cheshire. "It's economically destructive to you. It's psychologically destructive to you. It's physically destructive to you. The national media are chasing you to your car every day. It is one of the most awful things you could possibly go through. These gladiators are fighting and you are the prize, and if your gladiator loses, you die."

What can be done to protect against future Nifong-like abuses, and less extreme prosecutorial misconduct, in North Carolina and around the country?

Disbarring Nifong himself would be a good start. (Criminal prosecution of him and his accomplices would be even better.) As of May 2007, the North Carolina State Bar appeared very serious about disciplining the Durham DA. "What is most hopeful about what's happening to Nifong is that people will now pay attention," says Barry Scheck of the Innocence Project. If more prosecutors had to worry about being suspended or disbarred, fewer would abuse their powers.

A disbarment or prosecution of Nifong would, moreover, be a sharp departure from standard practice, as is illustrated by the North Carolina State Bar cases discussed above. Typically, even prosecutors caught in gross violations of the legal ethics rules are almost never held to account by their colleagues who run state bar associations, by other prosecutors, or by judges. "Many prosecutors . . . were cited multiple times for misconduct," the "Harmful Error" study found. "These prosecutors give recidivism—a word usually used to describe those they work to put behind bars—a disturbing new meaning." In a book entitled *Prosecutorial Misconduct*, Bennett L. Gershman documents hundreds of reported cases of misconduct so serious as to warrant state bar discipline. But hardly any of them led to such discipline. And even in those rare cases, the sanction was usually a slap on the wrist.

Perhaps the Nifong example will change this pattern of coddling even the most unethical prosecutors. It should.

Apart from professional discipline, perhaps the most important step that legislators can take to prevent rogue prosecutors from victimizing demonstrably innocent people is to undertake a serious reform of the grand jury process, to restore that institution to its mythical role as a bulwark against prosecutorial abuse.

While grand juries in most states provide no real protection against prosecutions of innocent people—because prosecutors control everything the grand jurors hear and see, sometimes without even a transcript to keep them honest—it doesn't have to be that way.

In New York and some other states, the rules allow grand juries to act as a real check. For example, in New York people targeted by prosecutors for indictment have a right to tell their stories to the grand jury, with counsel present. Other reforms that could mitigate some of the worst abuses in our criminal justice system include giving a state's governor, attorney general, or (as Roy Copper suggested) supreme court power to force a district attorney out of a case in which he has shown clear bias or used abusive tactics; requiring more reliable eyewitness-identification procedures and barring use of identifications obtained without them; requiring police to tape-record interrogations as a safeguard against officers misrepresenting what was said; adopting standards to prevent prosecutorial and expert-witness distortion of DNA and other forensic evidence;

putting more teeth in open discovery laws such as the one that Nifong so blatantly violated and passing such laws in every state; authorizing judges to dismiss before trial cases in which the evidence is clearly insufficient to establish guilt beyond a reasonable doubt; and removing the obstacles that many convicted defendants still encounter when they seek DNA tests that could establish their innocence.

Every one of these reforms (except the last) would have prevented one or more of the abuses that sustained Mike Nifong's wrongful prosecution of the Duke lacrosse defendants.

Perhaps the most potent reform of all would be to require the prosecution to reimburse the legal costs of, and pay compensation to, all criminal defendants who are found not guilty or otherwise exonerated. Unfortunately, the chance of any such law being adopted in the foreseeable future, anywhere, approaches zero.

For a thoughtful discussion of the above and other reforms to help innocent people, please visit www.innocenceproject.org and click on "FIX the system."

24. PRESUMED GUILTY:

FEMINIST OVERKILL

T O UNDERSTAND THE EAGERNESS with which many presumed the Duke lacrosse players guilty of a brutal rape allegation—and the stubbornness with which many journalists and academics brushed aside the mounting evidence of innocence—look back to a 1990 commencement speech at Yale Law School.

The speaker was Catharine MacKinnon, a Yale professor whose statuesque physical presence added force to her words. "Look to your left, look to your right, look in front of you, and look behind you," she began, as one of the graduating students that day recalls. "Statistics tell us you have just laid eyes on someone guilty of sexual assault."

This claim was nonsense, of course. MacKinnon was also talking nonsense in her 1989 magnum opus, *Toward a Feminist Theory of the State*, when she questioned "whether consent is a meaningful concept" and implied that *all* sex is akin to rape: "Perhaps the wrong of rape has proved so difficult to define because the unquestionable starting point has been that rape is defined as distinct from intercourse, while for women it is difficult to distinguish the two under conditions of male dominance." MacKinnon followed Andrea Dworkin's 1987 book *Intercourse*, which declared penetration itself a form of "occupation" and a "violation of female boundaries," however enthusiastically enjoyed by "the occupied person."

But so captivating was the rhetorical power of these radical feminists, and so readily does the academic world lap up absurd theories casting men (especially white men) as demons, that MacKinnon and Dworkin became cult figures. They were treated as leading authorities by a generation of law professors and students. Through like-minded journalists and others, the radical feminists' influence reached far beyond the academic world.

To a point, this movement was an overdue backlash against an era when real rape victims were not taken seriously and legal rules were rigged against them. Under the common law, men had a legal right to rape their wives. And under both the common law and the laws of most states until the 1960s, rape was defined so narrowly that women had to prove that they had resisted fiercely, even though many were and are advised to give in without struggle to a rapist lest they be killed or harmed. In addition, in many states no man could be convicted of rape based solely on the testimony of a woman. There had to be corroborating evidence, such as bruises or ripped clothing suggesting a struggle. And it was open season for defense lawyers to probe into the alleged victim's private life and drag out any history of less-than-virginal prior conduct.

Some of these old rules reflected a dilemma that remains as real today: In a large percentage of "he said, she said" sex crimes, the truth as to whether the woman consented or not is fundamentally unknowable. As the seventeenth-century English jurist Sir Matthew Hale wrote, rape "is an accusation easily to be made and hard to be proved, and harder to be defended by the party accused, tho never so innocent." Under the old criminal-law maxim that it is better for ten guilty people go free than for one innocent to be convicted, and the constitutional requirement of proof beyond a reasonable doubt, substantial numbers of rapists went free even in the face of strong evidence of guilt. This necessary cost of fairness to defendants left many victims humiliated by the legal system.

Whatever the rules, sexist attitudes were pervasive among police, prosecutors, and judges. Cops in the Baltimore police districts frequented by one of the authors of this book as a young reporter in the early 1970s, for example, often dismissed rape claims with mocking phrases such as "assault with a friendly weapon" and "unauthorized use," the charge brought against teenage kids for joyriding in other people's cars.

By the 1970s, a consensus emerged that these rules and attitudes needed to change. And change they did, so that women terrorized into involuntary sex could come forward with a reasonable chance of seeing their assailants convicted and without fear of seeing irrelevant details of their sex lives explored in open court.

But the changes have gone too far, driven by radical feminists' wild exaggerations of the extent of male sexual predation and female victimization and their empirically untenable view that women never (or hardly ever) lie about rape. In effect, the radical feminists' push has been for a regime that guarantees no rapist go unpunished, but any such regime would inevitably convict a great many innocent men. Simple morality, as well as the criminal-justice tradition, argues for an equilibrium in the difficult area of rape law that protects rape victims from undue humiliation without destroying the lives of innocent men. Terrible as it is for a victim to see a rapist escape punishment, it is far, far worse for an innocent person to be convicted of a sex crime.

By the time that the Duke lacrosse case was becoming a national sensation, the legal and cultural pendulums had swung so far as to invert the hallowed presumption that people are innocent until proven guilty. In today's politically correct world, men accused of rape often face a de facto presumption of guilt that is hard to dispel no matter how strong the evidence of innocence. Affluent white men accused of raping poor black women are especially ripe targets.

Indeed, two of the most publicized gang-rape claims in modern history—the 1987 Tawana Brawley case and the 2006 Duke lacrosse case—involved black women accusing white men, and both turned out to be frauds. Meanwhile, as Robert Woodson Sr. wrote in a syndicated column, "There are thousands of black women and children literally assaulted very day, and their condition and their plight is unnoticed and ignored—because their assailants are of their own same race."

The Duke lacrosse players were able to prove their innocence beyond a shadow of a doubt. But had the evidence of innocence been less overwhelming or the defense lawyers less effective, these innocent young men might well have been convicted and imprisoned for decades.

The presumed-guilty mind-set was epitomized by Wendy Murphy: "These guys, like so many rapists—and I'm going to say it because, at this point, she's entitled to the respect that she is a crime victim." Murphy's comment, on CNN's *Nancy Grace* show, came just hours after the April 10, 2006, release of stunningly powerful DNA evidence of the lacrosse players' innocence.

"For so long," Jim Cooney reflected after his client Reade Seligmann and the other lacrosse players had been declared innocent, "rape victims were poorly treated by the legal system and, as a result, there was much to be ashamed of. In the 1970s and 1980s, the pendulum began to swing and we entered an era in which rape victims were always believed and the defendant was presumed guilty because it became wrong to question a victim of rape. We see this in spades now in child molestation cases in which the same issues have taken place. The pendulum somehow needs to be brought back to the center to the point where legitimate victims do not have to have their entire sexual histories revealed, but defendants are permitted to make legitimate and real inquires into the truth of what is said."

False Rape Reports: How Common?

The entire extreme feminist project to import a presumption of guilt into the law and attitudes concerning rape has been erected on a false factual premise: that women hardly ever (or even never) lie about rape. Indeed, Professor

Dershowitz was once accused of sexual harassment merely for discussing the possibility of false rape reports in a Harvard Law School class. Many law professors avoid classroom discussion of rape lest they be similarly attacked.

A clear understanding of the frequency of false rape claims is critical to crafting just laws and rules of evidence for such cases. Were it true that women never lie, there *should be* a de facto presumption of guilt. In acquaintance-rape cases that do not present the pitfalls of eyewitness identification, the woman's word alone would be a smoking gun pointing to an inevitable conclusion, in every case.

But the fact is that "innocent men are arrested and even imprisoned as a result of bogus claims, and the precious resources of criminal justice agencies are wasted," as Linda Fairstein, former head of the sex-crimes unit of the Manhattan District Attorney's Office, wrote in "Why Some Women Lie About Rape," in *Cosmopolitan* magazine, in 2003. "These falsehoods trivialize the experience of every rape survivor." Fairstein also wrote: "There are about 4,000 reports of rape each year in Manhattan. Of these, about half simply did not happen."

The standard assertion by feminists that only 2 percent of rape claims are false, which traces to Susan Brownmiller's 1975 book *Against Our Will*, is without empirical foundation and belied by a wealth of empirical data. These data suggest that at least 9 percent and probably closer to half of all rape claims are false:

- FBI statistics say conservatively that about 9 percent of rape reports are "unfounded" in the sense of being dismissed without charges filed, usually because the accuser recants or her account is contradicted by other evidence.

- Forty-one percent of 109 rape complainants eventually admitted to police that no rape had occurred, according to a careful, highly regarded 1994 study of all rape reports in a midwestern town of about 70,000 between 1978 and 1987, by Purdue sociologist Eugene J. Kanin, Ph.D. The recantations made irrelevant the claims of many feminists that police often discount valid rape claims. And because there is no reason to suppose that *all* false accusers recanted, the total number of false reports probably exceeded 41 percent. The police in the study made serious efforts to polygraph both the accused and the accuser; it is now much more rare for police to polygraph rape accusers, due to pressure from feminist and victims' rights groups more interested in convictions than in truth.

Kanin also concluded that "these false charges were able to serve three major functions for the complainants: providing an alibi, a means of gaining revenge, and a platform for seeking attention/sympathy. This tripartite model resulted from the complainants' own verbalizations during recantation and does not constitute conjecture." Other experts note other motives for false rape claims; they include remorse after an impulsive sexual fling and escaping accountability when caught in an embarrassing consensual encounter.

- Fifty percent (32) of accusers recanted their rape charges in a study by Kanin of campus police reports on sixty-four rape claims at two large, unnamed Midwestern universities. In both universities, the taking of the complaint and the follow-up investigation were done by a ranking female officer. "Quite unexpectedly then," Kanin wrote, "we find that these university women, when filing a rape complaint, were as likely to file a false as a valid charge. Other reports from university police agencies support these findings."

- False rape accusations occur with scary frequency and "any honest veteran sex assault investigator will tell you that rape is one of the most falsely reported crimes," Craig Silverman, a former Colorado prosecutor known for his zealous pursuit of alleged rapists, said in 2004 as a commentator on the Kobe Bryant case for Denver's ABC affiliate. Silverman added that a Denver sex-assault unit commander had estimated that nearly 50 percent of reported rape claims are false.

- Fraudulent rape complaints were perceived as a problem by 73 percent of the women and 72 percent of the men in a survey of students at the Air Force Academy, West Point, and the Naval Academy, according to a March 2005 Defense Department report.

- One in four rape reports was unfounded in a 1990–1991 *Washington Post* investigation in seven Virginia and Maryland counties. When contacted by the *Post*, many of the alleged victims admitted that they had lied.

Apart from false rape claims, there is a very high incidence of mistaken identities (if a lower incidence of fabrication) when women accuse strangers of rape. "Every year since 1989, in about 25 percent of the sexual assault cases referred to the FBI where [DNA] results could be obtained, . . . the primary suspect has been excluded by forensic DNA testing," Peter Neufeld and Barry Scheck of the Innocence Project wrote in 1996. "Specifically, FBI officials report that out of roughly 10,000 sexual assault cases since 1989, about 2,000 tests have been inconclusive, . . . about 2,000 tests have excluded the primary suspect, and about 6,000 have 'matched' or included the primary suspect."

Media Bias Toward Presuming Guilt

Nobody dependent on the mainstream media for information about rape would have any idea how frequent false claims are. Most journalists simply ignore evidence contradicting the feminist line. They also slip sometimes into the habit of calling a rape complainant "the victim"—with no "alleged"—as did *The N&O* in its first big story on the Duke lacrosse case. Worse, they send a "victim" message in virtually every case through their policies of identifying all rape defendants while at the same time protecting the anonymity of almost all rape complainants.

The latter policy dates to the 1970s. It is rooted in a valid concern that women would suffer a social stigma if identified publicly as rape accusers (or victims), and that this would make others more reluctant to come forward and report rapes. "That is a powerful justification," as Duke student columnist Kristin Butler wrote on February 6 in *The Chronicle*. Indeed, 60 percent of rape and sexual assault victims do not report the crime to authorities, according to the Justice Department's National Crime Victimization Survey; most indicate that they would be less likely to report rapes if they knew their names would be published by the news media.

But Butler also wondered about the media double standard implicit in identifying rape defendants such as Dave Evans, Reade Seligmann, and Collin Finnerty, who were made into symbols of sexual assault from coast to coast. This double standard in effect presumes the guilt of all accused males and the truthfulness of all accusing females. And the stigma inherent in identifying a man as an alleged rapist is far, far worse than that inherent in identifying a woman as an alleged victim.

"If you are even accused of a sex crime, no matter how unjustly, your life is toast," columnist Tom Jicha wrote in the October 30, 2006, *Sun-Sentinel*. "As long as this stigma exists, basic fairness dictates that until there is a conviction, the accused deserves the same protection as the accuser. There is precedent. Some of society's most violent crimes are committed by minors. Yet no matter how heinous the offense, the identity of the alleged youthful offender is withheld by many news organizations. Given what has happened to their lives,

Seligmann, Evans and Finnerty would have been treated with more discretion by the media if they were remorseless 16-year-old serial killers."

Some in the media—including *The New York Times*, of course—continue to protect the anonymity of false accusers such as Crystal Mangum *even after* they have been proven beyond any doubt to be vicious liars bent on sending innocent men to prison. Tom Vaden, the public editor for *The N&O*, asserted on January 28 that his newspaper would continue to protect the Duke lacrosse accuser's anonymity even after the expected dismissal of the charges. He said this was necessary to assure "future victims that they can report a crime without wider exposure, even if the case goes against them." This view, wrote Butler, "takes an otherwise-justifiable double standard to an almost frightening extreme. For one thing, there is no especially compelling reason to believe that printing the names of false accusers will keep future victims from reporting rapes; there is, however, evidence to suggest that false rape allegations are much more common than many people are aware, and that the media's policies may even create a perverse incentive to cry rape. . . . I wonder, then, if we can continue justifying a media policy that creates a byproduct as serious as the problem it addresses."

The N&O eventually did publish Mangum's name, after the lacrosse players had been declared innocent by Attorney General Cooper. Perhaps it was shamed by Butler's evisceration of Vaden. Or perhaps the unmistakable clarity of the proof forced the newspaper to change its approach.

Professional Victim Advocates

Part of the drive to help rape victims has been the creation of a corps of professionals to examine them and tend to their needs, including SANE nurses such as trainee Tara Levicy in the Duke case and rape crisis counselors. These people often provide services to alleged victims of rape while the related criminal cases are being prepared or are pending.

These are welcome innovations, bringing specialized expertise to the process of determining the validity of rape claims as well as comfort for rape victims. But many of the women who choose such careers see themselves as advocates for rape accusers. And when advocates play critical roles in gathering and describing evidence, there is a danger that their ideological commitments will trump open-minded analysis of all available evidence.

Tara Levicy, for example, made it absolutely clear when interviewed by a defense lawyer in the Duke case that she'd never met a rape accuser whom she doubted. She also explained away the absence of any semen in Mangum after the alleged rape with the glib mantra that rape "is about power, not passion."

Of course, the same theorists who say that rape is about power also say that rapists seek power over women precisely *by inseminating them.*

"Tara Levicy's stridency and inability even to examine an opposite point of view had a lot to do with the genesis of this case," Joe Cheshire said as the case wound down. "There are people like her in hospitals all over this country. A lot of SANE nurses believe that if a woman comes in and says a penis raped her, then a penis raped her. It's a systemic problem all over this country."

"Victim advocate" support service providers have become an especially potent interest group in the Defense Department, which hires them to deal with sexual assault complaints by women at the service academies and in the military. These contractors have every incentive to exaggerate the amount of sexual assault. For them, "bad news is good news," Elaine Donnelly, president of the Center for Military Readiness, said in House testimony in June 2006. "This is a special interest like all others, with professional contractors seeking millions of Defense Department dollars for multi-year projects, career opportunities, prestigious offices, conferences, surveys, and provocative performances about date rape."

Police Practices

In past decades, polygraph tests were often a useful tool in rape investigations. While their scientific accuracy in detecting lies is very much in dispute, they are unquestionably effective in scaring many liars into coming clean. Dave Evans, Matt Zash, and Danny Flannery volunteering to take police polygraph tests was powerful (though not conclusive) evidence of their innocence. And when a rape accuser refuses to take such a test, it warrants suspicion that she may be lying.

Crystal Magnum was never even asked to take a polygraph. This was part of Nifong's pattern of conscious avoidance of evidence of innocence. The decision also reflects the success of rape victims' advocates in lobbying state and local governments to ban or discourage police from asking rape accusers to take polygraph tests. They have contended that women will be discouraged from reporting sexual assaults if police don't simply take them at their word, without question.

If accusers are asked to take polygraphs, "Reporting will just stop; then you'll have open season for the predators in the community," Sabrina Garcia, a sexual assault specialist for the Chapel Hill, North Carolina, Police Department, told *The N&O* in May 2006. The article reported that a recent proposed amendment to a federal law aimed to end police polygraphing of rape accusers by withholding millions in federal grants to states that don't stop using them by 2008.

Forensic Evidence

Some feminists have a perverse attitude toward the availability of DNA evidence, which can be a miraculous truth-finding device. Such evidence has supported many rape claims. But it has also helped prove that women claiming rape do lie in many cases and are mistaken about the alleged rapist's identity in many more. The radical feminist response? Don't trust DNA.

The Law Concerning Rape

Mike Nifong repeatedly suggested that he had no choice but to bring charges as long as the accuser claimed to have been assaulted, no matter how many times she contradicted herself or how strong the evidence that she was lying. This was false. But it's true that prosecutors often come under strong community pressure give the accuser "her day in court," as Durham minister Carl Kenney demanded in an October 16, 2006, *Herald-Sun* roundtable. It's also true that once a prosecutor decides to take a case to trial and an accuser testifies that the defendant raped her, the law of North Carolina and many states makes it hard for a judge to dismiss the charges no matter how implausible.

As Nifong showed so dramatically, not all prosecutors can be trusted to screen out even the most obviously bogus rape claims. And jurors are no more flawless than prosecutors. Indeed, in North Carolina and many other states, a defendant who can absolutely prove his innocence—most obviously Reade Seligmann in the lacrosse case—can nonetheless *still* be convicted, based solely on the word of the accuser. The relevant section from the North Carolina general statutes states that an accuser "naming the person accused, the date of the offense, the county in which the offense of rape was allegedly committed, and the averment 'with force and arms' . . . will support a verdict of guilty of rape in the first degree, rape in the second degree, attempted rape or assault on a female."

Nifong's defenders argued—perhaps correctly—that the sweeping nature of this statute would prevent a judge, as a matter of law, from dismissing the rape charge against Seligmann even though he could prove, through unimpeachable electronic evidence, that he could not possibly be guilty. Such provisions are unique to rape law—they do not exist for defendants charged with murder or simple assault—and are offensive to common sense and decency.

Rape Shield Laws

Some defendants are also unduly hobbled by the breadth of some of the rape shield laws adopted since the 1970s by every state and by Congress with the laudable goal of protecting rape accusers from humiliating public explorations into irrelevant details of their private sex lives. Many of these laws can be read as ruling out even quite *relevant* evidence that reasonable jurors would want to know before voting whether or not to convict.

The mere fact that a woman has been sexually promiscuous, for example, is properly excluded because its prejudicial impact outweighs its slight, or nonexistent, probative value. But evidence of prior sexual activities with the accused and of any prior rape claims that appear to have been false has obvious relevance. So does evidence that the accuser has used the same modus operandi to seduce other men that she used with the defendant (or that he claims she used). And so does evidence that the rape accuser is a prostitute, who may be claiming rape because of a disagreement over money.

Some rape shield laws, however, are so broadly worded that they can be read as barring such evidence. Indeed, such laws have produced some outrageous injustices.

Oliver Jovanovic, a thirty-two-year-old Columbia University student, had begun a relationship with a twenty-two-year-old Barnard student in 1996 with e-mail exchanges lasting about six months in which the two discussed their interest in sadomasochistic sex. Both of them testified that the woman had gone voluntarily to Jovanovic's apartment, stripped naked, and consented to being tied to a futon. Here their testimony diverged. She claimed that for the next twenty hours, he held her against her will, tortured, and sodomized her. Jovanovic said that she had consented to everything. The rape shield law kicked in when she testified that she had never expressed interest in sadomasochism. This was a lie, and defense lawyers sought to introduce e-mail exchanges to show it. But Manhattan Supreme Court Justice William Wetzel held that New York's rape shield law required excluding key e-mails because they described prior sexual encounters with other men. This decision allowed the woman to mislead the jury.

And in a 1997 case, sportscaster Marv Albert was accused in Arlington, Virginia, of assault and battery when an ex-lover alleged that he had bitten her during a sexual encounter. The judge allowed the prosecution to use testimony by other ex-lovers of Albert about his alleged proclivity for rough sex. But when Albert's lawyers asked to call witnesses who would testify that the accuser had a history of making false assault and rape accusations against former lovers, the judge said no, citing a rape shield law to justify the blatant double standard. Albert was forced into a plea bargain.

The danger of such miscarriages of justice persuaded the United Kingdom's Law Lords to rule in 2001 that Parliament's rape shield law breached defendants' fair trial rights. A 2004 study funded by the Criminal Bar Association and the University of Wales, Aberystwyth, based on interviews with seventy-seven British judges, reached the same conclusion.

Free Passes for False Accusers

Intentionally making a false accusation of criminal conduct against another person is itself a crime, as, of course, is lying under oath. Yet prosecutors almost never go after false rape accusers. Nor should they do so as in every case in which a rape defendant is found not guilty. The fact that proof of rape beyond a reasonable doubt is lacking does not necessarily establish that the accusation is false. And even accusers who admit that they have lied should usually be given a break lest other false accusers be deterred from recanting by fear of punishment.

But when it is clear that the accuser has lied and refuses to recant, the accuser should be prosecuted for trying to ruin an innocent person's life and to deter others from doing the same. At first blush, Crystal Mangum might appear a ripe target for prosecution, a malicious liar who deserves to rot in prison for a long time. But North Carolina attorney general Roy Cooper, alluding to her severe mental illnesses—details of which remain secret—said that he would not prosecute her because she seemed so deluded as to believe her own false accusations. It's also hard to imagine a Durham jury convicting her. And she might have a plausible insanity defense. And prosecutors are not supposed to bring cases they have no chance of winning. So the decision not to prosecute may be justifiable—in this case.

Unjust Prosecutions

The dangers of prosecuting and even convicting probably innocent men on weak rape charges, and of drumming innocent students out of universities, is very real. It has happened, and will continue to happen unless something changes.

A leading example is the case of Kobe Bryant. The NBA basketball star was indicted after a hotel clerk who had flirted with him, gone to his bedroom, and voluntarily engaged in passionate kissing claimed that he had raped her after she tried to stop. She had a long history of mental problems and falsely denied having had sex with other men not long before her encounter with

Bryant. She also brought a civil lawsuit seeking millions in damages. The criminal case was dropped when she refused to testify. Although she managed to extract a financial settlement in the civil suit, this reflected the risks faced by a very rich black defendant were he to stand trial before a white (or mostly white) jury on charges of raping a white woman.

The same forces that took the treatment of rape allegations to guilt-presuming extremes worked a similar change in the handling of child-sex-abuse allegations, especially in a rash of cases in the 1980s involving day-care centers, with bizarre tales of satanic rituals conducted in secret "clown rooms" and the like. The excesses of those prosecutions were epitomized by the conviction of Bernard Baran Jr. in 1985, when he was nineteen, of molesting five children at a Pittsfield, Massachusetts, day-care center. Reversing his conviction in an eighty-page June 2006 ruling, Superior Court Justice Francis Fecteau described how Baran had been indicted based on misleading snippets of videotaped interviews of small children. After years during which prosecutors claimed that the full tapes were "lost," they turned up. They showed, according to Harvey Silverglate, one of Baran's lawyers, that: "The crimes never occurred. No one molested these kids. They learned how to testify about where Bernie stuck his pee-pee by being brainwashed by social workers and cops using anatomically correct dolls."

The Campus Date-Rape Crusade

Part of the feminist revolution on rape was the creation at universities of rules and bureaucracies that often bring a heavy presumption of guilt to their assigned task of punishing male students and professors accused of raping female students. Some such cases develop into criminal prosecutions and ruin the lives of innocent (or at least not provably guilty) young men.

A heartbreaking article about such a case appeared in *The New York Times* in January 2007. It was about a Harvard student charged with rape by a fellow student in 1999, after they had climbed drunk into her bed, had sex, and she had become hysterical. Bewildered, the boy apologized profusely. This was used to help railroad him out of Harvard in a grossly unfair disciplinary proceeding. He was also criminally prosecuted and forced to plea-bargain to an indecent-assault charge—with eighteen months of house arrest, an electronic ankle bracelet, and rehabilitation counseling—to avoid the risk of a long prison term. The article was by Ashley Cross, who had become his girlfriend during all this and had learned not to "assume the guilt of intoxicated boys in the company of intoxicated girls everywhere." She explained how the rape charges had broken "this smart, gentle guy" and "extinguished the remaining spark he had left, the irreverence I'd originally fallen in love with." Cross closed: "I'll always regret what might have been. His ordeal will always haunt me. In my mind, he was not seeking to humiliate and subjugate a woman on that night many years ago. I believe he was a boy who endeavored for hours in the dark to express his drunken, fumbling desire in a way that, fair or not, ended up unraveling his life. I wish he had found me first."

LAMAR OWENS

A twenty-three-year-old African-American Naval Academy student and star football captain with limitless potential, Lamar Owens his career derailed by a bogus rape charge by a white woman whose violations of Navy rules were worse than his. Owens was resoundingly acquitted of rape in July 2006, after the evidence presented to a military jury showed clearly that his sexual encounter with a female midshipman six months before had been consensual; she had invited him to her room and into her bed after 3 A.M., while her roommate slept ten feet away and the hallway door was propped open with a trash can. The rape prosecution was widely seen as a travesty. But even after Owens was acquitted on the rape charge, he was denied his degree and officer's commission for his admitted act of having consensual sex with his accuser in Bancroft Hall, where all midshipmen are housed. Meanwhile, the false accuser—who had been called a victim in e-mails from top brass to the Naval Academy community and had been immunized in exchange for her testimony against Owens—has graduated and become an officer despite the military judge's finding that her credibility had been "eviscerated."

DAVID SCHAER

A twenty-year-old Brandeis junior, David Schaer was accused of rape in 1996 by a former girlfriend. After a night of drinking, the woman had called Schaer twice asking that he come to her room to "fool around" sexually. The initially reluctant boy arrived and they engaged in foreplay. But she later complained to the university that she had said she did not want to have sex, had gone to sleep, and had awakened to find him having sex with her. Weeks later, Schaer was summoned by Alwina Bennett, a Brandeis Student Life official. Together with the complaining woman, Bennett confronted him and asked why he felt he was there. Schaer, upset by the woman's evident unhappiness with the encounter, responded: "I think you feel I took advantage of a friend." Near tears, he also tried to tell Bennett that the woman had ardently urged him to have sex and had gotten a condom from her desk for him. The Brandeis official refused to hear him out, saying that "I am the complainant's support here." At Schaer's disciplinary hearing, the woman and Schaer told their stories; Bennett portrayed his response to her "why do you think you are here" question as an admission of guilt; another witness called Schaer an "egotistical bastard who had no respect for women"; and a female campus cop said that the woman "looked like a rape victim." The panel of six students and two faculty members found Schaer guilty of "unwanted sexual activity" and suspended him for more than three months over the summer. The woman's supporters confronted Schaer with "Rapist Go Home" signs and the school treated him as an outcast.

Schaer challenged the Brandeis process in the Massachusetts courts, showing that the disciplinary panel had allowed irrelevant and inflammatory evidence and violated the university's own procedural rules. With ten private colleges in the area filing friend-of-the-court briefs supporting Brandeis, the Massachusetts Supreme Judicial Court (SJC) ruled 3–2 that its treatment of Schaer was protected by academic freedom. This amounted to judicial encouragement of campus kangaroo courts, wrote moderate feminist Wendy Kaminer. She succinctly characterized the majority opinion: "The SJC does not consider it unfair for a private university to take an accusation of rape at face value, effectively presume the guilt of the accused, and find for the complainant after a sham, quasi-judicial proceeding."

RAMDAS LAMB

An assistant professor of religion at the University of Hawaii at Manoa, and a married Hindu monk, Ramdas Lamb was falsely accused of sexual harassment and rape in 1993 by Michelle Gretzinger, a student who had become distraught and angry during classroom discussion. Lamb had expressed skepticism when another student in the class had asserted that women never lie about rape or sexual harassment. Gretzinger—who had previously hung around Lamb's office and called his home late at night, to the annoyance of his wife—stopped participating in classes. This behavior caused Lamb to lower her grade to C at midterm. She complained to Susan Hippensteele, the university's "sexual harassment victims' advocate," who—according to a detailed and sensitive 1999 account of the case by moderate feminist Melanie Thernstrom in *George* magazine—exuded "the impassioned confidence of an ideologue." Gretzinger initially charged Lamb with "offensive language and statements in class regarding women." Hippensteele's initial response included a mandatory sexual harassment workshop for religion faculty, in which she asserted that sexual harassment is all "in the eye of the beholder," that "intention doesn't matter," and that the religion professors should redact from their curricula the "sexist" material that pervades most religious traditions. "My God, this is like Nazi Germany," exclaimed a professor who had grown up in Germany in the 1940s.

Gretzinger's story evolved during months spent conferring with Hippensteele. She now accused Lamb of kissing and fondling her, putting his hands down her pants, twice driving her home after class and raping her, and some fourteen other sexual encounters. Lamb emphatically denied all these charges and could prove that he had been elsewhere on most of these occasions. But a campus disciplinary panel allowed Gretzinger to change dates and other aspects of her story without notice to Lamb. Then, after a "hearing" at which Lamb was permitted neither to cross-examine the woman nor to call witnesses, the panel found that his classroom comments had been "outrageous and insensitive" and that he had sexually harassed Gretzinger by forcing her into a sexual relationship. The panel stressed its view that Gretzinger would not "make up something that would be so potentially damaging to her husband." Gretzinger left him soon thereafter and came out as a lesbian. Hippensteele had previously left her own husband and had a female lover. Lamb was savaged in the media. His guilt was assumed by much of the campus population. He received four death threats. His ten-year-old daughter was taunted at school by kids saying her father was a rapist. The university chancellor reversed the panel and dismissed the case. But Gretzinger and Hippensteele continued a publicity campaign against Lamb. Lamb later countersued Gretzinger (who had sued him and the university) for slander. He introduced evidence of her wildly changing stories and of another rape claim that she had filed, in California, that police elected not to pursue because they thought it was false. Lamb won the defamation suit. But his exoneration "received much less publicity than the allegations had," wrote Thernstrom. "Lamb is a person invested not only in being a good person but in being perceived as a good person—and the loss of that perception was devastating." Hippensteele, meanwhile, was given tenure in the university's Women's Studies Department.

Cathy Young described the trend underlying such cases in a 1999 *Boston Globe* column prompted by the Harvard case:

Once, feminists brought attention to real inequities in how our culture viewed rape. . . . But the pendulum has swung too far. The principle "no means no" is being interpreted so as to criminalize not only sexual coercion but any nonforcible, nonthreatening advances after the first "no."

Likewise, the principle that a woman has not consented to sex if she is violated while unconscious has been extended so far as to claim that a woman whose judgment is impaired by alcohol can retroactively change a "yes" to a "no." (In a notorious recent case at Brown University, the man was accused of sexual assault even though the woman apparently not only consented but initiated sex while intoxicated.) . . . When a woman gets into bed with a man and engages in sex play, she is not inviting rape. But she may be inviting a misunderstanding, particularly if her partner's judgment is impaired just like her own—a misunderstanding that people ought to be able to resolve on a personal level. . . . Our culture's laudable desire to empower women seems to have led to a situation in which the worst biases of the past are merely reversed.

"The distorting impact of political correctness on prosecutions of rape and what are seen as 'hate crimes,' motivated by the alleged victim's race or gender, is the logical outcome of the whole movement to remedy the problems of members of 'historically disadvantaged groups' by dispensing with some of the time-tested principles for keeping the criminal law fair and accurate," in the words of Harvey Silverglate. "This includes the tendency of much of the news media to allow PC to infect its reporting, lest the paper be deemed insufficiently sensitive to the needs of disadvantaged classes. All of this political correctness produces a danger of wrongful convictions, just as racism produced such dangers in prior generations where blacks were the presumed criminals rather than the presumed victims."

25. THE ASSAULT ON EXCELLENCE

T HE PRECEDING PAGES DESCRIBE how many professors and, to a lesser extent, administrators at one of the nation's finest universities chose to grind their radical political axes at the expense of both their own students' well-being and the academy's traditional fidelity to due process. And while the extreme nature of Mike Nifong's abuses of his law-enforcement powers can be seen as in some ways aberrational, the behavior of the Duke faculty and administration was all too representative of today's academy.

In the witch-hunt atmosphere of late March and early April 2006, dozens of Duke professors exploited the lacrosse case to advance their personal, pedagogical, or ideological agendas—at great cost to their own institution's students. The Group of 88 and campus allies such as Peter Wood and Orin Starn abandoned the academy's erstwhile respect for due process and dispassionate evaluation of evidence as an event unfolded before their own eyes that they were certain confirmed their extremist race/class/gender worldviews. Then, as Nifong's case collapsed, the Duke faculty activists not only refused to reconsider their actions but also continued to denounce the lacrosse players and other Duke students while ignoring myriad new facts, showing them to be wrong, that had emerged after the April 6, 2006, Group of 88 ad.

The performance of the Brodhead administration was scarcely better. Though privy to information that strongly suggested the players' innocence, the president's early actions conveyed an impression of guilt. Seemingly unable to move beyond his visceral personal distaste for the hiring of strippers by team leaders (not by sophomores Seligmann and Finnerty), Brodhead portrayed the entire team for months as monolithically of bad character. During the late spring and summer, the administration went out of its way to avoid being confronted with the accumulating evidence of innocence, spurning repeated offers of briefings by defense lawyers and of unfettered access to the entire discovery file. And despite the clear mandate of the Duke Faculty Handbook that professors treat *all* Duke students with respect as fellow members of the academic community, the administration did nothing to discipline—or even express disagreement with—professors who blatantly violated the standard.

Duke differs from most of its peer institutions in two respects. First, it is one of the handful of universities (including Stanford, Northwestern, Vanderbilt, and—except for football, in which it is Division 1-AA—Georgetown) that have attempted to combine academic with athletic excellence. Second, as an affluent, predominantly white institution in a city with a large black and poor population and a neighborhood (Trinity Park) full of politically correct whites, Duke must live with unusually stark town-gown tensions.

In most respects, however, Duke typifies higher education today—making the institution's response to the lacrosse case all the more alarming. Largely outside of public view, America's colleges and universities have dramatically changed in the last quarter century. The transformation dates from the late 1960s and early 1970s, when scholars active in the civil rights, feminist, antipoverty, and antiwar movements sought to make the academic structure more amenable to their political goals. At the same time, black and radical students demanded that universities establish Black Studies departments, often punctuating these demands with violence and threats, as when armed militants occupied Cornell's Student Union building in 1969. Programs or departments in women's studies and ethnic studies usually followed.

In contrast to the traditional disciplines of the liberal arts and sciences, such as history, English, biology, and chemistry, professors in these new fields entered the academy with explicitly political agendas. As Wahneema Lubiano herself explained in 2007, Black Studies faculty sought to "blur the line historically drawn between intellectual work as such and everything else that is recognized as 'political.'" Such attitudes are also spreading like metastasizing cancers through departments of sociology, history, English, anthropology, and other fields in the humanities and social sciences.

The transformation of the academy paralleled societal developments in the late 1960s and 1970s. But in the 1980s, popular attitudes dramatically shifted. Ronald Reagan won forty-four states in 1980 and forty-nine in 1984. The Equal Rights Amendment, which once seemed certain of passage, instead failed to gain support from a sufficient number of states. The change of heart in part reflected a more ambivalent attitude toward the ideologues who had appropriated the once-proud feminist label. More dramatically, a broad societal backlash developed against the increasingly large and rigid racial and gender preferences that had been engineered in the name of affirmative action.

In this newly moderate-to-conservative nation, educators might have explored whether some 1960s-era reforms went too far, and evolved intellectually along with the society around them. Instead, the 1980s witnessed the ascendance in the academy of a quasi-religious worship of diversity, which also boiled down mostly to racial and gender preferences, and which has infected curricular matters and come to affect hiring decisions university-wide.

By the late 1980s, most colleges and universities implemented new policies designed to purge from incoming students' minds the supposedly racist and sexist attitudes of American society. This agenda, which came to be known as "political correctness," aimed to teach students what and how to think about contentious issues involving race and gender, often at the expense of upholding students' civil liberties. The most common tactic was speech codes, vaguely written guidelines prohibiting speech or actions that college bureaucrats might interpret as hostile to women or minorities.

"In a nation whose future depends upon an education in freedom, colleges and universities are teaching the values of censorship, self-censorship, and self-righteous abuse of power," as Boston civil liberties lawyer Harvey Silverglate and Penn professor Alan Charles Kors wrote in their 1998 book, *The Shadow University: The Betrayal of Liberty on America's Campuses.* "Our students are being educated in so-called group rights and responsibilities, and in double standards to redress partisan definitions of historical wrongs. . . . [The norm is] intolerance of dissent from regnant political orthodoxy [and] the belief that universities not only may but should suspend the rights of some in order to transform students, the culture, and the nation according to their ideological vision and desire."

As it happens, one of Richard Brodhead's top advisors, Larry Moneta, played a key role in the highest-profile battle over a campus speech code. This was the notorious 1993 "water buffalo" episode at the University of Pennsylvania, the preeminent example of politically correct censorship gone mad.

Eden Jacobowitz, a freshman, was having trouble concentrating on an English paper because fifteen members of a sorority were loudly singing, chanting, and stomping underneath the windows of his dorm. "Please be quiet," he shouted.

After twenty minutes of even louder noise, Jacobowitz shouted again: "Shut up, you water buffalo." The women were black. That was all the university needed to prosecute the boy for "racial harassment," with potential penalties including expulsion.

No matter that "water buffalo" had never in history been deemed a racial slur, as was established by experts contacted by Jacobowitz's lonely but courageous faculty adviser, Alan Charles Kors. No matter that Jacobowitz had persuasively protested that he "would have said the same thing" had the noisemakers been Orthodox Jewish descendants of Holocaust survivors (like him). No matter that he had offered to meet with the offended women, to apologize for any hurt feelings, and to explain that he had not intended to impugn their race.

Moneta, then a midlevel university bureaucrat to whom Penn's judicial system reported, was instrumental in pressing racial harassment charges. At one point he preposterously stressed to Kors that he had found one dictionary listing Africa among the places where water buffalo roam.

When asked on NBC News whether he had ever heard of "water buffalo" being considered a racial slur, Moneta said: "Language in my mind is neutral. It's a question of the context in which language was used."

To most people, the context was that one student wanted a bunch of others to quiet down so he could work. To university administrators like Moneta, the context was their eagerness to show solidarity with black females in any conflict with a white male.

Kors once reduced the mind-set to a formula: "At universities in the current climate, sexual preference trumps merit; race trumps sexuality; gender, which used to be called sex, trumps race; and careerism trumps everything."

Penn officials knowingly falsified the record to suggest that Jacobowitz had used real racial slurs, not just "water buffalo." They lied to their students. They lied to Kors. They lied to the press. They tried imposing a gag order on Jacobowitz and Kors. They backed down only after publicity about their behavior created an international scandal.

Houston Baker, then a professor at Penn, joined the persecution of Eden Jacobowitz as faculty adviser to the women pressing the "racial harassment" charge. Baker had previously flung his standard "racist" smear at Kors for opposing the campus speech code and mandatory "sensitivity training." It didn't work. Kors was not intimidated by the likes of Baker. But the speech code and indoctrination went forward.

Years later, in 2002, Kors wrote a letter about the water buffalo episode to a student publication at Duke that had done a softball interview of Moneta when he moved up to a bigger job at Duke: "Check your history, and you'll find that Moneta's decision made Penn a national laughingstock. Asked to defend the absurdity of this prosecution, Moneta told the press, 'All speech is contextual.' After the trustees overturned Penn's speech code, the dutiful Moneta told the press, 'At Penn, all speech is free.'"

"If Strom Thurmond had become President of Penn, Larry Moneta would have had a Southern accent by day's end. Before he left Penn, he told me that he only had been following orders. Hold on to your liberties at Duke; watch those double standards; guard your principles dearly; and watch your back."

The water buffalo case was unusual only in the attention it received; such episodes are so common as to make plenty of work for the Foundation for Individual Rights in Education (FIRE), a civil liberties group created solely to defend student victims. But the vast publicity about the water buffalo case briefly shined a light onto the dark underbelly of political correctness in academia. And with lawsuits successfully challenging many speech codes on First Amendment grounds, Penn and most other colleges and universities either repealed or weakened their codes.

Yet the mind-set that led to speech codes remained firmly in place. Indeed, by the late 1990s, many reemerged in the form of pervasively adopted codes banning harassment of ethnic or racial minorities, women, or gays. Colleges justified the new approach by positioning the promotion of diversity as a key or even preeminent tenet of their educational philosophy. This strategy, of course, had the additional benefit of allowing faculty ideologues to maintain their belief systems free from considering new evidence. Sue Estroff, chair of the faculty at UNC from 2000 to 2003, boasted of her unwillingness to change in a 2002 interview with *The Chronicle*: "The cohort of people who are [senior faculty members] now on most university campuses are people like me, who went to college in the '60s and were part of that upheaval, who cut their teeth on a different kind of political activism and some radicalism."

The people who pay the bills—parents who make tuition payments and alumni who make donations—proved, by and large, oblivious to these changes. Alumni often see colleges and universities through the haze of affectionate allegiance, legacy preferences, and, for the largest donors, as places where they can get buildings named after them. Parents too often view institutions of higher education as credentialing bodies to ensure that their children can get good jobs rather than as centers of real education. Most parents and alumni, meanwhile, understandably feel reluctant to challenge professors on specific texts assigned in courses, or on decisions about who should be hired as new faculty members.

More sensible administrators and professors proved reluctant to challenge the ideologues within their midst. As *New York Times* reporter Richard Bernstein observed in his 1995 book, *Dictatorship of Virtue: How the Battle over Multiculturalism Is Reshaping Our Schools, Our Country, and Our Lives*,

"In the era of political correctness and craven university administrations, the charge of racism, unsubstantiated but accompanied by a few demonstrations and angry rhetorical perorations, suffices to paralyze a campus, to destroy a reputation, and to compel an administration into submission."

Those who did challenge the status quo suffered the consequences. The highest-profile example was Harvard president Lawrence Summers, who resigned under pressure in 2006. (That Bill Clinton's treasury secretary would prove far too right-wing for the contemporary academy gives some sense of the ideological midpoint in higher education today.) Summers first encountered trouble when he privately rebuked Cornel West—a university professor, the most prestigious faculty position at Harvard—for insufficient scholarly productivity. West complained that he had been insulted; pointed to the time he had spent recording a rap album and advising Al Sharpton on a possible presidential bid; and loudly decamped for Princeton, which was thrilled to have him. Next Summers angered campus ideologues by labeling a faculty proposal demanding that Harvard divest from businesses operating in Israel as "anti-Semitic in effect if not intent."

His downfall came in 2005, when Summers—under pressure to institute de facto hiring quotas for underrepresented women in mathematics, engineering, and some hard sciences—speculated that one possible explanation for the comparatively low numbers of women in those fields might be the copious data showing that men are overrepresented at both extremes of the aptitude scale relevant to those fields.

These remarks inflamed the academy nationwide, especially its feminist contingent. The Summers discussion of possible male-female differences came in an address urging academics to compile hard data regarding "what the quality of marginal hires are when major diversity efforts are mounted"—if only to rebut the "right-wing critics" who fear "clear abandonments of quality standards." (In the Duke context, such "marginal hires" would include Wahneema Lubiano, Grant Farred, or Thavolia Glymph.) If members of the academy want to sustain popular support for diversity initiatives, Summers noted, "they have to be willing to ask the question in ways that could face any possible answer that came out."

On diversity issues, however, Summers learned there was only one correct answer. In response to his remarks about women in science, the Harvard arts and sciences faculty considered a resolution of no confidence in the president, championed by what Harvard law professor Alan Dershowitz termed "a coalition of angry feminists, angry anti-Israeli people and angry leftists in general." Summers appeared before an emergency faculty meeting to offer groveling apologies for even *suggesting* the possibility of male-female differences in aptitude; Judaic Studies professor Ruth Wisse described him as "sounding more like a prisoner in a Soviet show trial than the original thinker that he is." Summers was supported by a sizable majority of Harvard students. He had backing from most editorial boards, even left-leaning ones. (*The Washington Post* cautioned that if "Summers loses his job for the crime of positing a politically incorrect hypothesis—or even if he pays some lesser price for it—the chilling effect on free inquiry will harm everyone.") But the faculty resolution passed anyway. Many of the president's critics, as Harvard History professor Stephan Thernstrom observed at the time, seemed intent on creating a university barricaded by a "mental Maginot Line," in which ideas—regardless of intellectual merit—that challenged their worldview would be excluded.

Within a year, the Harvard Corporation—led on the issue by former Duke president Nanerl Koehane—forced Summers out.

The Larry Summers case was complicated by the assertions of some of his critics that his difficult personality, mishandling of a faculty conflict-of-interest matter, and other factors might have been the main agents of his downfall. But his offenses against political correctness were clearly the main reasons for the faculty coup: the original draft of the no-confidence resolution mentioned only three items—his remarks about women in science, his opposition to divestment, and the West affair.

Harvey Silverglate placed this episode in its larger context in a piece in the *Boston Phoenix*: "The modern university is the culmination of a 20-year trend of irrationalism marked by an increasingly totalitarian approach to highly politicized issues. Students are subjected to mandatory gender- and racial-sensitivity training akin to thought reform . . . Faculty members and administrators are made to understand that their careers are at risk if they deviate from the accepted viewpoint."

Meanwhile, professorships increasingly look like self-perpetuating sinecures, and university presidents and boards (not unlike corporate boards) look increasingly like fearful faculty puppets. "You might think that presidents, provosts, deans, or trustees, with a broader view of the purposes of education, could see to it that the faculty become more cooperative," wrote the eminent scholar Donald Kagan, Sterling Professor of Classics and History at Yale, in the September 2006 *Commentary*. Instead,

> the twin purposes of a university are the transmission of learning and the
> free cultivation of ideas. Both are entrusted to the faculty, and both have
> been traduced at its hands. An imperial faculty that [selects] as colleagues
> only those who share their narrow political perspective is no longer serving

the purposes of higher education. It has instead become an agent of their degradation.

As things stand now, no president appears capable of taming the imperial faculty; almost none is willing to try; and no one else from inside the world of the universities or infected by its self-serving culture is likely to stand up and say, "enough," or to be followed by anyone if he does. Salvation, if it is to come at all, will have to come from without.

In the last decade, most administrators—like Brodhead at Duke—have bent to the wills of the campus activists, whether from a common belief in an extreme diversity agenda or from fear of ending up like Summers. The one thing that can most quickly ruin a careerist university bureaucrat is to run afoul of the left wing of the faculty.

The tactics advocated by the far left in the academy changed in the aftermath of the water buffalo case and the string of court defeats by universities whose speech codes violated the First Amendment. So diversity advocates launched a more comprehensive assault on academic norms. Since about the mid-1990s, Duke and many other colleges and universities have changed their hiring patterns to promote diversity at the expense of academic merit. In penance for Summers's politically incorrect stances, Harvard allocated $50 million—almost as much as the combined annual tuition of all 1,700 students in a Harvard entering class—to increase the number of women and minorities on the faculty.

In 2005, Columbia set aside $15 million for hiring women and minorities—and any white males who would "in some way promote the diversity goals of the university." The school's vice president for diversity emphasized that "the investment in and of itself is not sufficient to bring about the fundamental and far-reaching changes we are committed to make"; Columbia also needed procedural changes to ensure that more women and minority candidates wound up the top choice in job searches. President Lee Bollinger described this drive to lower academic standards as reaffirming the university's commitment to "academic excellence."

In 2005–2006, President Morton Shapiro of Williams, one of the nation's elite liberal arts colleges, solicited a report from Brown University diversity expert Evelyn Hu-DeHart on how Williams could achieve true diversity. Hu-DeHart recommended moving away from selecting faculty in the traditional disciplines of the liberal arts and sciences and instead undertaking new hires in interdisciplinary topics. Why? Because "scholars and teachers engaged in these studies are also predominately women and feminists, and men and women from racial/ethnic groups." The implication was that moderate white women and—of course—most white men were less desirable hires. Hu-DeHart also contended that Williams needed to look beyond the elite institutions from which, she implied, too many of the college's faculty had received Ph.D. degrees. As an example of the type of graduate program from which Williams should select new faculty, her report singled out the University of Texas at El Paso, generally considered a third- or fourth-tier school. The overriding goal: do whatever it takes to choose diverse or feminist candidates regardless of qualifications.

Hu-DeHart had, in fact, used these strategies when she chaired the University of Colorado's Ethnic Studies Department. In 1990, she cited diversity as the rationale for offering a faculty position to a minimally qualified figure named Ward Churchill, who claimed that he had Native American ancestry, which the relevant tribe disputes. In the spring of 2007, the Board of Regents fired Churchill—who had attracted national scorn for describing victims of the 9/11 attack on the World Trade Center as "little Eichmanns"—for massive plagiarism.

As the Colorado case suggested, less elite institutions have adopted equally or even more extreme diversity schemes. They have a somewhat freer hand in tossing aside tradition and excellence because alumni and donors have less power at the less elite places. Take Marquette, which in 2005 implemented a new policy *requiring* that one diverse finalist be considered for every new faculty hire. This in effect set up a two-track search process, in which quality was overtly subordinated to the applicant's race or ethnicity. Fields where few, if any, minority candidates would be likely to apply (such as, say, Russian history or early English literature) would simply be eliminated.

A few years before, Virginia Tech had taken some hiring decisions away from academic departments and given them to a pro-diversity dean. The University of Arizona's hiring blueprint includes requiring new faculty in some disciplines to "conduct research and contribute to the growing body of knowledge on the importance of valuing diversity." The school's faculty senate also recommended recruiting critical masses of "diverse professors who have shared intellectual interests." In other words, a mainstream economist who happened to be black would no longer be sufficiently diverse; minority candidates would need to fit in ideologically with their racial cohort.

And at the University of Oregon, a presidential commission proposed making "cultural competence" a key factor in all personnel decisions. This despite the fact that its release generated widespread criticism and hints from administrators that it would not be adopted.

In 2002, Duke Economics professor E. Roy Weintraub explained the problems with such policies in an unsuccessful effort to persuade Duke to return to the traditional ideal of a university education: professors committed to free intellectual exchange and pursuit of the truth teaching undergraduates the disciplines of the liberal arts canon, so that college graduates would possess the wide range of knowledge and skills necessary to function as democratic citizens.

"Any college has a limited resource of not only money but administrative energy," Weintraub noted. While Duke had "chosen to spend its money and energy on increasing diversity," he recommended academic excellence as the prime criterion in new hires. Political Science Department chairman Michael Munger, for one, had noticed that for all the emphasis on "diversity," diversity of thought seemed to be less valued. "In at least one case," he noted, "a department chair has [suggested] the function of Duke was to rid conservative students of their hypocrisies." Munger called for a return to a depoliticized classroom, long an ideal in the academy before the diversity crusade began.

Professors hired to promote diversity tend not to teach the traditional liberal arts courses—let alone mathematics or sciences. As colleges and universities embedded a diversity agenda within the curriculum, they also eliminated or dramatically reduced fields—such as political, legal, and diplomatic history—that the dominant ideologues perceive as focusing on "dead white men." Only a quarter, or fewer, of the American history professors in twenty-four of the nation's thirty largest public university history departments focus their research on politics, foreign policy, the law, religion, business, or the military—once the bread-and-butter courses. Other institutions have virtually abandoned these courses. Instead, students are propagandized with a campaign to portray the American past as an unrelieved horror show of dominant groups exploiting vulnerable and powerless ones, filtered through the analytic triumvirate of race, class, and gender.

A more direct drive to purge curricula of courses or themes perceived as politically incorrect came at the University of North Carolina in 2005. Seventy-one professors signed a letter criticizing the university for considering accepting a sizeable donation from the right-leaning Pope Center to establish a Western Cultures program at UNC. The foundation proposed contributing up to $700,000 annually to help fund the program, which would have created a new minor in Western cultures, honors courses, freshman seminars, undergraduate research awards, and study-abroad scholarships.

Sue Estroff, the former faculty president, opposed the grant on the grounds that UNC had "no need for more emphasis in Western studies." Such classes, Estroff fantastically reasoned, would threaten academic freedom and eliminate the possibility of the campus serving as a hotbed of dissent. In the post-9/11 era, she asserted, "universities were probably the only places where differing views of what 9/11 meant and what our responsibilities should be were actively aired." One of Estroff's most vociferous backers, anthropology professor Don Nonini, had previously taken his diversity agenda to unrecognizable extremes. He urged "the working class, poorer blacks, and other minorities" not to pay their income taxes as "another arena of resistance" against the "corporate economy." To deem such actions illegal, Nonini scoffed, is "the view of the IRS and of academics servicing the business community." UNC rejected the Pope Center's money and thus its students had less chance to learn about Western culture.

Diversity advocates justify their agenda by describing a world that no objective observer would recognize. Wagner College president Richard Guarasci, for instance, claimed that students arrived at Wagner "fearing encounters with 'the stranger'" (this in New York City, the most diverse city in the world) and in "deep denial about the contours of inequality." Undergraduates who harbored such inappropriate beliefs could only learn "the arts of democracy" through a reoriented curriculum based on "intercultural and diversity education" that would promote "the objectives of pluralist or multicentric democracy."

The new diversity policies have made the nation's college faculty much less intellectually diverse—as implied in the 2004 Duke Conservative Union study showing that Duke's humanities departments contained 142 registered Democrats and 8 registered Republicans. Duke's John Burness dismissed these numbers with the assertion that creativity in humanities and social science disciplines—oriented around issues of race, class, and gender—produced "perfectly logical criticism of the current society" in the classroom. The Burness rationale would be more persuasive if the criticism displayed by so many race-class-gender theorists of the society on whose prosperity they feed were more grounded in logic or in empirical fact.

According to a study of academics nationwide by professors Robert Lichter, Stanley Rothman, and Neil Nevitte, self-described liberals or leftists increased from 39 percent in 1984 to 72 percent in 2006, with higher percentages among the ranks of humanities and social science professors. For the general public, on the other hand, the number of self-identified liberals or leftists remained essentially unchanged in the same time period. As a result, by virtually any measurement, the ideological gap between the faculty and the students they teach is wider now than at any other point in American history. The views of many professors that most of their students are ideological enemies—or at best misguided waifs in need of reshaping by propaganda—weakens the traditional bonds between teacher and student. The malice exhibited by the Group of 88 toward white Duke students generally, as well as the lacrosse players specifically, fits this pattern.

A self-described "Duke mom" got to the heart of the matter in a perceptive November 27, 2006, essay posted on the Liestoppers blog:

When I see how agenda-driven is a core group of the humanities faculty at Duke inflaming an already inflamed situation at Duke, before the facts have become known, a group who would put their own personal passions above the welfare of, at least, portions of their student body, . . . I am very taken aback. . . . My feelings about Duke have changed, and I believe, sadly, it will probably be a permanent change, because of actions and words of the Group of 88 and the actions and words of President Brodhead and the Duke administration. . . .

For many, the biggest shock of this case has been to see, in the most bla-tant terms, that police and prosecutors would pursue a prosecution of three young men based on no evidence and refuse to accord them any of the hard-won protections of legal due process that this country has achieved.

For me, and probably for other moms, the bigger shock has been to see teachers, Duke faculty, whom we would hope would be shining beacons of learning and integrity to our kids their life long, . . . when we see them tak-ing time out in a very public statement to suggest there is something rotten about these very students, the young men and women with whom they share a campus and a university and whose education and growth as individuals is one of the primary missions of that university, . . . we are shocked and dis-mayed and saddened and changed. . . .

There are moms and dads and kids all across America who will be mak-ing educational decisions in the future. And yes, we are attracted by the wonderful educational opportunities that Duke will continue to offer, and yes, even by the prestige the university has and no doubt will retain. . . .

But we are not deaf, dumb and blind. We can't just ignore something so deeply shocking from such a large group of faculty, representing many de-partments.

Indeed, as Senator Lamar Alexander (R-Tenn.) told the Secretary of Edu-cation's Commission on the Future of Higher Education, the "absence of true diversity of opinion" on most campuses represents "the greatest threat to broader public support and funding for higher education." "The thought po-lice," Harvard professor Stephan Thernstrom recently observed, are now "not just outside, on some congressional or state legislative committee. They are inside too, in our midst." Brown University's president, Ruth Simmons, an African-American woman, has also expressed concern that the "chilling effect caused by the dominance of certain voices on the spectrum of moral and po-litical thought" might negatively affect a quality education.

But such moments of critical introspection seem increasingly rare in the self-satisfied, ideologically blinkered academic establishment. The norm is celebration of the ideological imbalance as proof that diversity policies are actually yielding the best and the brightest, and that only the intellectually deficient could be conservative or Republican—or, for that matter, moderate.

"Many conservatives may deliberately choose not to seek employment at top-tier research universities because they object, on philosophical grounds, to one of the fundamental tenets undergirding such institutions: the scientific method," wrote University of Pittsburgh professors Barry Ames, David C. Barker, Chris W. Bonneau, and Christopher J. Carman. SUNY-Albany's Ron McClamrock demonstrated his own commitment to the scientific method by declaring: "Lefties are overrepresented in academic because on average, we're just f-ing smarter."

In a stunning feat of self-unawareness, UCLA professor John McCumber told *The New York Times* that "a successful career in academia, after all, requires willingness to be critical of yourself and to learn from experience." He asserted that these qualities are "antithetical to Republicanism as it has recently come to be." Perhaps so. But the uncritical intellectual complacency that pervades the academic left resembles nothing so much as the most pigheaded brand of right-wing Republicanism.

Finally, defenders of the academic status quo fall back upon the familiar self-congratulatory theme that leftists predominate in the contemporary academy because "unlike conservatives, they believe in working for the public good and social justice, as well as knowledge and art for their own sake," in the words of Berkeley professor George Lakoff, also in *The New York Times*. Lakoff and similarly inclined figures seem unwilling or unable to recognize that people, in good faith, define "the public good" and "social justice" in very different ways, and so adopting such a goal amounts to having colleges take sides on political questions. Literally and theoretically, though never in practice, one could imagine a number of causes that would for many advance the public good and social justice—fund-raising for Israel, perhaps, by aiding the public good through defending innocent civilians against suicide murderers; or endorsing a Roman Catholic prolife campaign by promoting social justice through preventing destruction of innocent life.

How to explain the remoteness of so many academics from the world-views of most Americans? In an influential 2004 essay, Emory professor Mark Bauerlein traced the development of the groupthink infecting the contemporary academy: "At least in the humanities and social sciences . . . academics shun conservative values and traditions, so their curricula and hiring practices discourage non-leftists from pursuing academic careers. What allows them to do that, while at the same time they deny it, is that the bias takes a subtle form."

He added: "Some fields' very constitutions rest on progressive politics and make it clear from the start that conservative outlooks will not do. . . . The quasi-Marxist outlook of cultural studies rules out those who espouse capitalism. If you disapprove of affirmative action, forget pursuing a degree in African-American studies. If you think that the nuclear family proves the best unit of social well-being, stay away from women's studies."

Bauerlein listed three patterns of group behavior that especially characterize the culture of the academic herd: the "false consensus effect," in which "people think that the collective opinion of their own group matches that of the larger population"; the assumption that others whom one encounters are of like mind, or—in the academic context—that "all the strangers in the room at professional gatherings are liberals"; and the "law of group polarization," which holds that "when like-minded people deliberate as an organized group, the general opinion shifts toward extreme versions of their common beliefs."

These patterns of group behavior were on display in faculty responses to the lacrosse rape allegations. A classic example of the false consensus effect was Wahneema Lubiano's assertion that when the Group of 88 ad came out, "I did not hear from one colleague that there was something wrong with the ad." Shades of the (perhaps apocryphal) story of the late *New Yorker* film critic Pauline Kael's incredulousness at Richard Nixon's forty-nine-state trouncing of George McGovern in 1972: "How can that be? No one I know voted for Nixon." And Bauerlein's "law of group polarization" explains how, with virtually all of the 88 sharing a like-minded race/class/gender worldview, the group dynamic moved the content of the ad toward extreme versions of the common beliefs typified by Wahneema Lubiano and Karla Holloway.

In October 2006, the Institute for Jewish & Community Research produced the most comprehensive survey of faculty beliefs and ideology ever compiled. Its report contended that

faculty political culture is self-perpetuating. . . . Recruitment, hiring, and tenure review processes have either failed to adequately prevent this political imbalance within disciplines or have actually perpetuated and deepened political unity. . . . Significant percentages of faculty acknowledge that not only students but also other faculty may feel restricted in their expression of opinion if they conflict with dominant popular views on campus. . . . [M]ost faculty say . . . that their colleagues are reluctant to speak out against what they consider dominant or popular opinions at their institutions. . . . It would be equally unfortunate if conservatism or Buddhism or Evangelical religion were the dominant ideologies on campus. . . . Academic departments, especially in the social sciences and humanities, have become like exclusive political clubs, as hiring and promotion decisions are based on the "collegiality" of a candidate as well as the quality of his or her work. Someone has to "fit in."

The institute's report concluded, "It would be absurd to suggest that liberal faculty do not have an important place in American higher education. It should be equally disconcerting that faculty . . . may be rejected for positions or promotions because they are conservatives."

Disconcerting indeed. But that's American academia today. Professors control the searches for new hires. It is easy to screen out those who challenge the pedagogical or ideological worldview of people such as Wahneema Lubiano and Grant Farred. In this respect, academic extremism can be compared to a cancer on American higher education. Once ideologues achieve predominance, they replicate themselves, metastasize, and take over entire departments.

They also do much to bring about the larger sense of drift and dumbing-down described in a book by Harry R. Lewis, former dean of Harvard College, *Excellence Without a Soul: How a Great University Forgot Education*. Harvard's curriculum, he wrote, shows it to be "a university without a larger sense of educational purpose or a connection with its principal constituents." After three years of work by a faculty committee, billed by Summers himself as "the most comprehensive review of Harvard's curriculum in a century," Lewis assessed the result:

> *There is absolutely nothing that Harvard can expect students will know after they take three science or three humanities courses freely chosen from across the entire course catalog. The proposed general-education requirement gives up entirely on the idea of shared knowledge, shared values, even shared aspirations. In the absence of any pronouncement that anything is more important than anything else for Harvard students to know, Harvard is declaring that one can be an educated person in the 21st Century without knowing anything about genomes, chromosomes, or Shakespeare.*

Absent outside intervention—from alumni, trustees, parents, the media—academic culture is likely to grow more, not less, extreme. If so, the lacrosse case will be remembered as the forerunner of events to come, a new era in American higher education when faculty contempt for the students they teach overwhelms common sense and common decency.

EPILOGUE

I N EARLY JUNE 2007, after considering several Ivy League schools, Reade Seligmann announced that he was transferring to Brown. A few weeks before, Dave Evans had joined Morgan Stanley as an analyst. As of this writing, Collin Finnerty hadn't decided whether to return to Duke or to transfer. The trio's former teammates made a spirited run in the NCAA tournament before losing 12–11 to Johns Hopkins in the finals. The women's squad again reached the Final Four, but lost in the semifinals to Virginia.

Duke reached an out-of-court settlement with Mike Pressler, terms of which were not disclosed. Duke also settled with Dave Evans, Reade Seligmann, and Collin Finnerty for undisclosed sums, issuing a statement that "it is in the best interests of the Duke community to eliminate the possibility of future litigation and move forward." The settlement did not rule out lawsuits against Duke by other players. The three defendants, and perhaps teammates, were also widely expected to sue Nifong, other law enforcement officials, and the City of Durham for violating their constitutional rights.

In mid-June, the university announced that 42 percent of the students offered admission to the Class of 2011 would enroll at Duke—a slightly higher total than expected. The demographics of the class radically differed from its predecessors: applications and enrollments from African-Americans, Hispanics, and Asian Americans rose sharply, while the number of white students seeking to attend Duke plunged.

Responding to a flurry of alumni e-mails criticizing the administration for not doing more to protest the faculty's rush to judgment or Nifong's abuses, Duke board chairman Bob Steel sent out a mass e-mail calling for critics to put the past behind them so that "we can move forward together." As of June, the administration had given no indication that it saw any need to consider why so many Duke professors had so badly prejudged the case and launched such ugly attacks on innocent Duke students.

On May 11, City Manager Patrick Baker and Police Chief Steve Chalmers released a report denying that the Durham Police Department had mishandled the lacrosse case investigation. The two men claimed that the April 4 photo display used to indict Seligmann, Evans, and Finnerty was not a "lineup" and thus did not have to follow regular procedures. They also blamed the defense attorneys' supposed failure to present exculpatory evidence as the reason the prosecution had dragged on for a year before the defendants were declared innocent. The report generated widespread ridicule; Joe Cheshire dismissed it as "another attempt by the people in Durham responsible for this travesty of justice to engage in revisionist history in order to excuse their incompetence." The City Council responded by appointing an outside committee to investigate the police department's performance in the case.

The media equivalent of the Baker/Chalmers report came from *New York Times* public editor Byron Calame. In his final major column at the paper, Calame found that the past year's articles "generally reported both sides, and that most flaws flowed from journalistic lapses rather than ideological bias." *Times* editors continued to defend the paper's performance. Others in the media who had rushed to judgment likewise retained their early opinions in the post-exoneration atmosphere as if Roy Cooper had declared the players guilty rather than innocent. In perhaps the most astonishing such comment, John Feinstein asserted that he saw nothing wrong with his prior comment that Evans, Seligmann, and Finnerty were "probably guilty of everything but rape." He offered no evidence to corroborate his charge.

Finally, in June, the Disciplinary Hearing Commission held a five-day session deciding Mike Nifong's fate as a lawyer. After State Bar prosecutor Doug Brocker detailed the misconduct of the figure he derided as Durham County's "minister of injustice," Brad Bannon and other witnesses laid out the basic facts of the case. Reade Seligmann and others emotionally testified as to the effects of Nifong's behavior. The DA took the stand in his own defense, tearfully admitting some errors and promising to resign, but hoping to keep his law license. The most dramatic moment came when DHC chairman Lane Williamson asked whether Nifong accepted the findings of Roy Cooper's report. The DA paused for several seconds, leaned back in his chair, and then declared, "I think something happened in that bathroom." The panel, it was clear, disagreed.

The DHC panel ruled that Nifong had repeatedly and intentionally violated ethics guidelines and lied to the court, the defense counsel, and the State Bar. The panel stripped the DA of his law license. Lane Williamson summarized: The case was a "fiasco." Nifong was driven by "self-deception arising out of self-interest." And "those who made a rush to judgment based upon an unquestioning faith in what a prosecutor had told them were made to look foolish and many still do look foolish."

Williamson concluded by expressing his hope that the lacrosse case would "be a reminder to everyone that it's the facts that matter."

INDEX

ABC television network, 63–64, 123, 178, 185–186, 220, 288
Abrams, Dan, 86, 100, 123, 196, 205, 206, 271
Abrams Report, The (TV show), 86, 133, 161, 205, 327
academics, Duke University, 2, 5–6, 7–8, 15, 388
academy, politics and, 388–401
Actual Innocence Commission (North Carolina), 154–155, 156, 252
Adcock, David, 93
Addison, David, 63–64, 65, 89
admissions police, Duke University, 5–6
advocates, rape law, 377–378
African and African American Studies (AAAS) Program (Duke University), 299–300
Against Our Will (Brownmiller), 374
Albert, Marv, 380–381
Alexander, Lamar, 398
alibis. *See* exculpatory evidence
Allen, Charlotte, 122
Alleva, Joe, 7, 62, 63, 67, 68, 69, 70, 72, 91, 96, 141–142, 178, 278
Allison, Anne, 140, 339, 340, 341
Allison, F. Vincent, 134
American Psycho (book and movie), 138, 278
Ames, Barry, 399
Ammons, James, 134, 237
Anderson, Kurt, 122, 268
Anderson, William L., 44, 147
anti-Semitism, 189
Araton, Harvey, 233, 234
Archer, Breck, 110
Arico, Theresa, 252
Ashe, Mike, 204
Ashley, Bob, 258, 297
Ashton-James, Claire, 216
Associated Press (AP), 71, 101, 193, 245, 254, 318

athletics
    Duke University, 3–4, 5, 6, 7–8, 11, 93–94, 96, 129–130, 167–168
    forfeited games, 67–68, 70, 93
    lacrosse season cancellation, 119, 139–140, 149
    Nifong, Michael, 79
    Phantom Calls (Farred), 112–113
Atlanta Journal-Constitution (newspaper), 233–234

Baker, Houston A., Jr., 106–107, 108, 109, 135, 140, 141, 143–144, 167, 169, 211, 214, 215, 236, 247, 299, 338, 390
Baker, Lee, 329, 337
Baker, Patrick, 403
Baldwin, Steve, 135, 150, 284
Baltimore Sun (newspaper), 177–178, 245
Bannon, Brad, 95, 222, 223, 240
    media, 263
    Nifong, Michael, 97–98, 99–100, 285
    rape trial defense, 286–287, 288, 301–302, 307–308, 309–310
Baran, Bernard, Jr., 382
Barber, William J., II, 19, 134, 333
Barfield, Willie, 31
Barker, David C., 399
Barnett, Ross, 297
Bar-On, Rann, 74, 130
Barone, Michael, 151
Barstow, David, 318
Bauerlein, Mark, 399–400
Bayly, John H., Jr., 245–246
Bazelon, Emily, 319
Beason, William, 365
behavior code, Duke University, 274–276
Bell, Bill, 18–19, 82, 101, 134, 237, 316
Bench, Barry, 364–365
Bennett, Alwina, 383–384